The Bristol and Gloucestershire Archaeological Society
Gloucestershire Record Series

Hon. General Editor
C. R. Elrington, M.A., F.S.A., F.R.Hist.S.

Volume 20

Gloucestershire Feet of Fines
1300–1359

ABSTRACTS OF FEET OF FINES RELATING TO GLOUCESTERSHIRE 1300–1359

Edited by C. R. Elrington

The Bristol and Gloucestershire Archaeological Society

2006

The Bristol and Gloucestershire Archaeological Society
Gloucestershire Record Series

© The Bristol and Gloucestershire Archaeological Society

ISBN 0 900197 66 8

British Library Cataloguing in Publication Data
A catalogue entry for this book is available from the British Library

Printed in Great Britain by the Alden Press, Osney Mead, Oxford OX2 0EF

CONTENTS

ACKNOWLEDGEMENTS

Several people have given help or advice in the preparation of this edition, which is gratefully acknowledged. They include Dr. John Juřica of the Victoria County History of Gloucestershire and Dr. Nicholas Herbert, formerly his colleague, Mr. M. A. Davis of Cerney Wick, Dr. Robert Dunning of the Victoria County History of Somerset, Dr. Michael Roper, former Keeper of Public Records, and Mr. David Smith, former County and Diocesan Archivist and Hon. Secretary of the Bristol and Gloucestershire Archaeological Society. The staff of the Institute of Historical Research, University of London, of the Public Record Office, and of the Gloucestershire Record Office are also thanked for their assistance.

All the abstracts in this edition are from documents among the National Archives in the Public Record Office. Crown copyright material in the Public Record Office is reproduced by permission of the Controller of Her Majesty's Stationery Office.

June 2006

LIST OF ABBREVIATIONS

Berkeley Castle Mun.
: *Catalogue of the Medieval Muniments at Berkeley Castle*, 2 vols., Bristol and Gloucestershire Archaeological Society, Gloucestershire Record Series, vols. 17 and 18, 2004

Bigland, *Glos.*
: Ralph Bigland, *Historical, Monumental and Genealogical Collections relative to the County of Gloucester*, 4 vols., Bristol and Gloucestershire Archaeological Society, Gloucestershire Record Series, vols. 2, 3, 5, 8, 1989–95

Bristol Gt. Red Book
: *Great Red Book of Bristol*, ed. E. W. W. Veale, Bristol Record Society, vol. ii, 1931

CP 26
: Notes of Fines, in the Public Record Office

Cal. Inq. p.m. x
: *Calendar of Inquisitions post mortem*, vol. x, Public Record Office Texts and Calendars, 1921

Collinson, *Som.*
: John Collinson, *The History and Antiquities of Somerset*, 3 vols., 1791

Cornwall Fines, 1195–1377
: *Cornwall Fines, 1195–1377*, Devon and Cornwall Record Society, 1914

def.
: deforciant (i.e. defendant)

Devon Fines, 1272–1369
: *Devon Feet of Fines*, vol. ii, 1272–1369, Devon and Cornwall Record Society, 1939

Dorset Fines, 1195–1327, 1327–1485
: *Full Abstracts of Feet of Fines relating to the County of Dorset* [1195–1327, 1327–1485], Dorset Records, vols. v and x, 1869, 1910

Essex Fines, 1272–1326, 1327–1422
: *Feet of Fines for Essex*, vols. ii and iii, Essex Archaeological Society, 1913–49 (published in parts)

imp.
: impedient (i.e. defendant)

P.-N.G.
: *The Place-Names of Gloucestershire*, by A. H. Smith, English Place-Name Society, vols. xxxviii–xli, 1964–5

P.R.O.
: Public Record Office, Kew, London (The National Archives)

pet.
: *petens* (demandant, i.e. plaintiff)

quer.
: *querens* (complainant, i.e. plaintiff)

Reg. Martival, i
: *Register of Roger Martival, Bishop of Salisbury*, vol. i (Canterbury and York Society, 1959–60)

Rudder, *Glos.*
: Samuel Rudder, *A New History of Gloucestershire*, 1779, reprinted 1977

Som. Fines, 1307–46   *Pedes Finium, commonly called Feet of Fines, for the County of Somerset, 1307–1346*, Somerset Record Society, vol. xii, 1898

Staffs. Fines, 1327–1547   *The Final Concords, or Feet of Fines, 1327–1547*, in *Collections for a History of Staffordshire*, William Salt Society [original series], vol. xi, 1890

Sussex Fines, 1307–1509   *An Abstract of Feet of Fines relating to the County of Sussex from 1 Edward II to 24 Henry VII*, Sussex Record Society, vol. xxiii, 1916

V.C.H.   *The Victoria History of the Counties of England*, for all counties, in progress

Warws. Fines, 1284–1345   *Warwickshire Feet of Fines, 1284–1345*, Dugdale Society, vol. xv, 1939

Wilts. Fines, 1272–1327   *Abstracts of Feet of Fines relating to Wiltshire for the Reigns of Edward I and Edward II*, Wiltshire Archaeological and Natural History Society, Records Branch, vol. i, 1939

Wilts. Fines, 1327–77   *Abstracts of Feet of Fines Relating to Wiltshire for the Reign of Edward III*, Wiltshire Record Society, vol. xxix, 1974

INTRODUCTION

The introduction to the first part of this edition of Feet of Fines relating to Gloucestershire, published in 2003 as Volume 16 of the Gloucestershire Record Series, serves in many respects as an introduction to the later parts.

The second part includes abstracts of fines granted and recorded between 1300 and 1359. The abstracts are taken from the following files in the Public Record Office in the class Feet of Fines, Series I (CP 25/1):

Case	files	fines for	in regnal years
75	38–41	Gloucestershire	27–35 Edward I
76	42–55	Gloucestershire	1–20 Edward II
77	56–69	Gloucestershire	1–29 Edward III
78	70–72	Gloucestershire	29–36 Edward III
285	26	'Divers Counties'	33–35 Edward I
285	27	'Unknown and Various Counties'	1–35 Edward I
285	28–30	'Divers Counties'	1–11 Edward II
286	31–33	'Divers Counties'	11–20 Edward II
286	35–38	'Divers Counties'	1–11 Edward III
287	39–45	'Divers Counties'	11–32 Edward III
288	46	'Divers Counties'	32–35 Edward III
288	51	'Unknown and Various Counties'	1–49 Edward III

Where a foot of fine is not fully legible, an attempt has been made to supply any detail needed for the abstract by referring to the bundles of notes of fines (CP 26/1 in the Public Record Office), but notes have not invariably been found for fines that are filed among the feet.

The number of Gloucestershire fines in the 60 years 1300–1359 is nearly as large as that for the 101 years from 1199 to 1299. While the number of the surviving 13th-century fines would be greater had not the record of some been lost, there was a sharp increase, for reasons which are not altogether apparent, in the use of fines in the early 14th century, the yearly average of those relating to Gloucestershire more than doubling about 1305, from 7.5 in the decade to 1304 to 20 in that from 1305. The annual number of fines for a neighbouring county, Wiltshire, shows an equally sudden and even sharper increase between 1302 and 1308.

Whereas the first part of this edition finished at the year 1299 for no reason other than that that was a convenient point, there is more significance in the choice of 1359 as the year at which to finish the second part. Up to 1359 the granting and proclamation of a fine barred any claim to the property that was the subject of the fine by an outsider who had not put in a claim when the fine was proclaimed, such claims being endorsed on the feet of fines. A statute of 1360 removed the ability of a fine to bar claims in that way, thus reducing its usefulness as a means of conveying or settling property. There was consequently a gradual reduction in the number of fines that were levied, and the annual average number of fines for Gloucestershire fell from sixteen in the 55 years up to 1359 to between eight and nine a year in the forty years from 1360. Again, there was a similar reduction in the number of fines for Wiltshire.

In the 14th century the way in which fines were made differed in some respects from that of the 13th, and that has led to small changes in editorial method. First, after 1292 (see part 1, no. 956) no Gloucestershire fines made before justices in eyre have been found, all being made at Westminster or, when the king's court was in the north, at York, and therefore the abstracts below name the place where the fines were made only when instead of Westminster it was York. Secondly, the variety in the type of plea by which fines were initiated was reduced, the plea being one either of covenant or (decreasingly as the century went on) of warranty of charter; the abstracts below show only two exceptions (nos. 23 and 60) and unless it is otherwise indicated assume that the plea is stated in the fine to be of covenant. The fines of the 14th century also dealt with a more limited range of property rights than those of the 13th, as the relative shortness and simplicity of the index of subjects in the second part reflect.

The fines of the 14th century refer much more frequently than those of the 13th to the king's order or writ, whether for the making of a fine or for an attorney to represent one of the parties. That the record of the king's writ for the representation of a party by an attorney is to some extent haphazard is suggested by the occurrence of the same complainant in two fines of the same date, one of which records him as represented by an attorney by the king's writ and the other makes no mention of an attorney or the king's writ: an instance is nos. 201–2 below.

COLLATION OF THE NUMBERS IN THE FILES WITH THE NUMBERS IN THE PRINTED TEXT

The full reference for each document begins with the P.R.O. class letters and number for Feet of Fines, series I, i.e. CP 25/1. To order a file at the P.R.O. those letters and that number should be prefixed to the numbers of the case and file (the first two elements of the tripartite references given below and following each abstract in the text), and the number of the fine within the file (the last element in the tripartite reference) should be omitted.

number in file	number in text	regnal year	number in file	number in text	regnal year	number in file	number in text	regnal year
75/38/203	1	28 Edw. I	75/39/244	44	32 Edw. I	75/41/285	79	34 Edw. I
204	2	. . .	245	45	. . .	286	81	. . .
205	3	. . .	246	43	. . .	287	84	. . .
206	10	29 Edw. I	247	42	. . .	288	77	. . .
207	11	. . .	248	63	33 Edw. I	289	78	. . .
208	9	. . .	249	68	. . .	290	75	. . .
209	4	. . .	250	64	. . .	291	72	. . .
210	7	. . .	75/40/251	69	. . .	292	71	. . .
211	8	. . .	252	65	. . .	293	76	. . .
212	6	. . .	253	92	34 Edw. I	294	73	. . .
213	12	. . .	254	66	33 Edw. I	295	99	35 Edw. I
214	5	. . .	255	67	. . .	296	98	. . .
215	22	30 Edw. I	256	56	. . .	297	100	. . .
216	19	. . .	257	70	. . .	298	97	. . .
217	21	. . .	258	57	. . .	299	95	. . .
218	20	. . .	259	53	. . .	300	96	. . .
219	14	. . .	260	55	. . .	301	104	. . .
220	15	. . .	261	58	. . .	302	101	. . .
221	16	. . .	262	59	. . .	303	102	. . .
222	13	. . .	263	60	. . .	304	105	. . .
223	17	. . .	264	48	. . .	305	110	. . .
224	18	. . .	265	54	. . .	306	106	. . .
225	31	31 Edw. I	266	61	. . .	307	109	. . .
75/39/226	32	. . .	267	49	. . .	308	107	. . .
227	27	. . .	268	50	. . .	309	108	. . .
228	28	. . .	269	52	. . .	310	111	. . .
229	29	. . .	270	51	. . .	311	103	. . .
230	26	. . .	271	46	. . .	312	94	. . .
231	25	. . .	272	47	. . .	76/42/1	112	1 Edw. II
232	23	. . .	273	62	. . .	2	113	. . .
233	24	. . .	274	74	34 Edw. I	3	114	. . .
234	30	. . .	275	85	. . .	4	115	. . .
235	35	33 Edw. I	75/41/276	86	. . .	5	116	. . .
236	33	. . .	277	93	. . .	6	117	. . .
237	34	. . .	278	87	. . .	7	118	. . .
238	36	. . .	279	88	. . .	8	120	. . .
239	37	. . .	280	91	. . .	9	122	. . .
240	38	. . .	281	89	. . .	10	123	. . .
241	40	. . .	282	90	. . .	11	124	. . .
242	39	. . .	283	82	. . .	12	128	. . .
243	41	. . .	284	83	. . .	13	129	. . .

number in file	number in text	regnal year	number in file	number in text	regnal year	number in file	number in text	regnal year
76/42/14	127	1 Edw. II	76/44/64	178	4 Edw. II	76/46/113	232	7 Edw. II
15	125	. . .	65	180	. . .	114	222	. . .
16	126	. . .	66	179	. . .	115	237	8 Edw. II
17	121	. . .	67	181	. . .	116	234	. . .
18	119	. . .	68	182	. . .	117	240	. . .
19	138	2 Edw. II	69	183	. . .	118	235	. . .
20	130	. . .	70	185	. . .	119	238	. . .
21	131	. . .	71	184	. . .	120	236	. . .
22	132	. . .	72	186	. . .	121	241	. . .
23	133	. . .	73	189	5 Edw. II	122	244	. . .
24	141	. . .	74	187	. . .	123	243	. . .
25	142	. . .	75	190	. . .	124	247	. . .
76/43/26	145	. . .	77/45/76	191	. . .	125	245	. . .
27	143	. . .	77	188	. . .	76/47/126	248	. . .
28	146	. . .	78	200	. . .	127	249	. . .
29	147	. . .	79	193	. . .	128	250	. . .
30	149	. . .	80	194	. . .	129	246	. . .
31	148	. . .	81	199	. . .	130	239	. . .
32	134	. . .	82	197	. . .	131	233	. . .
33	139	. . .	83	198	. . .	132	255	9 Edw. II
34	140	. . .	84	201	. . .	133	252	. . .
35	136	. . .	85	202	. . .	134	256	. . .
36	137	. . .	86a	203	. . .	135	260	. . .
37	154	3 Edw. II	86b	196	. . .	136	253	. . .
38	151	. . .	87	205	6 Edw. II	137	254	. . .
39	152	. . .	88	206	. . .	138	261	. . .
40	150	. . .	89	207	. . .	139	257	. . .
41	156	. . .	90	208	. . .	140	258	. . .
42	153	. . .	91	204	. . .	141	266	. . .
43	161	. . .	92	210	. . .	142	265	. . .
44	159	. . .	93	211	. . .	143	263	. . .
45	173	. . .	94	209	. . .	144	262	. . .
46	163	. . .	95	196	5 Edw. II	145	270	. . .
47	164	. . .	96	217	7 Edw. II	146	264	. . .
48	165	. . .	97	218	. . .	147	268	. . .
49	166	. . .	98	214	. . .	148	267	. . .
50	167	. . .	99	215	. . .	149	259	. . .
76/44/51	168	. . .	100	220	. . .	150	269	. . .
52	169	. . .	76/46/101	216	. . .	76/48/151	271	. . .
53	170	. . .	102	219	. . .	152	275	10 Edw. II
54	171	. . .	103	223	. . .	153	281	. . .
55	172	. . .	104	224	. . .	154	282	. . .
56	155	. . .	105	221	. . .	155	276	. . .
57	157	. . .	106	228	. . .	156	279	. . .
58	160	. . .	107	225	. . .	157	277	. . .
59	162	. . .	108	229	. . .	158	272	. . .
60	176	4 Edw. II	109	226	. . .	159	273	. . .
61	177	. . .	110	227	. . .	160	283	. . .
62	174	. . .	111	230	. . .	161	274	. . .
63	175	. . .	112	231	. . .	162	284	. . .

number in file	number in text	regnal year	number in file	number in text	regnal year	number in file	number in text	regnal year
76/48/163	287	10 Edw. II	76/50/213	332	12 Edw. II	76/52/262	373	14 Edw. II
164	288	. . .	214	333	. . .	263	374	. . .
165	293	. . .	215	340	. . .	264	376	. . .
166	285	. . .	216	334	. . .	265	375	. . .
167	289	. . .	217	345	. . .	266	394	. . .
168	290	. . .	218	341	. . .	267	393	. . .
169	291	. . .	219	346	. . .	268	395	. . .
170	294	. . .	220	348	. . .	269	397	. . .
171	298	. . .	221	350	. . .	270	396	. . .
172	299	. . .	222	352	. . .	271	402	15 Edw. II
173	300	. . .	223	351	. . .	272	401	. . .
174	295	. . .	224	326	. . .	273	404	. . .
175	301	. . .	225	327	. . .	274	398	. . .
76/49/176	296	. . .	76/51/226	328	. . .	275	405	. . .
177	297	. . .	227	353	. . .	76/53/276	399	. . .
178	280	. . .	228	335	. . .	277	403	. . .
179	286	. . .	229	367	13 Edw. II	278	400	. . .
180	315	11 Edw. II	230	356	. . .	279	407	. . .
181	313	. . .	231	368	. . .	280	408	. . .
182	309	. . .	232	359	. . .	281	406	. . .
183	310	. . .	233	360	. . .	282	409	16 Edw. II
184	321	. . .	234	361	. . .	283	412	. . .
185	307	. . .	235	369	. . .	284	410	. . .
186	314	. . .	236	371	14 Edw. II	285	411	. . .
187	311	. . .	237	362	13 Edw. II	286	411	. . .
188	303	. . .	238	363	. . .	287	411	. . .
189	304	. . .	239	364	. . .	288	411	. . .
190	308	. . .	240	365	. . .	289	411	. . .
191	305	. . .	241	366	. . .	290	413	17 Edw. II
192	306	. . .	242	370	. . .	291	414	. . .
193	312	. . .	243	354	. . .	292	415	. . .
194	319	. . .	244	358	. . .	293	416	. . .
195	320	. . .	245	355	. . .	294	418	. . .
196	302	. . .	246a	371	14 Edw. II	295	417	. . .
197	324	. . .	246b	377	. . .	296	421	. . .
198	316	. . .	247	387	. . .	297	423	. . .
199	322	. . .	248	388	. . .	298	422	. . .
200	317	. . .	249	383	. . .	299	419	. . .
76/50/201	318	. . .	250	382	. . .	300	424	. . .
202	323	. . .	76/52/251	378	. . .	76/54/301	425	. . .
203	342	12 Edw. II	252	384	. . .	302	426	. . .
204	338	. . .	253	379	12 Edw. II	303	432	18 Edw. II
205	343	. . .	254	389	. . .	304	427	17 Edw. II
206	339	. . .	255	392	. . .	305	428	. . .
207	325	. . .	256	380	. . .	306	420	. . .
208	344	. . .	257	385	. . .	307	430	. . .
209	337	. . .	258	390	. . .	308	429	. . .
210	329	. . .	259	386	. . .	309	447	. . .
211	330	. . .	260	381	. . .	310a	432	18 Edw. II
212	331	. . .	261	372	. . .	310b	439	. . .

number in file	number in text	regnal year	number in file	number in text	regnal year	number in file	number in text	regnal year
76/54/311	433	18 Edw. II	77/56/5	487	1 Edw. III	77/58/55	527	4 Edw. III
312	434	. . .	6	492	. . .	56	538	. . .
313	435	. . .	7	493	. . .	57	616	8 Edw. III
314	441	. . .	8	488	. . .	58	539	4 Edw. III
315	437	. . .	9	483	. . .	59	540	. . .
316	445	. . .	10	489	. . .	60	535	. . .
317	442	. . .	11	494	2 Edw. III	61	536	. . .
318	443	. . .	12	501	. . .	62	571	5 Edw. III
319	436	. . .	13	496	. . .	63	576	. . .
320	446	. . .	14	498	. . .	64	574	. . .
321	444	. . .	15	499	. . .	65	577	. . .
322	449	. . .	16	500	. . .	66	575	. . .
323	438	. . .	17	497	. . .	67	572	. . .
324	448	. . .	18	502	. . .	68	579	6 Edw. III
325	450	. . .	19	520	3 Edw. III	69	564	5 Edw. III
76/55/326	455	. . .	20	523	. . .	70	573	. . .
327	456	. . .	21	495	2 Edw. III	71	565	. . .
328	451	. . .	22	517	3 Edw. III	72	566	. . .
328b	453	. . .	23	518	. . .	73	560	. . .
328c	472	. . .	24	522	. . .	74	561	. . .
329	459	. . .	25	519	. . .	75	562	. . .
330	457	. . .	77/57/26	521	. . .	77/59/76	555	. . .
331	458	. . .	27	512	. . .	77	557	. . .
332	466	19 Edw. II	28	513	. . .	78	567	. . .
333	460	. . .	29	516	. . .	79	569	. . .
334	467	. . .	30	514	. . .	80	558	. . .
335	468	. . .	31	508	. . .	81	559	. . .
336	469	. . .	32	504	. . .	82	589	6 Edw. III
337	464	. . .	33	507	. . .	83	580	. . .
338	461	. . .	34	503	. . .	84	597	. . .
339	462	. . .	35	505	. . .	85	592	. . .
340	463	. . .	36	515	. . .	86	594	. . .
341	465	. . .	37	509	. . .	87	595	. . .
342	471	. . .	38	510	. . .	88	596	. . .
343	470	. . .	39	546	4 Edw. III	89	581	. . .
344	473	. . .	40	547	. . .	90	582	. . .
345	474	. . .	41	548	. . .	91	583	. . .
346	476	. . .	42	551	. . .	92	584	. . .
347	477	. . .	43	543	. . .	93	586	. . .
348	478	20 Edw. II	44	553	. . .	94	587	. . .
349	481	. . .	45	545	. . .	95	588	. . .
350	453	18 Edw. II	46	524	. . .	96	598	. . .
351	479	20 Edw. II	47	525	. . .	97	590	. . .
352	472	18 Edw. II	48	526	. . .	98	585	. . .
353	482	20 Edw. II	49	550	. . .	99	599	. . .
354	480	. . .	50	529	. . .	100	602	7 Edw. III
77/56/1	485	1 Edw. III	77/58/51	530	. . .	77/60/101	600	. . .
2	491	. . .	52	541	. . .	102	610	. . .
3	486	. . .	53	537	. . .	103	601	. . .
4	490	. . .	54	542	. . .	104	606	. . .

number in file	number in text	regnal year	number in file	number in text	regnal year	number in file	number in text	regnal year
77/60/105	604	7 Edw. III	77/62/155	673	12 Edw. III	77/64/203	725	16 Edw. III
106	613	. . .	156	671	. . .	204	721	. . .
107	607	. . .	157	662	. . .	205	727	. . .
108	611	. . .	158	668	. . .	206	729	17 Edw. III
109	612	. . .	159	669	. . .	207	728	16 Edw. III
110	608	. . .	160	666	. . .	208	726	. . .
111	609	. . .	161	670	. . .	209	722	. . .
112	605	. . .	162	676	. . .	210	723	. . .
113	618	8 Edw. III	163	677	. . .	211a	729	17 Edw. III
114	619	. . .	164	678	. . .	211b	730	. . .
115	617	. . .	165	667	. . .	212	731	. . .
116	624	9 Edw. III	166	692	13 Edw. III	213	739	. . .
117	623	. . .	167	694	. . .	214	737	. . .
118	625	. . .	168	680	. . .	215	736	. . .
119	620	. . .	169	685	. . .	216	738	. . .
120	628	. . .	170	681	. . .	217	740	. . .
121	627	. . .	171	693	. . .	218	732	. . .
122	629	. . .	172	679	. . .	219	734	. . .
123	621	. . .	173	687	. . .	220	735	. . .
124	622	. . .	174	686	. . .	221	733	. . .
125	626	. . .	174 [bis]	682	. . .	222	756	18 Edw. III
77/61/126	630	. . .	175	683	. . .	223	741	. . .
127	638	10 Edw. III	77/63/176	684	. . .	224	742	. . .
128	639	. . .	177	690	. . .	225	743	. . .
129	637	. . .	178	688	. . .	77/65/226	744	. . .
130	636	. . .	179	689	. . .	227	757	. . .
131	633	. . .	180	695	. . .	228	761	. . .
132	632	. . .	181	707	14 Edw. III	229	760	. . .
133	631	. . .	182	703	. . .	230	758	. . .
134	634	. . .	183	706	. . .	231	746	. . .
135	635	. . .	184	697	. . .	232	747	. . .
136	640	. . .	185	701	. . .	233	745	. . .
137	655	11 Edw. III	186	698	. . .	234	751	. . .
138	656	. . .	187	699	. . .	235	752	. . .
139	657	. . .	188	705	. . .	236	748	. . .
140	658	. . .	189	704	. . .	237	753	. . .
141	659	. . .	190	708	15 Edw. III	238	750	. . .
142	641	. . .	191	714	. . .	239	754	. . .
143	642	. . .	192	713	. . .	240	749	. . .
144	648	. . .	193	712	. . .	241	763	. . .
145	643	. . .	194	710	. . .	241(a)	762	. . .
146	644	. . .	195	719	. . .	242	767	19 Edw. III
147	651	. . .	196	715	. . .	243	764	. . .
148	652	. . .	197	709	. . .	244	765	. . .
149	654	. . .	198	711	. . .	245	774	. . .
150	672	12 Edw. III	199	718	. . .	246	775	. . .
77/62/151	675	. . .	200A	716	. . .	247	769	. . .
152	663	. . .	200B	717	. . .	248	771	. . .
153	664	. . .	77/64/201	724	16 Edw. III	249	770	. . .
154	665	. . .	202	720	. . .	250	773	. . .

number in file	number in text	regnal year	number in file	number in text	regnal year	number in file	number in text	regnal year
77/66/251	772	19 Edw. III	77/68/301	834	24 Edw. III	77/69/350	885	29 Edw. III
252	776	. . .	302	832	. . .	78/70/351	886	. . .
253	777	. . .	303	831	. . .	352	887	. . .
254	778	. . .	304	835	. . .	353	891	. . .
255	780	20 Edw. III	305	842	25 Edw. III	354	890	. . .
256	781	. . .	306	839	. . .	355	888	. . .
257	791	. . .	307	840	. . .	356	889	. . .
258	782	. . .	308	837	. . .	357	897	. . .
259	783	. . .	309	844	. . .	358	893	. . .
260	784	. . .	310	836	. . .	359	895	. . .
261	786	. . .	311	843	. . .	360	894	. . .
262	788	. . .	312	841	. . .	361	898	. . .
263	789	. . .	313	845	26 Edw. III	362	899	30 Edw/ III
264	790	. . .	314	847	. . .	363	902	. . .
265	796	. . .	315	848	. . .	364	903	. . .
266	787	. . .	316	851	. . .	365	904	. . .
267	793	. . .	317	849	. . .	366	906	. . .
268	794	. . .	318	853	. . .	367	908	. . .
269	792	. . .	319	852	. . .	368	909	. . .
270	785	. . .	320	854	. . .	369	911	. . .
271	797	. . .	321	846	. . .	370	905	. . .
272	799	21 Edw. III	322	850	. . .	371	910	. . .
273	805	. . .	323	855	27 Edw. III	372	913	31 Edw. III
274	806	. . .	324	856	. . .	373	915	. . .
275	807	. . .	325	857	. . .	374	912	. . .
77/67/276	811	. . .	77/69/326	865	. . .	375	914	. . .
277	812	. . .	327	867	. . .	78/71/376	920	32 Edw. III
278	800	. . .	328	858	. . .	377	919	. . .
279	815	. . .	329	862	. . .	378	916	. . .
280	816	22 Edw. III	330	859	. . .	379	917	. . .
281	802	21 Edw. III	331	860	. . .	380	921	. . .
282	808	. . .	332	863	. . .	381	924	. . .
283	803	. . .	333	864	. . .	382	923	. . .
284	804	. . .	334	868	. . .	383	925	. . .
285	801	. . .	335	869	. . .	384	926	. . .
286	809	. . .	336	861	. . .	385	927	. . .
287	822	22 Edw. III	337(a)	870	. . .	386	928	. . .
288	821	. . .	337(b)	872	. . .	387	929	. . .
289	819	. . .	338	878	28 Edw. III	388	918	. . .
290	820	. . .	339	883	. . .	389	937	33 Edw. III
291	818	. . .	340	876	. . .	390	942	. . .
292	823	. . .	341	879	. . .	391	930	. . .
293	830	23 Edw. III	342	872	27 Edw. III	392	938	. . .
294	827	. . .	343	882	28 Edw. III	393	931	. . .
295	828	. . .	344	873	. . .	394	933	. . .
296	824	. . .	345	874	. . .	395	932	. . .
297	825	. . .	346	881	. . .	396	941	. . .
298	826	. . .	347	877	. . .	397	934	. . .
299	829	. . .	348	884	. . .	398	935	. . .
300	833	24 Edw. III	349	896	29 Edw. III	399	945	. . .

number in file	number in text	regnal year	number in file	number in text	regnal year	number in file	number in text	regnal year
78/71/400	939	33 Edw. III	286/35/50	528	4 Edw. III	287/41/338	755	18 Edw. III
78/72/401	943	. . .	286/36/53	531	. . .	342	759	. . .
402	940	. . .	54	532	. . .	287/42/363	779	19 Edw. III
403	944	. . .	55	533	. . .	367	766	. . .
285/26/320	80	34 Edw. I	56	534	. . .	373	768	. . .
285/27/40	22	30 Edw. I	67	544	. . .	382	795	20 Edw. III
285/28/11	135	2 Edw. II	71	552	. . .	389	798	. . .
18	144	. . .	74	554	. . .	287/43/403	810	21 Edw. III
32	158	3 Edw. II	82	556	5 Edw. III	407A	813	. . .
285/29/60	192	5 Edw. II	92	563	. . .	407B	814	. . .
61	195	. . .	96	568	. . .	412	817	22 Edw. III
72	212	6 Edw. II	99	570	. . .	287/44/457	838	25 Edw. III
84	213	7 Edw. II	286/37/109	578	. . .	485	866	27 Edw. III
285/30/107	242	8 Edw. II	122	591	6 Edw. III	487	866	. . .
112	251	. . .	124	593	. . .	488	866	. . .
132	278	10 Edw. II	137	603	7 Edw. III	492A	871	. . .
143	292	. . .	286/38/152	614	8 Edw. III	497	875	28 Edw. III
286/31/168	336	12 Edw. II	153	615	. . .	499	880	. . .
174	347	. . .	287/39/208	649	11 Edw. III	287/45/514	892	29 Edw. III
178	349	. . .	209	650	. . .	521	901	30 Edw. III
185	357	13 Edw. II	211	653	. . .	524	907	. . .
196	391	14 Edw. II	226	645	. . .	529	900	. . .
286/32/232	431	17 Edw. II	227	646	. . .	539	*	
237	440	18 Edw. II	229	647	. . .	547	922	32 Edw. III
247	452	. . .	240	660	. . .	548	922	. . .
286/33/253	454	. . .	245	674	12 Edw. III	549	922	. . .
266	475	19 Edw. II	247	661	. . .	288/46/564	936	33 Edw. III
286/35/1	484	1 Edw. III	287/40/261	691	13 Edw. III	288/51/5	847	26 Edw. III
34	506	3 Edw. III	275	700	14 Edw. III	6	847	. . .
39	511	. . .	287/40/285	702	14 Edw. III	288/51/(2)3	562	5 Edw. III
45	549	. . .	288	696	. . .			

* Reserved for a later volume, being recorded and granted in 38 Edw. II.

ABSTRACTS
OF FEET OF FINES FOR
GLOUCESTERSHIRE

28 Edward I

1300

1.   York. One week [12 June] from Trinity. Petronilla de Valeres quer. by William de Bentley (*Benteleye*); James de Valeres def. by William de Down Ampney (*Dounameneye*). A messuage, 1 ploughland, and 14*s*. 1*d*. rent in the Wick (*Wyk*) by Down Ampney. Right of James. For this, grant and render to Petronilla. To hold during her life, of James, paying a rose a year at St. John the Baptist and doing service to the chief lords. (Warranty.) Reversion to James.

75/38/203

2.   York. Morrow [25 June] of St. John the Baptist. Roger de la Green (*Grene*) of Bulley (*Bulleye*) quer.; Simon Guthlak' of *Putteleye* [Putloe in Standish or Putley, Herefs.] and Matilda his wife imp. Two messuages, 100 a. of land, 4 a. of meadow, 2 a. of pasture, and 12*s*. rent in Bulley. (Warranty of charter.) Right of Roger by gift of Simon and Matilda. (Warranty, specifying Simon's heirs.) Cons. 100 marks.

75/38/204

3.   York. Morrow [25 June] of St. John the Baptist. John Wellshot (*Welyshote*) quer. by William de Staunton; William le Cutler (*Cutiller*) of Gloucester (*Gloucestr'*) and Denise his wife imp. A messuage in Bristol (*Bristoll'*). (Warranty of charter.) Right of John by gift of William and Denise. (Warranty, specifying Denise's heirs.) Cons. 20 marks.

75/38/205

[Cf. *Bristol Gt. Red Book*, pp. 199–200, no. 66.]

29 Edward I

1300

4.   York. Two weeks [25 Nov.] from St. Martin. John Tropin and Felicia his wife quer. by Robert de Wilmington (*Wilmyndon*) in Felicia's place; John Crook (*Crok*) and Hawise his wife def. A messuage, 2 mills, 4 yardlands, 15 a. of pasture, and 10*s*. rent in Elberton (*Ailberton*). John Tropin acknowledged the right of John Crook. For this, grant by John Crook and Hawise to John Tropin and Felicia. To hold during their lives, of John Crook and Hawise and John Crook's heirs, paying a rose a year at St. John the Baptist. (Warranty.) Reversion to John Crook and Hawise and John Crook's heirs.

75/38/209

[For the identity of Elberton, Bigland, *Glos*. ii. 576.]

1301

5.   York. One week [9 Feb.] from the Purification. Peter de Stinchcombe (*Styntescumbe*) the elder quer. by John le Butler (*Butiller*); Thomas de Stinchcombe def. by Ralph son of Hugh le Clerk. A messuage, 2 ploughlands, 18 a. of wood, and 10 a. of pasture in Stinchcombe. Right of Thomas by Peter's gift. For this, grant back and render to Peter. To hold during his life, of Thomas, paying a rose a year at St. John the Baptist. (Warranty.) Reversion to Thomas.

75/38/214

6.   York. Two weeks [16 April] from Easter. John son of Robert Bennett (*Beneyt*) and Isabel his wife quer.; John de Frampton (*Frompton*) imp. One yardland and 4*s*. 3*d*. rent in Bisley (*Bisele*). (Warranty of charter.) Right of Isabel, as those which John and Isabel had by gift of John de Frampton. To hold to John and Isabel and Isabel's heirs. (Warranty.) Cons. 40*s*.

75/38/212

7.   York. One month [30 April] from Easter. William son of Henry Ithenard quer. by John de Middleton (*Middelton*); Henry de Ithenard of Paganhill (*Pagenhull*) def. by William de Dorchester (*Dorchestre*). A messuage, 1½ yardlands, 1 a. of meadow, 8*s*. 1½*d*. rent, a mill, and ½ a. of wood in Paganhill, and 2½ a. of land, 1 a. of meadow, and 3 a. of wood in the said township. Right of William by Henry's gift. For this, grant back and render to Henry. To hold during his life, of William, paying a rose a year at St. John the Baptist, and doing service to the chief lords. (Warranty.) Reversion to William. [*Worn and stained.*]

75/38/210

8.   York. One month [30 April] from Easter. Reynold Jordan (*Jurdan*) and Matilda his wife quer. by Adam de Cirencester (*Cyrencestr'*) in Matilda's place; Walter le Pope and Margery his wife imp. A messuage and ½ yardland in *Hauekescumbe*. (Warranty of charter.) Right of Reynold, as those which Reynold and Matilda had by gift of Walter and Margery. To hold to Reynold and Matilda and Reynold's heirs. (Warranty, specifying Margery's heirs.) Cons. 10 marks.

75/38/211

[*Hauekescumbe* may be the place in Duntisbourne Abbots given as Hanscumb in *P.-N.G.* i. 72.]

9.   York. Two weeks [11 June] from Trinity. John Burne and Denise his wife and John son of John Burne quer.; William de Hidcote (*Hudicotes*) imp. Two messuages, 4 yardlands, and a mill in Ebrington (*Ebrighton*). (Warranty of charter.) John Burne acknowledged the right of William. For this, grant to John Burne and Denise. To hold to them and their heirs in tail. Contingent remainders successively to John son of John Burne and his heirs in tail and to John Burne's heirs.

75/38/208

10. York. One week [1 July] from St. John the Baptist. John Wellshot (*Welishote*) quer. by William de Staunton; John son of Henry Horncastle (*Horncastel*) of Bristol (*Bristollia*) and Cecily his wife imp. A shop in Bristol (*Bristoll'*). (Warranty of charter.) Right of John Wellshot by gift of John and Cecily. (Warranty, specifying Cecily's heirs.) Cons. 100*s*.

75/38/206

[Cf. *Bristol Gt. Red Book*, p. 200, no. 67.]

1301

11. York. One week [1 July] from St. John the Baptist. John Wellshot (*Welishote*) quer. by William de Staunton; John son of Henry Horncastle (*Horncastel*) of Bristol (*Bristollia*) imp. A messuage in Bristol (*Bristoll'*). (Warranty of charter.) Right of John Wellshot by gift of John son of Henry. (Warranty.) Cons. 100*s*.

75/38/207

[Cf. *Bristol Gt. Red Book*, p. 200, no. 68.]

12. York. Two weeks [8 July] from St. John the Baptist. Adam de Gamages quer.; Henry de Ludlow (*Ludelowe*) and Agnes his wife imp. Twenty-eight acres of land and 24 a. of wood in Longhope (*Longehope*). (Warranty of charter.) Right of Adam by gift of Henry and Agnes. (Warranty, specifying Agnes's heirs.) Cons. 60 marks.

75/38/213

30 Edward I

1302

13. York. Two weeks [27 Jan.] from Hilary. John Donhead (*Dunheved*) and Isabel de Hagley (*Haggele*) quer. by Robert de Rottele; John de Middleton (*Middelton*) def. by John de Heyford. Four messuages and 1 ploughland in Sugarswell (*Sokerswelle*) and Shenington (*Shenindon*). John Donhead acknowledged the right of John de Middleton by gift of John and Isabel. For this, grant back and render to John and Isabel. To hold during their lives. Remainder to Isabel's son Edmund and his heirs in tail. Successive contingent remainders to Edmund's brother John and his heirs in tail, to John's brother Roland and his heirs in tail, and to John Donhead's heirs. [*Worn.*]

75/38/222

14. York. One month [20 May] from Easter. Adam son of Adam Scheld quer.; Adam Scheld of *Wytfeld* [Whitfield or Wightfield] and Matilda his wife def. A messuage and ½ yardland in *Wythfeld*. Right of Adam son of Adam by gift of Adam and Matilda. For this, grant back and render to Adam and Matilda. To hold during their lives, of Adam son of Adam, paying a rose a year at St. John the Baptist and doing service to the chief lords. (Warranty.) Reversion to Adam son of Adam.

75/38/219

15. York. One month [20 May] from Easter. Roger de Burghill (*Burghhull*) and Juliana his wife quer. by Adam Lucas; Mr. John de Chandos (*Chaundos*) def. by John de la Barrow (*Barwe*). A messuage, 1 ploughland, 6 a. of meadow, 2 a. of wood, and 20*s*. rent in Hatherley (*Haderleye*). Roger acknowledged the right of John. For this, grant and render to Roger and Juliana. To hold to them and their heirs in tail. Contingent remainder to Roger's heirs.

75/38/220

16. York. Five weeks [27 May] from Easter. Bartholomew Barron (*Barun*) of Churcham (*Chirgehamme*) quer.; Ralph Barron of Churcham and Cecily his wife imp. by Robert de Prestbury (*Prestebury*) in Ralph's place. A messuage and 1 yardland in Great Taynton (*Magna Teynton*). (Warranty of charter.) Right of Bartholomew by gift of Ralph and Cecily. (Warranty, specifying Cecily's heirs.) Cons. £20.

75/38/221

1302

17. York. Morrow [1 June] of Ascension. Hugh Sanekyn and Joan his wife quer. by John de Lyons (*Lyouns*); William de Wychewelle and Florence his wife and Robert de Bedford (*Bedeford*) and Margery his wife imp. by Richard de Bristol (*Bristoll'*) in Robert's place. A messuage in Bristol. (Warranty of charter.) Right of Hugh, as that which Hugh and Joan had by gift of William, Florence, Robert, and Margery. To hold to Hugh and Joan and Hugh's heirs. (Warranty, specifying Florence's and Margery's heirs.) Cons. £20.

75/38/223

[Cf. *Bristol Gt. Red Book*, pp. 200–1, no. 69.]

18. York. Morrow [1 June] of Ascension. Peter le Francis (*Fraunceys*) and Isabel his wife quer. by John de Lyons (*Lyouns*); Robert de Bedford (*Bedeford*) and Margery his wife imp. by Richard de Bristol (*Bristoll'*) in Robert's place. Rent of 9*s*. in Bristol. (Warranty of charter.) Right of Peter, as that which Peter and Isabel had by gift of Robert and Margery. To hold to Peter and Isabel and Peter's heirs. (Warranty, specifying Margery's heirs.) Cons. 10 marks.

75/38/224

[Cf. *Bristol Gt. Red Book*, p. 201, no. 70.]

19. York One week [24 June] from Trinity. Walter le Watevill the younger quer.; Walter le Watevill the elder imp. One yardland in Hidcote Bartrim (*Hudycote Bertram*). (Warranty of charter.) Right of Walter the younger by Walter the elder's gift. (Warranty.) Cons. £10.

75/38/216

20. York. One week [24 June] from Trinity. William de Garden (*Gardino*) and Isabel his wife quer.; Mr. William de Apperley (*Apperle*) imp. The manor of Cugley (*Coggele*). (Warranty of charter.) Right of Isabel, as that which William and Isabel had by Mr. William's gift. To hold to William and Isabel and Isabel's heirs. (Warranty.) Cons. 100 marks.

75/38/218

21. York. One week [1 July] from St. John the Baptist. Mr. William de Apperley (*Apperle*) quer.; William de Garden (*Gardino*) and Isabel his wife imp. The manor of Coverdine (*Culverden*) and 6 bovates of land and 6*s*. rent in Wallsworth (*Walesworth*). (Warranty of charter.) Right of Mr. William by gift of William and Isabel. (Warranty, specifying Isabel's heirs.) Cons. £100. *Endorsed* Ralph Barron (*Barun*) put in his claim. Agnes de Matson (*Mattesden*) and Eve her sister put in their claim.

75/38/217

22. York. Morrow [12 Nov.] of St. Martin. John le Brown (*Brun*) and Margery his wife quer. by John de Eyvill in John's place; John de Acton def. A messuage, 1 ploughland, and 40*s*. rent in Eycot (*Eycote*). Right of John de Acton by gift of John and Margery. For this, grant back and render to John and Margery. To hold during their lives. Remainder to John son of John de Acton and Elena his wife and Elena's heirs in tail. Successive contingent remainders to William Malherbe (*Malerbe*) and Elizabeth his wife and Elizabeth's heirs in tail and to Margery's heirs.

75/38/215

[A copy of this fine, indented neither at the top nor at the side, is filed as 285/27/40. It gives the final contingent remainder not to Margery's but to Elizabeth's heirs. It is endorsed 'These are fines of the manors of *Reppeford* and *West Schene* levied in the king's court'; the endorsement appears to have no relevance to the fine on which it is written, the places mentioned being perhaps Rofford (Oxon.) and West Sheen (Surrey).]

31 Edward I

1303

23. York. One week [9 Feb.] from the Purification. Gilbert FitzStephen (*Fiz Estevene*) pet. by Henry de Braundeston; Nicholas abbot of the church of St. Mary, Stanley (*Stanlegh*), tenant by John Turpyn. A messuage, a mill, 6 ploughlands, 60 a. of meadow, 20 a. of wood, 50 a. of pasture, and 5 marks rent in Codrington (*Cotherington*) by Pucklechurch (*Pokelchurche*). (Grand assize.) Right of the abbot. Remise and quitclaim to him. Cons. 100 marks. It was found by inquisition that long before the statute of Mortmain the abbot and his predecessors had seisin. *Endorsed* John de Cerne put in his claim. Henry de Haddon put in his claim. Margery de Mohun put in her claim. John de Brokenborough (*Brokebergh*) put in his claim.

75/39/232

24. York. Two weeks [21 April] from Easter. Nicholas Fader of Horton (*Horton*) quer.; Adam de Eccleshall (*Eccleshale*) def. A messuage, 43½ a. of land, 4 a. and 3 roods of meadow, and 1 a. and 3 roods of wood in Horton by Sodbury (*Sobbury*). Right of Adam by Nicholas's gift. For this, grant back and render to Nicholas. To hold during his life, of Adam, paying a rose a year at St. John the Baptist and doing service to the chief lords. (Warranty.) Reversion to Adam.

75/39/233

25. York. One month [5 May] from Easter. John le Brown (*Brun*) quer. by Gilbert Ash (*Asshe*); John de Acton def. by Adam Lucas. The manor of Elkstone (*Elkeston*) and the advowson of the church of the same manor. Right of John de Acton by John le Brown's gift. For this, grant back and render to John le Brown. To hold during his life, of the king. Remainder to John son of John de Acton and his wife Elena and their heirs in tail. Successive contingent remainders to William Malherbe (*Malerbe*) and his wife Elizabeth and their heirs in tail, and to John de Acton's heirs. Made by the king's order. [*Worn.*]

75/39/231

26. York. One week [9 June] from Trinity. John le Tanner (*Tannur*) of Leigh (*Leye*) and Joan his wife quer. by John de Lyons (*Lyouns*); Thomas Bonboef and Cristina his wife and Nicholas de Ufton (*Oftoune*) and Isabel his wife def. by Richard de Bristol (*Bristoll'*) in Thomas's place. A messuage in the suburb of Bristol. Right of John, as that which John and Joan had by gift of Thomas and Cristina and Nicholas and Isabel. To hold to John and Joan and John's heirs. (Warranty, specifying Cristina's and Isabel's heirs.) Cons. £10.

75/39/230

[Cf. *Bristol Gt. Red Book*, p. 201, no. 71.]

27. York. One week [1 July] from St. John the Baptist. Robert Hansum of Gloucester (*Gloucestr'*) the younger quer.; Richard Gabriel of Winchester (*Wynton'*) and Beatrice his wife imp. Two messuages, a mill, a garden, 6 a. of land, 4 a. of meadow, and 70*s.* 6*d.*

1303

rent in *Wykeham*, Sandhurst (*Sandhust*), Brook Street (*Brokestrete*) Gloucester, and the suburb of Gloucester (*Glouc'*). (Warranty of charter.) Right of Robert by gift of Richard and Beatrice. (Warranty, specifying Beatrice's heirs.) Cons. 100 marks.

75/39/227

[For *Wycham*, in Hempsted, see *P.-N.G.* ii. 167.]

28. York. One week [1 July] from St. John the Baptist. John Woodlock (*Wodelok*) of Cirencester (*Cyrencestr'*) and Avice his wife quer.; William Godwin (*Godwyne*) of Cirencester and Joan his wife imp. A messuage in Cirencester. (Warranty of charter.) Right of John, as that which John and Avice had by gift of William and Joan. To hold to John and Avice and John's heirs. (Warranty, specifying Joan's heirs.) Cons. £10.

75/39/228

29. York. One week [1 July] from St. John the Baptist. John abbot of the church of St. Mary of Bordesley (*Bordesleye*) quer. by John le Butler (*Botiller*); Guy de Beauchamp (*de Bello Campo*) earl of Warwick (*Warwyk*) def. by Roger Camp (*Caumpe*). The advowson of the church of Childswickham (*Wykewane*). Right of the abbot by the earl's gift. Remise and quitclaim to the abbot. (Warranty.) The abbot received the earl and his heirs into all future prayers and benefits in his church. Made by the king's order.

75/39/229

30. York. One week [1 July] from St. John the Baptist. Walter de Brinsop (*Bruneshope*) quer. by John Barrow (*Barewe*); Sibyl de Brinsop def. by Adam Lucas. Half of a messuage and a mill in Lydney (*Lydeneye*) and Purton (*Pyriton*) held by Ralph Hathaway (*Athewy*) for term of life. Right of Walter. Grant of the reversion to him. (Warranty.) Cons. 100*s*. Made in Ralph's presence and with his consent, and he did fealty to Walter.

75/39/234

31. York. One week [6 Oct.] from Michaelmas. Walter [de Wykewane] abbot of the church of St. Mary and St. Kenelm, Winchcombe (*Wynchechumbe*), quer. by John de Bledington (*Bladynton*); John le Brown (*Brun*) of Elkstone (*Elkeston*) and Margery his wife imp. A messuage, 1 ploughland, 1 a. of wood, and 20*s*. 3*d*. rent in Winchcombe, Coates (*Cotes*) by Winchcombe, Thropp (*Thorp*) by Winchcombe and Peasley (*Pyseleye*) by Winchcombe. (Warranty of charter.) Right of the abbot by gift of John and Margery. (Warranty, specifying Margery's heirs.) Cons. £200. Made by the king's order. [*Worn.*]

75/38/225

32. York. Morrow [12 Nov.] of St. Martin. William de Westbrook (*Westbrok*) of Thornbury (*Thornburi*) quer. by John le Butler (*Botiller*); Gilbert de Ruwes and Isolda his wife imp. Two messuages, 33 a. of land, 2 a. of meadow, 3 a. of pasture, and 5s. rent in Tockington (*Tokinton*) and *Whyteleye* [Wheatleaze?]. (Warranty of charter.) Right of William by gift of Gilbert and Isolda. (Warranty, specifying Isolda's heirs.) Cons. £20.

75/39/226

32 Edward I

1304

33. York. Two weeks [27 Jan.] from Hilary. Ellis de Axbridge (*Axebrigg*) quer. by John de Lyons (*Lyouns*); Adam de Bercham (*Berkham*) def. by John le Butler (*Botiller*). Rent of 40*s*. in the suburb of Bristol (*Bristoll'*). Right of Ellis by Adam's gift. (Warranty.) Cons. £20.

75/39/236

[Cf. *Bristol Gt. Red Book*, p. 201, no. 72.]

34. York. Three weeks [19 April] from Easter. John le Butler (*Botyller*) quer.; John de Bellew (*de Bella Aqua*) def. Seven messuages, 6 tofts, 4 yardlands and 7 a. of land, and 20 a. of meadow in Lechlade (*Lecchelade*). Right of John le Butler (*Botiller*). Remise and quitclaim to him. (Warranty.) Cons. 20 marks.

75/39/237

35. York. One month [26 April] from Easter. Thomas de Rodborough (*Rodebergh*) and Joan his wife quer. by John de Middleton (*Middelton*); Edmund son of Bartholomew de Turville (*Turbrevill*) def. by Simon de Welford (*Wellefford*). The manor of Notgrove (*Nategrave*) except for 2 yardlands in the same. (Warranty of charter.) Right of Thomas, as that which Thomas and Joan had by Edmund's gift. To hold to Thomas and Joan and Thomas's heirs. (Warranty.) Cons. £100.

75/39/235

36. York. One month [26 April] from Easter. Richard de Barton and Thomas Neel of Pirton (*Pyreton*) quer. by John de Slaughter (*Sloughtre*); Walter de Barton (*Berton*) imp. by Richard de Bickerton (*Bykerton*). Nine messuages, 10 yardlands, and one third of a messuage and a mill in Winstone (*Wyneston*). (Warranty of charter.) Right of Walter. For this, grant to Richard and Thomas and Richard's heirs in tail. Contingent remainder to Thomas's heirs. (Warranty.)

75/39/238

37. York. One month [26 April] from Easter. John de Slaughter (*Sloughtre*) quer.; Walter de Barton (*Berton*) def. by Richard de Bickerton (*Bykerton*). A messuage, 80 a. of land, 6 a. of meadow, and 4*s*. rent in South Cerney (*Suth Sarneye*). Right of John by Walter's gift. (Warranty.) Cons. 100 marks.

75/39/239

38. York. Two weeks [7 June] from Trinity. John le Brown (*Brun*) quer. by Gilbert Ash (*Asshe*); John de Acton (*Actone*) def. by Adam Lucas. One third of the manor of Winstone (*Wynneston*). Right of John de Acton by John le Brown's gift. For this, grant back and render to John le Brown. To hold during his life, of the king. Remainder to John son of John de Acton and Elena his wife and their heirs in tail. Successive contingent remainders to William Malherbe (*Malerbe*) and Elizabeth his wife and their heirs in tail and to John de Acton. Made by the king's order.

75/39/240

1304

39. York. Two weeks [7 June] from Trinity. William Randolf quer.; Walter Poitevin (*Peytevyn*) and Cecily his wife imp. A messuage in the suburb of Bristol (*Bristoll'*). (Warranty of charter.) Right of William by gift of Walter and Cecily. (Warranty, specifying Cecily's heirs.) Cons. £20.

75/39/242

[Cf. *Bristol Gt. Red Book*, p. 202, no. 73.]

40. York. Three weeks [14 June] from Trinity. Robert de Goldhill (*Goldhull*) quer.; William de Morwent (*Marewent*) def. A messuage, 1 yardland and 6 a. of land, and 2 a. of meadow in Hartpury (*Hardepyrye*), Morwent (*Marwent*), Rudford (*Rodeford*), and Maisemore (*Maysmore*). Right of Robert. Render to him. (Warranty.) Cons. 20 marks.

75/39/241

41. York. One month [21 June] from Trinity. John le Taverner of Bristol (*Bristoll'*) and Agnes his wife quer.; Walter Poitevin (*Peytevyn*) and Cecily his wife def. A messuage and 5 shops in Bristol and the suburb of the same town. Right of John, as those which John and Agnes had by gift of Walter and Cecily. To hold to John and Agnes and John's heirs. (Warranty, specifying Cecily's heirs.) Cons. £40.

75/39/243

[Cf. *Bristol Gt. Red Book*, p. 202, no. 74.]

42. York. One week [6 Oct.] from Michaelmas. Robert de Farndon clerk quer.; Robert de Kent of Campden (*Caumpeden*) chaplain def. One yardland in Broad Campden (*Brode Caumpeden*). Right of Robert de Farndon by Robert de Kent's gift. (Warranty.) Cons. 40 marks.

75/39/247

43. York. One month [27 Oct.] from Michaelmas. Stephen de Acton Turville (*Acton Turvill*) quer.; Warin son of William def. A messuage and 1 ploughland in Acton Turville. Right of Warin. For this, grant and render to Stephen. To hold during his life. Remainder to William son of the same Stephen and his heirs in tail. Successive contingent remainders to Robert brother of the same William and his heirs in tail and to Warin's heirs. *Endorsed* John son of Stephen de Acton put in his claim. [*Worn.*]

75/39/246

44. York. Morrow [12 Nov.] of St. Martin. Felicia de Chester (*Cestre*) quer.; Richard la Bank (*Labank*) and Lucy his wife imp. A messuage, a mill, 2 ploughlands, and 33*s.* rent in Longborough (*Langebergh*). (Warranty of charter.) Right of Felicia by gift of Richard and Lucy. For this, grant back and render to Richard and Lucy. To hold during their lives. Remainder to William de Chester of Campden (*Campeden*).

75/39/244

45. York. One week [18 Nov.] from St. Martin. Richard de Plumtre, Thomas de Pendock (*Penedok*), and William atte Verne quer.; Walter Aubrey (*Aubray*) and Agnes his wife def. A messuage, a shop, and 16*d.* rent in Gloucester (*Glouc'*). Right of William. To hold to Richard, Thomas, and William and William's heirs. (Warranty, specifying Agnes's heirs.) Cons. £4.

75/39/245

33 Edward I

1305

46. One week [9 Feb.] from the Purification. Robert de Hampton quer.; Thorald de la Mountain (*Muntaigne*) and Joan his wife def. A messuage in the suburb of Bristol (*Bristoll'*). Right of Robert by gift of Thorald and Joan. (Warranty, specifying Joan's heirs.) Cons. 10 marks.

75/40/271

[Cf. *Bristol Gt. Red Book*, p. 204, no. 81.]

47. One week [9 Feb.] from the Purification. Stephen de Beaumont (*de Bello Monte*) quer. by Walter de Compton; Thorald de la Mountain (*Mountaigne*) and Joan his wife imp. A messuage in Bristol (*Bristoll'*). (Warranty of charter.) Right of Stephen by gift of Thorald and Joan. (Warranty, specifying Joan's heirs.) Cons. 100*s*.

75/40/272

[Cf. *Bristol Gt. Red Book*, p. 204, no. 82. Thorald is called Theobald at one point in the document.]

48. Two weeks [2 May] from Easter. John de Heyford and Joan his wife quer.; John de Radbrook (*Rodbrok*) def. by Richard de Stanley (*Stonleye*). A messuage and 1 ploughland in Quinton (*Quenton*) and Radbrook. John de Heyford acknowledged the right of John de Radbrook. For this, grant and render to John de Heyford and Joan. To hold to them and their heirs in tail. (Warranty.) Contingent remainder to Joan's heirs.

75/40/264

49. Two weeks [2 May] from Easter. John le Taverner of Bristol (*Bristoll'*) quer.; Walter Poitevin (*Peytevyn*) of Bristol and Cecily his wife def. by John de Lyons (*Lyouns*) in Walter's place. Two shops in Bristol. Right of John. Remise and quitclaim, specifying Cecily's heirs, to him. (Warranty.) Cons. 20 marks.

75/40/267

[Cf. *Bristol Gt. Red Book*, p. 203, no. 77.]

50. Two weeks [2 May] from Easter. John le Parker quer.; Thorald de la Mountain (*Muntayne*) and Joan his wife def. Rent of 10*s*. in Bristol (*Bristoll'*). Right of John. Remise and quitclaim, specifying Joan's heirs, to him. (Warranty.) Cons. 100*s*.

75/40/268

[Cf. *Bristol Gt. Red Book*, p. 203, no. 78.]

51. Two weeks [2 May] from Easter. William Hayl and Matilda his wife quer.; Walter Poitevin (*Peytevyn*) and Cecily his wife def. A messuage in the suburb of Bristol (*Bristoll'*). Right of William. Render to him and Matilda. To hold to them and William's heirs. (Warranty, specifying Cecily's heirs.) Cons. 20 marks.

75/40/270

[Cf. *Bristol Gt. Red Book*, p. 204, no. 80.]

52. One month [16 May] from Easter. John le Long (*Lange*) of Bristol (*Bristoll'*) quer.; William de Horfield (*Horfeld*) and Joan his wife imp. A messuage in Bristol. (Warranty of charter.) Right of John by gift of William and Joan. (Warranty, specifying Joan's heirs.) Cons. £20.

75/40/269

[Cf. *Bristol Gt. Red Book*, p. 203, no. 79.]

1305

53. One week [20 June] from Trinity. Robert de Berkeley (*Berkeleye*) and Joan his wife quer.; William le Harper (*Harpur*) and Matilda his wife and Matilda's son John. A messuage, 80 a. of land, 5 a. of meadow, and 7*s*. 6*d*. rent in Cam (*Camme*). Right of Robert. Remise and quitclaim, specifying Matilda's heirs, to him and Joan and Robert's heirs. (Warranty.) Cons. £10.

75/40/259

54. One week [20 June] from Trinity. (Made York, morrow of St. John the Baptist, 32 Edward I [25 June 1304].) Thomas de Berkeley (*Berkeleye*) quer.; Richard son of John de Clifford def. The manor of Frampton on Severn (*Frompton super Sabrinam*), held by Robert son of Payn and Isabel his wife for term of life. Right of Thomas. Grant of the reversion to him. (Warranty.) Cons. £200. Made in the presence and with the consent of Robert and Isabel, who acknowledged that they had only a life-interest, and they rendered the manor to Thomas in court, and remised and quitclaimed it to him.

75/40/265

[Cf. *Berkeley Castle Mun.* i, p. 460, A2/23/4 (counterpart).]

55. Morrow [25 June] of St. John the Baptist. Ralph de Monthermer (*de Monte Hermeri*) earl of Gloucester (*Glouc'*) and Hertford (*Hertf'*) and Joan his wife quer. by Henry de Hexton; John de Cardiff (*Kerdif*) of Bristol (*Bristoll'*) the younger and Joan his wife def. A messuage, 2 ploughlands, and 1 yardland in Earthcott (*Erdecote*), Alveston (*Alweston*), and Row Earthcott (*Ruerdecote*). Right of Ralph, as those which he and Joan had by gift of John and Joan. To hold to Ralph and Joan and Ralph's heirs. (Warranty, specifying John's heirs.) Cons. 200 marks. *Endorsed* Robert de Acton put in his claim. Richard Devereux (*Deveroys*) put in his claim.

75/40/260

56. One week [1 July] from St. John the Baptist. William de Boxwell of Tetbury (*Tetteburi*) quer.; William Waleys and Alice his wife imp. A toft in Tetbury. (Warranty of charter.) Right of William de Boxwell by gift of William Waleys and Alice. (Warranty, specifying Alice's heirs.) Cons. 40*s*.

75/40/256

57. One week [1 July] from St. John the Baptist. Roger de la Green (*Grene*) of Bulley (*Bulleye*) and Alice his wife quer.; John de Okle (*Acle*) chaplain imp. A messuage, 200 a. of land, 8 a. of meadow, and 5 marks rent in Bulley. (Warranty of charter.) Right of Roger, as those which he and Alice had by John's gift. To hold to Roger and Alice and Roger's heirs. (Warranty.) Cons. £20.

75/40/258

58. One week [1 July] from St. John the Baptist. Margaret who was wife of John Giffard of Brimpsfield (*Brymesfeld*) quer.; John le White of Bristol (*Bristoll'*) def. A mill and 1 ploughland in Harry Stoke (*Stoke Henry*). Right of Margaret. Render to her. Cons. £20.

75/40/261

59. One week [1 July] from St. John the Baptist. John de Acton quer.; Nicholas son of Nicholas le Archer def. Sixty acres of land and 40*s*. rent in Winstone (*Wynneston*) held

1305

by William Absalon (*Apselon*) for term of life. Right of John. Grant of the reversion to him. To hold of the king. (Warranty.) Cons. 40 marks. William did fealty to John. Made by the king's order.

75/40/262

60. One week [1 July] from St. John the Baptist. Richard de Apperley (*Apperleye*) pet.; Geoffrey Murdoch (*Murdak*) and Margery his wife tenants. Two and a half yardlands, 35 a. of meadow, and 23*s.* rent in Lechlade (*Lechelad*). [Form of plea not specified.] Right of Richard. For this, grant to Geoffrey and Margery. To hold to them and their heirs in tail. Contingent remainder to Geoffrey's heirs.

75/40/263

61. One week [1 July] from St. John the Baptist. Thomas Russel quer.; Simon Hackespon of Bristol (*Bristoll'*) and Agnes his wife imp. A messuage in the suburb of Bristol. (Warranty of charter.) Right of Thomas by gift of Simon and Agnes. (Warranty, specifying Agnes's heirs.) Cons. 20 marks.

75/40/266

[Cf. *Bristol Gt. Red Book*, p. 203, no. 76.]

62. One week [1 July] from St. John the Baptist. William Ithenard and Eleanor his wife quer.; William de Burne def. A messuage and 1 yardland in Paganhill (*Pagenhull*). Right of William de Burne. For this, grant and render to William Ithenard and Eleanor. To hold to them and their heirs in tail. Contingent remainder to William Ithenard's heirs.

75/40/273

63. One week [6 Oct.] from Michaelmas. John le Rouse (*Rus*) and Hawise his wife quer. by Robert de Harescombe (*Harsecumbe*); Hugh de Almaly and Isabel Turbot def. by Robert de Prestbury (*Prestebury*). The manors of Duntisbourne Rouse (*Duntesburne*) and Harescombe (*Harescumbe*) and the advowsons of the churches of the same manors. Right of John. Render to John and Hawise. To hold to John and Hawise and John's heirs. Cons. £200.

75/39/248

64. One week [6 Oct.] from Michaelmas. Robert son of Payn and Isabel his wife quer.; Thomas de Berkeley (*Berkeleye*) the elder def. The manor of Frampton on Severn (*Frompton super Sabrinam*). Right of Thomas. For this, grant and render to Robert and Isabel. To hold to them and Robert's heirs in tail, of Thomas, paying 22 marks a year, at Michaelmas, Christmas, Easter, and St. John the Baptist, and doing service to the chief lords. Contingent reversion to Thomas.

75/39/250

[Cf. *Berkeley Castle Mun.* i, p. 460, A2/23/5 (counterpart).]

65. One week [6 Oct.] from Michaelmas. John de Abenhall (*Abbenhale*) and Clemency his wife quer.; Robert de Helion (*Helyun*) and Isabel his wife def. A messuage, 60 a. of land, and 6*s.* rent in Blaisdon (*Bletheden*). Right of Robert. For this, grant by Robert and Isabel to John and Clemency. To hold to them and John's heirs in tail. (Warranty, specifying Robert's heirs.) Contingent remainder to John's brother Reynold.

75/40/252

1305

66. One week [6 Oct.] from Michaelmas. John de Hillesley (*Hildesley*) and Joan his wife quer.; Stephen son of Laurence de Hillesley (*Hildesleye*) def. A messuage, 3 yardlands, 10 a. of meadow, and 10 a. of wood in Hawkesbury (*Haukesbury*). Right of Stephen by John's gift. For this, grant and render to John and Joan. To hold during their lives. Remainder to John's son Ellis and his heirs in tail. Successive contingent remainders to Ellis's sister Isabel and her heirs in tail, to Isabel's sister Margaret and her heirs in tail, to Margaret's sister Margery and her heirs in tail, and to Margery wife of Adam de Eyton. [*Worn.*]

75/40/254

67. One week [6 Oct.] from Michaelmas. John de Avening (*Avenyngg*) and Margery his wife quer.; Thomas de Beverston (*Beverstone*) def. A messuage and 1½ yardlands in Beverston (*Beverston*). Right of Thomas. For this, grant and render to John and Margery. To hold to them and their heirs in tail. (Warranty.) Contingent remainder to John's heirs.

75/40/255

68. Two weeks [13 Oct.] from Michaelmas. Guy de Beauchamp (*de Bello Campo*) earl of Warwick (*Warr'*) quer.; Alice who was wife of Walter de Beauchamp imp. Twenty-three messuages, 10 yardlands, 5 a. of meadow, and 3 a. of pasture in Kemerton (*Kynemarton*) and Aston on Carrant (*Astone*). (Warranty of charter.) Right of the earl by Alice's gift. For this, grant back and render to Alice. To hold during her life, of the earl, paying a rose a year at St. John the Baptist and doing service to the chief lords. Reversion to the earl.

75/39/249

69. Morrow [12 Nov.] of St. Martin. Walter de Gloucester (*Gloucestr'*) and Hawise his wife quer.; Richard Parfet and Margery his wife def. A messuage and 2 ploughlands in Brockworth (*Brocworth*). Right of Walter. Remise and quitclaim, specifying Margery's heirs, to Walter and Hawise and Walter's heirs. (Warranty.) Cons. £40.

75/40/251

70. One week [18 Nov.] from St. Martin. John son of Ralph de Dudbridge (*Dodebrygge*) quer.; Benedict de Dudbridge and Nichola his wife def. A messuage, 1½ a. of meadow, and half of 1 yardland in Paganhill (*Pagenhull*). Right of John by gift of Benedict and Nichola. For this, grant back and render to Benedict and Nichola. To hold to them and their heirs in tail. Contingent remainder to Benedict's heirs. [*Worn.*]

75/40/257

34 Edward I

1306

71. One week [20 Jan.] from Hilary. (Made York, one week from St. Martin 27 Edward I [18 Nov. 1299].) Walter de Cuylly quer.; John de Tessale and Matilda his wife def. A messuage, a garden, 26 a. of land, 8 a. of meadow, 1 a. of wood, 20*s.* rent, and one sixth of a mill in Charlton (*Cherleton*), Redland (*Thridelond*), and Lawrence Weston (*Weston Sancti Laurencii*). Right of Walter by gift of John and Matilda. And grant to Walter of the reversion of one third of a messuage, 3 ploughlands, a mill, and £10 rent held by

1306

Geoffrey de Ashland (*Asselond*) and Joan his wife in Joan's dower in the said townships, of Matilda's inheritance. (Warranty.) Cons. £40. Made in the presence of Geoffrey and Joan and with their consent, and they did fealty to Walter. [*Worn.*]

75/41/292

72. Two weeks [27 Jan.] from Hilary. John de Albrighton (*Albrightone*) quer.; Nicholas de Brent (*Brente*) def. A messuage and 1 yardland in Pucklechurch (*Pukelchurche*). Right of John. Render to him. Cons. 10 marks.

75/41/291

73. Two weeks [27 Jan.] from Hilary. Reynold Allway (*Eylwy*) quer.; Walter Allway imp. A messuage, a mill, 1 yardland, 3 a. of meadow, 1 a. of pasture, 6 a. of wood, and 4*s*. rent in Taynton (*Teyntone*). (Warranty of charter.) Right of Reynold by Walter's gift. For this, grant back and render to Walter. To hold during his life, of Reynold, paying a rose a year at St. John the Baptist and doing service to the chief lords. Reversion to Reynold.

75/41/294

74. One week [9 Feb.] from the Purification. (Made York, morrow of the Purification 32 Edward I [3 Feb. 1304].) Richard le Mercer of Worcester (*Wygorn'*) and Margery his wife and John son of Richard le Mercer of Worcester quer.; John de Morton and Elizabeth his wife def. Rents of 26*s*. and 1 lb. of pepper in Colesborne (*Colesburn*). Right of Richard, Margery, and John son of Richard, by gift of John and Elizabeth. To hold to Richard, Margery, John son of Richard, and Richard's heirs. (Warranty, by Elizabeth alone.) Cons. 20 marks.

75/40/274

[There is no clear indication that John's father was the same as the first-named Richard le Mercer.]

75. One week [9 Feb.] from the Purification. Maurice de Berkeley (*Berkeleye*) quer.; Ivo de Coombe (*Cumbe*) and Matilda his wife def. Two messuages, 1 yardland, and 3 a. of meadow in Wotton under Edge (*Wottone*). Right of Maurice. Render to him. (Warranty, specifying Matilda's heirs.) Cons. £10.

75/41/290

76. One week [9 Feb.] from the Purification. John atte Hall (*Halle*) of Little Badminton (*Parva Badmyntone*) quer.; Roger atte Hall of Little Badminton def. A messuage and 1 ploughland in Little Badminton. Right of John. For this, grant to Roger. To hold during his life, of John, paying a rose a year at St. John the Baptist and doing service to the chief lords. Reversion to John. [*Worn.*]

75/41/293

77. Two weeks [17 April] from Easter. John de Oxenton (*Oxindon*) quer.; Alice del Pount imp. by Henry de Sulstane. A messuage, 20 a. of land, and 2½ a. of meadow in Oxenton. (Warranty of charter.) Right of John by Alice's gift. For this, grant back and render to Alice. To hold during her life, of John, paying a rose a year at St. John the Baptist and doing service to the chief lords. Reversion to John.

75/41/288

1306

78. Three weeks [24 April] from Easter. Odo of Dumbleton (*Dumbeltone*) and Geva his wife quer.; Geoffrey Conquest def. A messuage, 1 ploughland, 7 a. of meadow, 3 a. of wood, and 15*s.* rent in Woolstone (*Wolstone*), Bishop's Cleeve (*Clive*), Woodmancote (*Wodemanecote*), and Gotherington (*Gotherynton*). Right of Geoffrey by gift of Odo and Geva. For this, grant back and render to Odo and Geva. To hold to them and their heirs in tail. Contingent remainder to Odo's heirs.

75/41/289

79. One week [5 June] from Trinity. Rose de Arden (*Arderne*) quer. by Jordan de Minworth (*Munneworth*); William de Tracy def. by John Bonsire of Toddington (*Tudyngton*). The manor of Doynton (*Doynton*). Right of Rose. Render to her. (Warranty.) Cons. 100 marks.

75/41/285

80. One week [5 June] from Trinity. (Made two weeks [17 April] from Easter in the said year.) Matilda daughter of Thomas de Sezincote (*Shesnecote*) quer.; Henry de Duffield (*Duffeld*) and Alice his wife def.) Peter dc Wallingford (*Walingeford*) and the said Matilda his wife quer.; the said Henry and Alice def. The manor of Sezincote, GLOS., and a messuage, 1 ploughland and 2 yardlands, 18 a. of meadow, 12 a. of wood, and 10 marks and 11*s.* rent in Harlaxton (*Herlauston*) by Grantham (*Grantham*) and Londonthorpe (*Lunderthorp*), LINCS. Right of Matilda, except for a messuage, 3 yardlands, and 12 a. of meadow in the said manor. Remise and quitclaim, specifying Alice's heirs, to Peter and Matilda and Matilda's heirs. For this, grant and render to Henry and Alice of the messuage, 3 yardlands, and 12 a. of meadow in the said manor. To hold to them and Alice's heirs. *Labelled* Glouc', Lincoln'. *Endorsed* Edward I (*E[dwardi] p[ri]mi*).

285/26/320

81. Two weeks [12 June] from Trinity. John del Cellar (*Celer*) quer.; William de Taunton and Alice his wife imp. A messuage and 4 shops in the suburb of Bristol (*Bristoll'*). (Warranty of charter.) Right of John by gift of William and Alice. (Warranty, specifying Alice's heirs). Cons. 10 marks. *Endorsed* John Andrew (*Andreau*) put in his claim.

75/41/286

[Cf. *Bristol Gt. Red Book*, pp. 204–5, no. 83.]

82. One week [1 July] from St. John the Baptist. William son of William Maunsell (*Mauncel*) and Joan daughter of Miles de Beauchamp (*de Bello Campo*) quer.; William Maunsell the elder def. A messuage, 2 ploughlands, and 20 a. of wood in Frampton Mansell (*Frampton*) by Sapperton (*Saberton*). Right of William son of William. Render to him and Joan. To hold to them and the heirs of William son of William. (Warranty.) Cons. £100.

75/41/283

83. One week [1 July] from St. John the Baptist. Simunda who was wife of Drew (*Drogo*) Dane quer. by Walter de Berkeley; William son of William Champneys (*Chaumpeneys*) def. A messuage, 1 yardland, pasture for 8 oxen and 8 cows, rents of 2*s.* 2*d.* and a rose in Henbury (*Hembury in Salso Marisco*), Elmington (*Aylmynton*), and Compton Greenfield (*Cumpton Grenevill*). Right of Simunda by William's gift. And

1306

grant to Simunda of the reversion of 8 a. of land held by Peter Crook (*Crok*) for term of life, of William's inheritance in the said townships. (Warranty.) Cons. £40. Made in Peter's presence and with his consent, and he did fealty to Simunda. [*Worn.*]

75/41/284

84. Two weeks [8 July] from St. John the Baptist. John de Langley (*Langeleye*) and Ela his wife quer.; William Foliot of Tarlton (*Torlton*) def. A messuage and 1 ploughland except for 5 a. of land and 1½ a. of meadow in Upper Siddington (*Over Sodynton*) held by Walter de Lilleybrook (*Lillebrok*) for term of life. Right of John. Grant to John and Ela and John's heirs of the reversion, of William's inheritance. And grant to John and Ela and John's heirs of the reversion of 3½ a. of land and ½ a. of meadow held by John Foliot (*Folyot*) for term of life and of 1½ a. of land and 1 a. of meadow held by the said John Foliot and Mabel his wife for term of life in the same township, of William's inheritance. (Warranty.) Cons. £20. Made in the presence of Walter, John Foliot, and Mabel and with their consent and they did fealty to John and Ela.

75/41/287

85. Two weeks [13 Oct.] from Michaelmas. William de Tracy and Denise his wife quer.; Rose de Arden (*Arderne*) def. The manor of Doynton (*Doynton*). William acknowledged the right of Rose. For this, grant and render to William and Denise. To hold to them and their heirs in tail. Contingent remainder to William's heirs.

75/40/275

86. Two weeks [13 Oct.] from Michaelmas. William de Ryons quer.; Thomas de Hinton (*Hynyton*) and Margery his wife imp. Four acres of meadow and 6*s.* 8*d.* rent in Sandhurst (*Sandhyrst*). (Warranty of charter.) Right of William by gift of Thomas and Margery. (Warranty, specifying Margery's heirs.) Cons. 20 marks.

75/41/276

87. Two weeks [13 Oct.] from Michaelmas. Robert Pope of Gloucester (*Gloucestr'*) quer.; John Allen (*Aleyn*) of *Meys* [Maisemore?] and Matilda his wife imp. A shop in Gloucester. (Warranty of charter.) Right of Robert by gift of John and Matilda. (Warranty, specifying Matilda's heirs.) Cons. 40*s.*

75/41/278

88. Two weeks [13 Oct.] from Michaelmas. Richard son of John de Monmouth (*Monemuth*) and Agnes de Mucegros quer.; Philip de Luda and Anabilla his wife imp. A messuage, 3 a. of meadow, 3*s.* 8¼*d.* rent, and half of 1 ploughland in Bulley (*Bulleye*). (Warranty of charter.) Right of Richard, as that which Richard and Agnes had by gift of Philip and Anabilla. For this, grant back and render to Philip and Anabilla. To hold during their lives, of Richard and Agnes and Richard's heirs, paying a rose a year at St. John the Baptist and doing service to the chief lords. Reversion to Richard and Agnes and Richard's heirs.

75/41/279

89. Two weeks [13 Oct.] from Michaelmas. Thomas de Colethrop quer.; Thomas le Butler (*Botiller*) and Agatha his wife def. A messuage and ½ yardland in Longney

1306

(*Longeneye*). Right of Thomas de Colethrop by gift of Thomas and Agatha. (Warranty, specifying Agatha's heirs.) Cons. 20 marks.

75/41/281

90. Morrow [3 Nov.] of All Souls. John son of Roger de Ravenshill (*Ravenhull*) quer.; Henry de Stroudford (*Strodeford*) def. A messuage, 1 yardland, and 4*d.* rent in Paganhill (*Pagenhull*). Right of John by Henry's gift. For this, grant back and render to Henry. To hold to Henry and his heirs in tail. Contingent remainder to Margery daughter of Roger de Ravenshill during her life and to Henry's heirs.

75/41/282

91. Morrow [12 Nov.] of St. Martin. John son of Stephen de Acton quer.; William de Acton def. A messuage, 39 a. of land, and 3 a. of pasture in Acton Turville (*Acton Turevill*). Right of William by John's gift. (Warranty.) Cons. 20 marks.

75/41/280

92. One week [18 Nov.] from St. Martin. (Made two weeks from Easter 33 Edward I [2 May 1305].) Richard Estmere of Bristol (*Bristoll'*) quer.; Nicholas Estmere and Olive his wife def. Three messuages, 2 shops, and £4 3*s.* 4*d.* rent in Bristol and the suburb of the same town. Right of Richard. Render to him. Remise and quitclaim, specifying Olive's heirs (Warranty.) Cons. 100 marks.

75/40/253

[Cf. *Bristol Gt. Red Book*, p. 202, no. 75. When the fine was made Olive was sole deforciant, named only as the daughter of Henry le Waleys of Bristol, she alone acknowledging Richard's right.]

93. One week [18 Nov.] from St. Martin. Giles de Avebury (*Avenebury*) quer.; Richard Organ of Harescombe (*Harscumbe*) and Agnes his wife imp. A messuage, 11 a. of land, 1 a. of meadow, 3*d.* rent, and half of 1 a. of pasture in Haresfield (*Harsfeld*) and Standish (*Stanedissh*). (Warranty of charter.) Right of Giles by gift of Richard and Agnes. (Warranty, specifying Agnes's heirs.) Cons. 20 marks. *Endorsed* John de la Hay (*Haye*) put in his claim.

75/41/277

35 Edward I

1306

94. Two weeks [25 Nov.] from St. Martin. John de Bradford (*Bradeford*) and Isabel his wife quer.; Walter de Cuylly def. Two messuages, a garden, 31 a. of land, 5½ a. of meadow, 1 a. of wood, rents of 7*s.* and 1 lb. of pepper, and one sixth of a mill in Charlton (*Cherleton*), Redland (*Thriddelond*), and Lawrence Weston (*Weston Sancti Laurencii*). Right of John, as those which John and Isabel had by Walter's gift. To hold to John and Isabel and John's heirs. And grant to John and Isabel and John's heirs of the reversion of one sixth of a messuage, a mill, 3 ploughlands, and £10 rent held by Geoffrey de Ashland (*Asshlond*) and Joan his wife in Joan's dower in the same townships, of Walter's inheritance. (Warranty.) Cons. 40 marks. Made in the presence of Geoffrey and Joan and with their consent, and they did fealty to John and Isabel.

75/41/312

[Cf. above, no. 71.]

1307

95. One week [20 Jan.] from Hilary. John Page and Emma his wife quer.; Laurence le Power and Margery his wife imp. A messuage and 3 yardlands in Lower Lemington (*Lemynton*) by Todenham (*Todenham*). (Warranty of charter.) Right of Emma, as those which John and Emma had by gift of Laurence and Margery. For this, grant back and render to Laurence and Margery. To hold during their lives, of John and Emma and Emma's heirs, paying a rose a year at St. John the Baptist and doing service to the chief lords. (Warranty.) Reversion to John and Emma and Emma's heirs.

75/41/299

96. One week [20 Jan.] from Hilary. Adam le Marshal (*Mareschal*) of Cirencester (*Cyrencestr'*) and Agnes his wife quer.; Roger son of Roger de Duntisbourne (*Duntesburn*) def. A messuage and 1½ yardlands in Duntisbourne Leer (*Duntesburn Lyre*) and Duntisbourne Abbots (*Duntesburn Abbatis Gloucestr'*). Right of Adam, as those which Adam and Agnes had by Roger's gift. To hold to Adam and Agnes and Adam's heirs. (Warranty.) Cons. 20 marks.

75/41/300

97. Two weeks [27 Jan.] from Hilary. Robert Snow of Bristol (*Bristoll'*) quer.; William Busy (*Busi*) and Avice his wife imp. A messuage in Bristol. (Warranty of charter.) Right of Robert by gift of William and Avice. (Warranty, specifying Avice's heirs.) Cons. 10 marks.

75/41/298

[Cf. *Bristol Gt. Red Book*, p. 205, no. 84.]

98. Morrow [3 Feb.] of the Purification. Walter le Felter (*Feltere*) quer.; Walter de Haurugge and Alice his wife imp. A messuage in Gloucester (*Gloucestr'*). (Warranty of charter.) Right of Walter le Felter by gift of Walter and Alice. (Warranty, specifying Walter de Haurugge's heirs.) Cons. 10 marks.

75/41/296

99. One week [9 Feb.] from the Purification. John de Aylburton clerk and Nicholas son of the same John quer.; Henry son of John Andrew (*Andreu*) imp. Fifteen acres of land and 1 a. of meadow in Aylburton (*Aylburton*) by Lydney *Lydeneye*). (Warranty of charter.) Right of Nicholas, as those which John and Nicholas had by Henry's gift. To hold to John and Nicholas and Nicholas's heirs. (Warranty.) Cons. £10.

75/41/295

100. One week [9 Feb.] from the Purification. Reynold de Norcott (*Northcote*) and Lucy his wife quer.; Henry de Scay def. A messuage and 3 yardlands in Shipton Moyne (*Shupton Moigne*). Reynold acknowledged the right of Henry by Reynold's gift. For this, grant and render to Reynold and Lucy. To hold to them and their heirs in tail. Contingent remainder to Reynold's heirs. (Warranty.)

75/41/297

101. Three weeks [16 April] from Easter. Richard son of Richard le Clerk of Paganhill (*Pagenhull*) quer.; Walter Downton (*Dounyntoun*) [*reading uncertain*] vicar of the church of Berkeley (*Berkeleye*) def. A messuage and 18 a. of land in Paganhill. Right of Walter by Richard's gift. For this, grant back and render to Richard. To hold during his life.

1307

Remainder to Joan and Agnes daughters of the same Richard and Joan's heirs in tail. Successive contingent remainders to Agnes's heirs in tail and to Richard's heirs. [*Badly worn.*]

75/41/302

102. Three weeks [16 April] from Easter. Walter de Lilleybrook (*Lillebrok*) and Matilda his wife quer.; Thomas de Hynkole and Elena his wife def. Rent of 31*s.* in Trewsbury (*Trusebury*) by Coates (*Cotes*). Right of Walter. Render to Walter and Matilda. To hold to them and Walter's heirs. (Warranty, specifying Elena's heirs.) Cons. £20.

75/41/303

103. Three weeks [16 April] from Easter. Richard atte Oak (*Ok*) and Margaret his wife quer.; William de East Chelworth (*Estecheleworth*) and Isabel his wife imp. A messuage in the suburb of Bristol (*Bristoll'*). (Warranty of charter.) Right of Richard, as that which Richard and Margaret had by gift of William and Isabel. To hold to Richard and Margaret and Richard's heirs. (Warranty, specifying Isabel's heirs.) Cons. 100*s.*

75/41/311

[Cf. *Bristol Gt. Red Book*, p. 205, no. 85.]

104. One month [23 April] from Easter. Isabel who was wife of William de Birmingham (*Bermyngeham*) quer. by Roger de Lichfield (*Lychefeld*); Stephen de Beaubras [*reading uncertain*] and Sibyl his wife def. A messuage, 120 a. of land, 21 a. of meadow, 8 a. of wood, and 12*s.* 6*d.* rent in Thornbury (*Thornbury*) and Alveston (*Halweston*). Right of Isabel by gift of Stephen and Sibyl. For this, grant back and render to Stephen and Sibyl. To hold during their lives, of Isabel, paying a rose a year at St. John the Baptist and doing service to the chief lords. Remainder to John de Birmingham and his heirs in tail, to hold of Isabel by the said services. Successive contingent remainders to John's brother Henry and his heirs in tail, to Henry's brother Nicholas and his heirs in tail, and to Isabel. [*Badly worn.*]

75/41/301

105. One month [23 April] from Easter. Bartholomew de Grenville (*Greynvill*) and Anne his wife quer.; William Giffard def. The manor of Compton Greenfield (*Cumpton Greyvill*) and the advowson of the chapel of the same manor. Bartholomew acknowledged the right of William by his gift. For this, grant and render to Bartholomew and Anne. To hold to them and Bartholomew's heirs.

75/41/304

[Cf. *Berkeley Castle Mun.* i, p. 456, A2/20/3 (i) (copy).]

106. Two weeks [4 June] from Trinity. William de la Green (*Grene*) quer.; Florence (*Florentius*) de Stoke Bishop (*Stok Episcopi*) def. A messuage and 1 yardland in Stoke Bishop. Right of William. Render to him. (Warranty.) Cons. 20 marks.

75/41/306

107. Morrow [25 June] of St. John the Baptist. John Gullifer (*Golaffre*) quer.; Henry le Chamberlain (*Chaumberleng*) and Matilda his wife def. Two yardlands and 2 messuages and one third of a messuage in Batsford (*Bachesore*). Right of Matilda. For this, grant and render by Henry and Matilda to John. To hold during his life, of Henry and Matilda

1307

and Matilda's heirs, paying a rose a year at St. John the Baptist and doing service to the chief lords. (Warranty.) Reversion to Henry and Matilda and Matilda's heirs. [*Worn.*]

75/41/308

108. Morrow [25 June] of St. John the Baptist. John de Bradford (*Bradeford*) and Isabel his wife quer.; Walter de Pelevill and Nesta his wife and Mr. Adam de Abbotsbury (*Abbodesburi*) and Elena his wife def. A messuage, 4 bovates of land, and 33*s*. rent in Lawrence Weston (*Weston Sancti Laurencii*), Redland (*Thriddelond*), and Charlton (*Cherleton*). Right of John, as in homages and services of free men and villeins holding those villeinages and their families, meadows, feedings, pastures, rents, reliefs, escheats, and all else. Remise and quitclaim, specifying Nesta's and Elena's heirs, to John. (Warranty.) Cons. £40.

75/41/309

109. One week [1 July] from St. John the Baptist. John de Slaughter (*Sloghtre*) and Elena his wife quer.; William de Chester (*Cestre*) of Broad Campden (*Brodecaumpeden*) def. A messuage, 8 yardlands, 6 a. of meadow, 33*s*. rent, and rents of 1 qr. of oats, 6½ qr. of wheat, 6½ qr. beans and peas, and 1 lb. of cumin in Longborough (*Langebergh*) held by Lucy who was wife of Richard la Bank (*Labaunk*) for term of life. Right of John. Grant of the reversion, of William's inheritance, to John and Elena and John's heirs. (Warranty.) Cons. 100 marks. Made in Lucy's presence and with her consent, and she did fealty to John and Elena.

75/41/307

110. Two weeks [8 July] from St. John the Baptist. William de Grumvill quer.; William de Leach (*Lecche*) and Margery his wife imp. A messuage and 2 ploughlands in Eastleach (*Estlecche*). (Warranty of charter.) William de Leach acknowledged the right of William de Grumvill by his gift. For this, grant and render to William de Leach and Margery. To hold to them and William de Leach's heirs.

75/41/305

111. Two weeks [8 July] from St. John the Baptist. John le Butler (*Botiller*) of Llantwit (*Lanultye*) and Beatrice his wife quer.; William [de Rya] abbot of St. Mary's, Flaxley (*Flexlie*), def. by Brother William de Malmesbury. A messuage and 1 ploughland in Brawn (*Breuerne*) and Sandhurst (*Sandhurst*) held by Alexander de Bicknor (*Bykenore*) for term of life by the abbot's demise, paying to the abbot 6 marks and 20 cartloads of hay a year. Right of John. Grant of the reversion to John and Beatrice and John's heirs. Cons. £20. Made in Alexander's presence and with his consent, and he acknowledged that he had only a life tenure. And he rendered, remised, and quitclaimed the holding to John and Beatrice and John's heirs. [*Worn.*]

75/41/310

1 Edward II

1307

112. One week [18 Nov.] from St. Martin. Geoffrey de Dunster (*Dunsterre*) and Isabel his wife quer.; William de Burne def. A messuage and 1 ploughland in Olveston (*Olveston*) and Tockington (*Tokynton*). Geoffrey acknowledged the right of William by Geoffrey's gift. For this, grant and render to Geoffrey and Isabel. To hold to them and their heirs in tail. Contingent remainder to Geoffrey's heirs. [*Worn.*]

76/42/1

113. Two weeks [25 Nov.] from St. Martin. (Made the morrow of St. John the Baptist 35 Edward I [25 June 1307].) William de Ryons (*Ryuns*) and Amice his wife quer.; Thomas de Hinton (*Hyneton*) and Margery his wife imp. Three messuages, 20 a. of land, and 4½ a. of meadow in Brickhampton (*Brighthampton*). (Warranty of charter.) Right of William, as those which William and Amice had by gift of Thomas and Margery. To hold to William and Amice and William's heirs. (Warranty, specifying Thomas's heirs.) Cons. 20 marks.

76/42/2

1308

114. One week [20 Jan.] from Hilary. (Made one week from St. John the Baptist 35 Edward I [1 July 1307].) Thomas Russel quer.; Ellis le Keu and Mariota his wife def. A messuage and 2 shops in the suburb of Bristol (*Bristoll'*). Right of Thomas by gift of Ellis and Mariota. (Warranty, specifying Mariota's heirs.) Cons. £30.

76/42/3

[Cf. *Bristol Gt. Red Book*, p. 205, no. 86. Mariota's name, on the first occurrence only, is spelled Moriota.]

115. One week [20 Jan.] from Hilary. (Made one week from Trinity 35 Edward I [28 May 1307].) Thomas de Salop' of Bristol (*Bristoll'*) quer.; Thomas de Glastonbury (*Glaston'*) and Alice his wife imp. A messuage in the suburb of Bristol. (Warranty of charter.) Right of Thomas de Salop' by gift of Thomas and Alice. (Warranty, specifying Alice's heirs.) Cons. 100*s*. [*Worn.*]

76/42/4

[Cf. *Bristol Gt. Red Book*, p. 206, no. 87.]

116. One week [20 Jan.] from Hilary. John de la Marine quer.; William Tyard of Bristol (*Bristoll'*) imp. A messuage in the suburb of Bristol. (Warranty of charter.) Right of John by William's gift. (Warranty.) Cons. 20 marks. *Endorsed* Robert le Knight (*Kneygth'*) son of Alexander le Knight (*Kneyft*) of Bristol, Edith daughter of the said Robert, [and] John son of Cristiana Wombestrongg' sister of the said Robert put in their claim.

76/42/5

[Cf. *Bristol Gt. Red Book*, p. 206, no. 88.]

117. One week [20 Jan.] from Hilary. John son of William de Leach (*Lecche*) quer.; William de Leach def. A messuage and 200 a. of land in Eastleach (*Estlecche*). Right of John by William's gift. For this, grant back and render to William. To hold during his

1308

life, of John, paying a rose a year at St. John the Baptist and doing service to the chief lords. Reversion to John.

76/42/6

118. Two weeks [28 April] from Easter. William Gold and Cristiana his wife quer.; Walter le Webber (*Webbe*) and Joan his wife def. Eight acres of land in Alkington (*Alkynton*) by Berkeley (*Berkele*). Right of William, as that which William and Cristiana had by gift of Walter and Joan. To hold to William and Cristiana and William's heirs. (Warranty, specifying Joan's heirs.) Cons. 10 marks.

76/42/7

[Cf. *Berkeley Castle Mun.* i, pp. 51–2, A1/3/183, 192 (counterparts).]

119. Two weeks [28 April] from Easter. William le Gold and Cristiana his wife quer.; William le Clerk and Alice his wife def. Eight acres of land in Alkington (*Alkynton*) by Berkeley (*Berkeleye*). Right of William le Gold, as that which William and Cristiana had by gift of William and Alice. To hold to William and Cristiana and William le Gold's heirs. (Warranty, specifying Alice's heirs.) Cons. 10 marks.

76/42/18

120. Three weeks [5 May] from Easter. (Made two weeks from St. John the Baptist 35 Edward I [8 July 1307].) John son of Richard de Brokenborough (*Brokeneberewe*) quer.; Geoffrey de Mohun and Margery his wife def. A messuage, 4 bovates of land, 3 a. of meadow, 3 a. of wood, and 60s. rent in Winterbourne (*Wynterburn*) by Codrington (*Cutherington*). Right of John. Render to him. (Warranty, specifying Margery's heirs.) Cons. £40.

76/42/8

121. Morrow [24 May] of Ascension. Robert son of Stephen Whateman and Joan his wife quer.; William de Burne def. A messuage in the suburb of Bristol (*Bristoll'*). Robert acknowledged the right of William by Robert's gift. For this, grant and render to Robert and Joan. To hold to them and their heirs in tail, of William, paying a rose a year at St. John the Baptist and doing service to the chief lords. Contingent reversion to William. [*Worn.*]

76/42/17

[Cf. *Bristol Gt. Red Book*, p. 206, no. 89.]

122. One week [16 June] from Trinity. William de Ryons (*Ryuns*) quer.; Adam de Rumney (*Romeneye*) and Margery his wife imp. by Richard de Saul (*Salle*) in Adam's place by the king's writ. A messuage in Gloucester (*Gloucestr'*). (Warranty of charter.) Right of William by gift of Adam and Margery. (Warranty, specifying Margery's heirs.) Cons. 100s.

76/42/9

123. One week [16 June] from Trinity. Adam de la Woodhall (*Wodehalle*) quer.; John le Butcher (*Boghiare*) of Tewkesbury (*Teukesbury*) and Cristiana his wife def. Two messuages in Tewkesbury. Right of Adam. Render to him. (Warranty, specifying Cristiana's heirs.) Cons. 10 marks.

76/42/10

1308

124. One week [16 June] from Trinity. (Made one week from Hilary 35 Edward I [20 Jan. 1307].) Miles de Rodborough (*Rodeberwe*) and Matilda his wife quer.; Sampson Caperun of Horsley (*Horslee*) and Agnes his wife imp. A messuage and 30 a. of land in Minchinhampton (*Munechenehampton*). (Warranty of charter.) Right of Miles, as those which Miles and Matilda had by gift of Sampson and Agnes. To hold to Miles and Matilda and Miles's heirs. (Warranty, specifying Agnes's heirs.) Cons. £20. [*Worn.*]

76/42/11

125. One week [16 June] from Trinity. Alexander de Bicknor (*Bykenore*) the younger quer.; John de Hanley (*Hanleye*) and Agnes his wife def. Rent of 12*s*. 4*d*. in Ruardean (*Rewardyn*). Right of Alexander by gift of John and Agnes. (Warranty, specifying Agnes's heirs.) Cons. £10.

76/42/15

126. One week [16 June] from Trinity. William Howard quer.; Henry de Walpole (*Walpol*) and Alice his wife def. Eight messuages, 6 yardlands, and 40*s*. rent in King's Weston (*Kyngesweston*) and the Saltmarsh (*Salso Marisco*). Right of William by gift of Henry and Alice. (Warranty, specifying Henry's heirs.) Cons. 100 marks.

76/42/16

127. Two weeks [23 June] from Trinity. (Made the morrow of Ascension 35 Edward I [5 May 1307].) John de Bradford (*Bradeford*) and Isabel his wife quer.; Mr. Adam de Abbotsbury (*Abbotesbury*) and Elena his wife def. One sixth of a messuage, 2 ploughlands, and £10 rent in Lawrence Weston (*Weston Sancti Laurencii*), Redland (*Thriddelond*), and Charlton (*Cherleton*) held by Joan who was wife of Geoffrey de Ashland (*Asshelond*) in dower, of Elena's inheritance. Right of John. Grant of the reversion to John and Isabel and John's heirs. (Warranty.) Cons. £20. Made in Joan's presence and with her consent, and she did fealty to John and Isabel. [*Worn.*]

76/42/14

128. Morrow [25 June] of St. John the Baptist. Richard de Apperley (*Apperleye*) and Joan his wife quer.; William de Bonham clerk imp. A messuage and 2 ploughlands in Coverdine (*Colverden*). (Warranty of charter.) Right of Richard, as those which Richard and Joan had by William's gift. To hold to Richard and Joan and Richard's heirs. (Warranty.) Cons. £100.

76/42/12

129. Morrow [25 June] of St. John the Baptist. John de Leadon (*Ledene*) and Alice his wife quer.; Richard de Apperley (*Apperleye*) and Joan his wife imp. A messuage and 1 ploughland in Leadon. (Warranty of charter.) Richard acknowledged the holdings to be the right of Alice, as those which John and Alice had by Richard's gift. To hold to John and Alice and Alice's heirs. (Warranty, specifying Richard's heirs.) Cons. 100 marks.

76/42/13

2 Edward II

1308

130. One week [6 Oct.] from Michaelmas. Henry de Charingworth (*Chaueryngworth*) and Matilda his wife quer.; John atte Ash (*Asshe*) and Agnes his wife def. A messuage and 2½ yardlands in Shenington (*Shenyndon*). Right of Henry, as those which Henry and Matilda had by gift of John and Agnes. To hold to Henry and Matilda and Henry's heirs. (Warranty, specifying John's heirs.) Cons. 20 marks.

76/42/20

131. One week [6 Oct.] from Michaelmas. Richard de Hatherley (*Hatherleye*) clerk quer.; Stephen de Fulbourn (*Fuleburn*) and Olive his wife imp. A toft and 1 a. of land in the suburb of Gloucester (*Gloucestre*). (Warranty of charter.) Right of Richard by gift of Stephen and Olive. (Warranty, specifying Stephen's heirs.) Cons. 10 marks.

76/42/21

132. One week [6 Oct.] from Michaelmas. Adam le Franklin (*Fraunkeleyn*) of Tibberton (*Tyberton*) quer.; William le Franklin of Tibberton def. A messuage, 1 yardland, and 5 a. of meadow in Tibberton. Right of Adam by William's gift. For this, grant back and render to William. To hold during his life, of Adam, paying a rose a year at St. John the Baptist and doing service to the chief lords. Reversion to Adam.

76/42/22

133. One week [6 Oct.] from Michaelmas. Hugh of Aldithelegh and Isolda his wife quer. by Henry de Hexton; William Basset and Matilda his wife def. A messuage and 1 yardland in Eastington (*Estenton*). Right of Hugh, as those which Hugh and Isolda had by gift of William and Matilda. To hold to Hugh and Isolda and Hugh's heirs. (Warranty, specifying Matilda's heirs.) Cons. 20 marks.

76/42/23

134. One week [6 Oct.] from Michaelmas. Laurence de Cary quer.; William de Burham of Childswickham (*Wykwane*) and Elena his wife def. A messuage in Bristol (*Bristoll'*). Right of Laurence. Remise and quitclaim, specifying Elena's heirs, to him. (Warranty.) Cons. £10.

76/43/32

[Cf. *Bristol Gt. Red Book*, p. 207, no. 90.]

135. Two weeks [13 Oct.] from Michaelmas. John Wrong and Juliana his wife quer.; Fraric son of Walter de Down Ampney (*Dunameneye*) def. Four messuages, 3 yardlands, 10 a. of meadow, and 8*s.* rent in Down Ampney, GLOS., 30*s.* rent in Stretton on Fosse (*Stratton super Fosse*), WARWS., and 20*s.* rent in Cricklade (*Crekelad*), WILTS. Right of John, as those which John and Juliana had by Fraric's gift. For this, grant back and render to Fraric. To hold during his life, of John and Juliana and John's heirs, paying a rose a year at St. John the Baptist and doing service to the chief lords. Reversion to John and Juliana and John's heirs. *Labelled* Glouc', Warr', Wiltes'; *also* J. Beneger. [*Worn and torn.*]

285/28/11

[Cf. *Warws. Fines, 1284–1345*, p. 61, no. 1286; *Wilts. Fines, 1272–1327*, p. 123.]

1308

136. One month [27 Oct.] from Michaelmas. John Tentefur and Agnes his wife quer.; John Jenkin (*Jonkyn*) of Gloucester (*Gloucestr'*) and Agnes his wife imp. A messuage and a shop in Gloucester (*Glouc'*). (Warranty of charter.) Right of John Tentefur, as those which he and Agnes had by gift of John Jenkin and Agnes. To hold to John Tentefur and Agnes and John Tentefur's heirs. (Warranty, specifying the heirs of Agnes Jenkin.) Cons. 20 marks.

76/43/35

137. One month [27 Oct.] from Michaelmas. Thomas de Wickham (*Wykham*) quer. by Richard de Saul (*Salle*); Henry de Charingworth (*Chaueryngworth*) and Matilda his wife def. A messuage and 2 yardlands in Shenington (*Shenyngdon*). Right of Thomas. Render to him. Cons. £20.

76/43/36

138. Morrow [12 Nov.] of St. Martin. William Damsel (*Damoysele*) and Matilda his wife quer.; Roger de Aldwick (*Aldewyke*) and Elena his wife imp. A toft, 30 a. of land, and half of 1 yardland in Painswick (*Paynneswyk*) and Upton St. Leonards (*Upton Sancti Leonardi*). (Warranty of charter.) Right of William, as those which William and Matilda had by gift of Roger and Elena. To hold to William and Matilda and William's heirs. (Warranty, specifying Roger's heirs.) Cons. £10.

76/42/19

139. Morrow [12 Nov.] of St. Martin. William Damsel (*Damoysele*) and Matilda his wife quer.; Roger de Aldwick (*Aldewyk*) imp. A messuage and 1 ploughland in Painswick (*Paynneswyk*). (Warranty of charter.) Right of William, as those which he and Matilda had by Roger's gift. To hold to William and Matilda and William's heirs. (Warranty.) Cons. £10.

76/43/33

140. Morrow [12 Nov.] of St. Martin. Nicholas de Portbury and Amice his wife quer.; Roger de Brackley (*Brackeleye*) and Isabel his wife imp. A messuage in Bristol (*Bristoll'*). (Warranty of charter.) Right of Nicholas, as that which he and Amice had by gift of Roger and Isabel. To hold to Nicholas and Amice and Nicholas's heirs. (Warranty, specifying Isabel's heirs.) Cons. 10 marks.

76/43/34

[Cf. *Bristol Gt. Red Book*, p. 207, no. 91.]

141. One week [18 Nov.] from St. Martin. Henry le Moyne and Joan his wife quer.; Mr. Thomas de Cobham def. The manor of Shipton Moyne (*Shipton Moyne*) and the advowson of the church of the same manor. Right of Thomas by Henry's gift. For this, grant and render to Henry and Joan. To hold to them and their heirs in tail. Contingent remainder to Henry's heirs.

76/42/24

1309

142. One week [20 Jan.] from Hilary. Geoffrey son of Hugh de Weston quer.; Walter le Butler (*Boteler*) of Weston Subedge (*Weston under Egge*) def. A messuage and 1 yardland in Weston Subedge. Right of Geoffrey. Render to him. (Warranty.) Cons. £10.

76/42/25

1309

143. One week [20 Jan.] from Hilary. William de Pidgemore (*Pyddesmore*) and Rose his wife quer.; Mr. Walter de Stratton def. A messuage and ¾ yardland in Randwick (*Ryndewyk*). William acknowledged the right of Walter by William's gift. For this, grant and render to William and Rose. To hold to them and their heirs in tail. Contingent remainder to William's heirs. [*Worn.*]

76/43/27

144. One week [20 Jan.] from Hilary. John de Aungens quer.; William de Burne def. Three messuages, 3 ploughlands, 1 yardland, and 8 a. of land, and £21 8s. 9d. rent in Maiden Bradley (*Maydenebradelegh*), Porton (*Porton*), Netheravon (*Netheravene*), Amesbury (*Ambresbury*), and Little Langford (*Parva Langeford*) and the advowson of the church of Little Langford, WILTS., and 10s. rent in Bristol (*Bristoll'*), GLOS. Right of William by John's gift. For this, grant back to John and render to him of all except £21 8s. 9d. of the rent. To hold during his life. And grant to him of the reversion of £10 16s. 9d. rent in Porton and Bristol held by Jordan de Aungens for term of life and of £10 12s. rent in Netheravon held by Walter de Sutton and Joan his wife for term of Joan's life, of William's inheritance. To hold as above. Remainder to Walter de Sutton and Joan his wife and their heirs in tail. Successive contingent remainders to Jordan de Aungens and his heirs in tail, and to John's heirs. Made in the presence of Jordan, Walter, and Joan and with their consent, and they did fealty to John. *Labelled* Wyltes', Glouc'. [*Worn and stained.*]

285/28/18

[Cf. *Wilts. Fines, 1272–1327*, p. 123.]

145. One week [9 Feb.] from the Purification. Walter le Carpenter of Haresfield (*Sherrevesharsefeld*) and Richard his son quer.; Walter Onyot and Alice his wife def. One third of a messuage, 1 yardland, 4 a. of meadow, and 2 a. of pasture in Haresfield (*Shirrevesharsefeld*) and Colethrop (*Colethorp*). Right of Walter le Carpenter. Remise and quitclaim, specifying Alice's heirs, to Walter and Richard and Walter's heirs. (Warranty.) Cons. £20.

76/43/26

146. One week [9 Feb.] from the Purification. Walter de Gloucester (*Gloucestr'*) quer.; Walter de Banbury (*Bannebur'*) and Joan his wife def. A messuage and 1 ploughland in Elm Bridge (*Elbrigge*). Right of Walter de Gloucester. Remise and quitclaim, specifying Joan's heirs, to him. (Warranty.) Cons. 40 marks.

76/43/28

147. Two weeks [13 April] from Easter. Roger de Aldwick (*Aldewyk*) and Elena his wife quer. by William de Eycot (*Eycote*) in their place by the king's writ; William Damsel (*Dammoysele*) and Matilda his wife def. A messuage, a toft, 1 ploughland, 30 a. of land, and half of 1 yardland in Painswick (*Payneswyk*) and Upton St. Leonards (*Upton Sancti Leonardi*). Grant and render to Roger and Elena. To hold during their lives, of William and Matilda and William's heirs, paying a rose a year at St. John the Baptist and doing service to the chief lords. (Warranty.) Reversion to William and Matilda and William's heirs.

76/43/29

1309

148. Two weeks [8 June] from Trinity. Richard de Brickhampton (*Brighthampton*) and Margery his wife quer.; Thomas de Hinton (*Hynton*) and Margery his wife def. A messuage, 2½ yardlands, 7 a. of meadow, 1 a. of pasture, and rents of 12*s.* 8½*d.* and 1 lb. of pepper and a clove in Brickhampton. Right of Richard. Remise and quitclaim, specifying the heirs of Margery de Hinton, to Richard and Margery and Richard's heirs. Cons. 100*s.*

76/43/31

149. One week [1 July] from St. John the Baptist. William Russel quer.; John de Staunden def. Two messuages, 8 yardlands, and 23 a. of meadow in Dyrham (*Durham*) and Hinton (*Henton*) by Dyrham. Right of John by William's gift. For this, grant back and render to William. (Warranty.)

76/43/30

3 Edward II

1309

150. One week [6 Oct.] from Michaelmas. John Mautravers and Elcanor his wife quer.; William Ithenard the elder and Cristina his wife def. A messuage and 1 yardland in Woodchester (*Wodecestr'*). Right of John, as those which he and Eleanor had by gift of William and Cristina. To hold to John and Eleanor and John's heirs. (Warranty, specifying Cristina's heirs.) Cons. £20.

76/43/40

151. Two weeks [13 Oct.] from Michaelmas. Nicholas de Seymour (*Seymor*) quer.; Clemency de Seymour imp. A messuage, 1 yardland, 2 a. of meadow, 2 a. of wood, and 3*s.* rent in Paganhill (*Pagenhulle*). (Warranty of charter.) Right of Nicholas by Clemency's gift. (Warranty.) Cons. £20.

76/43/38

152. Two weeks [13 Oct.] from Michaelmas. Roger son of Philip Barbast of Wickwar (*Wykewarre*) quer.; Alice who was wife of Philip Barbast def. A messuage and 1 yardland in Wickwar. Right of Roger. Render to him. (Warranty.) Cons. 20 marks. *Endorsed* Thomas son of Philip Barbast of Wickwar put in his claim.

76/43/39

153. One month [27 Oct.] from Michaelmas. Robert FitzPayne (*fiz Paen*) and Isabel his wife quer. by John de Middleton (*Middelton*) in Isabel's place; Richard de Clifford and Sarah his wife def. Rent of 6 marks and 6*s.* 8*d.* in Frampton on Severn (*Frompton super Severne*). Right of Robert, as that which Robert and Isabel had by gift of Richard and Sarah. To hold to Robert and Isabel and Robert's heirs. (Warranty, specifying Sarah's heirs.) Cons. £60.

76/43/42

154. Morrow [12 Nov.] of St. Martin. Robert de Perrers (*Perers*) of Prestbury (*Prestbury*) quer.; John Ragun and Sarah his wife def. A messuage, 1 ploughland, and 2*s.* rent in Up Hatherley (*Uphatherleye*). Right of Robert. Render to him. (Warranty, specifying John's heirs.) Cons. 100 marks.

76/43/37

1309

155. Morrow [12 Nov.] of St. Martin. Simon Forstal of Bristol (*Bristoll'*) quer.; Alexander Roop of Bristol and Alice his wife def. A messuage in Bristol. Right of Simon by gift of Alexander and Alice. (Warranty, specifying Alexander's heirs.) Cons. 100*s*.

76/44/56

[Cf. *Bristol Gt. Red Book*, p. 208, no. 93.]

156. One week [18 Nov.] from St. Martin. Margaret Giffard (*Gyffard*) of Brimpsfield (*Brimesfeld*) and John Giffard of Brimpsfield quer. by Robert de Prestbury (*Presteburi*); John de Lambourn (*Lamburn*) and Matilda his wife def. A messuage, 50 a. of land, and 4 a. of meadow in Weston Birt (*Brettesweston*) and the advowson of the church of the same township. Right of John Giffard. Render to Margaret and John. To hold to Margaret and John and John's heirs. (Warranty, specifying Matilda's heirs.) Cons. 100 marks.

76/43/41

1310

157. One week [9 Feb.] from the Purification. William de Asthall (*Esthalle*) and Ela his wife quer.; Henry de Kingston (*Kyngeston*) and Margaret his wife def. A messuage, a garden, and 1 a. of meadow in Shenington (*Shenyndon*). Right of Ela, as that which William and Ela had by gift of Henry and Margaret. To hold to William and Ela and Ela's heirs. (Warranty, specifying Margaret's heirs.) Cons. 20 marks.

76/44/57

158. Two weeks [3 May] from Easter. John Pypard quer.; Edmund le Butler (*Boteller*) def. The manor of Rotherfield Peppard (*Rutheresfeld Pypard*) and a messuage, 80 a. of land, 1 a. of meadow, and 6 marks and 2*s*. 2*d*. rent in Fritwell (*Fretewell*), OXON., the manor of Belluton (*Belweton*) and £7 rent in Brean (*Breen*) by Bleadon (*Bledon*), SOM., the manor of Cold Ashton (*Cold Asshton*), GLOS., and the manor of Great Linford (*Magna Lynford*), BUCKS. Right of Edmund by John's gift. For this, grant back and render to John. To hold during his life, of Edmund, paying a rose a year at St. John the Baptist and doing service to the chief lords. Reversion to Edmund. *Labelled* Oxon', Somers', Glouc', Buk'. *Endorsed* William de Grandison (*Grandissono*) and Sibyl his wife put in their claim. [*Worn*.]

285/28/32

[Cf. *Som. Fines, 1307–46*, p. 112.]

159. Three weeks [10 May] from Easter. John de Bitton (*Button*) quer.; Henry le Cheyney (*Chanu*) def. A messuage, a mill, 2 ploughlands, 13 a. of meadow, 50 a. of pasture, 60 a. of wood, and 50*s*. 8¾*d*. rent in Upton Cheyney (*Upton*). Right of John by Henry's gift. For this, grant back and render to Henry. To hold during his life, of John, paying a rose a year at St. John the Baptist and doing service to the chief lords. Reversion to John.

76/43/44

160. One month [17 May] from Easter. Henry de Kingston (*Kyngeston*) and Margaret his wife quer.; William de Asthall (*Esthalle*) and Ela his wife def. A messuage and half of a garden in Shenington (*Shenyndon*). Right of Margaret, as those which Henry and Margaret had by gift of William and Ela. To hold to Henry and Margaret and Margaret's heirs. (Warranty, specifying Ela's heirs.) Cons. £10.

76/44/58

1310

161. Morrow [29 May] of Ascension. Roger atte Well (*Welle*) of Dorn (*Dorne*) quer.; Henry le Chamberlain (*Chaumberleyn*) of Batsford (*Bacheshore*) and Matilda his wife def. Thirteen acres and 1 rod of land and 2 a. and 1 rod of meadow in Batsford by Bourton on the Hill (*Bourton*). Right of Roger by gift of Henry and Matilda. (Warranty, specifying Matilda's heirs.) Cons. 20 marks.

76/43/43

162. Morrow [29 May] of Ascension. Roger atte Well (*Welle*) of Dorn (*Dorne*) and William his son quer.; Henry le Chamberlain (*Chaumberleyn*) of Batsford (*Bacheshore*) and Matilda his wife def. Six acres of land and 1 a. and two thirds of a rood of meadow in Batsford by Bourton on the Hill (*Bourton*). Right of Matilda, as those which Henry and Matilda had by gift of Roger and William. For this, grant back and render to Roger and William. To hold during their lives. (Warranty, specifying Matilda's heirs.) Reversion to Matilda's heirs.

76/44/59

[The clause about the reversion does not allow for the possibility that Matilda might survive Roger and William.]

163. One week [21 June] from Trinity. Robert Dastyn and Margery his wife quer.; John de Boxore def. A messuage and 2 ploughlands in Dumbleton (*Dumbelton*) and Littleton (*Lutlynton*). Robert acknowledged the right of John by Robert's gift. For this, grant and render to Robert and Margery. To hold to them and their heirs in tail. Contingent remainder to Robert's heirs.

76/43/46

164. One week [21 June] from Trinity. Richard de Ampney (*Ammeneye*) quer.; Maurice de Weston and Alesia his wife def. A messuage in Cirencester (*Cyrencestr'*). Right of Richard by gift of Maurice and Alesia. (Warranty, specifying Maurice's heirs.) Cons. £10.

76/43/47

165. One week [21 June] from Trinity. Richard de Croupes quer.; Peter within the Gate (*Wythyntheyate*) of Ampney (*Ameneye*) def. The manor of Withington (*Wytinton*). Right of Peter by Richard's gift. For this, grant back and render to Richard. To hold during his life, of the king. Remainder to Richard son of the same Richard the elder and his heirs in tail. To hold of the king. Contingent remainder to the heirs of Richard de Croupes. Made by the king's order.

76/43/48

166. One week [21 June] from Trinity. Thomas son of Leticia de Longborough (*Langeberegh*) quer.; Henry de Longborough (*Langebergh*) def. Two messuages and 2 yardlands in Longborough. Right of Thomas by Henry's gift. For this, grant back and render to Henry. To hold during his life, of Thomas, paying a rose a year at St. John the Baptist and doing service to the chief lords. Reversion to Thomas.

76/43/49

167. One week [21 June] from Trinity. John abbot of the church of St. Mary, Kingswood (*Kyngeswode*), quer.; Robert Wither (*Wyther*) and Sibyl his wife def. A messuage,

1310

1 yardland, and 26 a. of land in Hill (*Hulle*). Right of the abbot by gift of Robert and Sibyl. (Warranty, specifying Robert's heirs.) Cons. £40. Made by the king's order.

76/43/50

[Cf. *Berkeley Castle Mun.* i, p. 252, A1/34/9 (counterpart).]

168. One week [21 June] from Trinity. Joan daughter of Robert atte Water (*Watere*) of Staverton (*Staverton*) quer.; Robert son of John atte Water imp. One yardland and 1 a. of meadow in Huntley (*Hunteleye*). (Warranty of charter.) Right of Joan by Robert's gift. Cons. 20 marks.

76/44/51

[The clause in which Robert acknowledges Joan's right gives his name as Richard.]

169. One week [21 June] from Trinity. Alice daughter of Reynold Jordan quer.; Reynold Jordan (*Jordain*) and Matilda his wife def. Two messuages, 2 yardlands, 3 a. of meadow, and 2 a. of wood in Edgeworth (*Eggesworthe*). Right of Alice by gift of Reynold and Matilda. For this, grant back and render to Reynold and Matilda. To hold during their lives, of Alice, paying a rose a year at St. John the Baptist and doing service to the chief lords. Reversion to Alice.

76/44/52

170. One week [21 June] from Trinity. John Fleming (*Flemyngg*) and Joan his wife quer.; William de Aston Subedge (*Aston subtus Egge*) def. A messuage and 3 ploughlands in Aston Subedge and the advowson of the church of the same township. John acknowledged the right of William. For this, grant and render to John and Joan. To hold to them and their heirs in tail. (Warranty.) Contingent remainder to Alexander de Besford. [*Worn.*]

76/44/53

171. One week [21 June] from Trinity. Stephen de Saltmarsh (*de Salso Marisco*) quer.; John Test def. A messuage, 1 ploughland, and 10*s.* rent in Sibland (*Sibbelond*) by Thornbury (*Thornburi*). Right of John by Stephen's gift. For this, grant back and render to Stephen. To hold during his life. Successive remainders to Stephen's son John during his life and to Stephen's heirs.

76/44/54

172. One week [21 June] from Trinity. William de Hanningfield (*Hanyngfeld*) and Felicia his wife quer.; Thomas de Shirwell (*Shyrewell*) of Bristol (*Bristoll'*) def. Seven shops and half of a messuage in Bristol and the suburb of the same town held by Nicholas de Burton and Olive his wife in Olive's dower. Right of William. Grant to William and Felicia and William's heirs of the reversion, of Thomas's inheritance. (Warranty.) Cons. £10. Made in the presence of Nicholas and Olive and with their consent, and they did fealty to William and Felicia. *Endorsed* William de Lyons (*Lyuns*) and Matilda his wife and Adam de Lyons put in their claim.

76/44/55

[Cf. *Bristol Gt. Red Book*, p. 207, no. 92.]

173. One week [1 July] from St. John the Baptist. John de Bitton (*Button*) quer.; Adam le Mason (*Machun*) of Saltford (*Saltford*) and Agnes his wife def. A messuage, 26 a. of

1310

land, and 1 a. of meadow in Upton Cheyney (*Upton*) by Bitton (*Button*). Right of John by gift of Adam and Agnes. (Warranty, specifying Agnes's heirs.) Cons. £20. *Endorsed* William Becket (*Beket*) of Farnborough (*Ferneberwe*) put in his claim.

76/43/45

4 Edward II

1310

174. One week [6 Oct.] from Michaelmas. Martin Horncastle (*Horncastel*) of Bristol (*Bristoll'*) quer. by William Gylemyn; Matilda Pokerel (*Pukerel*) def. A messuage and 8 a. of land in Clifton (*Clifton*) by Bristol. Right of Martin. Render to him. (Warranty.) Cons. 20 marks.

76/44/62

[Cf. *Bristol Gt. Red Book*, p. 208, no. 94.]

175. One week [6 Oct.] from Michaelmas. Robert Tumbrel quer. by William Gylemyn; William de Siston and Emma his wife def. A messuage in the suburb of Bristol (*Bristoll'*). Right of Robert. Render to him. (Warranty, specifying Emma's heirs.) Cons. £10.

76/44/63

[Cf. *Bristol Gt. Red Book*, p. 208, no. 95.]

176. One week [18 Nov.] from St. Martin. Richard de Monmouth (*Monemuthe*) quer.; John Barron (*Barun*) and Juliana his wife imp. A messuage, 1 yardland, 4 a. of meadow, 4 a. of wood, and 14s. rent in Great Taynton (*Magna Teynton*). (Warranty of charter.) Right of Richard by gift of John and Juliana. (Warranty, specifying Juliana's heirs.) Cons. £20. *Endorsed* Walter le Young (*Jovene*) of Taynton (*Teynton*) put in his claim. [*Worn*.]

76/44/60

177. Two weeks [25 Nov.] from St. Martin. Henry le Kec quer.; Thomas le Kec def. A messuage, 1 yardland, and 4 a. of meadow in Standish (*Stanedisch*). Right of Henry by Thomas's gift. For this, grant back and render to Thomas. To hold during his life, of Henry, paying a rose a year at St. John the Baptist and doing service to the chief lords. Reversion to Henry.

76/44/61

178. Two weeks [25 Nov.] from St. Martin. Thomas de Amersham (*Agmodesham*) quer.; Walter Onyot of Tirley (*Trynle*) and Alice his wife imp. A messuage and 13 a. of land in Southam (*Sutham*) by Bishop's Cleeve (*Clyve Episcopi*). (Warranty of charter.) Right of Thomas by gift of Walter and Alice. (Warranty, specifying Alice's heirs.) Cons. 20 marks.

76/44/64

1311

179. One week [20 Jan.] from Hilary. Robert de Okle (*Acle*) quer.; Walter de Okle def. A messuage, 80 a. of land, 11 a. of meadow, 3 a. of pasture, 3 a. of wood, and 3 a. of moor in Okle and Malswick (*Maleswyk*) by Newent (*Newent*). Right of Robert by Walter's gift. For this, grant back and render to Walter. To hold during his life. Successive remainders

1311

to Matilda Crook (*Crok*) during her life and to Walter son of Walter de Okle and his heirs in tail. Successive contingent remainders to that Walter's brother John and his heirs in tail, and to John's brother Thomas and his heirs. *Endorsed* Margery daughter of Roger de Okle put in her claim. [*Worn.*]

76/44/66

180. One week [9 Feb.] from the Purification. Richard de la Hale quer.; William le Freeman (*Freman*) and Emma his wife def. Three acres in Longney (*Langeneye*). Right of Richard. Remise and quitclaim, specifying Emma's heirs, to him. Cons. 10 marks.

76/44/65

181. One week [13 June] from Trinity. Thomas son of Nicholas de Coldicote (*Caldicote*) and Margery his wife quer.; William de Preston parson of the church of Barton on the Heath (*Barton*) def. Three messuages, 5½ yardlands, 29 a. of meadow, and 6*s.* 4*d.* rent in Coldicote, Moreton in Marsh (*Morton*), Bourton on the Hill (*Bourton*), and Longborough (*Longebergh*). Thomas acknowledged the right of William by Thomas's gift. For this, grant and render to Thomas and Margery. To hold to them and Thomas's heirs in tail. Contingent remainder to Thomas's heirs.

76/44/67

182. One week [13 June] from Trinity. John Boverel quer.; Edith daughter of William Curtis (*Curteys*) def. A messuage, 50 a. of land, and 12 a. of wood in Newent (*Newent*), Stallion (*Stallynge*), and Cugley (*Cuggeleye*). Right of John. For this, grant and render to Edith. To hold during her life. Remainder to Edith's son John and his heirs in tail. Successive contingent remainders to John's sister Alice and her heirs in tail, to Alice's sister Edith and her heirs in tail, to Reynold Allway (*Aylwy*) and Clemency his wife and their heirs in tail, and to Reynold's heirs.

76/44/68

183. One week [13 June] from Trinity. Richard de Saul (*Salle*) clerk quer.; Henry de Cam (*Camme*) the elder def. A messuage, 2 ploughlands, 7 a. of meadow, 3 a. of pasture, and 20*s.* rent in Cam and Coaley (*Coueleye*). Right of Richard by Henry's gift. For this, grant back and render to Henry. To hold during his life. Remainder to Henry de Cam the younger and Lucy his wife and their heirs in tail. Contingent remainder to the heirs of Henry the elder.

76/44/69

184. One week [13 June] from Trinity. Thomas de Salop' of Bristol (*Bristoll'*) quer.; John de Bridges (*Brugges*) of Bristol and Isabel his wife def. Two shops in Bristol. Right of Thomas by gift of John and Isabel. (Warranty, specifying Isabel's heirs.) Cons. 100*s.*

76/44/71

[Cf. *Bristol Gt. Red Book*, p. 208, no. 96.]

185. Morrow [25 June] of St. John the Baptist. Odo of Dumbleton (*Dombelton*) and Matilda his wife quer.; Robert parson of the church of Alderton (*Aldrinton*) def. Two messuages, 2 ploughlands, 8 a. of meadow, 8 a. of wood, and 13*s.* 4*d.* rent in

1311

Woolstone (*Wolston*), Gotherington (*Goderinton*), Bishop's Cleeve (*Clyve*), Woodmancote (*Wodemancote*), and Dixton (*Diclesdon*). Right of Robert by Odo's gift. For this grant and render to Odo and Matilda. To hold to them and their heirs in tail. Contingent remainder to Odo's heirs.

76/44/70

186. One week [1 July] from St. John the Baptist. Hugh le Despenser the elder quer.; Malcolm Musard def. The manors of Upper Siddington (*Oversuthynton*) and Greenhampstead (*Grenhamstede*) [*i.e.* Miserden] and the advowson of the church of the township of Greenhampstead. Right of Hugh. Remise and quitclaim to him. (Warranty.) Cons. £200.

76/44/72

<h2 style="text-align:center">5 Edward II</h2>

1311

187. Two weeks [13 Oct.] from Michaelmas. Richard son of Laurence de Little Compton (*Parva Cumpton*) quer.; Roger le Seler and Agnes his wife def. One yardland except 3½ a. of land in Little Compton. Right of Richard by gift of Roger and Agnes. (Warranty, specifying Agnes's heirs.) Cons. £10. *Endorsed* William de Compton put in his claim.

76/44/74

188. Two weeks [13 Oct.] from Michaelmas. John de Chew (*Cheu*) quer.; Agnes who was wife of Roger de Pembroke (*Penbrok*) def. A messuage in Bristol (*Bristoll'*). Right of John by Agnes's gift. (Warranty.) Cons. £10.

76/45/77

[Cf. *Bristol Gt. Red Book*, p. 209, no. 97.]

189. One month [27 Oct.] from Michaelmas. Maurice de Ash (*Asshe*) quer.; Robert Gregory (*Gregori*) of Leigh (*la Lee*) and Agnes his wife def. A messuage and ½ yardland in Leigh. Right of Maurice by gift of Robert and Agnes. (Warranty, specifying Agnes's heirs.) Cons. £10.

76/44/73

190. Morrow [12 Nov.] of St. Martin. Thomas de Brockworth quer.; Henry de Brockworth def. Three messuages and 1½ yardlands in Brockworth (*Brockworth*). Right of Thomas by Henry's gift. For this, grant back and render to Henry. To hold during his life. Remainder to Henry's son John and his heirs in tail. Contingent remainder to Henry's heirs.

76/44/75

191. One week [18 Nov.] from St. Martin. John de Besemountsel and Alice his wife quer. by Walter Torel in Alice's place by the king's writ; Robert le Vicarsman (*Vikeresman*) of 'Seint Johan' of Worcester (*Wygorn'*) def. Six messuages, 4 yardlands, 7 a. of meadow, and 7 a. of pasture in Alderton (*Aldrinton*) and Gretton (*Gretton*) by Winchcombe (*Wynchecombe*). John acknowledged the right of Robert by John's gift. For this, grant and render to John and Alice. To hold during their lives. Remainder to their son John and his heirs in tail. Contingent remainder to that John's sister Katherine.

76/45/76

1312

192. One week [20 Jan.] from Hilary. Joan who was wife of John de Newington (*Newenton*), Mr. Henry de Newington, and William de Ditchford (*Dichford*) and Agnes his wife quer. by Reynold Bagge of Aston (*Aston*) in Agnes's place by the king's writ; William son of William de Ditchford def. Five messuages and 2 yardlands and 14½ a. of land in Mollington (*Mollynton*), OXON., a messuage and ½ yardland in Alderton (*Aldrynton*), GLOS., and 1 a. and 3 roods of meadow and half of 1 yardland in Shotteswell (*Shoteswell*), WARWS. Joan and Henry acknowledged the right of William son of William by gift of Joan and Henry. For this, grant and render to Joan, Henry, and William de Ditchford and Agnes. To hold during their lives, of William son of William, paying a rose a year at St. John the Baptist and doing service to the chief lords. Reversion to William son of William. *Labelled* Oxon', Glouc', Warr'. [*Worn.*]

285/29/60

[Cf. *Warws. Fines, 1284–1345*, p. 73, no. 1353.]

193. Two weeks [27 Jan.] from Hilary. Walter Wyth quer.; Isabel daughter of Walter de Wick (*Wyk*) def. A messuage, 30 a. of land, and 1 a. of meadow in Arlingham (*Erlyngham*). Right of Walter by Isabel's gift. For this, grant back and render to Isabel. To hold during her life, of Walter, paying a rose a year at St. John the Baptist and doing service to the chief lords. Reversion to Walter.

76/45/79

194. Two weeks [27 Jan.] from Hilary. William de Asthall (*Esthalle*) and Ela his wife quer.; Henry son of Nicholas de Fonte of Upton (*Opton*) def. Two messuages, 4 ploughlands, 18 a. of meadow, 5 a. of wood, 13s. rent, and one fifth of 2 mills in Shenington (*Shenyndon*). Right of Henry by gift of William and Ela. For this, grant back and render to William and Ela. To hold during their lives. Remainder to their son John and his heirs in tail. Contingent remainder to John's sister Joan. *Endorsed* Henry de Kingston (*Kyngiston*) and Margaret his wife put in their claim.

76/45/80

195. Two weeks [27 Jan.] from Hilary. William Tuchet quer.; Bartholomew de Badlesmere (*Badelesmere*) def. The manor of Lyonshall (*Lenhales*), HEREFS., and the manor of Oxenton (*Oxendon*), GLOS. Right of Bartholomew by William's gift. For this, grant back and render to William. To hold to him and his heirs in tail, of Bartholomew, paying a rose a year at St. John the Baptist and doing service to the chief lords. Contingent reversion to Bartholomew. *Labelled* Heref', Glouc'. *Endorsed* Philip de Neville (*Nevile*) of Brampton (*Brampton*) and Robert his son put in their claim. Richard Tuchet put in his claim. Roger de Mortain (*Morteyn*) and Isabel his wife put in their claim.

285/29/61

196. One week [9 Feb.] from the Purification. Richard de la Marche quer.; John Adrian def. A messuage in Bristol (*Bristoll'*). Right of Richard. Remise and quitclaim to him. (Warranty.) Cons. 100s.

76/45/86b (formerly 76/45/95)

[Cf. *Bristol Gt. Red Book*, p. 209, no. 99.]

1312

197. Two weeks [9 April] from Easter. John de Saltmarsh (*de Salso Marisco*) quer.; Hugh Cheyney (*Chanu*) def. A messuage, 15 a. of land, and 1 rood of meadow in Bitton (*Button*). Right of John by Hugh's gift. For this, grant back and render to Hugh. To hold during his life, of John, paying a rose a year at St. John the Baptist and doing service to the chief lords. (Warranty.) Reversion to John.

76/45/82

198. Two weeks [9 April] from Easter. Nicholas Burdun and Denise his wife quer.; Denise who was wife of Robert le Wyne def. A messuage, 4 ploughlands, 20 a. of meadow, 34 a. of wood, and 6 marks and 10*s.* rent in Oldbury on the Hill (*Oldebury*) and Didmarton (*Dudemerton*) by Badminton (*Badmynton*) and the advowson of the church of Oldbury. Nicholas acknowledged the right of Denise who was wife of Robert by Nicholas's gift. For this, grant and render to Nicholas and Denise. To hold to them and Nicholas's heirs.

76/45/83

199. Morrow [5 May] of Ascension. Benedict Serun of Bourton (*Burton*) and Agnes his wife quer. by William de Elmore (*Elmor*) in Agnes's place by the king's writ; Adam le Northerner (*Northerne*) of Bristol (*Bristoll'*) def. Two messuages, 28 a. of land, and 4 a. of meadow in Horfield (*Horfelde*) and Stapleton (*Stapelton*) by Bristol. Right of Benedict, as those which Benedict and Agnes had by Adam's gift. To hold to Benedict and Agnes and Benedict's heirs. (Warranty.) Cons. 40 marks.

76/45/81

200. One week [28 May] from Trinity. Richard de Priddy (*Pridie*) quer.; William de Kingston (*Kyngeston*) and Alice his wife def. A messuage in Bristol (*Bristoll'*). Right of Richard by gift of William and Alice. (Warranty, specifying Alice's heirs.) Cons. 10 marks.

76/45/78

[Cf. *Bristol Gt. Red Book*, p. 209, no. 98.]

201. One week [1 July] from St. John the Baptist. Thomas de Berkeley (*Berkeleye*) the elder quer. by Robert de Prestbury (*Prestebury*); John de Lindsey (*Lyndeseye*) and Agnes his wife def. Seventeen and a half acres of land in Stone (*Stone*) by Berkeley. Right of Thomas. Render to him. (Warranty, specifying Agnes's heirs.) Cons. £20.

76/45/84

[Cf. *Berkeley Castle Mun.* i, p. 238, A1/31/17 (counterpart).]

202. One week [1 July] from St. John the Baptist. Thomas de Berkeley (*Berkele*) quer. by Robert de Prestbury (*Prestebury*) in his place by the king's writ; William Priddy (*Pridy*) and Juliana his wife def. Six acres of land in Ham (*Hamme*). Right of Thomas. Render to him. (Warranty, specifying Juliana's heirs.) Cons. 10 marks.

76/45/85

203. One week [1 July] from St. John the Baptist. Thomas Neel of Pirton (*Pyriton*) quer.; Margery who was wife of John le Brown (*Brun*) of Elkstone (*Elkeston*) def. Fifteen messuages, 2 mills, 2 ploughlands, 60 a. of wood, 4 a. of meadow, and 5*s.* rent in Eycot (*Eycote*), Nether Rendcomb (*Nethereryndecumbe*), North Cerney (*Northserneye*), and

1312

Woodmancote (*Wodemannecote*). Right of Margery. For this, grant and render to Thomas. To hold to him and his heirs in tail. Successive contingent remainders to Juliana de Blunsdon (*Blontesdon*) during her life, to Geoffrey son of [another] Thomas Neel and his heirs in tail, and to John de Bourton (*Burghton*). (Warranty.) [*Worn.*]

76/45/86a

6 Edward II

1312

204. Two weeks [8 July] from St. John the Baptist. John Calf of Campden (*Caumpedene*) quer.; Nicholas le Purser (*Pursere*) of Reading (*Redyng*) and Alice his wife def. Three messuages in Chipping Campden (*Caumpedene*) held by Nicholas le French (*Frensche*) for term of life. Right of John. Grant to him of the reversion, of Alice's inheritance. Cons. 10 marks. Made in the presence of Nicholas le French and with his consent, and he did fealty to John.

76/45/91

205. One week [6 Oct.] from Michaelmas. William le Mohun and Alice his wife quer.; John de Abson (*Abbodeston*) def. Five messuages, 144 a. of land, 20 a. of meadow, 30 a. of pasture, and 10 a. of wood in Siston (*Cyston*) and Redford (*Ritford*). William acknowledged the right of John by William's gift. For this, grant and render to William and Alice. To hold to them and their heirs in tail. Successive contingent remainders to William's son William and his heirs in tail, to that William's brother John and his heirs in tail, to John's brother Thomas and his heirs in tail, and to William le Mohun's heirs.

76/45/87

1313

206. One week [20 Jan.] from Hilary. Agnes daughter of Henry le Teynturer quer. by Robert de Malvern (*Malverne*); Henry le Teynturer of Winchcombe (*Wynchecumbe*) imp. A messuage and 12*d.* rent in Winchcombe. (Warranty of charter.) Right of Agnes by Henry's gift. (Warranty.) Cons. 100 marks.

76/45/88

207. Two weeks [29 April] from Easter. Nicholas de Valeres (*Valers*) and Margaret his wife quer. by John de Macey in Margaret's place by the king's writ; Peter de Cusancia def. The manor of Down Ampney (*Dounameney*). Nicholas acknowledged the right of Peter by Nicholas's gift. For this, grant and render to Nicholas and Margaret. To hold during their lives, of Peter, paying £10 a year, at Whitsun and St. Martin, and doing service to the chief lords. Reversion to Peter. [*Worn.*]

76/45/89

208. Two weeks [29 April] from Easter. Matilda who was wife of Henry de Charingworth (*Chaueringworth*) quer.; John de Ash (*de Fraxino*) and Agnes his wife def. A messuage and 2 yardlands in Charingworth. Right of Matilda. Render to her. (Warranty, specifying John's heirs.) Cons. £40.

76/45/90

1313

209. One week [17 June] from Trinity. John de Wincot (*Wonnecote*) and Eleanor his wife quer.; Mr. Simon de Wincot def. Fourteen messuages, 2 ploughlands and 2½ yardlands, and 17*s*. rent in Ullington (*Ollynton*). Right of Mr. Simon by gift of John and Eleanor. For this, grant back and render to John and Eleanor. To hold to them and their heirs in tail. Contingent remainder to Eleanor's heirs.

76/45/94

210. Morrow [25 June] of St. John the Baptist. Henry de Bulmville of Gloucester (*Gloucestr'*) quer.; Geoffrey Gamel of Bicknor (*Bikenore*) and Agnes his wife imp. A messuage in Gloucester. (Warranty of charter.) Right of Henry by gift of Geoffrey and Agnes. (Warranty, specifying Agnes's heirs.) Cons. 40*s*.

76/45/92

211. Morrow [25 June] of St. John the Baptist. Robert le Skey and Isabel his wife quer. by William le Messager in Isabel's place by the king's writ; Agnes who was wife of Peter de Braose (*Brewosa*) def. Three messuages, 2 yardlands and 25 a. of land, 3½ a. of meadow, pasture for 2 draught animals (*affros*) and 8 oxen and cows, and 15*s*. rent in Tetbury (*Tettebury*) and Tetbury Upton (*Upton*). Robert acknowledged the right of Agnes by Robert's gift. For this, grant and render to Robert and Isabel. To hold to them and their heirs in tail, of Agnes, paying a rose a year at St. John the Baptist and doing service to the chief lords. Successive contingent remainders to John de Braose and his heirs in tail and to John's brother Peter and his heirs in tail. Contingent reversion to Agnes. [*Worn.*]

76/45/93

212. Morrow [25 June] of St. John the Baptist. John Mautravers the younger quer.; John Mautravers the elder def. The manors of Witchampton (*Wichhampton*), Langton Matravers (*Langeton*), and Woolcombe (*Wolecumbe*), DORSET, the manors of Great Somerford (*Sumerford*) and Coate (*Cotes*), WILTS., and the manor of Woodchester (*Wodechestr'*), GLOS. Right of John the younger by gift of John the elder. For this, grant back and render to John the elder. To hold during his life, of John the younger, paying a rose a year at St. John the Baptist and doing service to the chief lords. Reversion to John the younger. *Labelled* Dors', Wyltes', Glouc'.

285/29/72

[Cf. *Dorset Fines, 1195–1327*, p. 321; *Wilts. Fines, 1272–1327*, p. 125.]

7 Edward II

1313

213. Two weeks [8 July] from St. John the Baptist. Gilbert de Clare earl of Gloucester (*Gloucestr'*) and Hertford (*Hertford*) and Matilda his wife quer. by Adam de Broom (*Brom*) in Matilda's place; Gilbert de St. Owen (*de Sancto Audoeno*) def. The manor of Old Sodbury (*Sobbury*), GLOS., and the manor of Betchworth (*Bechesworth*), SURREY. Gilbert de Clare acknowledged the right of Gilbert de St. Owen by gift of Gilbert de Clare. For this, grant and render to the earl and Matilda. To hold to them and their heirs in tail, of the king. Contingent remainder to the earl's heirs. Made by the king's order. *Labelled* Glouc', Surr'.

285/29/84

[For the identity of Old Sodbury, Rudder, *Glos*. 678.]

1313

214. One week [6 Oct.] from Michaelmas. John le Eyre (*Eyr*) of Oxenton (*Oxindon*) and Cristina his wife quer.; Richard de la Sale of Hazleton (*Haselton*) def. Two messuages and 1 yardland in Pamington (*Pamynton*) and Oxenton. John acknowledged the right of Richard by John's gift. For this, grant and render to John and Cristina. To hold to them and their heirs in tail. Contingent remainder to John's heirs.

76/45/98

215. One week [6 Oct.] from Michaelmas. Walter Warin (*Waryn*) and Reynold his brother quer.; John son of Thomas Warin def. A messuage, 10 a. of land, and 1 a. of meadow in Lydney (*Lideneye*) Right of John. For this, grant and render to Walter and Reynold. To hold during their lives. Remainder to Walter son of John Warin. (Warranty.) [*Worn.*]

76/45/99

216. Two weeks [13 Oct.] from Michaelmas. William de Lambourn quer.; John de Guise (*Gyse*) the elder def. The manor of Elmore (*Elmor*). Right of William. For this, grant and render to John of two thirds of the manor. To hold during his life. And grant of the reversion of the third part of the manor held in dower by Beatrice who was wife of Anselm de Guise, of William's inheritance. To hold as above. Remainder to John son of John de Guise (*Gise*) and his heirs in tail. Contingent remainder to the heirs of the said John de Guise. Made in Beatrice's presence and with her consent, and she did fealty to John. [*Worn.*]

76/46/101

217. Three weeks [20 Oct.] from Michaelmas. John de Great Wormington (*Magna Wormynton*) and Agnes his wife quer.; John son of Hugh atte Wood (*Wode*) def. Two messuages, 10 a. of land, and 1 a. of meadow in Winchcombe (*Wynchecumbe*) and Greet (*Grete*) by Winchcombe. Right of John son of Hugh by gift of John and Agnes. For this, grant back and render to John and Agnes. To hold during their lives, of John son of Hugh, paying a rose a year at St. John the Baptist and doing service to the chief lords. Reversion to John son of Hugh. [*Worn.*]

76/45/96

218. Morrow [3 Nov.] of All Souls. Robert Moryn and Margaret his wife quer.; Richard Fouward def. A messuage and 1 yardland in Aston Subedge (*Aston under Egge*). Right of Margaret. For this, Robert and Margaret granted and rendered the holdings to Richard. To hold to him and his heirs in tail, of Robert and Margaret and Margaret's heirs, paying 1*d.* a year at Christmas and doing service to the chief lords. Contingent reversion to Robert and Margaret and Margaret's heirs. *Endorsed* William de Mickleton (*Mikelton*) chaplain put in his claim.

76/45/97

219. Morrow [12 Nov.] of St. Martin. Walter Guge quer.; Richard le Norris (*Norays*) and Lucy his wife def. One quarter of a messuage in Tewkesbury (*Teukesbury*). Right of Walter by gift of Richard and Lucy. (Warranty, specifying Lucy's heirs.) Cons. a young sparrowhawk.

76/46/102

1313

220. Two weeks [25 Nov.] from St. Martin. John de la River (*Ryvere*) quer.; John atte Well (*Welle*) of Tormarton (*Tormerton*) and Alice his wife def. A messuage, 1 yardland, and 2 a. of meadow in Tormarton. Right of John de la River. Render to him. (Warranty, specifying John atte Well's heirs.) Cons. a young sparrowhawk.

76/45/100

1314

221. Morrow [3 Feb.] of the Purification. William de Brockworth (*Brokworth*) quer. by John de Elkstone (*Elkeston*) in his place by the king's writ; Thomas Orchard (*atte Norcharde*) def. A messuage, 3 yardlands, and 15*s*. 5*d*. rent in Elkstone. Right of William. Render to him. (Warranty.) Cons. a young sparrowhawk.

76/46/105

222. Morrow [3 Feb.] of the Purification. William de Brockworth (*Brokworth*) quer.; William Alsy def. by John de Elkstone (*Elkeston*) in his place by the king's writ. A messuage and ½ yardland in Elkstone. Right of William de Brockworth. Render to him. (Warranty.) Cons. a young sparrowhawk.

76/46/114

[It may be noted that in the two fines above, of the same date with the same querelant, John de Elkstone appears as attorney in one for the querelant and in the other for the deforciant.]

223. One week [9 Feb.] from the Purification. Peter de Edgeworth (*Egesworth*) quer.; Roger de la Green (*Grene*) of Bulley (*Bulleye*) and Margaret his wife def. Five marks rent in Bulley. Roger acknowledged the right of Peter by Roger's gift. For this, grant and render to Roger and Margaret. To hold to them and Roger's heirs.

76/46/103

224. One week [9 Feb.] from the Purification. John de Annesley (*Annesleye*) and Lucy who was wife of Robert de la Mare quer. by William de Bentley (*Benteleye*); William de Yetminster (*Yetmynstre*) def. Eight messuages, a mill, 225 a. and 3 roods of land, 15 a. of meadow, 4 a. of pasture, 15 a. of wood, and 35*s*. 4*d*. rent in Down Hatherley (*Dunhatherleye*). Grant and render to John and Lucy. To hold during John's life. Remainder to Hawise who was wife of John de Ferrers (*Ferers*). Cons. a young sparrowhawk.

76/46/104

225. Three weeks [28 April] from Easter. William de Brockworth (*Brokworth*) quer. by John de Elkstone (*Elkeston*) in his place by the king's writ; Thomas Orchard (*Attenorcharde*) def. Rent of 32*s*. in Mickleton (*Mukelton*) held by John de Trillowe for term of life as demised by Thomas. Right of William. Grant to him of the reversion. (Warranty.) Cons. a young sparrowhawk. Made in the presence of John de Trillowe who acknowledged that he had only a life-interest, and he rendered the rent to William.

76/46/107

226. Morrow [17 May] of Ascension. William de Odiham quer.; Anselm de Gurney (*Gurnay*) def. A messuage, 1 ploughland, and 2*s*. rent in King's Weston (*Kyngesweston*). Right of Anselm by William's gift. For this, grant back and render to William. To hold

1314

during his life, of Anselm, paying a rose a year at St. John the Baptist and doing service to the chief lords. Reversion to Anselm. [*Worn.*]

76/46/109

227. Morrow [17 May] of Ascension. William le Devenish (*Deveneys*) of Didmarton (*Dudemerton*) quer.; Robert Child and Margery his wife def. Two messuages, 1½ yardlands, 7 a. of meadow, and 10 a. of wood in Hawkesbury (*Hauekesbury*), Kilcott (*Kylecote*), and Leighterton (*Leghtrinton*). Right of William by gift of Robert and Margery. For this, grant back and render to Robert and Margery. To hold during their lives, of William, paying a rose a year at St. John the Baptist and doing service to the chief lords. Reversion to William.

76/46/110

228. One week [9 June] from Trinity. John Giffard of Boyton (*Boyton*) quer.; Adam de Harvington (*Herwynton*) def. The manors of Norton (*Norton*) and Weston Subedge (*Weston Underegge*) and the advowson of the church of the same manor of Weston. Right of Adam by John's gift. For this, grant back and render to John. To hold during his life, of the king. Remainder to John son of John Giffard and his legitimate heirs in tail. Contingent remainder to John Giffard's heirs. Made by the king's order.

76/46/106

229. One week [9 June] from Trinity. Adam son of William Roger (*Rogger*) of Newland (*la Newelonde*) quer.; Robert Pratt (*Prat*) and Margery his wife imp. A messuage, 7 a. of land, 1 a. and 3 roods of meadow, 1 a. and 1 rood of wood, and 2*s*. rent in Newland. (Warranty of charter.) Right of Adam by gift of Robert and Margery. (Warranty, specifying Robert's heirs.) Cons. a young sparrowhawk.

76/46/108

230. One week [9 June] from Trinity. John Orger quer.; Richard Orger def. A messuage, 3 a. of meadow, 4 a. of wood, 4*s*. rent, and half of 1 yardland in Harescombe (*Harsecombe*). Right of John by Richard's gift. (Warranty.) Cons. a young sparrowhawk.

76/46/111

231. One week [9 June] from Trinity. Odo de Acton and Elizabeth his wife quer.; Roger Quantock (*Cantok*) def. Two messuages, 1 ploughland, 30 a. of meadow, 20 a. of pasture, and 100*s*. rent in Kingston (*Kyngeston*) and Gossington (*Gosynton*). Odo acknowledged the right of Roger by Odo's gift. For this, grant and render to Odo and Elizabeth. To hold to them and Odo's heirs.

76/46/112

[Cf. *Berkeley Castle Mun.* i, p. 279, A1/43/50 (counterpart).]

232. One week [9 June] from Trinity. Richard de Foxcote quer.; William de Bath (*Bathon'*) of Cirencester (*Cirencestr'*) and Alice his wife def. Two messuages, 1 ploughland, 4 a. of wood, and rents of 12*d*. and 1 lb. of pepper in Duntisbourne Abbots (*Duntesbourn Hotot*). Right of Richard by gift of William and Alice. (Warranty, specifying Alice's heirs.) Cons. a young sparrowhawk.

76/46/113

8 Edward II
1314

233. One week [6 Oct.] from Michaelmas. Roger Pluf of Gloucester (*Gloucestr'*) and Margery his wife quer.; John Tentefur of Gloucester and Agnes his wife def. A messuage in the suburb of Gloucester. Right of Roger. Render to Roger and Margery. To hold to them and Roger's heirs. (Warranty, specifying John's heirs.) Cons. a young sparrowhawk.

76/47/131

234. Two weeks [13 Oct.] from Michaelmas. John de Norwich (*de Norwyco*) quer.; Robert Davy and Alice his wife imp. A messuage in Gloucester (*Gloucestr'*). (Warranty of charter.) Right of John by gift of Robert and Alice. (Warranty, specifying Alice's heirs.) Cons. 20*s*.

76/46/116

235. Two weeks [13 Oct.] from Michaelmas. Henry del Oak (*Ok*) quer.; Robert Davy and Alice his wife imp. Seven acres of land in Parton (*Parton*). (Warranty of charter.) Right of Henry by gift of Robert and Alice. (Warranty, specifying Alice's heirs.) Cons. 100*s*.

76/46/118

236. Two weeks [13 Oct.] from Michaelmas. John de Marshfield (*Marsfeld*) quer.; William Seend (*Seynde*) and Margaret his wife def. A messuage in the suburb of Bristol (*Bristoll'*). Right of John by gift of William and Margaret. (Warranty, specifying Margaret's heirs.) Cons. 20*s*.

76/46/120

[Cf. *Bristol Gt. Red Book*, p. 210, no. 101.]

237. Three weeks [20 Oct.] from Michaelmas. John Delerobe and Alice his wife quer.; Anselm son of Robert de Gurney (*Gornay*) def. Four messuages and a shop in the suburb of Bristol (*Bristoll'*) outside the new gate. John acknowledged the right of Anselm by John's gift. For this, grant and render to John and Alice. To hold to them and their heirs in tail. Contingent remainder to John's heirs. [*Split.*]

76/46/115

[Cf. *Bristol Gt. Red Book*, p. 209, no. 100.]

238. Three weeks [20 Oct.] from Michaelmas. Katherine daughter of Nicholas de Apperley (*Apperle*) quer.; Richard de Apperley def. Two messuages, 50 a. of land, 17 a. of meadow, and 29*s*. rent in Apperley. Right of Richard by Katherine's gift. For this, grant back and render to Katherine. To hold to her and her heirs in tail, of Richard, paying a rose a year at St. John the Baptist and doing service to the chief lords. Contingent reversion to Richard.

76/46/119

239. Three weeks [20 Oct.] from Michaelmas. Stephen Brown (*Broun*) the younger quer.; Adam de Stanley (*Stanleye*) and Matilda his wife imp. Two shops in Gloucester (*Gloucestr'*). (Warranty of charter.) Right of Stephen by gift of Adam and Matilda. (Warranty, specifying Matilda's heirs.) Cons. 40*s*.

76/47/130

1314

240. Morrow [3 Nov.] of All Souls. Walter de Maisemore (*Maysemor*) quer.; Philip le Tailor (*Taillour*) and Margery his wife imp. A messuage in the suburb of Gloucester (*Gloucestr'*). (Warranty of charter.) Right of Walter by gift of Philip and Margery. (Warranty, specifying Margery's heirs.) Cons. 100*s*.

76/46/117

1315

241. One week [20 Jan.] from Hilary. Thomas Hastang and Matilda his wife quer.; John atte Box (*Boxe*) and Ismania his wife def. One fifth of the manor of Shenington (*Shenyndon*). Thomas acknowledged the right of Ismania. For this, grant and render to Thomas and Matilda. To hold to them and their heirs in tail. Contingent remainder to Matilda's heirs. (Warranty, specifying Ismania's heirs.)

76/46/121

242. One week [9 Feb.] from the Purification. William Gerald of Matson (*Mattesdon*) and Katherine his wife quer.; William de Gardens (*de Gardinis*) of Matson and Isabel his wife def. A messuage, 1 ploughland, 20 a. of wood, and 50*s*. rent in Reslaw (*Russheleie*), *Savereye*, and Withymoor (*Wythemere*), HEREFS., and the manor of Matson and a messuage, 1 ploughland, 20 a. of wood, and 15*s*. rent in Cugley (*Cuggeleye*) by Newent (*Neuwent*), GLOS. William Gerald acknowledged the right of Isabel. For this, William de Gardens and Isabel granted and rendered the holdings to William Gerald and Katherine. To hold to them and their heirs in tail, of William de Gardens and Isabel and Isabel's heirs, paying a rose a year at St. John the Baptist and doing service to the chief lords. (Warranty.) Contingent reversion to William de Gardens and Isabel and Isabel's heirs. *Labelled* Hereford', Glouc'. *Endorsed* Ralph Barron (*Baroun*) put in his claim. Agnes de Matson (*Matesdon*) put in her claim. John de la Hill (*Hulle*) put in his claim. [*Stained.*]

285/30/107

243. Two weeks [6 April] from Easter. John de Brokenborough (*Brokenberwe*) quer.; Robert atte Nash (*Nasshe*) and Agnes his wife def. A messuage, 4 a. of meadow, and half of 1 yardland in Over (*Oure*) by Almondsbury (*Almondesbury*). Right of John by gift of Robert and Agnes. (Warranty, specifying Agnes's heirs.) Cons. 10 marks.

76/46/123

244. Three weeks [13 April] from Easter. William le Sumpter (*Sumeter*) and Isabel his wife quer. by Richard de Saul (*Salle*) in their place by the king's writ; William de Elmore and Simunda his wife def. Four acres of land in Ham (*Homme*) by Berkeley (*Berkele*). Right of William le Sumpter. Remise and quitclaim, specifying Simunda's heirs, to William le Sumpter and Isabel and William le Sumpter's heirs. (Warranty.) Cons. 40*s*.

76/46/122

245. Three weeks [13 April] from Easter. Henry le Gardener (*Gardyner*) and Isabel his wife quer. by Richard de Saul (*Salle*) in their place by the king's writ; William de Elmore and Simunda his wife imp. A messuage in Berkeley (*Berkeleye*). (Warranty of charter.) Right of Henry, as that which Henry and Isabel had by gift of William and Simunda. To hold to Henry and Isabel and Henry's heirs. (Warranty, specifying Simunda's heirs.) Cons. 30*s*.

76/46/125

1315

246. Three weeks [13 April] from Easter. Stephen Brown (*Broun*) quer.; Thomas Marmion and Elicia his wife imp. Rent of 20*s*. in Gloucester (*Gloucestre*). (Warranty of charter.) Right of Stephen by gift of Thomas and Elicia. (Warranty, specifying Elicia's heirs.) Cons. 10 marks.

76/47/129

247. Morrow [2 May] of Ascension. John de Stonor (*Stonore*) quer.; Thomas de la Hay def. Twelve messuages, 2 ploughlands and 100 a. of land, 40 a. of meadow, 100 a. of wood, 16 a. of pasture, and 12*d*. rent in Henbury (*Hembury in Salso Marisco*). Right of John by Thomas's gift. (Warranty.) Cons. 200 marks.

76/46/124

248. One week [25 May] from Trinity. William de Shenington (*Shenyndon*) quer.; William de Ryons (*Ryuns*) and Avice his wife imp. Three messuages, 20 a. of land, and 4½ a. of meadow in Brickhampton (*Bryghthamptone*). (Warranty of charter.) Right of William de Shenington by gift of William de Ryons and Avice. (Warranty, specifying the heirs of William de Ryons.) Cons. £60.

76/47/126

249. Two weeks [1 June] from Trinity. Richard Cromelyn of Hoddington (*Hodinton*) quer.; Thomas de Hoddington chaplain def. Rent of £10 in Broad Campden (*Brodecaumpeden*). Right of Thomas by Richard's gift. For this, grant back and render to Richard. To hold during his life. Remainder to Richard's son John and Margaret his wife and their heirs in tail. Successive contingent remainders to John's brother Richard and his heirs in tail, to that Richard's brother Alexander and his heirs in tail, to Alexander's brother Baldwin and his heirs in tail, to Baldwin's brother Nicholas and his heirs in tail, to Nicholas's brother William and his heirs in tail, and to Richard Cromelyn's heirs. [*Worn.*]

76/47/127

250. Two weeks [1 June] from Trinity. Richard de Saul (*Salle*) quer.; William de Berton and Denise his wife def. A messuage in Berkeley (*Berkeleye*). Right of Richard by gift of William and Denise. (Warranty, specifying Denise's heirs.) Cons. 40*s*.

76/47/128

251. Two weeks [1 June] from Trinity. Thomas son of John de Newington (*Newynton*) and Joan his wife quer. by Henry de Wenland (*Wenlond*) in Joan's place; John son of Robert Jones of Longdon (*Longedon*) def. A messuage, a mill, 2 yardlands, and 5*s*. rent in Twyning (*Tweyngg*), GLOS., and 49*s*. 6½*d*. rent in Strensham (*Strengesham*), WORCS. Thomas acknowledged the right of John by Thomas's gift. For this, grant and render to Thomas and Joan. To hold to them and their heirs in tail. Contingent remainder to Thomas's heirs. *Labelled* Gloucestr', Wygorn'.

285/30/112

9 Edward II

1315

252. One week [6 Oct.] from Michaelmas. Richard de Apperley (*Apperloye*) quer.; Walter le Passer (*Passour*) of the Haw (*de Haghe*) and Katherine his wife def. A messuage, 5 a. of land, and 1½ a. of meadow in Apperley (*Apperleye*). Right of Richard by gift of Walter and Katherine. (Warranty, specifying Walter's heirs.) Cons. 10 marks.

76/47/133

253. Two weeks [13 Oct.] from Michaelmas. Robert Skay and Isabel his wife quer. by John de Horsley in Isabel's place by the king's writ; Stephen Clinchaunt of Rodmarton (*Rodmarton*) and Lucy his wife def. A messuage, 3 yardlands, and 22*s*. 6*d*. rent in Rodmarton (*Rodemarton*) and the advowson of the church of the same township. Right of Robert. Render to him and Isabel. To hold to them and Robert's heirs. (Warranty, specifying Lucy's heirs.) Cons. 100 marks. *Endorsed* John Burdon and Alice his wife put in their claim.

76/47/136

254. Two weeks [13 Oct.] from Michaelmas. Robert de Alne quer.; Stephen Clinchaunt of Rodmarton (*Rodmarton*) def. A messuage, 2 yardlands, and 20*s*. rent in Rodmarton. Right of Robert. Render to him. (Warranty.) Cons. £40.

76/47/137

255. Three weeks [20 Oct.] from Michaelmas. Thomas de Dowdeswell (*Doudeswelle*) and Katherine his wife quer.; John de la Hussey (*Hoese*) parson of the church of Meysey Hampton (*Hampton Meysy*) def. A messuage, a mill, 1 ploughland and 10 yardlands, 15 a. of meadow, 50 a. of wood, and 7*s*. 8*d*. rent in Castlett (*Cadeslade*) and Cutsdean (*Cotesdene*). Thomas acknowledged the right of John by Thomas's gift. For this, grant and render to Thomas and Katherine. To hold to them and their heirs in tail. Contingent remainder to Thomas's heirs.

76/47/132

[Cutsdean was transferred to Glos. from Worcs. in 1931.]

256. Three weeks [20 Oct.] from Michaelmas. William atte Southend (*Suthende*) of Longborough (*Longebergh*) quer.; Adam Porcy of Ashton (*Asshton*) def. Half of a messuage, of 1 yardland and 1 a. of land, and of 1 a. of meadow in Longborough. Right of Adam by William's gift. For this, grant back and render to William. To hold during his life. Remainder to William's son Adam and that Adam's sister Matilda [jointly] and Matilda's heirs in tail. Contingent remainder to William's heirs.

76/47/134

257. Three weeks [20 Oct.] from Michaelmas. Robert Sapy (*Sapi*) and Aline his wife quer. by John de Chinnor (*Chynnore*) in Aline's place; Thomas Prick (*Prycke*) and Joan his wife def. A messuage, 29 a. and 1 rood of land, and 1⅓ a. of meadow in Huntley (*Huntele*). Right of Robert, as those which Robert and Aline had by gift of Thomas and Joan. To hold to Robert and Aline and Robert's heirs. (Warranty, specifying Joan's heirs.) Cons. £20.

76/47/139

1315

258. Three weeks [20 Oct.] from Michaelmas. Roger de Barley (*Berleye*) quer.; Thomas de la Chamber (*Chaumbre*) of Sherborne (*Shireburn*) and Denise his wife def. A messuage and 36 a. of land in Calmsden (*Calmundesden*). Right of Roger by gift of Thomas and Denise. (Warranty, specifying Denise's heirs.) Cons. 100*s*.

76/47/140

259. Three weeks [20 Oct.] from Michaelmas. Roger le Devenish (*Devenyssh*) quer.; Walter le Devenish and Isabel his wife def. A messuage in Gloucester (*Gloucestr'*). Right of Roger. Render to him. (Warranty, specifying Isabel's heirs.) Cons. 20*s*.

76/47/149

260. Morrow [12 Nov.] of St. Martin. Thomas de Breadstone (*Bradeston*) and Isabel his wife quer. by Richard Wrenche in Isabel's place by the king's writ; Thomas son of Thomas de Billow (*Beleye*) def. A messuage, 2 ploughlands, 20 a. of meadow, 7 a. of pasture, and 100*s*. rent in Cam (*Camme*), Alkington (*Alkynton*), and Ham (*Homme*). Thomas de Breadstone acknowledged the right of Thomas son of Thomas by gift of Thomas de Breadstone. For this, grant and render to Thomas de Breadstone and Isabel. To hold to them and their heirs in tail. Contingent remainder to the heirs of Thomas de Breadstone.

76/47/135

261. Morrow [12 Nov.] of St. Martin. William de Shenington (*Shenyndon*) quer.; Nicholas le Spicer def. Rent of 10 marks in Elm Bridge (*Elbrugg*) by Gloucester (*Gloucestr'*). Nicholas acknowledged the rent with all the service of Olive who was wife of Stephen de Fulbourn (*Fulburn*) and her heirs from all the holdings which she held of Nicholas in the said township to be the right of William. (Warranty.) Cons. £40. Made in Olive's presence and with her consent, and she did fealty to William.

76/47/138

1316

262. One week [20 Jan.] from Hilary. Adam de la Fenne quer.; Richard Burgess (*Burgeys*) of Lechlade (*Lecchelade*) and Isabel his wife imp. A messuage, 2½ a. of meadow, and half of 1 yardland in Lechlade. (Warranty of charter.) Right of Adam by gift of Richard and Isabel. (Warranty, specifying Isabel's heirs.) Cons. 20 marks.

76/47/144

263. Two weeks [27 Jan.] from Hilary. Walter Aubrey quer.; Nicholas de Capel (*Capele*) and Isabel his wife def. Rent of 40*s*. in Pebworth (*Pebbeworthe*). Right of Walter by gift of Nicholas and Isabel. Remise and quitclaim, specifying Isabel's heirs, to him. (Warranty.) Cons. 10 marks.

76/47/143

264. Two weeks [27 Jan.] from Hilary. Robert de Hampton quer.; Walter le Glover (*Glovere*) and Elena his wife def. A messuage in Bristol (*Bristoll'*). Right of Robert by gift of Walter and Elena. (Warranty, specifying Elena's heirs.) Cons. 100*s*.

76/47/146

[Cf. *Bristol Gt. Red Book*, p. 210, no. 103.]

1316

265. Morrow [3 Feb.] of the Purification. Thomas le Fox quer.; Richard Dawe and Alice his wife def. Half of a messuage in Chipping Sodbury (*Chepyng Sobbury*). Right of Thomas. Render to him. (Warranty, specifying Alice's heirs.) Cons. 20*s*.

76/47/142

266. One week [9 Feb.] from the Purification. William le Blake of Hatfield (*Hatfeld*) vicar of the church of Henbury (*Hembury in Salso Marisco*) quer.; William Savage (*Sauvage*) def. A messuage, 2½ yardlands, 8 a. of meadow, 3 a. of pasture, and rents of 8*s*. and ½ lb. of cumin in Shirehampton (*Hampton*) by Henbury. Right of William le Blake by William Savage's gift. For this, grant and render to William Savage of the messuage, 12 a. of land, 4 a. of meadow, and the rent. To hold during his life, of William le Blake, paying a rose a year at St. John the Baptist and doing service to the chief lords. Reversion to William le Blake.

76/47/141

267. Three weeks [2 May] from Easter. Richard de Sutton and Agnes his wife quer. by John de Pateshall (*Pateshill*) in Agnes's place; William de Baunton (*Baudynton*) and Margaret his wife def. One fifth of the manor of Shenington (*Shenyndon*). Richard acknowledged the right of Margaret. For this, William and Margaret granted and rendered the fifth to Richard and Agnes. To hold to them and their heirs in tail. Contingent remainder to Richard's heirs. (Warranty, specifying Margaret's heirs.)

76/47/148

268. One week [13 June] from Trinity. Roger Turtle (*Tourtle*) of Bristol (*Bristoll'*) quer. by Peter de la Rockley (*Rokele*); Walter Pelevill (*Pelevyle*) and Nesta his wife imp. Two messuages in Bristol. (Warranty of charter.) Right of Roger by gift of Walter and Nesta. (Warranty, specifying Walter's heirs.) Cons. 100*s*.

76/47/147

[Cf. *Bristol Gt. Red Book*, p. 210, no. 104. Part of the surname Rokele has been lost in the filing hole.]

269. One week [13 June] from Trinity. John la Warre quer.; Roger la Warre def. The manor of Wickwar (*Wykewarre*) and the advowson of the church of the same manor. Right of John by Roger's gift. For this, grant back and render to Roger. To hold during his life, of John, paying a rose a year at St. John the Baptist and doing service to the chief lords. Reversion to John.

76/47/150

270. Two weeks [20 June] from Trinity. Bernard atte Wolde of Bristol (*Bristoll'*) quer.; Alexander le Tucker (*Tokere*) of Bristol and Alice his wife def. A messuage in Bristol. Right of Bernard by gift of Alexander and Alice. (Warranty, specifying Alice's heirs.) Cons. 20*s*.

76/47/145

[Cf. *Bristol Gt. Red Book*, p. 210, no. 102.]

1316

271. Two weeks [20 June] from Trinity. John de Bromwich (*Bromwych*) quer.; Walter de Staundon and Agnes his wife imp. A messuage and 10 a. of land in Lydney (*Lydeneye*). (Warranty of charter.) Right of John by gift of Walter and Agnes. (Warranty, specifying Agnes's heirs.) Cons. 10 marks.

76/48/151

10 Edward II

1316

272. One week [6 Oct.] from Michaelmas. William son of Thomas le Venour (*Venur*) and Elena his wife quer. by Robert d'Abitot (*de Abetot*) in Elena's place by the king's writ; Robert le Venour and Robert de Bromfield (*Bromfeld*) and Joan his wife def. A messuage and 8 a. of land in Great Shurdington (*Magna Schurdinton*). Grant and render to William and Elena. To hold to them and their heirs in tail. Contingent remainder to Elena's heirs. (Warranty by Robert le Venour.) Cons. 20 marks.

76/48/158

273. One week [6 Oct.] from Michaelmas. Richard de Saul (*Salle*) clerk quer.; Geoffrey de Fretherne (*Frethorn*) def. A messuage and 1 yardland in Fretherne, Saul, and Framilode (*Fromylode*) held by Alice who was wife of Walter de Saul for term of life. Right of Geoffrey. For this, grant of the reversion to Richard. To hold during his life, of Geoffrey, paying 20s. a year, at St. Thomas the Apostle [21 Dec.] and St. John the Baptist, and doing service to the chief lords. Successive remainders to Richard's brother John and to John's brother Robert, each to hold during his life, of Geoffrey, for the said services. Reversion to Geoffrey. This agreement was made after Alice's death, Richard acknowledging that he was seised for term of life of the holdings which Alice formerly held. [*Worn.*]

76/48/159

274. One week [6 Oct.] from Michaelmas. Richard le Hayward (*Heyward*) quer.; Walter Hardegray and Margaret his wife def. A messuage, 18 a. of land, and 1 a. of meadow in Down Hatherley (*Dounhatherleye*). Right of Richard. Render to him. (Warranty, specifying Margaret's heirs.) Cons. 20 marks.

76/48/161

275. Two weeks [13 Oct.] from Michaelmas. John de Berkeley (*Berkeleye*) and Hawise his wife quer. by Peter de Edgeworth (*Eggesworth*) in Hawise's place; Anselm de Gurney (*Gurneye*) def. The manor of Dodington (*Dodinton*). John acknowledged the right of Anselm by John's gift. For this, grant and render to John and Hawise. To hold to them and their heirs in tail. Contingent remainder to John's heirs.

76/48/152

276. Two weeks [13 Oct.] from Michaelmas. Ellis le Gardiner and Agnes his wife quer. by Robert de Saul (*Salle*) in their place by the king's writ; John Warin (*Waryn*) def. Twelve acres of land in *Pyriton* [Parton, Pirton, or Purton]. Grant and render to Ellis and Agnes. To hold to them and their heirs in tail. Contingent remainder to John's son Walter. (Warranty.) Cons. 20 marks.

76/48/155

1316

277. Two weeks [13 Oct.] from Michaelmas. (Made three weeks from Michaelmas 7 Edward II [20 Oct. 1313].) John de Olney (*Olneye*) quer.; Stephen de Fulbourn (*Fulburne*) and Olive his wife def. (Stephen was dead by the time that the fine was granted and recorded, and Olive was then the sole def.) A messuage, a mill, and 1 ploughland in Elm Bridge (*Elbrigge*) by Churchdown (*Chirchedon*). Stephen and Olive acknowledged the right of John. For this, grant and render to Stephen and Olive. To hold during their lives, of John, paying a rose a year at St. John the Baptist and doing service to the chief lords. Reversion to John. *Endorsed* Henry de Compton (*Cumpton*) chaplain put in his claim. Edmund de Banbury (*Bannebury*) put in his claim. William de Shenington (*Shenyndone*) put in his claim. Joan who was wife of Walter de Banbury put in her claim.

76/48/157

278. Two weeks [13 Oct.] from Michaelmas. Herbert son of John and Eleanor his wife quer. by Richard de Saul (*Salle*) in Eleanor's place; John de Standish (*Stanedish*) def. The manors of Londesborough (*Lounesburgh*) and Weaverthorpe (*Wytherthorp*), YORKS., a messuage, 1 ploughland, 6 a. of meadow, and 12 a. of wood in Southam (*Sutham*), GLOS., and two thirds of the manor of Stanford (*Stanford*), BERKS. Herbert acknowledged the right of John by Herbert's gift. For this, grant and render to Herbert and Eleanor. To hold to them and Herbert's heirs. *Labelled* Ebor', Glouc', Berk'.

285/30/132

[Stanford is more likely to be Stanford Dingley than Stanford in the Vale: *V.C.H. Berks.* iv. 111, 479–82.]

279. One month [27 Oct.] from Michaelmas. Henry le Gardiner quer.; Robert Bastard def. A messuage, 40 a. of land, and 1 a. of meadow in *Pyriton* [Parton, Pirton, or Purton]. Right of Robert by Henry's gift. For this, grant back and render to Henry. To hold during his life. Remainder to Ellis le Gardiner and Agnes his wife and Ellis's heirs in tail. Contingent remainder to Henry's heirs.

76/48/156

280. Morrow [3 Nov.] of All Souls. Walter de Nass (*Nasse*) and Robert his son quer. by Richard de Saul (*Salle*) in their place by the king's writ; Walter Warin (*Waryn*) imp. Rent of 62*s*. 6*d*. in Lydney (*Lydeneye*). (Warranty of charter.) Right of Walter de Nass, as that which he and Robert had by Walter Warin's gift. To hold to Walter de Nass and Robert and that Walter's heirs. (Warranty.) Cons. 100 marks.

76/49/178

281. Morrow [12 Nov.] of St. Martin. John de Estoft quer.; John de Wysham and Matilda his wife imp. A messuage, 12½ a. of land, and 1½ a. of meadow in Upper Siddington (*Oversodington*). (Warranty of charter.) Right of John de Estoft by gift of John de Wysham and Matilda. (Warranty, specifying Matilda's heirs.) Cons. 20 marks.

76/48/153

282. One week [18 Nov.] from St. Martin. William Whitenough (*Whitynogh*) quer.; John Whitenough (*Witynogh*) def. A messuage, 12 a. of land, and 1 a. of meadow in Hope (*Hope*) by Thornbury (*Thornbury*). Right of William by John's gift. For this, grant back

1316

and render to John. To hold during his life, of William, paying a rose a year at St. John the Baptist and doing service to the chief lords. Reversion to William. [*Faded.*]

76/48/154

283. One week [18 Nov.] from St. Martin. John de Chausy and Joan his wife quer. by Richard de Saul (*Salle*) in Joan's place by the king's writ; Henry Everard (*Everad*) def. A messuage and 2 ploughlands in Alderley (*Alreleye*). John acknowledged the right of Henry by John's gift. For this, grant and render to John and Joan. To hold to them and John's heirs.

76/48/160

1317

284. One week [20 Jan.] from Hilary. William son of Thomas le Venour and Elena his wife quer. by Robert d'Abitot (*de Apetot*) in their place by the king's writ; Ralph Wyberd and Agnes his wife imp. A messuage and 8 a. of land in Shurdington (*Shurdynton*). (Warranty of charter.) Right of Elena, as those which William and Elena had by gift of Ralph and Agnes. To hold to William and Elena and Elena's heirs. (Warranty, specifying Agnes's heirs.) Cons. 10 marks.

76/48/162

285. One week [20 Jan.] from Hilary. Thomas de Amersham (*Agmondesham*) quer.; Peter de Apperley (*Apperleye*) and Juliana his wife imp. A messuage and one third of 1 yardland in Southam (*Sutham*) by Bishop's Cleeve (*Clyve Episcopi*). (Warranty of charter.) Right of Thomas by gift of Peter and Juliana. (Warranty, specifying Juliana's heirs.) Cons. 10 marks.

76/48/166

286. One week [20 Jan.] from Hilary. Robert de Lydney (*Lydeneye*) quer.; Richard Maynard and Alice his wife def. Rent of 20*s.* in Lydney. Right of Robert. Render to him. (Warranty, specifying Alice's heirs.) Cons. 100*s.*

76/49/179

287. Morrow [3 Feb.] of the Purification. John Athelam of Tewkesbury (*Teukesbury*) quer.; Robert de Cricklade (*Crickelad*) of Tewkesbury and Matilda his wife imp. Half of a messuage and of 1 a. of meadow in Tewkesbury. (Warranty of charter.) Right of John by gift of Robert and Matilda. (Warranty, specifying Robert's heirs.) Cons. 100*s.*

76/48/163

288. Two weeks [17 April] from Easter. John de Acton and Milisent his wife quer. by John de Elkstone (*Elkestan*) in Milisent's place by the king's writ; John de Hawkesbury (*Hauekesbury*) chaplain def. The manor of Iron Acton (*Irenacton*). John de Acton acknowledged the right of John de Hawkesbury by gift of John de Acton. For this, grant and render to John de Acton and Milisent. To hold to them and their heirs in tail. Contingent remainder to the heirs of John de Acton.

76/48/164

1317

289. Three weeks [24 April] from Easter. Thomas de Berkeley (*Berkeleye*) the elder quer. by Richard de Saul (*Salle*) in his place by the king's writ; William atte Wood (*Wode*) and Matilda his wife imp. A messuage, 1 yardland, and 4 a. of meadow in Alkington (*Alkynton*) by Berkeley. (Warranty of charter.) Right of Thomas by gift of William and Matilda. (Warranty, specifying Matilda's heirs.) Cons. 20 marks.

76//48/167

290. Three weeks [24 April] from Easter. Thomas de Berkeley (*Berkeleye*) the elder by Richard de Saul (*Salle*) in his place by the king's writ; Hugh de Croweford and Margery his wife def. A messuage, 16 a. of land, and 2 a. of meadow in Ham (*Hamme*) and Alkington (*Alkinton*). Right of Thomas. Render to him. (Warranty, specifying Margery's heirs.) Cons. 20 marks.

76/48/168

[Cf. *Berkeley Castle Mun.* i, p. 239, A1/31/22 (counterpart).]

291. Three weeks [24 April] from Easter. Roger de Barley (*Berleye*) quer.; Thomas de la Chamber (*Chaumbre*) of Sherborne (*Shyreburn*) and Denise his wife def. A messuage and 1 hide of land in Calmsden (*Calmondesden*) held by Walter Burgess (*Burgeys*) of Baunton (*Baudynton*) for term of life. Right of Roger. Grant to Roger of the reversion, of Denise's inheritance. (Warranty.) Cons. 100 marks. Made in Walter's presence and with his consent, and he did fealty to Roger.

76/48/169

292. Three weeks [24 April] from Easter. Hugh le Despenser (*Despens'*) the elder and William de Haudlo clerk quer.; John de Haudlo and Matilda his wife def. The manor of Billingford (*Byllyngford*) and 20 a. of land in Foxley (*Foxle*) and the advowson of the church of the same manor of Billingford, NORF., the manor of Haselbech (*Haselbeche*) and the advowson of the church of the same manor, NORTHANTS., 24 marks and 10*s.* rent in Biddestone (*Budeston*) and Sutton Veny (*Fennysutton*), two thirds of the manor of Great Cheverell (*Magna Chiverel*), and the advowson of the churches of the said manor and of the township of Sutton Veny, WILTS., and 8 messuages, 12 shops, 15 cellars, 2 gardens, and 62*s.* rent in Bristol (*Bristoll'*), GLOS. Right of Hugh and William by gift of John and Matilda. For this, grant back and render to John and Matilda. To hold to them and their heirs in tail male, the land in Foxley of the chief lords and all the other holdings of the king. Contingent remainder to Matilda's heirs. Made by the king's order except as to the land in Foxley. *Labelled* Norff', Norht', Wyltes', Gloucestr'. *Endorsed twice, horizontally and vertically,* Edward Charles and Alice his wife put in their claim. [*Worn.*]

285/30/143

[Cf. *Wilts. Fines, 1272–1327*, pp. 127–8.]

293. One month [1 May] from Easter. John de Thormerton quer.; John de Frocester (*Froucestre*) and Joan his wife def. A messuage, a mill, 8 a. of land, and 2 a. of meadow in Maisemore (*Mayesmore*), Sandhurst (*Sandhurst*), Churchdown (*Churchesdon*), and Brook Street (*Brocstrete*) by Gloucester (*Gloucestre*). Right of John de Thormerton. Render to him. (Warranty, specifying John de Frocester's heirs.) Cons. 20 marks.

76/48/165

1317

294. One week [5 June] from Trinity. Walter Sewaker quer.; Robert Beaugraunt and Matilda his wife def. Six acres of land in Alkington (*Alkynton*) by Berkeley (*Berkeleye*). Right of Walter. Render to him. (Warranty, specifying Matilda's heirs.) Cons. 10 marks.

76/48/170

295. One week [5 June] from Trinity. Roger Damory quer.; Richard Thork of Hampen (*Hannepenne*) and Susan his wife imp. The manor of Hampen. (Warranty of charter.) Right of Roger. Remise and quitclaim, specifying Susan's heirs, to him. (Warranty.) Cons. 100 marks. *Endorsed* Jordan de Hengham put in his claim.

76/48/174

296. One week [5 June] from Trinity. Philip de la Wall (*Walle*) quer.; Isaac de Stone and Matilda his wife def. A messuage and 14 a. of land in Ham (*Hamme*) and Thornbury (*Thorniburi*). Right of Philip by gift of Isaac and Matilda. (Warranty, specifying Matilda's heirs.) Cons. 20 marks.

76/49/176

297. One week [5 June] from Trinity. Robert de Bittiscombe (*Bytlescumb*) quer.; Robert Sturdy (*Stourdy*) and Cristiana his wife imp. A messuage, 1 ploughland, 20 a. of meadow, 80 a. of wood, 100 a. of pasture, and 30s. rent in Cromhall (*Croumhale*). (Warranty of charter.) Right of Robert de Bittiscombe by gift of Robert Sturdy and Cristiana. (Warranty, specifying Cristiana's heirs.) Cons. 100 marks. *Endorsed* Robert son of John de Radington (*Radyngton*) put in his claim.

76/49/177

298. Two weeks [12 June] from Trinity. Richard de Guiting (*Gutynge*) of Campden (*Caunpedene*) quer.; John Vactus of Campden (*Campeden*) and Sibyl his wife def. One third of a messuage in Campden (*Campedene*). Right of Richard by gift of John and Sibyl. (Warranty, specifying Sibyl's heirs.) Cons. 20s.

76/48/171

299. Morrow [25 June] of St. John the Baptist. Andrew de Pendock (*Penedok*) and Isabel his wife quer.; Thomas de Braose (*Brewosa*) def. A messuage, 4 bovates of land, 10 a. of meadow, 6 a. of pasture, and 26s. rent in Forthampton (*Forthampton*). Right of Andrew, as those which Andrew and Isabel had by Thomas's gift. For this, grant back and render to Thomas. To hold during his life, of Andrew and Isabel and Andrew's heirs, paying a rose a year at St. John the Baptist and doing service to the chief lords. Reversion to Andrew and Isabel and Andrew's heirs.

76/48/172

300. Morrow [25 June] of St. John the Baptist. Robert Gille (*Gylle*) of Great Bentham (*Magna Benetham*) quer.; Ralph Wyberd (*Wybert*) and Agnes his wife def. A messuage, 12 a. of land, 1½ a. of pasture, and half of 1 a. of meadow in Little Witcombe (*Parva Wydecumbe*) and Great Bentham. Right of Robert. Render to him. (Warranty, specifying Agnes's heirs.) Cons. 20 marks. *Endorsed* Thomas de Bentham (*Benetham*) put in his claim. William de Bentham put in his claim.

76/48/173

1317

301. Morrow [25 June] of St. John the Baptist. William de la Grave of Wightfield (*Wyghtfeld*) quer. by Peter de Edgeworth (*Eggesworth*) in his place by the king's writ; Richard le Roo of Gloucester (*Gloucestre*) 'pestour' [*i.e. baker*] and Denise his wife and John le Meys of Gloucester and Matilda his wife def. A shop and 8*s*. rent in Gloucester. Right of William. Render to him. (Warranty, specifying Denise's and Matilda's heirs.) Cons. 10 marks.

76/48/175

11 Edward II

1317

302. Two weeks [8 July] from St. John the Baptist. Nicholas de Pechesleye of Campden (*Caumpedene*) and Joan his wife quer.; Robert de Pechesleye of Campden def. Five messuages, a shop, 1½ yardlands and 2 a. of land, and 2 a. of meadow in Westington (*Westinton*) and Campden. Right of Robert by gift of Nicholas and Joan. For this, grant back and render to Nicholas and Joan. To hold to them and their heirs in tail. Contingent remainder to Nicholas's heirs.

76/49/196

303. One week [6 Oct.] from Michaelmas. Matilda who was wife of Henry Guge of Tewkesbury (*Teukesbury*) quer. by Henry de Wenland in their place by the king's writ; Richard de Houghton (*Hoghton*) and Alice his wife def. A messuage, 9 a. of land, and 1½ a. of meadow in Gupshill (*Gopeshull*) by Tewkesbury. Right of Matilda by gift of Richard and Alice. (Warranty, specifying Alice's heirs.) Cons. 20 marks.

76/49/188

304. One week [6 Oct.] from Michaelmas. Geoffrey de la Hill (*Hulle*) of Ketford (*Ketford*) quer. by Roger de Wallington (*Walinton*) in his place by the king's writ; John son of William de Okle (*Ocle*) and Elena his wife def. A messuage, 6 a. of land, and 3 a. of meadow in Newent (*Newent*). Right of Geoffrey. Render to him. (Warranty, specifying Elena's heirs.) Cons. 10 marks.

76/49/189

305. One week [6 Oct.] from Michaelmas. Robert d'Abitot (*Dabetot*) and Joan his wife quer. by Peter de Edgeworth (*Eggeworth*) in Joan's place by the king's writ; William le Freeman (*Freman*) of Elmore (*Elmor*) def. A messuage, 18 a. of land, and 2 a. of meadow in Elmore. Grant and render to Robert and Joan. To hold to them and their heirs in tail. Contingent remainder to Robert's heirs. (Warranty.) Cons. £20.

76/49/191

306. One week [6 Oct.] from Michaelmas. Robert de Winchester (*Wynton'*) quer.; Richard son of Walter de Saul (*Salle*) and Alice his wife def. Three [*reading uncertain*] messuages, a mill, 32 a. of land, and 1 a. of meadow in Cam (*Camme*). Right of Alice. For this, Richard and Alice granted and rendered the holdings to Robert. To hold during his life, of Richard and Alice and Alice's heirs, paying 20*s*. a year, at Michaelmas, Christmas, Easter, and St. John the Baptist, and doing service to the chief lords. Reversion to Richard and Alice and Alice's heirs. [*Worn.*]

76/49/192

1317

307. Two weeks [13 Oct.] from Michaelmas. Adam de la Fenne and Alice his wife quer. by the said Adam in Alice's place by the king's writ; Boniface de Coate (*Cotes*) of Southrop (*Suthrop*) and Alice his wife def. A messuage [and] 2 yardlands in Coate, Eastleach (*Estleche*), and Southrop. Right of Adam, as that which Adam and Alice had by gift of Boniface and Alice. To hold to Adam and Alice and Adam's heirs. (Warranty, specifying the heirs of Alice wife of Boniface.) Cons. 20 marks.

76/49/185

308. Three weeks [20 Oct.] from Michaelmas. Geoffrey atte Heath (*Hethe*) of Bristol (*Bristoll'*) quer.; Richard Avery (*Averay*) of Bedminster (*Bedemenstre*) and Agnes his wife def. A messuage in Bristol. Right of Geoffrey. Render to him. (Warranty, specifying Agnes's heirs.) Cons. 10 marks.

76/49/190

[Cf. *Bristol Gt. Red Book*, p. 211, no. 105.]

309. One month [27 Oct.] from Michaelmas. John Giffard of Brimpsfield (*Brimmesfeld*) and William de Perrers (*Perers*) of Prestbury (*Prestebury*) quer. by John de Elkstone (*Elkeston*) in John's place; Robert de Prestbury def. The manor of Up Hatherley (*Uphatherleye*). Right of John. Render to John and William. To hold to John and William and John's heirs. Cons. 100 marks. *Endorsed* Henry de Hatherley (*Hatherleye*) put in his claim.

76/49/182

310. One month [27 Oct.] from Michaelmas. Reynold le Bestman (*Bestemon*) and Matilda his wife quer. by Peter de Edgeworth (*Eggesworth*) in their place by the king's writ; Walter de Capel (*Capele*) and Isabel his wife imp. A messuage in Gloucester (*Gloucestr'*). (Warranty of charter.) Right of Reynold, as that which Reynold and Matilda had by gift of Walter and Isabel. To hold to Reynold and Matilda and Reynold's heirs. (Warranty, specifying Walter's heirs.) Cons. 100*s*. [*Torn*.]

76/49/183

311. One month [27 Oct.] from Michaelmas. Hugh de Bisley (*Byseleye*) quer.; Reynold Cotheridge (*Coterich*) and Matilda his wife def. Two acres of wood and one third of a messuage and 1 yardland in Bisley (*Byseley*). Right of Hugh by gift of Reynold and Matilda. For this, grant back and render to Reynold and Matilda. To hold during their lives, of Hugh, paying a rose a year at St. John the Baptist and doing service to the chief lords. Reversion to Hugh.

76/49/187

312. One month [27 Oct.] from Michaelmas. John de Morton and Cristiana his wife and John son of John de Morton and Eleanor his wife quer.; William parson of the church of Hampnett (*Hamptonet*) def. The advowson of the church of Hampnett and the manor of Hampnett except for one quarter of the manor. John de Morton and Cristiana acknowledged the right of William by gift of John de Morton and Cristiana. For this,

1317

grant back and render to John de Morton and Cristiana. To hold during their lives. Remainder to John the son and Eleanor and their heirs in tail. Contingent remainder to the heirs of that John. [*Worn.*]

76/49/193

313. Morrow [12 Nov.] of St. Martin. Robert de Aston and Katherine his wife quer. by Peter de Edgeworth (*Eggesworth*) in their place by the king's writ; Henry de Aston def. Four messuages, 2 ploughlands and 20 a. of land, 8 a. of meadow, and 2*s.* 6*d.* rent in Ampney Crucis (*Ameneye Sancti Crucis*) and Aston Blank (*Coldaston*). Robert acknowledged the right of Henry by Robert's gift. For this, grant and render to Robert and Katherine. To hold to them and Robert's heirs.

76/49/181

314. Morrow [12 Nov.] of St. Martin. Robert Brown (*Broun*) of Campden (*Caumpeden*) and Joan his wife quer. by the said Robert in Joan's place; John Watts (*Wattes*) of Campden and Sibyl his wife def. One third of a messuage in Campden. Right of Robert. Render, specifying Sibyl's heirs, to Robert and Joan. To hold to Robert and Joan and Robert's heirs. (Warranty.) Cons. 100*s.*

76/49/186

315. One week [18 Nov.] from St. Martin. Henry de Clissold (*Clyveshale*) quer.; Richard de Clissold def. Two messuages, 1¾ yardlands, and 2 a. of meadow in Througham (*Throughham*) and Clissold. Right of Henry by Richard's gift. For this, grant back and render to Richard. To hold during his life, of Henry, paying a rose a year at St. John the Baptist and doing service to the chief lords. Remainder to Emma daughter of William de Bisley (*Biseley*) during her life. Reversion to Henry.

76/49/180

1318

316. One week [20 Jan.] from Hilary. John de Baysam of Gloucester (*Gloucestr'*) and Alice his wife quer.; Philip le Tailor (*Taillur*) of Gloucester and Margery his wife imp. A messuage and a toft in the suburb of Gloucester. (Warranty of charter.) Right of John, as those which John and Alice had by gift of Philip and Margery. To hold to John and Alice and John's heirs. (Warranty, specifying Margery's heirs.) Cons. 10 marks.

76/49/198

317. One week [20 Jan.] from Hilary. Henry Winpenny (*Wynepeny*) 'shipman' quer. by Robert de Hampton in his place by the king's writ; John de Wybyngton and Agnes his wife def. Three shops in Bristol (*Bristoll'*). Right of Henry by gift of John and Agnes. (Warranty, specifying Agnes's heirs.) Cons. 100 marks. *Endorsed* John Wellshot (*Welhyshote*) of Bristol put in his claim.

76/49/200

[Cf. *Bristol Gt. Red Book*, p. 211, no. 106.]

1318

318. One week [20 Jan.] from Hilary. Robert de Spaxton (*Spakston*) quer.; William Busy of Bristol (*Bristoll'*) and Amice his wife def. A messuage in Bristol. Right of Robert by gift of William and Amice. (Warranty, specifying Amice's heirs.) Cons. 40*s*.

76/50/201

[Cf. *Bristol Gt. Red Book*, p. 211, no. 107.]

319. One week [9 Feb.] from the Purification. Mr. Ellis de St. Albans (*de Sancto Albano*) quer.; John de Arle and Isabel his wife def. One ploughland, 30*s*. rent, and half of a messuage in Cold Ashton (*Asshton*) and Bath (*Bathon'*). Right of Isabel. For this, John and Isabel granted back and rendered the holdings to Mr. Ellis. To hold during his life, of John and Isabel and Isabel's heirs, paying a rose a year at St. John the Baptist and doing service to the chief lords. Reversion to John and Isabel and Isabel's heirs.

76/49/194

[The two places are confidently identified as Cold Ashton and Bath, so that the fine should have been a 'divers counties' fine, for Glos. and Som.]

320. Two weeks [7 May] from Easter. John de Annesley and Lucy his wife quer. by John de Elkstone (*Elkestan*) in Lucy's place by the king's writ; John de Bures and Hawise his wife def. Thirty-nine messuages, 2 mills, 8 ploughlands, 37 a. of meadow, 25 a. of pasture, 18 a. of wood, and £4 6*s*. 2*d*. rent in Down Hatherley (*Dunhatherleye*), Kemerton (*Kynemarton*), and Aston on Carrant (*Aston super Carente*). John de Annesley acknowledged the right of Hawise. For this John de Bures and Hawise granted and rendered the holdings to John de Annesley and Lucy. To hold during their lives, of John de Bures and Hawise and Hawise's heirs, paying a rose a year at St. John the Baptist and doing service to the chief lords. (Warranty.) Reversion to John de Bures and Hawise and Hawise's heirs. [*Worn*.]

76/49/195

321. One week [25 June] from Trinity. John atte Hazel (*Hasele*) and Joan his wife quer.; John le Walker (*Wakyare*) of Syde (*Syde*) and Agnes his wife def. A messuage in Hampnett (*Hamptonet*) by Northleach (*Northlech*). Right of Joan, as that which John atte Hazel and Joan had by gift of John le Walker and Agnes. To hold to John atte Hazel and Joan and Joan's heirs. (Warranty, specifying Agnes's heirs.) Cons. £10.

76/49/184

322. One week [25 June] from Trinity. John atte Hill (*Hulle*) quer.; Ralph le Tiler (*Tylare*) and Juliana his wife imp. A messuage in Gloucester (*Gloucestr'*). (Warranty of charter.) Right of John by gift of Ralph and Juliana. (Warranty, specifying Ralph's heirs.) Cons. 40*s*.

76/49/199

323. One week [25 June] from Trinity. Walter de Upton 'apprentiz' quer. by Adam Read (*Red*) in his place by the king's writ; Richard Avery (*Averay*) of Bedminster (*Bedemenst'*) and Agnes his wife def. Two shops in Bristol (*Bristoll'*). Right of Walter by gift of Richard and Agnes. (Warranty, specifying Agnes's heirs.) Cons. 10 marks.

76/50/202

[Cf. *Bristol Gt. Red Book*, pp. 211–12, no. 108.]

1318

324. Two weeks [2 July] from Trinity. William son of William de la Wick (*Wyke*) of Daglingworth (*Dagelyngeworth*) quer.; William de la Wick of Daglingworth def. A messuage and 2 yardlands in Daglingworth. Right of William son of William. Render to him. (Warranty.) Cons. 10 marks.

76/49/197

12 Edward II

1318

325. Two weeks [8 July] from St. John the Baptist. Thomas Coke quer.; Vincent le Read (*Rede*) and Margery his wife def. A messuage in Gloucester (*Gloucestr'*). Right of Thomas by gift of Vincent and Margery. (Warranty, by Vincent alone.) Cons. 10 marks.

76/50/207

326. Two weeks [8 July] from St. John the Baptist. William de Chilton quer.; John le White of Bristol (*Bristoll'*) 'deyere' [*i.e. dyer*] and Juliana his wife def. A messuage in the suburb of Bristol. Right of William. Remise and quitclaim, specifying Juliana's heirs, to him. Cons. 100*s.*

76/50/224

[Cf. *Bristol Gt. Red Book*, p. 212, no. 110.]

327. Two weeks [8 July] from St. John the Baptist. Nicholas Bruse and Matilda his wife quer.; Thomas Lewin (*Lewyn*) def. A messuage and 1 ploughland in Elmstone (*Aylmundeston*) by Uckington (*Okynton*). Nicholas acknowledged the right of Thomas by Nicholas's gift. For this, grant and render to Nicholas and Matilda. To hold to them and Nicholas's heirs.

76/50/225

328. Two weeks [8 July] from St. John the Baptist. John Fylus of Bishop's Cleeve (*Clyve*) and Cecily his wife quer. by Peter de Edgeworth (*Eggeworth*) in Cecily's place by the king's writ; Nicholas Bruse (*Breuse*) and Matilda his wife def. One seventh of a messuage, 2 ploughlands, 16 a. of meadow, 6 a. of pasture, 2 a. of wood, and 40*s.* rent in Staverton (*Staverton*) and Deerhurst (*Derhurst*). Right of Matilda. For this, Nicholas and Matilda granted the one seventh to John and Cecily. To hold to them and their heirs in tail, of Nicholas and Matilda and Matilda's heirs, paying a rose a year at St. John the Baptist and doing service to the chief lords. (Warranty.) Contingent reversion to Nicholas and Matilda and Matilda's heirs. [*Worn.*]

76/51/226

329. One week [6 Oct.] from Michaelmas. Nicholas de Morton (*Moreton*) of Tewkesbury (*Teukesbury*) quer.; William Lovecock (*Lovecok*) of Tewkesbury and Alice his wife imp. A messuage, 3 a. of land, and 22*s.* rent in Tewkesbury. (Warranty of charter.) Right of Nicholas by gift of William and Alice. (Warranty, specifying Alice's heirs.) Cons. £20.

76/50/210

330. One week [6 Oct.] from Michaelmas. John le Butler (*Botiller*) of Llantwit (*Lanultyt*) and Beatrice his wife quer.; Thomas le Butler def. A messuage and 1 ploughland in Murcott (*Morcote*). Right of Thomas by gift of John and Beatrice. For this, grant back

1318

and render to John and Beatrice. To hold to them and their heirs in tail. Contingent remainder to Beatrice's heirs.

76/50/211

[Geographical proximity indicates Murcott in Minsterworth: cf. below, nos. 537–8.]

331. One week [6 Oct.] from Michaelmas. Richard atte Wood (*Wode*) and Joan his wife quer. by Peter de Edgeworth (*Eggesworth*) in Joan's place by the king's writ; Odo de Acton def. A messuage and 2 ploughlands in Chedworth (*Cheddeworthe*). Richard acknowledged the right of Odo by Richard's gift. For this, grant and render to Richard and Joan. To hold to them and their heirs in tail. Contingent remainder to Richard's heirs.

76/50/212

332. One week [6 Oct.] from Michaelmas. Robert de Prestbury (*Prestebury*) and Elizabeth his wife quer. by John de Elkstone (*Elkeston*) in Elizabeth's place; William de Prestbury def. The manor of Up Hatherley (*Ophatherleye*), and a messuage, 2 tofts, and 1 ploughland in Prestbury. Robert acknowledged the right of William by Robert's gift. For this, grant and render to Robert and Elizabeth. To hold to them and Robert's heirs. *Endorsed* Thomas son of John de Up Hatherley (*Uphatherleye*) put in his claim.

76/50/213

333. One week [6 Oct.] from Michaelmas. John le Butler (*Botiller*) of Llantwit (*Lanultyt*) and Beatrice his wife quer.; Thomas le Butler def. The manor of the Park (*parco*). Right of Thomas by gift of John and Beatrice. For this, grant back and render to John and Beatrice. To hold to them and their heirs in tail. Contingent remainder to Beatrice's heirs.

76/50/214

[For the identity of the Park, below, no. 537.]

334. One week [6 Oct.] from Michaelmas. Walter de Didcot (*Dudycote*) of Tewkesbury (*Theukesbury*) quer.; William Lovecock (*Lovecok*) of Tewkesbury and Alice his wife imp. Half of a messuage in Tewkesbury. (Warranty of charter.) Right of Walter by gift of William and Alice. (Warranty, specifying Alice's heirs.) Cons. 100*s*. [*Worn.*]

76/50/216

335. One week [6 Oct.] from Michaelmas. William Hereward (*Hurward*) quer.; Bartholomew de Grenville (*Grenevill*) and Anne his wife def. The manor of Compton Greenfield (*Comton Grenevill*) and the advowson of the chapel of the same manor. Right of William, of which he had the advowson and one third and two thirds of two thirds of the manor by gift of Bartholomew and Anne. And grant to William of the reversion of one third of two thirds of the manor held by Richard de Thorverton (*Thoverton*) and Katherine his wife in Katherine's dower, of Bartholomew's inheritance. (Warranty.) Cons. 100 marks. Made in the presence and with the consent of Richard and Katherine, and they did fealty to William. *Endorsed* Henry de Grenville (*Grenevile*) put in his claim. [*Worn.*]

76/51/228

[Cf. *Berkeley Castle Mun.* i, p. 456, A2/20/3 (ii) (copy).]

336. One week [6 Oct.] from Michaelmas. William Reynald of Eyford (*Eyford*) quer.; Margaret who was wife of Nicholas de Valeres (*Valers*) def. Two messuages, 23 a. of land, 30 a. of wood, 13*s*. 1½*d*. rent, half of a messuage, and one third of 1 knight's fee in

1318

Uley (*Iwelegh*), Cam (*Camme*), and Baunton (*Baudynton*), GLOS., and a messuage, 36 a. of land, 4 a. of meadow, 17 a. of pasture, and one third of a mill in Winford (*Wynfrith*), Regil or Ridgehill (*Ragel*), Dundry (*Dundray*), Cranmore (*Cranemere*), and *Calecote*, SOM. Right of William by Margaret's gift. For this, grant back and render to Margaret. To hold during her life. Remainder to Walter de Romsey (*Romeseye*) and Katherine his wife and their heirs in tail. Successive contingent remainders to Walter's son John and Margaret his wife and their heirs in tail and to Katherine's heirs. *Labelled* Gloucestr', Sumers'. *Endorsed* Thomas de Berkeley (*Berkeleye*) the elder put in his claim. [*Worn.*]

286/31/168

[Cf. *Som. Fines, 1307–46*, p. 118.]

337. Two weeks [13 Oct.] from Michaelmas. Reynold de Abenhall (*Abbenhale*) and Sibyl his wife quer. by John de Cirencester (*Cirencestre*) in Sibyl's place by the king's writ; Peter de Edgeworth (*Egesworth*) def. A messuage, 1 ploughland, 4 a. of meadow, 30 a. of wood, 6 marks rent, and a mill in Blaisdon (*Blechedon*) and half of the advowson of the church of the same township. Reynold acknowledged the right of Peter by Reynold's gift. For this, grant and render to Reynold and Sibyl. To hold to them and Reynold's heirs.

76/50/209

338. One month [27 Oct.] from Michaelmas. Thomas Russel quer.; Benedict de Soweye and Agnes his wife imp. A shop in Lewins Mead (*Lewelinesmede*) [Bristol]. (Warranty of charter.) Right of Thomas by gift of Benedict and Agnes. (Warranty, by Benedict alone.) Cons. 20*s*.

76/50/204

[Omitted from *Bristol Gt. Red Book*.]

339. One month [27 Oct.] from Michaelmas. John atte Hazel (*Hasele*) and Joan his wife quer.; Walter de Campden (*Caumpeden*) and Felicia his wife def. One yardland and 8 a. of land, 2 a. of meadow, and one third of 2 messuages in Hampnett (*Hamptonet*) by Northleach (*Northlech*). Right of Joan. Render to John and Joan. To hold to them and Joan's heirs. (Warranty, specifying Felicia's heirs.) Cons. 20 marks.

76/50/206

340. One month [27 Oct.] from Michaelmas. William son of Adam Bras, Elena daughter of William de Crikefeld, and William de Crikefeld quer.; Walter Musket def. A messuage, 1 yardland, and 4*s*. 10½*d*. rent in English Bicknor (*Bikenore*). Grant and render to William son of Adam, Elena, and William de Crikefeld. To hold to them and Elena's heirs in tail. Contingent remainder to Elena's sister Agnes. Cons. 10 marks. [*Worn.*]

76/50/215

341. One month [27 Oct.] from Michaelmas. John de la Bussere and William his brother quer.; Roger de la Bussere of Broad Marston (*Brodemerston*) imp. A messuage, 3 yardlands, and 12 a. of meadow in Broad Marston. (Warranty of charter.) Right of John, as those which John and William had by Roger's gift. To hold to John and William and John's heirs. (Warranty.) Cons. 20 marks.

76/50/218

1318

342. Morrow [3 Nov.] of All Souls. Richard le White of Bristol (*Bristoll'*) quer.; Richard Blanket and Alice his wife and Richard atte Hay and Agnes his wife def. A messuage and a shop in the suburb of Bristol. Right of Richard le White. Remise and quitclaim, specifying Alice's and Agnes's heirs, to Richard le White. Cons. £20. *Endorsed* John Clof put in his claim. John Clof of Bristol and Juliana his wife put in their claim. Agnes sister of the same Juliana put in her claim.

76/50/203

[Cf. *Bristol Gt. Red Book*, p. 212, no. 109.]

343. Morrow [3 Nov.] of All Souls. Nicholas de Kingston (*Kyngeston*) the elder and Joan his wife quer. by Nicholas de Kinnersley (*Kynardesle*) in Joan's place; William FitzWarren (*fitz Warin*) def. The manor of Tortworth (*Torteworth*) and 2 messuages, 2 ploughlands and 1 yardland, 20 a. of meadow, and 4 a. of wood in Oldbury upon Severn (*Oldebyry*), Thornbury (*Thornbury*), Thatcham (*Thacham*), and Falfield (*Valefeld*), and the advowson of the church of the same township of Tortworth. Nicholas acknowledged the right of William by Nicholas's gift. For this, grant and render to Nicholas and Joan. To hold to them and Nicholas's heirs.

76/50/205

344. Morrow [3 Nov.] of All Souls. Robert Pope of Gloucester (*Gloucestr'*) quer. by Peter de Edgeworth (*Eggesworth*); Richard le Roo and Denise his wife and John le Meys and Matilda his wife def. A messuage in Gloucester. Right of Robert. Remise and quitclaim, specifying Denise's and Matilda's heirs, to Robert. (Warranty.) Cons. 20 marks.

76/50/208

345. Morrow [3 Nov.] of All Souls. Richard de Apperley (*Apperleye*) and Joan his wife quer.; Peter de Edgeworth (*Egesworth*) def. Two messuages, 2 ploughlands, 40 a. of meadow, and 60s. rent in Apperley, Deerhurst Walton (*Walton*), Deerhurst (*Derhurst*), Sandhurst (*Sondhurst*), Gloucester (*Gloucestr'*), and Rudford (*Rodeford*). Richard acknowledged the right of Peter by Richard's gift. For this, grant and render to Richard and Joan. To hold to them and their heirs in tail. Contingent remainder to Richard's heirs.

76/50/217

346. Morrow [12 Nov.] of St. Martin. John atte Hazel (*Hasele*) and Joan his wife quer.; Walter de Campden (*Caumpedene*) and Felicia his wife and John le Walker (*Wakyare*) and Agnes his wife def. Two thirds of a messuage, 42 a. of land, and 3 a. of meadow in Hampnett (*Hamptenet*). Right of John atte Hazel. Remise and quitclaim, specifying Felicia's and Agnes's heirs, to John atte Hazel and Joan and John's heirs. (Warranty.) Cons. £20.

76/50/219

347. Morrow [12 Nov.] of St. Martin. Bogo de Knovill and Joan his wife quer. by Oliver de Serynton in Joan's place by the king's writ; Robert le Teyntour and Warin de Queryndon def. The manors of Kilcot (*Killecote*) and Little Taynton (*Parva Teynton*), GLOS., and the manor of Ditteridge (*Dycherigg*) and the advowson of the church of the same manor, WILTS. Bogo acknowledged the right of Robert, as those which Robert and

1318

Warin had by Bogo's gift. For this, grant and render to Bogo and Joan. To hold to them and Bogo's heirs. *Labelled* Gloucestr', [*in different ink*] Wiltes'.

286/31/174

[Cf. *Wilts. Fines, 1272–1327*, p. 128.]

1319

348. One week [20 Jan.] from Hilary. John son of William de Eastleach Turville (*Lecche Turvill*) and Alice his wife quer. by Nicholas de Stratford in Alice's place by the king's writ; Henry de Wincot (*Wynnecote*) parson of the church of Bonnington (*Bunynton*) def. A messuage and 200 a. of land in Eastleach Turville. John acknowledged the right of Henry by John's gift. For this, grant and render to John and Alice. To hold to them and their heirs in tail. Contingent remainder to John's heirs.

76/50/220

349. One week [20 Jan.] from Hilary. John de Bradley (*Bradelegh*) and Isabel his wife quer. by John Gacelyn in Isabel's place by the king's writ; Nicholas de Caldecote def. Three messuages, 3 tofts, 3 gardens, 6 bovates of land, 11 a. of meadow, 3 a. of wood, rents of 40s. and 1 lb. of pepper, and one third of a mill in Charlton (*Cherleton*), Redland (*Tridelond*), and Lawrence Weston (*Weston Sancti Laurencii*) by Henbury (*Hembury*), GLOS., 3 messuages, a dovecot, and 14 a. of land in Bradford-on-Avon (*Bradeford*), WILTS., and 3 messuages, a garden, 47 a. of land, 10½ a. of meadow, 5s. rent, and half of a pasture in Thatcham (*Thachham*) and Colthrop (*Coldrop*), BERKS. Right of John. Remise and quitclaim to John and Isabel and John's heirs. (Warranty.) Cons. 100 marks. *Labelled* Glouc', Wyltes', Berk'. [*Torn, worn, and stained.*]

286/31/178

[Cf. *Wilts. Fines, 1272–1327*, p. 129.]

350. Three weeks [29 April] from Easter. Roger le Norman (*Normaund*) of Cirencester (*Cyrencestr'*) quer.; William de Asthall (*Estehalle*) and Ela his wife def. Seven messuages, 3½ yardlands, and 2s. rent in Arlington (*Alurynton*) by Bibury (*Bybury*) and one fifth of the manor of Arlington. Right of Roger. Remise and quitclaim, specifying Ela's heirs, to him of the messuages, land, and rent. And grant to him of the reversion of the one fifth of the manor held by John de Pembridge (*Penebrugge*) and Alice his wife in Alice's dower, of Ela's inheritance. (Warranty.) Cons. £40. Made in the presence and with the consent of John and Alice, and they did fealty to Roger.

76/50/221

351. One month [6 May] from Easter. Walter le Carpenter of Haresfield (*Harsefeld*) and Richard son of Alice de Caldecote of Haresfield quer. by Peter de Edgeworth (*Eggesworth*) in Walter's place by the king's writ; Richard Veal (*Vyel*) of Rodley (*Rodleye*) def. Two messuages, 60 a. of land, and 5 a. of meadow in Haresfield (*Shirrevesharsefeld*), Oakey (*Okheye*), Colethrop (*Colethrop*), and Standish (*Stanedissh*). Richard son of Alice acknowledged the right of Richard Veal. For this, grant and render to Walter and Richard son of Alice. To hold to them and Richard's heirs in tail. Contingent remainder to Alice la Clerk (*Clerkes*) of Fyfield (*Fifhide*). *Endorsed* John de la Hay of Haresfield put in his claim.

76/50/223

1319

352. Morrow [18 May] of Ascension. Robert Brown (*Broun*) of Campden (*Caumpeden*) quer.; William Noverey of Campden and Alice his wife def. A messuage in Campden. Right of Robert by gift of William and Alice. (Warranty, specifying Alice's heirs.) Cons. 10 marks.

76/50/222

353. Morrow [25 June] of St. John the Baptist. Robert de Hawley (*Haulee*) and Matilda his wife quer. by John de Cirencester (*Cyrencestr'*) in Matilda's place; Geoffrey le Despenser (*le Despens'*) of Upton (*Upton*). Four messuages in Chipping Campden (*Cheping Caumpeden*). Robert acknowledged the right of Geoffrey by Robert's gift. For this, grant and render to Robert and Matilda. To hold to them and their heirs in tail. Contingent remainder to Robert's heirs. [*Worn.*]

76/51/227

13 Edward II

1319

354. York. Two weeks [13 Oct.] from Michaelmas. John de Olney (*Olneye*) and Matilda his wife quer.; Henry del Oak (*Ok*) def. A messuage, 1 ploughland, and 6 marks rent in Churchdown (*Circhedon*), Noke (*Oke*), Hucclecote (*Hokelecote*), and the suburb of Gloucester (*Gloucestr'*). Right of John. Render to John and Matilda. To hold to them and John's heirs. (Warranty.) Cons. £20. *Endorsed* Olive daughter of Henry del Oak put in her claim; Matilda who was wife of William de Witcombe (*Wydecumbe*) put in her claim.

76/51/243

355. York. One month [27 Oct.] from Michaelmas. Thomas de Brockworth (*Brocworth*) and Margery his wife quer. by Peter de Edgeworth (*Eggesworth*) in Margery's place; Robert d'Abitot (*Dabetot*) def. A messuage, a toft, 1 yardland and 40 a. of land, and 2 a. of wood in Pauntley (*Paunteleye*) and Dymock (*Dymmok*). Thomas acknowledged the right of Robert by Thomas's gift. For this, grant and render to Thomas and Margery. To hold to them and Thomas's heirs.

76/51/245

1320

356. York. Two weeks [27 Jan.] from Hilary. Roger son of Thomas East (*Est*) of Broad Campden (*Brodecampedene*) and Alice his wife quer. by William de Northwick (*Northewyk*) in Alice's place; Alexander son of Richard de Hoddington (*Hodynton*) def. Three messuage, 2½ yardlands, 10 a. of meadow, and 13*s.* rent in Broad Campden and Chipping Campden (*Chepingecampeden*). Roger acknowledged the right of Alexander by Roger's gift. For this, grant and render to Roger and Alice. To hold during their lives. Remainder to Roger's son Richard and his heirs in tail. Contingent remainder to Roger's heirs. *Endorsed* Hugh Foward of Weston (*Weston*) put in his claim.

76/51/230

357. York. Two weeks [27 Jan.] from Hilary. William de Chester (*Cestre*) and Alice his wife quer. by William de Northwick (*Northwyk*) in Alice's place by the king's writ;

1320

Walter Gullifer (*Golafre*) def. A messuage, 2 yardlands, 12 a. of meadow, rents of 30*s.* and 7 qr. of wheat, 7 qr. of barley, and 7 qr. of peas and beans in Rous Lench (*Lench Randolf*) and Aston Magna (*Hongende Aston*) by Blockley (*Blockele*), WORCS., and a messuage, 2 yardlands, and 10 a. of meadow in Longborough (*Langeberghe*), GLOS. William acknowledged the right of Walter by William's gift. For this, grant and render to William and Alice. To hold during their lives. Remainder to William's son John and his heirs in tail. Successive contingent remainders to John's brother Thomas and his heirs in tail and to William's heirs. *Labelled* Wygorn', Glouestr'.

286/31/185

358. Three weeks [20 April] from Easter. Roger le Norman (*Normand*) of Cirencester (*Cyrencestre*) quer.; William son of Robert de Pennington (*Penynton*) and Margaret his wife def. One fifth of the manor of Arlington (*Alurynton*) held by John de Pembridge (*Penebrigge*) and Alice his wife in Alice's dower. Right of Roger. Grant to him of the reversion, of Margaret's inheritance. (Warranty.) Cons. 20 marks. Made in the presence and with the consent of John and Alice, and they did fealty to Roger.

76/51/244

359. One week [1 June] from Trinity. Roger le Norman (*Normaund*) of Cirencester (*Cyrencestre*) quer.; Robert de Wickham (*Wykham*) and Elizabeth his wife def. One fifth of the manor of Arlington (*Alurynton*) held by John de Pembridge (*Penebrugg*) and Alice his wife in Alice's dower. Right of Roger. Grant to him of the reversion, of Elizabeth's inheritance. (Warranty.) Cons. £20. Made in the presence and with the consent of John and Alice, and they did fealty to Roger. [*Worn.*]

76/51/232

360. One week [1 June] from Trinity. Walter de Stapleton (*Stapeldon*) bishop of Exeter (*Exon'*) quer.; William Hereward def. The manor of Compton Greenfield (*Compton Greynevyle*), rent of 1 lb. of pepper, and half a knight's fee in Elmington (*Almyngton*) and the advowson of the chapel of the said manor. Right of the bishop. For this, grant and render to William of the holdings and advowson except for one third of two thirds of the manor. To hold to William and his heirs in tail. And grant to William of the reversion of the one third of two thirds held by Richard de Thorverton (*Thunverdon*) and Katherine his wife in Katherine's dower, of the bishop's inheritance. To hold as above. Successive contingent remainders to Richard de Stapleton and his heirs in tail and to William's heirs. *Endorsed* Henry de Grenville (*Greyneville*) put in his claim; Henry de Grenville (*Greynevile*) put in his claim.

76/51/233

[Cf. *Berkeley Castle Mun.* i, p. 456, A2/20/3 (iii) (copy).]

361. One week [1 June] from Trinity. John le Rouse (*Rous*) and Hawise his wife quer.; John parson of the church of Harescombe (*Harsecombe*) def. The manor of Harescombe. Right of John the parson by gift of John le Rouse and Hawise. For this, grant back and render to John and Hawise. To hold during their lives. Remainder to John son of John le Rouse and his heirs in tail. Contingent remainder to the heirs of John le Rouse.

76/51/234

1320

362. One week [1 June] from Trinity. Philip Joyce (*Joce*) quer.; William Joyce imp. A messuage, a mill, 20 a. of land, and 1 a. of meadow in the township of St. Briavels (*de Sancto Breavello*). (Warranty of charter.) Right of Philip by William's gift. (Warranty.) Cons. 10 marks.

76/51/237

363. One week [1 June] from Trinity. John de Carrant (*Carent*) quer.; William le Sectere and Alice his wife def. A messuage in Tewkesbury (*Teukesbury*). Right of John by gift of William and Alice. (Warranty, specifying Alice's heirs.) Cons. 100*s*. *Endorsed* William le Portreeve (*Portereve*) of Tewkesbury put in his claim.

76/51/238

364. One week [1 June] from Trinity. Philip Joyce (*Joce*) quer.; William Joyce def. A messuage, 1 ploughland and 92 a. of land, and 60*s*. rent in Newland (*Neweland*). Right of Philip. Render to him. To hold of the king. (Warranty.) Cons. 100 marks. Made by the king's order.

76/51/239

365. One week [1 June] from Trinity. John Giffard (*Gyffard*) of Brimpsfield (*Brymmesfeld*) quer. by John de Elkstone (*Elkeston*); Philip de Gomeldon (*Gomelden*) and Agnes his wife imp. The advowson of the church of Winterbourne (*Wynterburn*) by Stoke Gifford (*Stok' Giffard*) and a quarter of half of the same manor of Winterbourne. (Warranty of charter.) Right of John by gift of Philip and Agnes. (Warranty, specifying Agnes's heirs.) Cons. £100.

76/51/240

366. One week [1 June] from Trinity. Richard de Apperley (*Apperleye*) and Joan his wife quer. by Peter de Edgeworth (*Eggesworth*) in Joan's place by the king's writ; Robert de Masindon and Margery his wife def. Twenty-five acres of land, 4 a. of meadow, 2 a. of pasture, and 5*s*. rent, a quarter of 1 a. of wood, and one seventh of a messuage in Staverton (*Staverton*), Deerhurst (*Derhurst*), and Down Hatherley (*Dunhatherleye*). Right of Richard, as those which Richard and Joan had by gift of Robert and Margery. To hold to Richard and Joan and Richard's heirs. (Warranty, specifying Margery's heirs.) Cons. £20.

76/51/241

367. Two weeks [8 June] from Trinity. Roger de la Garston and Sarah his wife quer.; Richard de East Dean (*Estden*) clerk def. One and a half ploughlands, 6½ a. of meadow, 11 a. of wood, and 18*s*. 1½*d*. rent in Stone (*Stone*) by Berkeley (*Berkele*). Right of Richard by gift of Roger and Sarah. For this, grant back and render to Roger and Sarah. To hold during their lives. Remainder to Roger's son Thomas and Alice his wife and their heirs in tail. Contingent remainder to Sarah's heirs.

76/51/229

368. Two weeks [8 June] from Trinity. Walter son of Roger Aubrey quer.; John de Corse (*Cors*) and Alice his wife def. Two messuages, 1½ yardlands, and 2 a. of meadow in

1320

Bromsberrow (*Broumsberwe*) by Dymock (*Dymmok*). Right of Walter by gift of John and Alice. (Warranty, specifying Alice's heirs.) Cons. £10.

76/51/231

369. Two weeks [8 June] from Trinity. Walter son of Walter Wyth of Arlingham (*Erlyngham*) and Isabel his wife quer. by Peter de Edgeworth (*Eggesworth*) in their place by the king's writ; Walter son of John Wyth of Arlingham def. A messuage, 80 a. of land, 8 a. of meadow, and 20*s*. rent in Arlingham. Grant and render to Walter son of Walter and Isabel. To hold to them and their heirs in tail, of Walter son of John, paying a rose a year at St. John the Baptist and doing service to the chief lords. Contingent reversion to Walter son of John. Cons. £100.

76/51/235

370. Two weeks [8 June] from Trinity. John son of John le Rouse (*Rous*) and Mabel his wife quer.; John le Rouse and Hawise his wife def. The manor of Duntisbourne Rouse (*Duntesburne*), except for 1 a. of land and except for the advowson of the church of the same township. Grant and render to John son of John and Mabel. To hold to them and their heirs in tail, of John le Rouse and Hawise and that John's heirs, paying a rose a year at St. John the Baptist and doing service to the chief lords. (Warranty, by John le Rouse alone.) Contingent reversion to John le Rouse and Hawise and that John's heirs

76/51/242

14 Edward II

1320

371. Two weeks [8 July] from St. John the Baptist. Hugh le Despenser (*Despens'*) the younger and Eleanor his wife quer.; Hugh de Audley (*Audele*) the younger and Margaret his wife def. The castle and manor of Newport (*de Novo Burgo*), the manors of Stow (*Stowe*), Rumney (*Rempny*), *Diveleys* [Dyffryn?], Machen (*Maghay*), and *Freneboth* [Dyffryn Ebbwy or Pentre Poeth?], 3¾ knights' fees in Bassaleg Ebbwy (*Basselek Ebboz*), Coedkernew (*Coickarnan, Coyckarnan*) by *Diveleys*, *Becaneslegh* [Began?], the townships of St. Bride's (*Sancta Brigida*) and St. Mellons (*Sancto Melano*), and the advowsons of the priory of Malpas (*de Malo Passu*) and of the churches of Machen and Llanvihangel (*Lanihangel*) in Wentlooge (*Wenthelok*) [MON.]. Grant and render to Hugh le Despenser and Eleanor. To hold to them and Eleanor's heirs, of the king, in exchange for the manor Ryhall (*Rihale*), RUTLAND, the manor of Rotherfield (*Retherfeld*) and 7,000 a. of wood in Rotherfield, SUSSEX, 1,000 a. of wood in West Peckham (*Westpekham*) and Tonbridge (*Tonbrigge*), KENT, 300 a. of pasture and 200 a. of wood in Bushey (*Busseye*), MIDDX., 3 knights' fees in Chelsham (*Chelsham*) and Warlingham (*Warlingham*), SURREY, the advowsons of the churches of Caldecote (*Caldecote*) and Barton Bendish (*Berton Sancti Andree*), NORF., the advowson of the church of All Hallows (*Omnium Sanctorum*) the Great, LONDON (*London*), half a knight's fee in Ashreigney (*Esshe Reigne*) and the manors of Langtree (*Langetrewe*) and Chittlehampton (*Chitilhampton*) except for 73¼ knights' fees and one twenty-fourth of a knight's fee in the same manors of Langtree and Chittlehampton, the hundred of Winkleigh (*Wynkele*) in the said manor of Chittlehampton, and the advowson of the church of the same manor of Langtree, DEVON, the manor of Bushey (*Bisseye*) except for 300 a. of pasture and 200 a.

1320

of wood in the same manor of Bushey, HERTS., and a knight's fee in North Weald (*Welde*) and the manor of Weald except for 5½ knights' fees in the same manor of Weald, ESSEX, granted and rendered to Hugh de Audley and Margaret by Hugh le Despenser and Eleanor. (Warranty by Hugh de Audley and Margaret, specifying Margaret's heirs.) Made by the king's order. [*Worn and holed.*]

76/51/246a (formerly 76/51/236)

[The fine should have been filed among those for Divers Counties. It is labelled with the single county name *Gloucestr'*, because Monmouthshire, which is not specified in the fine, adjoined Glos. All the places conveyed with Newport are apparently in the area immediately west of Newport. For the identity of North Weald, *V.C.H. Essex*, iv. 287. The corresponding fine of the same date, by which Hugh and Eleanor le Despenser conveyed the estates named above other than in Monmouthshire, of Eleanor's inheritance, to Hugh and Margaret de Audley, in exchange for the estates in Monmouthshire, is filed with those for Divers Counties (case 286, file 31, no. 191) and is abstracted in *Essex Fines, 1272–1326*, p. 201 (which identifies Dyffryn Ebbwy and Bassaleg Ebbwy) and *Sussex Fines, 1307–1509*, pp. 48–9, no. 1587.]

372. One week [6 Oct.] from Michaelmas. William son of Thomas Ace quer.; Alice who was wife of Thomas Ace def. A messuage, 1 yardland, and 3 a. of meadow in Weston Subedge (*Weston Underegge*). Right of Alice. For this, grant and render to William. To hold to him and his heirs in tail, of Alice, paying a rose a year at St. John the Baptist and doing service to the chief lords. Successive contingent remainders to William's brother Thomas and his heirs in tail, to Thomas's brother John and his heirs in tail, to John's brother Geoffrey and his heirs in tail, and to Alice and her heirs.

76/52/261

373. One week [6 Oct.] from Michaelmas. Robert de Sapy and Aline his wife quer. by Hugh de Ham (*Hamme*) in Aline's place by the king's writ; Ellis Winter (*Wynter*) of Huntley (*Huntelegh*) and Petronilla his wife def. Ten acres of land in Huntley. Right of Robert, as that which Robert and Aline had by gift of Ellis and Petronilla. To hold to Robert and Aline and Robert's heirs. (Warranty, by Ellis alone.) Cons. 10 marks.

76/52/262

374. One week [6 Oct.] from Michaelmas. William Maunsell (*Maunsel*) quer.; John son of John Alexander (*Alisaundre*) of Duntisbourne (*Dontesburne*) def. The manor of Over Lypiatt (*Overelupeyat*). Right of John by William's gift. For this, grant back and render to William. To hold during his life. Remainder to William's son William and his heirs in tail. Contingent remainder to William Maunsell's heirs.

76/52/263

375. One week [6 Oct.] from Michaelmas. Reynold atte Townsend (*attetounesende*) and Cristiana his wife and Robert atte Townsend quer.; John de Paris (*Parys*) def. A messuage and 20 a. of land in Staverton (*Staverton*). Reynold acknowledged the right of John by Reynold's gift. For this, grant and render to Reynold, Cristiana, and Robert. To hold during their lives. Remainder to Robert's heirs.

76/52/265

1320

376. Two weeks [13 Oct.] from Michaelmas. John le Duke (*Duk*) of Kingston (*Kyngeston*) and Alice his wife quer. by Robert d'Abitot (*de Abetot*) in Alice's place by the king's writ; Simon Passemer def. A messuage, 53 a. of land, 7½ a. of meadow, and 5*s*. rent in Slimbridge (*Slymbrugg*), Kingston, Gossington (*Gosynton*), and Uley (*Iwele*). John acknowledged the right of Simon by John's gift. For this, grant and render to John and Alice. To hold to them and their heirs in tail. Successive contingent remainders to John's daughter Katherine and her heirs in tail and to John's heirs.

76/52/264

377. Three weeks [20 Oct.] from Michaelmas. William Leonard and Ascelina his wife quer.; Nicholas Neel of Wightfield (*Wyghtfeld*) def. Two messuages, 20 a. of land, and 4 a. of meadow in Wightfield and Apperley (*Apperleye*) by Deerhurst (*Derhurst*). William acknowledged the right of Nicholas by William's gift. For this, grant and render to William and Ascelina. To hold to them and William's heirs.

76/51/246b

378. Three weeks [20 Oct.] from Michaelmas. Howel son of John ap Howel (*aphowel*) quer.; John ap Howel and Erneburga his wife def. A messuage, 3 ploughlands, and 63*s*. 4*d*. rent in Newland (*La Newelonde*). Right of Howel. Render to him. To hold of the king. (Warranty, specifying Erneburga's heirs.) Cons. 40 marks. Made by the king's order.

76/52/251

379. Three weeks [20 Oct.] from Michaelmas. John Osborne (*Osebarn*) of Leigh (*Leye*) and Isabel his wife quer. by John de Elkstone (*Elkeston*) in Isabel's place by the king's writ; Roger le Warner (*Waryner*) of Tetbury (*Tettebury*) and Alice his wife imp. A messuage in Tetbury. (Warranty of charter.) Right of John, as that which John and Isabel had by gift of Roger and Alice. To hold to John and Isabel and John's heirs. (Warranty, specifying Alice's heirs.) Cons. 100*s*.

76/52/253

[Cf. below, no. 383.]

380. Three weeks [20 Oct.] from Michaelmas. Thomas de Dowdeswell (*Doudeswell*) and Katherine his wife quer.; John de la Hussey (*Heose*) parson of the church of Meysey Hampton (*Hampton Meysy*) def. The manor of Dowdeswell and the advowson of the church of the same manor. Thomas acknowledged the right of John, of which he had the advowson and two thirds of the manor by Thomas's gift. For this, grant and render to Thomas and Katherine. To hold to them and their heirs in tail. And grant to them of the reversion of one third of the manor held in dower by Matilda who was wife of William de Dowdeswell, of John's inheritance. To hold as above. Contingent remainder to Thomas's heirs. Made in Matilda's presence and with her consent, and she did fealty to Thomas and Katherine.

76/52/256

1320

381. Three weeks [20 Oct.] from Michaelmas. John Botetourt and Matilda his wife quer.; Ralph Sharp chaplain def. The manor of Woodmancote (*Wodemancote*). Right of Ralph by gift of John and Matilda. For this, grant back and render to John and Matilda. To hold during their lives. Remainder to John's son John and his heirs in tail. Contingent remainder to Matilda's heirs.

76/52/260

382. One month [27 Oct.] from Michaelmas. John de Eastington (*Estynton*) and Agnes his wife quer. by Peter de Edgeworth (*Eggesworth*) in Agnes's place by the king's writ; William de Yetminster (*Yetemenstr'*) def. Two messuages, 96 a. of land, 8 a. of meadow, 1½ a. of wood, and 2s. 6d. rent in Eastington (*Estynton*) by Stonehouse (*Stonhous*) and Acton (*Eggeton*) by Berkeley (*Berkelegh*). John acknowledged the right of William by John's gift. For this, grant and render to John and Agnes. To hold to them and their heirs in tail. Contingent remainder to John's heirs.

76/51/250

383. Morrow [3 Nov.] of All Souls. John Osborne (*Osebarn*) of Leigh (*Leye*) and Isabel his wife quer. by John de Elkstone (*Elkeston*) in Isabel's place by the king's writ; Robert son of Roger le Warner of Tetbury (*Tettebury*) and Alice his wife imp. A messuage in Tetbury. (Warranty of charter.) Right of John, as that which John and Isabel had by gift of Robert and Alice. To hold to John and Isabel and John's heirs. (Warranty, specifying Alice's heirs.) Cons. 100s.

76/51/249

[Cf. no. 379 above, made two weeks earlier. The only substantive difference in the terms of the fines is that the impedients were Roger and his wife Alice in the first but Robert son of Roger and his wife Alice in the second. Father and son may each have had a wife Alice, but in each fine it was the wife's heirs who were specified and it is unlikely that the son's wife was the heir of his father's wife. If both fines related to the same transaction the earlier one may have had to be replaced because it was defective.]

384. Morrow [3 Nov.] of All Souls. John Giffard of Brimpsfield (*Brinmesfeld*) quer. by John de Elkstone (*Elkeston*); Thomas Grasenloyl and Amice his wife def. The advowson of the church of Winterbourne (*Wynterbourn*) by Stoke Gifford (*Stoke Giffard*) and a quarter of half of the manor of the same township. Right of John. Remise and quitclaim, specifying Amice's heirs, to him. (Warranty.) Cons. 10 marks.

76/52/252

385. Morrow [3 Nov.] of All Souls. John de Bures and Hawise his wife quer.; William de Yetminster (*Yetemenstr'*) def. A messuage, 280 a. of land, 60 a. of meadow, and 2s. rent in Longford (*Longeford*) by Gloucester (*Gloucestriam*) and the manors of Boddington (*Botinton*) and Great Taynton (*Magna Teynton*). Right of William by gift of John and Hawise. For this, grant back and render to John and Hawise. To hold to them and Hawise's heirs, except for the manor of Taynton, which they were to hold during their lives with remainder to Hawise's son Robert and his heirs in tail male, with contingent remainder to Hawise's heirs. [*Worn.*]

76/52/257

1320

386. Morrow [3 Nov.] of All Souls. William Davy of Longney (*Longeneye*) quer.; Thomas le Walker (*Walkare*) of Slimbridge (*Slymbrugge*) and Lucy his wife def. A messuage and 2½ a. of land in Longney. Right of William. Render to him. (Warranty, specifying Lucy's heirs.) Cons. 10 marks.

76/52/259

387. Morrow [12 Nov.] of St. Martin. Hugh de Audley (*Audele*) the younger and Margaret his wife quer. by James de Podimore (*Podemor*); Stephen Beaubras and Sibyl his wife def. A messuage, 160 a. of land, 31 a. of meadow, 12 a. of wood, and 16*s.* 8*d.* rent in Thornbury (*Thornbury*) and Alveston (*Aluston*). Grant to Hugh and Margaret. To hold to them and Hugh's heirs during the life of Stephen and Sibyl. Remise and quitclaim to Hugh and Margaret of whatever Stephen and Sibyl had in the holdings for term of life. Cons. £100.

76/51/247

388. Morrow [12 Nov.] of St. Martin. John de Gloucester (*Gloucestr'*) and Joan his wife quer. by the said John in Joan's place by the king's writ; Robert de Gloucester def. A messuage, 2 ploughlands, 12 a. of meadow, 10 a. of pasture, 3 a. of wood, and 30*s.* rent in Alkerton (*Alcrinton*). John acknowledged the right of Robert by John's gift. For this, grant and render to John and Joan. To hold during their lives, of Robert, paying a rose a year at St. John the Baptist and doing service to the chief lords. Reversion to Robert.

76/51/248

389. Morrow [12 Nov.] of St. Martin. Hugh de Audley (*Audele*) the younger and Margaret his wife quer. by James de Podimore (*Podmor*); Stephen Beaubras and Sibyl his wife def. Seven acres of land and 10 a. of meadow in Thornbury (*Thornbury*). Right of Hugh, as those which Hugh and Margaret had by gift of Stephen and Sibyl. To hold to Hugh and Margaret and Hugh's heirs. (Warranty, specifying Sibyl's heirs.) Cons. 10 marks.

76/52/254

390. Morrow [12 Nov.] of St. Martin. Robert Richman (*Richeman*) quer.; Simon Passemer def. A messuage, 4 a. of meadow, and 1 a. of land and half of 1 yardland in Wotton St. Mary (*Wotton*) and Sandhurst (*Sondhurst*). Right of Simon by Robert's gift. For this, grant back and render to Robert. To hold during his life. Remainder to Stephen Brown (*Broun*) and Amice his wife and their heirs in tail. Contingent remainder to Robert's heirs.

76/52/258

391. Morrow [12 Nov.] of St. Martin. Hugh le Despenser (*Despens'*) the elder quer.; Hugh le Despenser the younger and Eleanor his wife def. The manor of Stanford in the Vale (*Staneford*), BERKS., the manor of Fairford (*Faireford*), GLOS., and the hundred of Chadlington (*Chadelyngton*), OXON. Right of Eleanor. For this, grant and render by Hugh the younger and Eleanor to Hugh the elder. To hold during his life, of the king. Reversion to Hugh the younger and Eleanor and Eleanor's heirs. Made by the king's order. *Labelled* Berk', Gloucestr', Oxon'. *Endorsed* Agnes who was wife of Ingram de Horton put in her claim.

286/31/196

[For the identity of Stanford in the Vale, *V.C.H. Berks.* iv. 480.]

1320

392. One week [18 Nov.] from St. Martin. Henry de Brockworth (*Brokworth*) and Alice his wife quer.; Gilbert de Rues and Agnes his wife def. Two messuages, 1 yardland, and 7 a. of wood in Upton St. Leonards (*Upton Sancti Leonardi*) and Pincott (*Pynicote*). Henry acknowledged the right of Gilbert. For this, Gilbert and Agnes granted and rendered the holdings to Henry and Alice. To hold during their lives. Remainder to Henry's son John and his heirs in tail. Successive contingent remainders to John's brother Thomas and his heirs in tail and to Thomas's heirs. (Warranty by Gilbert and his heirs.)

76/52/255

1321

393. One week [20 Jan.] from Hilary. Mr. Richard de Clare quer.; John de Carrant (*Carente*) def. A toft, 3 yardlands, and a quarter of a messuage in Notgrove (*Nategrave*). Right of John by Mr. Richard's gift. For this, grant back and render to Mr. Richard. To hold during his life. Remainder to Richard de Carrant and Margery his wife and their heirs in tail. Contingent remainder to Richard de Carrant's heirs.

76/52/267

394. Two weeks [27 Jan.] from Hilary. Walter de Colseth and Cristiana his wife quer.; Walter le Passer (*Passour*) of the Haw (*Hawe*) and Katherine his wife def. A messuage, 6 a. of land, and 6 a. of meadow in Tirley (*Trynleye*) and Hasfield (*Hasfeld*). Walter de Colseth acknowledged the right of Walter le Passer. For this, Walter [le Passer] and Katherine granted and rendered the holdings to Walter de Colseth and Cristiana. To hold to them and Walter de Colseth's heirs. (Warranty by Walter le Passer and his heirs.)

76/52/266

395. Two weeks [27 Jan.] from Hilary. Walter le Passer (*Passour*) of the Haw (*Hawe*) and Katherine his wife quer.; Walter de Colseth and Cristiana his wife def. A messuage, 6 a. of land, and 6 a. of meadow in Tirley (*Trynleye*). Walter le Passer acknowledged the right of Walter le Colseth. For this, Walter [de Colseth] and Cristiana granted and rendered the holdings to Walter le Passer and Katherine. To hold to them and Walter le Passer's heirs. (Warranty by Walter de Colseth and his heirs.)

76/52/268

[The relationship between nos. 394 and 395 is not clear.]

396. One month [17 May] from Easter. William le Eyre (*Eyr*) quer.; John de Whitby (*Whiteby*) and Alice his wife def. A messuage and 50 a. of land in Winstone (*Wyneston*). Right of William. Remise and quitclaim, specifying Alice's heirs, to him. (Warranty.) Cons. £40.

76/52/270

397. Morrow [25 June] of St. John the Baptist. Edmund [FitzAlan] earl of Arundel (*Arundell*) quer. by William de Northwick (*Norwyk*); Gilbert de Rues (*Ruus*) and Agnes his wife def. A messuage, a mill, 1 yardland, 13 a. of meadow, 7 a. of pasture, and 15*s.* 4*d.* rent in Upton St. Leonards (*Upton Sancti Leonardi*) by Gloucester (*Gloucestr'*). Right of the earl by gift of Gilbert and Agnes. To hold to the earl, of the king. (Warranty by Gilbert and his heirs.) Cons. 100 marks. Made by the king's order.

76/52/269

15 Edward II

1321

398. One week [6 Oct.] from Michaelmas. William Flambard and Matilda his wife quer.; John Flambard def. The manor of Sezincote (*Shesencote*) and the advowson of the church of the same manor. Right of John by gift of William and Matilda. For this, grant back and render to William and Matilda. To hold to them and their heirs in tail. Successive contingent remainders to Matilda's son John and his heirs in tail, to that John's sister Katherine and her heirs in tail, and to William's heirs.

76/52/274

399. One week [6 Oct.] from Michaelmas. William le Small (*Smale*) of Tewkesbury (*Teukesbury*) quer.; William Lovecock (*Lovecok*) of Tewkesbury and Alice his wife def. A messuage in Tewkesbury. Right of William le Small by gift of William and Alice. (Warranty, specifying Alice's heirs.) Cons. 100*s*.

76/53/276

400. One week [6 Oct.] from Michaelmas. Simon de Yardley (*Yerdeleye*) of Tewkesbury (*Teukesbury*) and Margery his wife quer. by the said Simon in Margery's place by the king's writ; William Lovecock (*Lovecok*) and Alice his wife imp. A messuage in Tewkesbury. (Warranty of charter.) Right of Simon, as that which Simon and Margery had by gift of William and Alice. To hold to Simon and Margery and Simon's heirs. (Warranty, specifying Alice's heirs.) Cons. 10 marks.

76/53/278

401. Two weeks [13 Oct.] from Michaelmas. William Sharp of Cirencester (*Cirencestre*) and Margery his wife quer. by John de Cirencester in their place by the king's writ; Roger de Aston of Cirencester and Edith his wife def. A messuage in Cirencester. Right of William, as that which William and Margery had by gift of Roger and Edith. To hold to William and Margery and William's heirs. (Warranty, specifying Edith's heirs.) Cons. 100*s*.

76/52/272

402. Three weeks [20 Oct.] from Michaelmas. Robert Dastyn (*Dasteyn*) quer.; Walter Powick (*Poywyk*) of Dumbleton (*Dumbilton*) chaplain, def. Two messuages and 2 yardlands in Great Wormington (*Magna Wormynton*). Right of Robert. Render to him. Cons. 20 marks. *Endorsed* John de Witley (*Wythylegh*) and Cristina his wife, John le Walsh (*Walshe*) of Paganhill (*Pagenhull*) and Amice his wife, John le Freeman (*Freman*) of Aston (*Aston*) and Alice his wife, and Amice daughter of William Gupshill (*Gopeshull*), and Alice put in their claim.

76/52/271

403. Three weeks [20 Oct.] from Michaelmas. Robert de Carrant (*Karent*) and Alice his wife quer. by Robert de Malvern (*Malverne*) in Alice's place; Laurence Bruton def. A messuage, a mill, and 1 yardland in Tewkesbury (*Theukesbury*). Robert acknowledged the right of Laurence by Robert's gift. For this, grant and render to Robert and Alice. To hold to them and their heirs in tail. Contingent remainder to Robert's heirs.

76/53/277

1321

404. Morrow [3 Nov.] of All Souls. Mr. Roger de Quantock (*Cantok*) quer.; Robert de Hardwick (*Herdewyk*) parson of the church of Wanstrow (*Wendestre*) def. A messuage, 2 ploughlands, 40½ a. of meadow, and £4 rent in Aust (*Auste*) and Elberton (*Albrighton*) and half of the passage over the water [of Severn] of Aust Cliff (*Austeclyve*). Right of Robert by Mr. Roger's gift. For this, grant back and render to Mr. Roger. To hold during his life. Remainder to Odo de Acton and Roger his son and that Roger's heirs in tail. Contingent remainder to Mr. Roger's heirs.

76/52/273

405. Morrow [3 Nov.] of All Souls. Richard de Panes and Benedicta his wife quer. by John Valet in their place by the king's writ; Robert le Clerk 'deghere' [*i.e.* dyer] of Bristol (*Bristoll'*) and Margery his wife def. A messuage and 2 shops in the suburb of Bristol. Right of Richard, as those which Richard and Benedicta had by gift of Robert and Margery. To hold to Richard and Benedicta and Richard's heirs. (Warranty by Robert alone.) Cons. 10 marks.

76/52/275

[Cf. *Bristol Gt. Red Book*, pp. 212–13, no. 111.]

406. Morrow [3 Nov.] of All Souls. John de Chedworth (*Cheddeworth*) quer.; Laurence de la Hay (*Haye*) and Joan his wife def. A messuage in the suburb of Gloucester (*Gloucestr'*). Right of John by gift of Laurence and Joan. (Warranty, specifying Joan's heirs.) Cons. 100*s*.

76/53/281

1322

407. One week [20 Jan.] from Hilary. Nicholas Buyrsy of Longney (*Longeneye*) quer.; Walter le Devenish (*Deveneys*) 'taillour' and Isabel his wife def. A messuage and a shop in Gloucester (*Gloucestr'*). Right of Nicholas by gift of Walter and Isabel. (Warranty, specifying Isabel's heirs.) Cons. 10 marks.

76/53/279

408. One week [20 Jan.] from Hilary. Geoffrey Herdman (*Hirdman*) of Gloucester (*Gloucestr'*) and Edith his wife quer. by the said Geoffrey; Richard de Straddle (*Straddel*) of Gloucester and Matilda his wife def. A messuage in Gloucester. Right of Geoffrey, as that which Geoffrey and Edith had by gift of Richard and Matilda. To hold to Geoffrey and Edith and Geoffrey's heirs. (Warranty, specifying Matilda's heirs.) Cons. 100*s*.

76/53/280

16 Edward II

1322

409. York. One week [6 Oct.] from Michaelmas. John de Aston of Gloucester (*Gloucestr'*) quer. by Peter de Edgeworth (*Eggesworth*); John le Earl (*Erl*) of Winchcombe (*Wynchecoumbe*) and Justina his wife def. A messuage in Gloucester. Right of John de Aston by gift of John le Earl and Justina. (Warranty, specifying Justina's heirs.) Cons. 100*s*.

76/53/282

1322

410. York. Two weeks [13 Oct.] from Michaelmas. Geoffrey Herdman (*Hirdman*) of Gloucester (*Gloucestre*) and Edith his wife quer. by the said Geoffrey; John le Earl (*Erl*) of Winchcombe (*Wynchecoumbe*) and Justina his wife def. Ten acres of land and 20*s*. rent in Gloucester (*Gloucestr'*) and Upton St. Leonards (*Upton Sancti Leonardi*) by Gloucester. Right of Geoffrey, as those which Geoffrey and Edith had by gift of John and Justina. To hold to Geoffrey and Edith and Geoffrey's heirs. (Warranty, specifying Justina's heirs.) Cons. 20 marks.

76/53/284

411. York. Morrow [3 Nov.] of All Souls. [1] Hugh le Despenser the younger and Eleanor his wife quer.; Elizabeth who was wife of John de Burgh (*de Burgo*) def. The castles and manors of Usk (*Usk*), Llangybi (*Tregruk*), and Caerleon (*Kaerlion*), the manors of Liswerry (*Lyswyry*), Tintern Parva (*Parva Tynterne*), New Grange (*Nova Grangia*), Little Llantrisant (*Parva Lantrissan*), Trelleck (*Trillek*), Mitchel Troy (*Troye*), Llangwm (*Lamcom*), and Undy (*Woundy*), and the advowsons of the churches of Tredunnock (*Tredenauch*), Llansoy (*Landisseye*), Mitchel Troy, Llangybi, Panteg (*Pentok*), Kemeys (*Kemmeys*), and Llandegveth (*Landegewyth*), of the abbey of Caerleon, of the priory of Usk, of the chapel of Cwmcarvan (*Conkarvan*), and of the hospital of Usk. [2] The same Elizabeth quer.; the same Hugh and Eleanor def. The castles and manors of Swansea (*Swayneseye*), Oystermouth (*Oystremuth*), Penmark (*Penmarch*), *Loghherne* [Laugharne?], and *Lunan* and the advowsons of the churches of Swansea, Talybont-on-Usk (*Talbont*), and Oystermouth and of the priory of Llangennith (*Langwynyth in Gower*). As to the castles, manors, and advowsons in [1], right of Hugh, and render of them to Hugh and Eleanor. To hold to them and Hugh's heirs, of the king. (Warranty.) For this, as to the castles, manors, and advowsons in [2], right of Elizabeth, and render of them to her in exchange. To hold of the king. (Warranty, specifying Hugh's heirs.) Made by the king's order. *Endorsed* Alice daughter of William de Rocolf put in her claim. [*Worn*.]

76/53/285

[Although labelled *Gloucestr'* and filed as a Glos. fine, this agreement relates to places in Monmouthshire and Glamorgan and perhaps elsewhere in Wales. The four documents which follow it in the file are a copy of the fine (53/286), copies of a writ dated 8 Feb. 1 Edw. III [1327] to the treasurer and chamberlain for the fine to be sent to the king and council in parliament (53/287 and 53/289), and the return to the writ from the treasurer and barons of the Exchequer, dated 21 Feb. (53/288).]

1323

412. York. Two weeks [5 June] from Trinity. Robert de Swinburne (*Swynburne*) quer.; John Botetourt (*Botetourte*) and Matilda his wife def. The manor of Woodmancote (*Wodemannescote*). Right of Robert by gift of John and Matilda. (Warranty, specifying Matilda's heirs.) Cons. 100 marks.

76/53/283

17 Edward II

1323

413. York. Two weeks [13 Oct.] from Michaelmas. Henry de Brockworth (*Brokworth*) and Alice his wife quer. by Walter de Cheltenham in Alice's place by the king's writ;

1323

Richard Ernes def. A toft, 48 a. of land, 3 a. of meadow, and 3*s*. 4*d*. rent in Brockworth. Henry acknowledged the right of Richard. For this, grant and render to Henry and Alice. To hold during their lives. Remainder to Henry's son John and his heirs in tail. Contingent remainder to Henry's heirs. (Warranty.) [*Faded.*]

76/53/290

414. York. Two weeks [13 Oct.] from Michaelmas. John Petch (*Pecche*) the elder quer.; William de Asthall (*Esthalle*) and Ela his wife def. One fifth of the manor of Shenington (*Shenyngdon*). Right of John by gift of William and Ela. For this, grant back and render to William and Ela. To hold during their lives, of John, paying a rose a year at St. John the Baptist and doing service to the chief lords. Reversion to John. [*Worn.*]

76/53/291

415. York. Two weeks [13 Oct.] from Michaelmas. John Petch (*Pecche*) the elder quer.; William de Asthall (*Esthall*) and Ela his wife def. Four messuages, 6 yardlands, and 4 a. of meadow in Shenington (*Shenyndon*). Right of John by gift of William and Ela. (Warranty by William alone.) Cons. 100 marks.

76/53/292

416. York. Two weeks [13 Oct.] from Michaelmas. William de la Green (*Grene*) quer.; William de Harpenden (*Harepeden*) and Elizabeth his wife def. Three messuages, 2 tofts, 2 yardlands, 1½ a. of meadow, 2*s*. rent, and half of a messuage in Marshfield (*Marsfeld*). Right of William de la Green. Render to him of the tofts, meadow, rent, a messuage, and half of a messuage and of the 2 yardlands except for 2 a. And grant to him of the reversion of half of a messuage held by James le Draper and Agnes his wife for term of life, of half of a messuage held by William Hart (*Hert*) and Joan his wife for term of life, of half of a messuage held by Thomas le Skinner (*Skynner*) and Matilda his wife for term of life, and of 2 a. of land and half of a messuage held by Henry Peppercorn (*Peprecorn*) and Agnes his wife for term of life, of Elizabeth's inheritance. Cons. 20 marks. [*Worn.*]

76/53/293

1324

417. One week [20 Jan.] from Hilary. William son of John Marky and Juliana his wife quer. by Robert Munning (*Monnyng*) in Juliana's place by the king's writ; John Marky def. Five messuages, 90 a. of land, and 8*s*. rent in Ruardean (*Ruardyn*). Right of William, as those which William and Juliana had by John's gift. To hold to William and Juliana and William's heirs. (Warranty.) Cons. 20 marks.

76/53/295

418. One week [9 Feb.] from the Purification. William le Fryg quer.; Robert Beaugrant (*Beugraunt*) and Matilda his wife def. Two and a half acres of land in Ham (*Hamme*) by Berkeley (*Berkeleye*). Right of William by gift of Robert and Matilda. (Warranty by Robert alone.) Cons. 100*s*.

76/53/294

1324

419. Two weeks [29 April] from Easter. John Athelam and Joan his wife quer.; William le Sectere and Alice his wife def. A messuage in Tewkesbury (*Teukesbury*). Right of John. Remise and quitclaim, specifying Alice's heirs, to John and Joan and John's heirs. (Warranty.) Cons. 100*s*.

76/53/299

420. Two weeks [29 April] from Easter. Robert de Cameley (*Cameleye*) of Bristol (*Bristoll'*) quer. by Philip Payn in his place by the king's writ; John le Bond (*Bonde*) of Bristol and Cristiana his wife def. A messuage in the suburb of Bristol. Right of Robert. Render to him. (Warranty, specifying Cristiana's heirs.) Cons. 100*s*.

76/54/306

[Cf. *Bristol Gt. Red Book*, p. 213, no. 112.]

421. Three weeks [6 May] from Easter. Robert de Haudlo clerk quer.; John de Haudlo and Matilda his wife def. The manor of Little Rissington (*Rysyndon Basset*), held by Aline who was wife of Edward Burnel for term of life. Right of Robert. Grant to him of the reversion, of Matilda's inheritance. (Warranty.) Cons. £100. Made in Alina's presence and with her consent, and she did fealty to Robert.

76/53/296

422. One month [13 May] from Easter. Robert Mandeville (*Maundevill*) of Weston (*Weston*) and Isabel his wife quer.; Walter de Wilton (*Wylton*) and Isabel his wife def. Five messuages, 20 a. and 2½ yardlands of land, and 2 a. of wood in Painswick (*Payneswyk*), Edge (*Egge*), and Pitchcombe (*Pychenecoumbe*). Grant and render to Robert and Isabel. To hold during their lives. Successive remainders to Robert's son William during his life, to William's brother Thomas during his life, and to Thomas's brother John and his heirs in tail. Contingent remainder to the heirs of Robert's wife Isabel. Cons. £20. [*Worn.*]

76/53/298

423. Morrow [25 May] of Ascension. Robert de Mandeville (*Maundevill*) of Weston (*Weston*) and Isabel his wife quer.; Walter de Wilton (*Wylton*) and Isabel his wife def. One ploughland and 22*s*. rent in Pitchcombe (*Pichenecombe*). Grant and render to Robert and Isabel. To hold to them and their heirs in tail, of the king. Contingent reversion to Walter and Isabel and that Isabel's heirs. Cons. 40 marks. Made by the king's order.

76/53/297

424. One week [17 June] from Trinity. Walter de Cauntelo (*Cantilupo*) parson of the church of Snitterfield (*Snytenfeld*) and Thomas Beton parson of the church of Avon Dassett (*Avene Dersete*) quer.; Robert de Grousewolde chaplain def. Twenty-five messuages, 9 yardlands and 270½ a. of land, 40½ a. of meadow, 10 a. of pasture, and rents of 50*s*. and a pair of gloves in Welford (*Welneford*), Weston on Avon (*Weston Cauntelo*), and Chipping Campden (*Chepyng Caumpedene*). Walter acknowledged the right of Robert. For this, grant and render to Walter and Thomas of a messuage, the 270½ a. of land, the meadow, pasture, and rent. To hold during their lives. And grant to them of the reversion of 24 messuages and 9 yardlands held by Robert le Blunt (*Blount*)

1324

for term of life, of the inheritance of Robert de Grousewolde. To hold as above. Remainder of all to Thomas West and Eleanor his wife and that Thomas's heirs. [*Stained.*]

76/53/300

425. One week [17 June] from Trinity. Walter le Southern (*Southerne*) of Gloucester (*Gloucestr'*) quer.; Roger Mayflyn and Margery his wife def. A messuage, 18½ a. of land, and 1½ a. of meadow in Down Hatherley (*Dounhatherleye*). Right of Walter by gift of Roger and Margery. For this, grant back and render to Roger and Margery. To hold during their lives, of Walter, paying 4 bushels of wheat a year at Michaelmas and doing service to the chief lords. Reversion to Walter.

76/54/301

426. One week [17 June] from Trinity. John de Sutton and Emma his wife quer. by William de Wick (*Wyke*); Roger de la Green (*Grene*) of Bulley (*Bulleye*) and Margaret his wife imp. Rent of 5 marks in Bulley. (Warranty of charter.) Right of John, as that which John and Emma had by gift of Roger and Margaret. To hold to John and Emma and John's heirs. (Warranty by Roger alone.) Cons. £20.

76/54/302

427. One week [17 June] from Trinity. Richard Billing and Elena his wife quer.; William Holt of Boseley (*Boseleye*) def. Two messuages, a mill, 2 ploughlands, 7 a. of meadow, 1 a. of pasture, 3 a. of wood, and 5*s*. rent in Boseley and Adsett (*Adesete*). Richard acknowledged the right of William. For this, grant and render to Richard and Elena. To hold to them and their heirs in tail, of William, paying a rose a year at St. John the Baptist and doing service to the chief lords. Contingent reversion to William.

76/54/304

428. One week [17 June] from Trinity. Ralph de Marston (*Mersshton*) and Eleanor his wife quer. by the said Ralph in Eleanor's place by the king's writ; Walter Moryn of Cirencester (*Cyrencestr'*) and Eleanor his wife def. A messuage in Cirencester (*Cirencestr'*). Right of Ralph, as that which Ralph and Eleanor had by gift of Walter and Eleanor. To hold to Ralph and Eleanor and Ralph's heirs. (Warranty by Walter alone.) Cons. 10 marks.

76/54/305

429. Morrow [25 June] of St. John the Baptist. John Tentefur (*Tyndefur*) quer.; John le Meys (*Moys*) and Matilda his wife and Richard le Roo and Denise his wife def. A shop in Gloucester (*Gloucestr'*). Right of John Tentefur by gift of John le Meys, Matilda, Richard, and Denise. (Warranty, specifying Matilda's and Denise's heirs.) Cons. 40*s*.

76/54/308

430. One week [1 July] from St. John the Baptist. Roger le Teslare of Bristol (*Bristoll'*) quer.; Robert Grauntpee of Warwick (*Warrewyk*) and Isabel his wife def. A messuage in the suburb of Bristol. Right of Roger by gift of Robert and Isabel. (Warranty, specifying Isabel's heirs.) Cons. £10.

76/54/307

[Cf. *Bristol Gt. Red Book*, p. 213, no. 113.]

1324

431. One week [1 July] from St. John the Baptist. John de Montfort (*de Monte Forti*) parson of the church of Combe Hay (*Comb Hauway*) and Walter de Sampford (*Saumpford*) quer.; Ellis Cotel def. The manor of Corscombe (*Corscumbe*), SOM., and the manor of Coomb's End (*Cotelescombe*), GLOS., held in dower by Matilda who was wife of William Cotel. Right of John. Grant of the reversion, of Ellis's inheritance, to John and Walter and John's heirs. Cons. £200. *Labelled* Somers', Gloucestr'.

286/32/232

[Cf. *Som. Fines, 1307–46*, p. 122. *P.-N.G.* i. 160 identifies *Cotelescombe* as Combend in Elkstone, but *V.C.H. Glos.* vii. 212–13 implicitly rejects the identification. That it was in fact Coomb's End in Old Sodbury (Nat. Grid 750808; cf. *P.-N.G.* iii. 54) is clear from a fine of 1432, P.R.O., CP 25/1/79/88, no. 44, of which an abstract is to be published in *Glos. Fines, 1360–1509*, no. 517 (forthcoming).]

18 Edward II

1324

432. Two weeks [8 July] from St. John the Baptist. John de Stonor (*Stonore*) quer.; William de Condicote (*Cundicote*) def. The manor of Condicote and pasture for 4 oxen and 200 sheep in Upper Swell (*Overeswell*) and the advowson of the church of the said manor. Right of John by William's gift. (Warranty.) Cons. £100.

76/54/310a (formerly 76/54/303)

433. One week [6 Oct.] from Michaelmas. William de la Green (*Grene*) quer.; Edmund de Knowle (*Knolle*) and Matilda his wife def. Three messuages, 2 tofts, 2 yardlands, 1½ a. of meadow, 10*s.* rent, and half of a messuage in Marshfield (*Marsfelde*). Right of William. Remise and quitclaim, specifying Matilda's heirs, to him. (Warranty.) Cons. 100*s.*

76/54/311

434. One week [6 Oct.] from Michaelmas. John Cole of Tewkesbury (*Teukesbury*) quer.; Walter de Didcot (*Dudecote*) of Tewkesbury and Matilda his wife def. Two messuages, 9 a. of land, and 1½ a. of meadow in Tewkesbury and Gupshill (*Gopushull*) by Tewkesbury. Right of John. Render to him. (Warranty, specifying Matilda's heirs.) Cons. 10 marks.

76/54/312

435. One week [6 Oct.] from Michaelmas. Richard Alwyn (*Ailwyne*) quer.; John Levison (*Levesone*) and Alice his wife def. A messuage and 1 yardland in Ampney Crucis (*Upameneye*). Right of Richard by gift of John and Alice. (Warranty by John alone.) Cons. 20 marks.

76/54/313

436. One week [6 Oct.] from Michaelmas. Mr. Jordan de Baunton (*Baudynton*) and Alice his wife quer.; Mr. Robert de Worth def. Two messuages, 3½ yardlands, and 6 a. of meadow in South Cerney (*Southerneye* [*sic*]) and Baunton. Mr. Jordan acknowledged the right of Mr. Robert by Mr. Jordan's gift. For this, grant and render to Mr. Jordan and Alice. To hold to them and their heirs in tail. Successive contingent remainders to Mr. Jordan's brother Robert during his life, to Robert's brother Walter during his life, to

1324

Walter's son Richard and his heirs in tail, and to William de Froxmere of *Wychet* [Wyegate?]. *Endorsed* Thomas son of Thomas atte Ford (*Forde*) put in his claim. [*Worn.*]

76/54/319

437. Two weeks [13 Oct.] from Michaelmas. Nicholas atte Chyrcheye of Stroud (*la Strode*) and Alice his wife quer.; Benedict Bennett (*Benet*) def. A messuage, 40 a. of land, and ¼ a. of meadow in Bisley (*Byseleye*) and Lypiatt (*Lepeyat*). Nicholas acknowledged the right of Benedict by Nicholas's gift. For this, grant and render to Nicholas and Alice. To hold to them and their heirs in tail. Contingent remainder to Nicholas's heirs.

76/54/315

438. Two weeks [13 Oct.] from Michaelmas. William Somerville (*Somervill*) quer.; Walter Gullifer (*Golafre*) def. The manor of Aston Somerville (*Aston Somervill*). Right of Walter. For this, grant and render of two thirds of the manor to William. To hold during his life. And grant to William of the reversion of the one third of the manor held by Geoffrey de Wickham (*Wykewane*) and Hawisc his wife for term of Hawise's life, of Walter's inheritance. To hold as above. Remainder to Isabel de Rivers (*Ryvers*) during her life and to Isabel's son John and his heirs in tail. Successive contingent remainders to John's sister Alice and her heirs in tail, to Alice's sister Eleanor and her heirs in tail, and to William's heirs. Made in the presence of Geoffrey and Hawise and with their consent, and they did fealty to William.

76/54/323

439. One month [27 Oct.] from Michaelmas. Thomas de la Ford (*Forde*) and Eleanor his wife quer.; John le Widow (*Wydewe*) chaplain def. A messuage, 2 yardlands, 8 a. of meadow, 6 a. of pasture, and 3 a. of wood in Boddington (*Botynton*). Thomas acknowledged the right of John by Thomas's gift. For this, grant and render to Thomas and Eleanor. To hold to them and Thomas's heirs.

76/54/310b

440. One month [27 Oct.] from Michaelmas. John de Langley (*Langeleye*) and Ela his wife quer. by Thomas de Solihull in Ela's place by the king's writ; Robert de Farndon, parson of the church of Harborough Magna (*Herdeberge*) def. The manors of Stivichall (*Styvychale*) and Wyken (*Wyke*), WARWS., and the manor of Weston Maudit (*Weston Mauduyt*), GLOS. John acknowledged the right of Robert by John's gift. For this, grant and render to John and Ela. To hold during their lives. Remainder to John's son Geoffrey and Mary his wife and their heirs in tail. Contingent remainder to Geoffrey's heirs. *Labelled* Warr', Gloucestr'. *Endorsed* Thomas son of John de Langley (*Langeleye* [replacing *Langelegh* crossed out]) put in his claim. [*Worn.*]

286/32/237

[Cf. *Warws. Fines, 1284–1345*, p. 123, no. 1611.]

441. Morrow [3 Nov.] of All Souls. John le Butler (*Botiller*) of Llantwit (*Lanultit*) quer.; Andrew de Pendock (*Pendok*) and Isabel his wife def. A messuage, 1 ploughland, 10 a. of meadow, and 20s. rent in Forthampton (*Forthampton*). Right of John. Remise and

1324

quitclaim, specifying Andrew's heirs, to John. (Warranty by Andrew alone.) Cons. 10 marks.

76/54/314

442. Morrow [3 Nov.] of All Souls. John le Butler (*Botiller*) of Llantwit (*Lanultyt*) and Beatrice his wife quer. by Robert Malemayns in Beatrice's place by the king's writ; Gilbert de Masinton and Cristina his wife def. A messuage, 1 ploughland, and 6 a. of meadow in Hardwicke (*Herdewyk*) by Longney (*Longeneye*) and Moreton Valence (*Morton*) by Wheatenhurst (*Whitenhurst*). John acknowledged the right of Gilbert, as those which Gilbert and Cristina had by John's gift. For this, grant and render to John and Beatrice. To hold to them and their heirs in tail. Contingent remainder to John's heirs.

76/54/317

443. Morrow [3 Nov.] of All Souls. William Brown (*Brun*) parson of the church of Tortworth (*Torteworth*) quer.; Nicholas de Kingston (*Kyngeston*) and Joan his wife def. The manor of Tortworth and 2 messuages, 2 ploughlands, 1 yardland, 20 a. of meadow, and 4 a. of wood in Oldbury upon Severn (*Oldebury*), Thornbury (*Thornbury*), Thatcham (*Tacham*), and Falfield (*Valefeld*) and the advowson of the church of Tortworth. Right of William by gift of Nicholas and Joan. For this, grant back and render to Nicholas and Joan. To hold to them and their heirs in tail. Successive contingent remainders to Henry [Burghersh] bishop of Lincoln (*Lincoln'*) during his life, to Peter Veal (*Veel*) and Cecily his wife and their heirs in tail, and to Nicholas's heirs. [*Worn and stained.*]

76/54/318

444. Morrow [3 Nov.] of All Souls. Thomas Abraham and Matilda his wife quer. by Philip Payn in Matilda's place by the king's writ; Robert le Porker and Isabel his wife def. A messuage in the suburb of Bristol (*Bristoll'*). Right of Thomas. Render to him and Matilda. To hold to them and Thomas's heirs. (Warranty, specifying Isabels's heirs.) Cons. 100*s. Endorsed* Nicholas de Rowberrow (*Rougbergh*) put in his claim.

76/54/321

[Cf. *Bristol Gt. Red Book*, pp. 213–14, no. 114.]

445. Morrow [12 Nov.] of St. Martin. John de Annesley (*Annesleye*) and Lucy his wife quer.; William de Yetminster (*Yetemenestre*) def. A messuage, a mill, 1 ploughland, and 16 a. of meadow in Churchdown (*Chirchesdon*). John acknowledged the right of William by John's gift. For this, grant and render to John and Lucy. To hold to them and their heirs in tail. Contingent remainder to Thomas son of Robert de la Mare during his life and to Thomas's brother Peter.

76/54/316

446. Morrow [12 Nov.] of St. Martin. John son of Richard Laurence of Little Compton (*Parva Compton*) and Nicholas brother of the same John quer.; William Thatcher (*Thechare*) and Cristina his wife imp. A messuage and 9 a. of land in Little Compton. (Warranty of charter.) Right of John. Remise and quitclaim, specifying Cristina's heirs, to John and Nicholas and John's heirs. (Warranty.) Cons. 10 marks.

76/54/320

1325

447. One week [20 Jan.] from Hilary. John son of John de Bitton (*Button*) and Hawise his wife quer. by Walter de Compton (*Cumpton*) in Hawise's place by the king's writ; William de Bourne (*Burne*) and Richard de Compton def. Four messuages and 7 ploughlands in Bitton, Hanham (*Hanam*), Oldland (*Oldelond*), West Hanham (*Westhanam*), Upton Cheyney (*Uptone Chanu*), Siston (*Siston*), Pucklechurch (*Pokelechirch*), and Churchley (*Chirchleye*). John acknowledged the right of William. For this, William and Richard granted the holdings to John and Hawise and rendered to them a messuage and 2 ploughlands in Bitton, Hanham, Oldland, and Siston. To hold to John and Hawise and John's heirs in tail. And grant to John and Hawise of the reversion of a messuage and 2 ploughlands in West Hanham held by John de Widdenhill (*Widihull*) and Margery his wife for term of Margery's life, of a messuage and 1 ploughland in Pucklechurch and Churchley held by Ellis Brown (*Brun*) and Adam his son for term of life, of two thirds of a messuage and 2 ploughlands in Upton Cheyney held by Henry 'le Fiz' John Cheyney (*Johan Chanu*) for term of life, of the remaining third of the messuage and 2 ploughlands in Upton Cheyney held by John Percy (*Percehay*) and Margery his wife in Margery's dower, all of William's inheritance. To hold as above. Successive contingent remainders to Thomas brother of John son of John and his heirs in tail and to Thomas de Berkeley (*Berkelay*) the elder. Made in the presence of John de Widdenhill and Margery and of Henry and with their consent, and they did fealty to John son of John and Hawise. *Endorsed* Stephen de la More, Richard le Blunt (*Blount*), and John Marmion (*Marmyoun*) put in their claim. [*Faded and stained.*]

76/54/309

448. One week [20 Jan.] from Hilary. Robert FitzPayne (*le fiz Payn*) and Ela his wife quer. by Thomas de Lutteswell in Ela's place by the king's writ; Jordan de Byntre parson of the church of *Wroxhale* def. The manor of Frampton on Severn (*Frompton super Sabrinam*). Robert acknowledged the right of Jordan by Robert's gift. For this, grant and render to Robert and Ela. To hold to them and Robert's heirs.

76/54/324

449. Morrow [3 Feb.] of the Purification. Thomas Diggel of Bristol (*Bristoll'*) quer.; Richard le Barber of Cardiff (*Kerdyf*) imp. A messuage in the suburb of Bristol. (Warranty of charter.) Right of Thomas by Richard's gift. (Warranty.) Cons. 100*s*. *Endorsed* Richard son of Robert Truelove (*Trulof*) of Bristol put in his claim.

76/54/322

[Cf. *Bristol Gt. Red Book*, p. 214, no. 115.]

450. Morrow [3 Feb.] of the Purification. John de Langley (*Langeleye*) and Ela his wife quer. by James de Podimore (*Podemor*) in Ela's place by the king's writ; Robert de Farndon clerk def. The manor of Lower Siddington (*Northersodynton*) and a messuage, 2 ploughlands, and 4*s*. rent in Tarlton (*Torleton*) and Rodmarton (*Rodmerton*). John acknowledged the right of Robert by John's gift. For this, grant and render to John and Ela. To hold during their lives, two thirds of the manor of the king and the residue of the holdings of the chief lords. Remainder to Geoffrey de Langley and Mary his wife and their heirs in tail. Contingent remainder to Geoffrey's heirs. Made as to the two thirds of the manor by the king's order. *Endorsed* Thomas son of John de Langley put in his claim. [*Worn.*]

76/54/325

1325

451. Two weeks [21 April] from Easter. William de la Hay quer.; William de Hasfield (*Hasfeld*) vicar of the church of Henbury (*Hembury*) def. A messuage, 1 ploughland, and 3*s*. rent in Shirehampton (*Sherny Hampton*) by Henbury. Right of William de la Hay by gift of William de Hasfield. For this, grant back and render to William de Hasfield. To hold during his life, of William de la Hay, paying a rose a year at St. John the Baptist and doing service to the chief lords. Remainder to Stephen Cappenore and Alice his wife and their heirs in tail. Successive contingent remainders to William son of the said William de la Hay and his heirs in tail, and to that William's brother John and his heirs in tail. Contingent reversion to the heirs of William de la Hay. [*Worn.*]

76/55/328

452. Two weeks [21 April] from Easter. Hugh le Despenser (*Despens'*) quer.; Ebulo le Strange (*Lestraunge*) and Alesia his wife def. Seventy-five knights' fees in Alton Barnes (*Aulton Berners*), Creslow (*Carselewe*), Searchfield (*Secchevill*), Wilsford (*Wyvelesford*), Shrewton (*Shirreveton*), Winterbourne Earls (*Wynterbourn*), Little Cheverell (*Parva Cheverell*), Etchilhampton (*Echelhampton*), Marten (*Merton*), Coate (*Cotes*), Hill Deverill (*Deverel*), Chaddenwick (*Chadewych*), Norridge (*Norrigge*), Chitterne St. Mary (*Chitterne Mayden*), Winterbourne Stoke (*Wynterbourn Stoke*), Burcombe (*Bredecoumbe*), Little Langford (*Langeford*), Deptford (*Depeford*), Chicklade (*Chikkelade*), Poole Keynes (*La Pole*), Boyton (*Boyton*), Orcheston St. George (*Orcheston*), *Clandon* [Steeple Claydon, Bucks.?], Maddington (*Madynton*), Middleton (*Middelton*), Zeals (*Seles*), Homington (*Homynton*), Corton (*Cortyngton*), Asherton (*Asserton*), Fisherton Anger (*Fissherton Auch'*), Burcombe (*Brudecoumbe*), Maddington (*Wynterbourn*) by Chitterne (*Chitterne*), Langley Burrell (*Langele Burel*), Box (*La Boxe*), North Wraxall (*Wroxhale*), Nabal's (*Knabbewell*), Hartham (*Hertham*), Portishead (*Portesheved*), Great Chalfield (*Chaldefeld*), Whaddon (*Waddon*), Timsbury (*Tymbresbarwe*), *Lyllynton* [Lillington, Dorset?], *Plumbury* [Pomeroy?], Baycliff (*Bailleclyff*), Stratton St. Margaret (*Stratton*), *Cotsetle* [Cottles?], Hilperton (*Hulprynton*), Littlecote (*Littelecote*), Yatesbury (*Yatebury*), Whitcombe (*Wydecoumbe*), Broughton Giffard (*Broghton*), Monkton (*Moneketon*), Avon (*Avene*), Allington (*Aldyngton*), North Tidworth (*Todeworth Melewys*), Durnford (*Durneford*), Little Durnford (*Parva Derneford*), Amesbury (*Aumbresbury*), Porton (*Porton*), Great Durnford (*Magna Derneford*), Lake (*Lake*), West Wellow (*Welewe*), Bramshot (*Bremelshet*), Little Amesbury (*Westaumbresbury*), Netton (*Netton*), Netheravon (*Netheravene*), *Maperton* [Maperton, Som., *or* Mapperton, Dorset?], Melbury Sampford (*Melebury*), *Plumbere* [Pomeroy?], Kington Magna (*Kyngton*), Blunsdon Gay (*Bluntesdon*), Wanborough (*Wamberge*), Mildenhall (*Mildenhale*), and Compton Bassett (*Coumpton Basset*), WILTS., 15 knights' fees in Tuxwell (*Tokeswell*), Norton St. Philip (*Norton*), Ashcombe (*Esthesshecoumbe*), West Ashcombe (*Westhesshecoumbe*), Stogumber (*Stokegowere*), *Sotton*, Charlton Horethorne (*Cherleton*), Iford (*Iford*), Langford Budville (*Langeford*), Ham (*Hamme*), Henstridge (*Hengstrigg*), Kinson (*Kynstanton*), North Stoke (*Stoke Basset*), Luckington (*Lokynton*), and Durleigh (*Durleye*), SOM., 11¼ knights' fees in Combe Hay (*Coumbhaweye*), East Dewlish (*Estdouelys*), West Dewlish (*Westdouelys*), Winterborne Houghton (*Wynterbourn Houton*), Woodyates (*Wodegate*), *Meleburn*, Tollard Farnham (*Tollard*), Tarrant Crawford (*Crauford*), *Merton* [Moreton?], and

1325

Wakyngham [Wokingham?, formerly partly Wilts.], DORSET, 8 knights' fees in Lus Hill (*Lusteshull*), Shrivenham (*Shryvenham*), Stalpits (*Staupult*), Drayton (*Dreyton*) by Abingdon (*Abyndon*), Wantage (*Wanetynge*), and Ardington (*Ardynton*), BERKS., 12 knights' fees in Oldbury upon Severn (*Aldebury*), Iron Acton (*Irenacton*), King's Weston (*Kyngeston Weston*), *Capenore*, Ampney Crucis (*Amene Sancte Crucis*), Hatherop (*Hatherop*), GLOS., 1½ knights' fees in Borcombe (*Bourcoumbe*), DEVON, 9 knights' fees in North Charford (*Cherdeford*), Bickton (*Byketon*), Hambledon (*Hameldon*), Portsea (*Porteseye*), and Copnor (*Coupenore*), HANTS., and 2½ knights' fees in North Aston (*Northeston*), OXON. Right of Hugh. Remise and quitclaim, specifying Alesia's heirs, to him. (Warranty.) Cons. £1,000. *Labelled* Wyltes', Somers', Dors', Berk', Glouc', Devon', Sutht', Oxon'. [*Worn and stained.*]

286/32/247

[Cf. *Devon Fines, 1272–1369*, pp. 236–7, no. 1177; *Dorset Fines, 1195–1327*, pp. 328–9; *Som. Fines, 1307–46*, p. 122; *Wilts. Fines, 1272–1327*, pp. 132–3. The counties in which the fine locates the fees are in several instances wrong: besides the uncertain *Clandon*, *Lyllynton*, *Maperton*, and *Wakyngham*, Creslow was in Bucks., Searchfield and Bramshot in Hants., Portishead, Timsbury, and Combe Hay in Som., Melbury Sampford, Kington Magna, and Kinson in Dorset, North Stoke in Oxon., and Luckington and Lus Hill in Wilts., while Burcombe, Pomeroy, and Maddington are apparently each named twice.]

453. Three weeks [28 April] from Easter. William Corbet of Chaddesley Corbett (*Chaddesleye*) quer.; Richard de Bromhull parson of the church of Chaddesley def. The manor of Tytherington (*Tydrynton*). Right of Richard by William's gift. For this, grant back and render to William. To hold during his life. Remainder to John Clinton (*Clynton*) of Maxstoke (*Maxstoke*) and Margery his wife and their heirs in tail. Contingent remainder to William's heirs. [*Worn.*]

76/55/328b (formerly 76/55/350)

454. One month [5 May] from Easter. William de Walton (*Wauton*) quer.; Philip Tyrel and Richard de Walton def. Two thirds of half of the manors of Sutton Veny (*Magna Sutton*) and Little Sutton (*Parva Sutton*), WILTS., and one quarter of the manor of Cromhall (*Crumhale*) and the advowson of the church of the same manor, GLOS. Right of Richard, as those which Richard and Philip had by William's gift. For this, grant back and render to William. To hold during his life. Remainder to William's son John and his heirs in tail. Successive contingent remainders to John's brother Andrew and his heirs in tail, to William's brother John and his heirs in tail, to that John's sister Isabel and her heirs in tail, and to William de Walton's heirs. *Labelled* Wyltes', Glouc'. [*Worn and stained.*]

286/33/253

[Cf. *Wilts. Fines, 1272–1327*, p. 133.]

455. Morrow [17 May] of Ascension. Hugh le Despenser earl of Winchester (*Wynton'*) quer.; Elizabeth Comyn def. The manor of Painswick (*Payneswyk*). Right of the earl. Render to him. To hold of the king. (Warranty.) Cons. £50. Made by the king's order.

76/55/326

1325

456. Morrow [17 May] of Ascension. Hugh le Despenser the younger quer.; Elizabeth Comyn def. The castle and manor of Castle Goodrich (*Castel Goderich*) in the Welsh march (*marchia Wall'*). Right of Hugh. Render to him. To hold of the king. (Warranty.) Cons. £50. Made by the king's order.

76/55/327

457. One week [9 June] from Trinity. William son of Robert de Pennington (*Penynton*) quer.; Cristina who was wife of Robert de Pennington def. A messuage and 1 ploughland in Baunton (*Baudynton*) and the advowson of the church of St. Mary of Cricklade (*Crekkelade*). Grant and render to William. To hold to him and his heirs in tail. Successive contingent remainders to William's brother Robert and his heirs in tail, to Robert's brother Henry and his heirs in tail, to Henry's brother Nicholas and his heirs in tail, to William George (*Jorge*) and Alice his wife and their heirs in tail, and to Alice's heirs. (Warranty.) Cons. £20. [*Worn*.]

76/55/330

[Since Cricklade was in Wilts. this fine, labelled only *Glouc'*, should have been a 'divers counties' fine.]

458. One week [9 June] from Trinity. John le Butler (*Botyler*) of Llantwit (*Lanultyt*) quer.; Richard le Hatter (*Hattere*) and Amice his wife def. A messuage, 22 a. and 3 roods of land, 3 a. of meadow, and 9s. 11½d. rent in Gupshill (*Gopushull*), Southwick (*Suthewyk*), and Fiddington (*Fidenton*). Right of John. Render to him. (Warranty, specifying Amice's heirs.) Cons. £20. *Endorsed* Between John le Butler (*Botiller*) of Llantwit [*unfinished*].

76/55/331

459. Two weeks [16 June] from Trinity. (Made two weeks from St. Martin 12 Edward II [25 Nov. 1318].) John de Bradley (*Bradelegh*) and Isabel his wife quer. by John Gacelyn in Isabel's place by the king's writ; Nicholas de Caldecote def. (Nicholas was dead by the time that the fine was granted and recorded, and was replaced as def. by his brother and heir Walter). One sixth of a messuage, a mill, 3 ploughlands, and £10 rent in Charlton (*Cherletone*), Redland (*Tridelonde*), and Lawrence Weston (*Weston Sancti Laurencii*) by Henbury (*Hembury*) held in dower by Joan who was wife of William le Veym. Nicholas acknowledged the right of John and granted the reversion to John and Isabel and John's heirs. (Warranty.) Cons. £20. [*Worn*.]

76/55/329

19 Edward II

1325

460. Two weeks [8 July] from St. John the Baptist. Adam Gamage quer.; Thomas Aubrey (*Aubray*) and Leticia his wife def. A messuage, 4 a. of land, and 3s. rent in Gloucester (*Gloucestr'*) and Upton St. Leonards (*Upton Sancti Leonardi*). Right of Adam. Remise and quitclaim, specifying Leticia's heirs, to him. (Warranty.) Cons. £10.

76/55/333

1325

461. One week [6 Oct.] from Michaelmas. William Archibald (*Archebaud*) and Matilda his wife quer.; John le Widow (*Wodewe*) def. Four messuages, 1 ploughland, 6 a. of meadow, 6 a. of pasture, and 8*s*. 9*d*. rent in Cirencester (*Cirencestr'*). William acknowledged the right of John by William's gift. For this, grant and render to William and Matilda. To hold to them and their heirs in tail. Contingent remainder to William's heirs. [*Worn*.]

76/55/338

462. One week [6 Oct.] from Michaelmas. Robert de Bodenham (*Bodeham*) and Margery his wife quer. by John de Monnington (*Monyton*) in Margery's place by the king's writ; Richard de Mansell Gamage (*Malmeshull Gammage*) and Walter ap David def. The manor of Wormington (*Wormynton*). Robert acknowledged the right of Richard, as that which Richard and Walter had by Robert's gift. For this, grant and render to Robert and Margery. To hold to them and their heirs in tail male. Contingent remainder to Robert's heirs.

76/55/339

463. One week [6 Oct.] from Michaelmas. Henry le Farmer (*Fermer*) quer.; Walter le Farmer def. Two messuages, 44 a. of land, 3 a. of meadow, and 5 a. of wood in Paganhill (*Pagenhull*). Right of Walter by Henry's gift. For this, grant back and render to Henry. To hold during his life. Remainder to Margery daughter of Walter Blackman (*Blakeman*). To hold during her life. Remainder to Henry's son Henry and his heirs in tail. Successive contingent remainders to that Henry's brother Walter and his heirs in tail and to Henry le Farmer's heirs. *Endorsed* Richard son of Henry le Farmer of Paganhill put in his claim.

76/55/340

464. Two weeks [13 Oct.] from Michaelmas. John le Dyer (*Dyghere*) of Tewkesbury (*Teukesbury*) and Alice his wife quer. by John de Tewkesbury in Alice's place by the king's writ; William de Mitton (*Mutton*) of Tewkesbury and Alice his wife def. A messuage in Tewkesbury. Right of John, as that which John and Alice had by gift of William and Alice. To hold to John and Alice and John's heirs. (Warranty, specifying the heirs of Alice wife of William.) Cons. 40*s*.

76/55/337

465. Three weeks [20 Oct.] from Michaelmas. Jordan Bishop (*Bisshop*) and Joan his wife quer. by John de Barford (*Bereford*) in Joan's place; John Sewerby (*Sywardeby*) def. The manor of Little Sodbury (*Parva Sobbury*) and the advowson of the church of the same manor. Jordan acknowledged the right of John by Jordan's gift. For this, grant and render to Jordan and Joan. To hold to them and their heirs in tail. Successive contingent remainders to Jordan's brother Thomas and his heirs in tail, to Thomas's brother John and his heirs in tail, to John's sister Sibyl and her heirs in tail, to Sibyl's brother William and his heirs in tail, to William's sister Juliana and her heirs in tail male, and to Jordan's heirs. [*Worn*.]

76/55/341

1325

466. Morrow [3 Nov.] of All Souls. Richard Foward of Campden (*Caumpeden*) quer.; Richard le Tailor (*Taillour*) of Tredington (*Tredynton*) and Agnes his wife def. A messuage in Campden. Right of Richard Foward by gift of Richard le Tailor and Agnes. (Warranty, specifying Agnes's heirs.) Cons. 40*s*.

76/55/332

467. Morrow [12 Nov.] of St. Martin. Geoffrey de Wickham (*Wykewane*) of Aston Somerville (*Aston Somervill*) and Hawise his wife quer. by Richard de Chalk in Hawise's place by the king's writ; John de Slaughter (*Sloghtre*) and Elena his wife def. A messuage, 8 yardlands, 26 a. of meadow, and rents of 3*s*. and 1 qr. of oats and 1 lb. of cumin in Longborough (*Longeberwe*). Geoffrey acknowledged the right of John. For this, John and Elena granted to Geoffrey and Hawise the reversion of the holdings held by Richard de Hoddington (*Hodynton*) and Lucy his wife for term of Lucy's life, of John's inheritance. To hold during their lives. Remainder to Geoffrey's son John and his heirs in tail. Successive contingent remainders to John's brother Walter and his heirs in tail, to Walter's sister Matilda and her heirs in tail, and to Geoffrey's heirs. (Warranty by John de Slaughter and his heirs.) Made in the presence of Richard and Lucy and with their consent, and they did fealty to Geoffrey and Hawise. [*Worn.*]

76/55/334

468. One week [18 Nov.] from St. Martin. Hugh le Despenser earl of Winchester (*Wynton'*) quer.; John de Rale and Ida his wife def. One third of half of the manor of Barnsley (*Bardesleye*). Right of the earl. Remise and quitclaim, specifying Ida's heirs, to him. Cons. £30.

76/55/335

469. One week [18 Nov.] from St. Martin. John son of Richard Laurence of Little Compton (*Parva Cumpton*) and Nicholas brother of the same John quer.; John de Barnwell (*Bernewell*) and Agnes his wife def. A messuage, 17 a. of land, and 1 a. of meadow in Little Compton. Right of John son of Richard. Render to him and Nicholas. (Warranty by John de Barnwell and his heirs.) Cons. 20 marks.

76/55/336

1326

470. Morrow [3 Feb.] of the Purification. John le Arblaster of Hasfield (*Hasfeld*) quer.; Nicholas Sneed (*Snede*) of Eldersfield (*Eldesfeld*) def. Four messuages, 30 a. of land, 6 a. of meadow, and 4*s*. rent in Hasfield, Tirley (*Trynleye*), and Ashleworth (*Asshelworth*). Right of Nicholas by John's gift. For this, grant back and render to John. To hold during his life. Remainder to Robert de Carrant (*Carente*) and Joan his wife and their heirs in tail. Contingent remainder to John's heirs.

76/55/343

1326

471. One week [9 Feb.] from the Purification. William de Northlew (*Northloue*) and Joan his wife quer.; Robert le Mason (*Masoun*) of Stone (*Stone*) def. A messuage, 21 a. of land, and 1 a. of meadow in Stone and Ham (*Hamme*) by Berkeley (*Berkeleye*). William acknowledged the right of Robert by William's gift. For this, grant and render to William and Joan. To hold during their lives, of Robert, paying a rose a year at St. John the Baptist and doing service to the chief lords. Reversion to Robert.

76/55/342

472. Two weeks [6 April] from Easter. Peter son of William de Wincot (*Wynecote*) and Katherine his wife quer.; William de Wincot def. A messuage and 4 ploughlands in Wincot by Lower Quinton (*Netherquenton*). Peter acknowledged the right of William. For this, grant to Peter and Katherine and their heirs in tail of the reversion of the messuage and 2½ ploughlands held by John de Heyford for term of 4½ years and of 1½ ploughlands held by Nicholas de Beenham for term of 30 years as demised by the said William. To hold of William, paying a rose a year at St. John the Baptist and doing service to the chief lords. Contingent reversion to William. Made in the presence of John and Nicholas and with their consent, and they did fealty to Peter and Katherine. [*Worn.*]

76/55/328c (formerly 76/55/352)

[This fine, earlier filed as though dated 20 Edward II, has been moved to a position in the file among those for 18 Edward II though in fact dated 19 Edward II.]

473. Three weeks [13 April] from Easter. Henry de Hauville (*Hauvile*) quer.; Nicholas de Grey and Agnes his wife def. The manor of Shenington (*Shenyngton*). Right of Henry by gift of Nicholas and Agnes. For this, grant back and render to Nicholas and Agnes. To hold to them and Agnes's heirs.

76/55/344

474. One month [20 April] from Easter. John Champneys (*Chaumpeneys*) of Oakenhill (*Okenhull*) quer. by John de Winstone (*Wyneston*) in his place by the king's writ; John Lydiard (*Lydyerd*) of Wotton under Edge [*Wode...*] def. A messuage, a mill, and 1 ploughland in Elberton (*Albryghton*) by Thornbury (*Thornbury*). Grant and render to John Champneys. To hold to him and his heirs in tail. Successive contingent remainders to John son of Agnes de Cowhill (*Couhill*) and his heirs in tail, to John's brother Geoffrey and his heirs in tail, to Geoffrey's sister Joan and her heirs in tail, and to Henry son of John Champneys of Wilmington (*Wylmyngdon*). Cons. 100 marks. [*Worn.*]

76/55/345

475. One month [20 April] from Easter. Ellis Cotel quer. by John de Chidgley (*Chiddelegh*); John de Montfort (*de Monte Forti*) parson of the church of Combe Hay (*Combhauweye*) and Walter de Sampford (*Saumpford*) def. The manor of Corscombe (*Corscombe*), SOM., and the manor of Coomb's End (*Cotelescombe*), GLOS., held by Matilda who was wife of William Cotel in dower. Grant to Ellis of the reversion, of John's inheritance. To hold to Ellis during his life. Remainder to John de Palton and Joan his wife and their heirs in tail. Contingent remainder to that John's heirs. *Labelled* Somers', Glouc'.

286/33/266

[Cf. *Som. Fines, 1307–46*, p. 123; above, no. 431.]

1326

476. Two weeks [1 June] from Trinity. John le Butler (*Botiller*) of Llantwit (*Lanultit*) quer.; Thomas de Braose (*Brewouse*) def. A messuage and 1 ploughland in Forthampton (*Forthampton*). Right of John. Remise and quitclaim to him. (Warranty.) Cons. 10 marks.

76/55/346

477. One week [1 July] from St. John the Baptist. Ranulph le Wheeler (*Wheolare*) of Gloucester (*Gloucestr'*) quer.; William de Ryons (*Ryuns*) of Gloucester and Amice his wife def. A messuage, 43 a. of land, 16 a. of meadow, and 5 a. of pasture in Over (*Ovre*), Highnam (*Hynehamme*), Lassington (*Lassyndon*), and Maisemore (*Mayesmore*). Right of Ranulph. Render to him. (Warranty by William alone.) Cons. 10 marks.

76/55/347

20 Edward II

1326

478. One week [6 Oct.] from Michaelmas. Ralph de Dorset (*Dercet*) quer.; John de Sudeley (*Sudley*) def. The manor of Sudeley. Right of Ralph by John's gift. For this, grant back and render to John. To hold during his life, of the king. Remainder to John son of Bartholomew de Sudeley and Eleanor de Scales and their heirs in tail. Contingent remainder to John de Sudeley's heirs. Made by the king's order.

76/55/348

479. Two weeks [13 Oct.] from Michaelmas. John atte Playstead (*Pleystede*) and Alice his wife quer.; Nicholas de Thame and Elena his wife def. A messuage and half of 1 yardland in Badgeworth (*Beggeworth*). Right of John. Render to John and Alice. To hold to them and John's heirs. Cons. 10 marks. [*Worn.*]

76/55/351

480. Two weeks [13 Oct.] from Michaelmas. John Falcons (*Faucons*) quer.; Adam de Walgrave (*Waldegrave*) and Margery his wife def. A messuage, 2 tofts, 30 a. of land, and 1 a. of meadow in *Quenynton* [Quenington *or* Quinton]. Right of John by gift of Adam and Margery. (Warranty by Adam alone.) Cons. £10.

76/55/354

481. Morrow [3 Nov.] of All Souls. John Athelam of Tewkesbury (*Teukesbury*) quer.; Edmund de Barton (*Bauyrton*) and Agnes his wife def. A messuage in Tewkesbury. Right of John by gift of Edmund and Agnes. (Warranty, specifying Edmund's heirs.) Cons. 100*s*.

76/55/349

482. Morrow [12 Nov.] of St. Martin. Laurence de Ruyton of Tewkesbury (*Teukesbury*) and Joan his wife quer.; Hugh Ward (*Warde*) of Fenny Compton (*Fenycompton*) and Alice his wife def. A toft, 18 a. of land, and 1 a. of meadow in Hidcote Bartrim (*Hudicote Bartram*). Right of Joan, as those which Laurence and Joan had by gift of Hugh and Alice. To hold to Laurence and Joan and Joan's heirs. (Warranty by Hugh alone.) Cons. 20 marks.

76/55/353

1 Edward III

1327

483. Two weeks [26 April] from Easter. (Made 2 weeks from Michaelmas 20 Edward II [13 Oct. 1326].) Thomas de Chester (*Cestre*) of Bibury (*Bybury*) quer.; William le Marshal (*Mareschal*) of Shorncote (*Cernecote*) and Agnes his wife def. Two messuages and 1½ yardlands in Bibury. Right of Agnes. For this, William and Agnes granted and rendered the holdings to Thomas. To hold to him and his heirs in tail male. Successive contingent remainders to Thomas's daughter Alice and her heirs in tail male, to Henry de Chester of Bibury and his heirs in tail male, and to Thomas's heirs. (Warranty, specifying Agnes's heirs.) *Endorsed* The fines of Easter term of 1 Edward III contain 36. [*Worn.*]

77/56/9

484. Two weeks [26 April] from Easter. Richard son of Gilbert Talbot (*Talebot*) and Elizabeth his wife quer.; Gilbert Talbot and Thomas his brother def. The manor and hundred of Bampton (*Bampton*), OXON., the manor of Hertingfordbury (*Hertfordyngbury*), HERTS., the manor of Winterbourne (*Wynterburn*), WILTS., the manors of Moreton Valence (*Morton*) and Whaddon (*Whaddon*), GLOS., and the manor of Pollicott (*Policote*), BUCKS. Right of Gilbert and Thomas by gift of Richard and Elizabeth. For this, grant back and render to Richard and Elizabeth. To hold to them and their heirs in tail, of the king. Contingent remainder to Richard's heirs. Made by the king's order. *Labelled* Oxon', Hertford', Wyltes' Gloucestr', Buk'.

286/35/1

[Cf. *Wilts. Fines, 1327–77*, p. 14, no. 1.]

485. One week [14 June] from Trinity. John Athelam quer.; John le Marshal (*Mareschal*) of Tewkesbury (*Teukesbury*) and Gunnilda his wife def. One and a half acres of land in Tewkesbury. Right of John Athelam. Remise and quitclaim, specifying Gunnilda's heirs, to him. (Warranty.) Cons. 100*s*. *Endorsed* Fines of Gloucester county from the first year of Edward III to the seventh year. [*Worn.*]

77/56/1

486. One week [14 June] from Trinity. John de Keynsham (*Keynesham*) of Redcliffe Street (*Redeclyvestrete*) quer. by John Manship; John le Bond (*Bonde*) and Cristina his wife def. A messuage in the suburb of Bristol (*Bristoll'*). Right of John de Keynsham by gift of John and Cristina. (Warranty, specifying Cristina's heirs.) Cons. 100*s*.

77/56/3

[Cf. *Bristol Gt. Red Book*, p. 214, no. 117.]

487. One week [14 June] from Trinity. Walter de Shipton and Alice his wife quer.; John son of John de Cleeve (*Clyve*) of Gupshill (*Gopushull*) and Margery his wife def. A messuage, 32½ a. of land, 5½ a. of meadow, and 2*s*. 8*d*. rent in Southwick (*Suthewyk*) by Tewkesbury (*Teukesbury*). Right of Walter. Remise and quitclaim, specifying Margery's heirs, to Walter and Alice and Walter's heirs. (Warranty.) Cons. 100 marks.

77/56/5

1327

488. One week [14 June] from Trinity. (Made one week from Trinity 18 Edward II [9 June 1325].) John Bennett (*Benet*) and Isabel his wife quer.; Walter de Yanworth (*Yaneworth*) chaplain def. Two messuages, 1 ploughland and ½ yardland, 5 a. of meadow, and 4*s.* rent in Bisley (*Byseleye*). Right of Walter, of which he had one messuage, the ploughland, meadow, and rent by gift of John and Isabel. For this, grant back and render to John and Isabel. To hold during their lives. And grant to them of the reversion of one messuage and the ½ yardland held by Adam atte Rook Wood (*Rokewode*) and Margery his wife for term of life, of Walter's inheritance. To hold as above. Remainder to Robert son of the same John and Isabel and his heirs in tail. Contingent remainder to Isabel's heirs. Made in Adam's presence and with his consent, and he did fealty to John and Isabel. [*Worn and stained.*]

77/56/8

[The year in which the agreement was made, the surname *Benet*, and the amount of rent are illegible in the foot of fine and have been supplied from the note of fine, CP 26/1/5, Trin. 1 Edw. III.]

489. One week [14 June] from Trinity. John le Bond (*Bonde*) and Cristina his wife quer.; Geoffrey le Felter (*Veltere*) and Cristina his wife def. A messuage in the suburb of Bristol (*Bristoll'*). Right of Cristina wife of John, as that which John and Cristina had by gift of Geoffrey and Cristina. To hold to John and Cristina and Cristina's heirs. (Warranty, specifying the heirs of Geoffrey's wife Cristina.) Cons. 10 marks.

77/56/10

[Cf. *Bristol Gt. Red Book*, p. 215, no. 118.]

490. Two weeks [21 June] from Trinity. Thomas de Swinburne (*Swynburn*) and Margery his wife quer.; Robert de Swinburne def. The manor of Woodmancote (*Wodemanscote*) by Dursley (*Dersleye*). Thomas acknowledged the right of Robert by Thomas's gift. For this, grant and render to Thomas and Margery. To hold to them and their heirs in tail male. Contingent remainder to Thomas's heirs.

77/56/4

491. Two weeks [8 July] from St. John the Baptist. Robert George (*Gyorge*) [*reading uncertain*] of Bristol (*Bristoll'*) quer.; Howell (*Houwellus*) de Roilly and Matilda his wife def. A messuage in Bristol. Right of Robert by gift of Howell and Matilda. (Warranty, specifying Matilda's heirs.) Cons. 100*s. Endorsed* Adomar de Lisle (*de Insula*), John de Romsey (*Romeseye*), and Arnald Frombaud, executors of the will of Raymond Frombaud, put in their claim. [*Worn.*]

77/56/2

[Cf. *Bristol Gt. Red Book*, p. 214, no. 116.]

492. Two weeks [8 July] from St. John the Baptist. Thomas son of Gilbert Aylard of Stanshawe (*Stanshawe*) quer.; Gilbert Aylard of Stanshawe def. The manor of Stanshawe. Right of Thomas by Gilbert's gift. For this, grant back and render to Gilbert. To hold during his life, of Thomas, paying a rose a year at St. John the Baptist and doing service to the chief lords. Reversion to Thomas.

77/56/6

1327

493. Two weeks [8 July] from St. John the Baptist. Walter de Combe (*Coumbe*) and Margaret his wife quer.; Ellis de Combe def. Two ploughlands and 10 a. of meadow in Wick Dangerville (*Wyke Daungerevill*). Right of Ellis by gift of Walter and Margaret. For this, grant back and render to Walter and Margaret. To hold to them and their heirs in tail. Contingent remainder to Margaret's heirs. [*Worn.*]

77/56/7

[Wick Dangerville, of which the name has gone out of use, is represented by Upper or Lower Wick, in Berkeley.]

2 Edward III

1328

494. York. Three [24 April] weeks from Easter. (Made Westminster, two weeks from Easter, 1 Edward III [26 April 1327].) Robert de Ashton and Elizabeth his wife quer. by John de Sevenhampton in Elizabeth's place; Walter Waleys def. Two messuages, 2 ploughlands, 36 a. of meadow, 5 a. of wood, and 70*s*. rent in Winterbourne (*Wynterbourn*) and *Otryngton*. Robert acknowledged the right of Walter. For this, grant to Robert and Elizabeth and their heirs in tail of the reversion of the holdings held by Florence who was wife of John de Ashton for term of life, of Walter's inheritance. Contingent remainder to Robert's heirs. Made in the presence of Florence and with her consent, and she did fealty to Robert and Elizabeth.

77/56/11

[The reading *Otryngton* is uncertain, the tops of the first two letters being lost in the hole made for filing. The place-name may have been lost: the spelling is difficult to reconcile with the known forms for Elberton, Elmington, Olveston, Tockington, or Tytherington.]

495. York. One week [5 June] from Trinity. John le Small (*Smale*) clerk quer.; Osbert d'Abitot (*Dabitot*) clerk def. A messuage in Tewkesbury (*Teukesbury*). Right of John. Render to him. (Warranty.) Cons. 100*s*. [*Faded.*]

77/56/21

[This fine is of 2 Edward III but is placed in the file among those for 3 Edward III. The year date is legible under ultra-violet.]

496. York. One week [6 Oct.] from Michaelmas. Robert de Overton of Edgeworth (*Eggesworth*) and Alice his wife quer. by Peter de Edgeworth in Alice's place by the king's writ; John Jenkin (*Janekyn*) of Oxenton (*Oxindon*) def. A messuage and one third of a messuage, half of 1 yardland, and one third of 2 yardlands in Edgeworth. Robert acknowledged the right of John by Robert's gift. For this, grant and render to Robert and Alice. To hold during their lives. Remainder as to the messuage and the half to Robert's daughter Juliana and her heirs in tail. Successive contingent remainders to Juliana's sister Margery and her heirs in tail and to Robert's heirs. Remainder as to the thirds to the said Margery and her heirs in tail. Successive contingent remainders to the said Juliana and her heirs in tail and to Robert's heirs. [*Worn.*]

77/56/13

1328

497. York. Two weeks [13 Oct.] from Michaelmas. Reynold atte Townsend (*Tounesende*) of Staverton (*Staverton*) quer.; Robert son of Reynold atte Townsend of Staverton def. A messuage and 2 ploughlands in Staverton. Right of Robert by Reynold's gift. For this, grant back and render to Reynold. To hold during his life, of Robert, paying a rose a year at St. John the Baptist and doing service to the chief lords. Reversion to Robert.

77/56/17

498. York. Three weeks [20 Oct.] from Michaelmas. Robert de Prestbury quer. by Peter de Edgeworth (*Eggesworth*) in his place by the king's writ; Mr. Richard le Mason (*Mazoun*) of Uley (*Iweleye*) and Matilda his wife def. Two messuages, a toft, 1 ploughland, 3 a. of meadow, and 10 a. of pasture in Badgeworth (*Beggeworth*), Hatherley Wood (*Hatherleywode*), Up Hatherley (*Uphatherleye*), Down Hatherley (*Dunhatherleye*), Brickhampton (*Brighthampton*), and Shurdington (*Shurdynton*). Right of Robert. Remise and quitclaim, specifying Mr. Richard's heirs, to him. Cons. 20 marks. *Endorsed* William Damsel (*Damoysel*) put in his claim. Henry Cropet put in his claim.

77/56/14

499. York. One month [27 Oct.] from Michaelmas. William de Whatcote and Alice his wife quer.; Agnes de la Chamber (*Chaumbre*) of Weston Subedge (*Weston Underegge*) def. Four messuages and 3½ yardlands in Weston Subedge. Grant and render to William and Alice. To hold to them and their heirs in tail, of Agnes, paying during Agnes's life 20 marks a year, at Michaelmas and Easter, and to Agnes's heirs a rose a year at St. John the Baptist and doing service to the chief lords. Contingent reversion to Agnes. Cons. £20. *Endorsed* John son of John atte Chamber (*Chaumbre*) of Weston Subedge (*Weston under egge*) put in his claim. [*Worn.*]

77/56/15

500. York. One month [27 Oct.] from Michaelmas. John Damsel (*Damoisele*) quer.; William Damsel and Matilda his wife def. A messuage, 1 ploughland, and 40*s.* rent in Painswick (*Payneswyke*). Right of John by gift of William and Matilda. For this, grant back and render to William and Matilda. To hold to William and Matilda during their lives, of John, paying a rose a year at St. John the Baptist and doing service to the chief lords. Reversion to John.

77/56/16

501. York. Morrow [3 Nov.] of All Souls. (Made Westminster, one week from St. John the Baptist, 1 Edward III [1 July 1327].) Thomas de Berkeley (*Berkele*) quer.; Roger de Burghill (*Burghull*) and Sibyl his wife def. One ploughland in Down Hatherley (*Dunhatherle*), held by William de Hathaway (*Hathewy*) and Agnes his wife for term of life. Right of Thomas. Grant, specifying Roger's heirs, of the reversion of the holding, which William and Agnes had by demise of Roger and Sibyl, to Thomas. Cons. 10 marks. Made in the presence of William and Agnes and with their consent, and they did fealty to Thomas. *Endorsed* Reynold de la Mare of Little Hereford (*Parva Hereford*) put in his claim.

77/56/12

[Cf. *Berkeley Castle Mun.* i, p. 469, A2/25/1 (counterpart).]

1329

502. York. One week [20 Jan.] from Hilary. Thomas de Prayers quer.; Roger [Northburgh] bishop of Coventry and Lichfield (*Coventr' et Lichefeld*) def. The manor of Dorsington (*Dersyngton*). Right of the bishop by Thomas's gift. For this, grant back and render to Thomas. To hold during his life. Remainder to Thomas's son Henry and Sarah his wife and their heirs in tail. Contingent remainder to Thomas's heirs.

77/56/18

3 Edward III

1329

503. Two weeks [7 May] from Easter. Gilbert de Kinnersley (*Kynardesleye*) quer.; John de Paris (*Parys*) def. Nine messuages, 2 ploughlands and 42 a. of land, 36 a. of meadow, 12 a. of pasture, 30 a. of wood, and 100*s*. rent in Leigh (*Leye*) by Deerhurst (*Derhurst*), Staverton (*Staverton*), Haydon (*Heydone*), and the Haw (*Hawe*). Right of Gilbert. Render to him. (Warranty.) Cons. 100 marks.

77/57/34

504. One week [25 June] from Trinity. William de St. George (*de Sancto Georgio*) and Joan his wife quer.; Thomas de Scalers (*Scalariis*) the elder def. The manor of Hatley St. George (*Hungri Hattele*) [Cambs.] and the advowson of the church of the same manor. William acknowledged the right of Thomas by William's gift. For this, grant and render to William and Joan and their heirs in tail. Contingent remainder to William's heirs.

77/57/32

[This fine, clearly relating to Cambs., is wrongly labelled *Gloucestr'* and filed with the Glos. fines.]

505. One week [25 June] from Trinity. Roger le Teslare and Cristiana his wife quer.; John de Bures of Essex (*Essex'*) and Alice his wife def. A messuage in Bristol (*Bristoll'*). Right of Roger. Render to Roger and Cristina. To hold to them and Roger's heirs. (Warranty, specifying Alice's heirs.) Cons. 10 marks.

77/57/35

[Cf. *Bristol Gt. Red Book*, p. 215, no. 120.]

506. One week [25 June] from Trinity. John de Bures and Hawise his wife quer.; John de Sollers (*Solers*) def. The manor of Brewham (*Bruham*), 24 a. of pasture, and 100 a. of wood in Charlton Musgrove (*Cherleton Mussegros*), SOM., and the manor of Boddington (*Botynton*) except for 1 toft, 36 a. of land, and 4 a. of meadow in the same manor, GLOS. Right of John de Sollers by gift of John de Bures and Hawise. For this, grant back and render to John de Bures and Hawise. To hold during their lives. Remainder to Giles de Beauchamp (*de Bello Campo*) and Katherine his wife and their heirs in tail. Contingent remainder to Hawise's heirs. *Labelled* Somers', Gloucestr'.

286/35/34

[Cf. *Som. Fines, 1307–46*, p. 238.]

507. One week [1 July] from St. John the Baptist. Thomas de Breadstone (*Bradeston*) and Isabel his wife quer.; John de Marsh (*Mareys*) def. Eight messuages, 120 a. of land, 15 a. of meadow, 8 a. of pasture, 10 a. of wood, and 100*s*. rent in Cam (*Camme*) and Stinchcombe (*Styntescombe*). Thomas acknowledged the right of John by Thomas's gift. For this, grant and render to Thomas and Isabel. To hold to them and Thomas's heirs.

77/57/33

1329

508. Two weeks [2 July] from Trinity. Robert de Sapy and Aline his wife quer.; William vicar of the church of Westbury on Severn (*Westbury*) def. Half of the manor of Westbury, and the advowson of the church of Westbury. Right of William by gift of Robert and Aline. For this, grant back and render to Robert and Aline. To hold to them and their heirs in tail. Contingent remainder to Aline's heirs.

77/57/31

509. Two weeks [2 July] from Trinity. Robert de Sapy and Aline his wife and John de Wysham quer.; John de Carswall (*Carsewall*) def. The manor of Huntley (*Hunteleye*) and the advowson of the church of the same manor. Robert and Aline acknowledged the right of John de Carswall by gift of Robert and Aline. For this, grant back and render to Robert and Aline. To hold to them and their heirs in tail. Contingent remainder to John de Wysham. *Endorsed* Thomas de Huntley (*Huntelegh*) put in his claim.

77/57/37

510. Two weeks [2 July] from Trinity. Reynold de Abenhall (*Abbehale*) quer.; John de Sutton and Emma his wife def. A messuage, a mill, 2 ploughlands, 12 a. of meadow, 4 a. of pasture, and 6 marks rent in Bulley (*Bulley*) and Tibberton (*Tyberton*). Right of Reynold by gift of John and Emma. For this, grant back and render to John and Emma. To hold to them during their lives, of Reynold, paying a rose a year at St. John the Baptist and doing service to the chief lords. Reversion to Reynold.

77/57/38

511. Two weeks [8 July] from St. John the Baptist. John de Olney (*Olneye*) and Agnes his wife quer.; William de Burgh clerk def. The manor of Hardmead (*Hardemede*), BUCKS., and a messuage, 1 ploughland, and 6 marks rent in Churchdown (*Chirchedon*), Oakey (*Okei*), Hucclecote (*Hokelecote*), and the suburb of Gloucester (*Glouc'*), GLOS. John acknowledged the right of William by John's gift. For this, grant and render to John and Agnes. To hold to them and their heirs in tail. Contingent remainder to John's heirs. *Labelled* Buk', Glouc'. *Endorsed* Richard de Windsor (*Wyndesore*) put in his claim.

286/35/39

512. One week [6 Oct.] from Michaelmas. Mr. Henry de Amberley (*Amberesleye*) clerk and Reynold Musard chaplain quer.; Robert de Laverton (*Laberton*) and Joan his wife def. Five messuages, 3 yardlands and 8 a. of land, and 2 a. of meadow in Saintbury (*Seynesbury*). Right of Mr. Henry, as those which Mr. Henry and Reynold had by gift of Robert and Joan. For this, grant back and render to Robert and Joan. To hold to them and Joan's heirs.

77/57/27

513. One week [6 Oct.] from Michaelmas. Thomas de Seymour (*de Sancto Mauro*) and Alice his wife quer. by John de Helpston (*Helpiston*) in Alice's place by the king's writ; Laurence de Seymour parson of the church of Higham Ferrers (*Hegham Ferers*) def. The manor of Meysey Hampton (*Hempton Meysy*). Thomas acknowledged the right of Laurence by Thomas's gift. For this, grant and render to Thomas and Alice. To hold to

1329

them and Thomas's heirs in tail. Successive contingent remainders to Thomas's brother Alan and his heirs in tail, to Alan's brother Nicholas and his heirs in tail, to Laurence de Seymour and his heirs in tail, and to Thomas's heirs. *Endorsed* John Meysey (*Meisy*) put in his claim. [*Worn.*]

77/57/28

514. One week [6 Oct.] from Michaelmas. Henry de Brockworth (*Brokworth*) quer.; Ralph le Parker and Agnes his wife def. A messuage, 1 a. of wood, and half of 1 yardland in Alstone (*Alweston*). Right of Henry. Render to him. (Warranty, specifying Agnes's heirs.) Cons. 10 marks.

77/57/30

515. One week [6 Oct.] from Michaelmas. Richard le White quer. by John de Winstone (*Wynston*) in his place by the king's writ; Geoffrey de Eldersfield (*Eldresfeld*) and Cristiana his wife def. A messuage in the suburb of Bristol (*Bristoll'*). Right of Richard. Remise and quitclaim, specifying Cristiana's heirs, to him. (Warranty.) Cons. 10 marks.

77/57/36

[Cf. *Bristol Gt. Red Book*, pp. 215–16, no. 121.]

516. Three weeks [20 Oct.] from Michaelmas. Richard Morris (*Moryce*) of Bristol (*Bristoll'*) quer.; Robert de Stroud (*de la Strode*) and Emma his wife and Thomas Barron (*Barun*) chaplain def. A messuage and 2 yardlands in Churcham (*Chirchehamme*) and Morton (*Morton*). Right of Richard by gift of Robert and Emma and Thomas. (Warranty, by Robert alone.) Cons. 100*s.*

77/57/29

517. One month [27 Oct.] from Michaelmas. John de Bewbush (*de Bellobosco*) and Isabel his wife quer.; John Ashwy and William Percy (*Percehay*) def. Five messuages, 1 ploughland and 4 yardlands, 7 a. of meadow, 3 a. of wood, and rents of 2*s.* and ½ lb. of pepper in Shipton Moyne (*Shupton Moygne*). Right of John Ashwy, as those which John and William had by gift of John de Bewbush and Isabel. For this, grant back and render to John and Isabel. To hold during their lives. Remainder to Nicholas son of John de Bewbush and Isabel his sister [jointly] and that Isabel's heirs in tail. Successive contingent remainders to Nicholas's brother William and his heirs in tail, to William's brother Gilbert and his heirs in tail, to Gilbert's sister Joan and her heirs in tail, and to the heirs of Isabel wife of John de Bewbush. [*Worn.*]

77/56/22

518. One month [27 Oct.] from Michaelmas. Richard de Renham quer.; John de Mount Gilbert (*de Monte Gilberti*) of Withington (*Wythyndon super le Wolde*) and John son Peter de Norton and Alice his wife def. A messuage, 32 a. of land, and 2 a. of meadow in Withington. Right of Richard by gift of John, John, and Alice. (Warranty, specifying Alice's heirs.) Cons. 10 marks.

77/56/23

1329

519. Morrow [3 Nov.] of All Souls. William de Quinton (*Quenton*) quer.; Laurence de Ruyton (*Ruton*) of Tewkesbury (*Teukesbury*) and Joan his wife def. Two messuages, 22 a. of land, and 1 a. of meadow in Hidcote Bartrim (*Hudicote Bertram*). Right of William by gift of Laurence and Joan. (Warranty, specifying Joan's heirs.) Cons. 10 marks.

77/56/25

520. Morrow [12 Nov.] of St. Martin. Thomas Crook (*Crok*) of Gloucester (*Gloucestre*) clerk quer.; Thomas le Goldsmith (*Goldsmyth*) and Alice his wife def. Two messuages, 1½ yardlands, 8 a. of meadow, 3 a. of pasture, and 2*s.* rent in Wightfield (*Wyghtfeld*) and Apperley (*Apperleye*). Right of Thomas Crook by gift of Thomas le Goldsmith and Alice. For this, grant back and render to Thomas and Alice. To hold during their lives. Remainder to Richard de Bramshill (*Bromshull*) and Isabel his wife and their heirs in tail. Contingent remainder to Edward son of Thomas le Goldsmith and his heirs in tail, to Edward's sister Amice and her heirs in tail, to Amice's brother Ralph and his heirs in tail, and to Thomas le Goldsmith's heirs. [*Worn.*]

77/56/19

521. Morrow [12 Nov.] of St. Martin. Richard de Scarning (*Skarnyngge*) quer.; William Kipping (*Kyppyng*) of Minchinhampton (*Munechenehampton*) and Juliana his wife def. A messuage in Cirencester (*Cyrencestre*). Right of Richard by gift of William and Juliana. (Warranty, specifying Juliana's heirs.) Cons. 100*s.*

77/57/26

522. One week [18 Nov.] from St. Martin. Walter le White 'fisshere' quer.; John de Newton (*Neuton*) 'smyth' def. A messuage in the suburb of Bristol (*Bristoll'*). Right of Walter. Render to him. (Warranty.) Cons. 10 marks. *Endorsed* Thomas de Whittokesmede and Joan his wife co-executrix of the will of Gilbert Derby of Bristol put in their claim.

77/56/24

[Cf. *Bristol Gt. Red Book*, p. 215, no. 119.]

523. Two weeks [25 Nov.] from St. Martin. William de la Green (*Grene*) and John de Badgeworth (*Baggeworthe*) quer.; John de Saltmarsh (*Sautemareys*) def. The manor of West Hanham (*Westhanam*). Right of William, as that which William and John de Badgeworth had by gift of John de Saltmarsh. To hold to William and John and William's heirs. (Warranty.) Cons. 100 marks.

77/56/20

4 Edward III

1330

524. Two weeks [27 Jan.] from Hilary. Thomas le Monks (*Monekes*) of Codrington (*Codrynton*) quer.; Roger le Monks of Codrington and Alice his wife def. A messuage and 4 yardlands in Codrington. Right of Thomas by gift of Roger and Alice. For this, grant back and render to Roger and Alice. To hold during their lives, of Thomas, paying a rose a year at St. John the Baptist and doing service to the chief lords. Reversion to Thomas.

77/57/46

1330

525. Two weeks [27 Jan.] from Hilary. William son of John le Scrip' of Gloucester (*Gloucestre*) quer.; John Lutekene and Isabel his wife def. A messuage in Gloucester. Right of William by gift of John and Isabel. To hold to William. (Warranty, specifying Isabel's heirs.) Cons. 100*s*.

77/57/47

526. Morrow [3 Feb.] of the Purification. Ranulph de Beckford (*Bekkeford*) 'fishere' and Agnes his wife quer.; Robert Michel and Margery his wife def. Two shops in Gloucester (*Gloucestr'*). Right of Ranulph. Remise and quitclaim, specifying Margery's heirs, to Ranulph and Agnes and Ranulph's heirs. (Warranty.) Cons. 10 marks.

77/57/48

527. Morrow [3 Feb.] of the Purification. Elizabeth who was wife of John de Burgh (*de Burgo*) quer.; William la Zouche (*Zousche*) and Eleanor his wife def. The castles and manors of Usk (*Usk*), Llangybi (*Tregruk*), and Caerleon (*Kaerlion*) and the manors of Liswerry (*Lyswyry*), Tintern Parva (*Parva Tynterne*), New Grange (*Nova Grangia*), Little Llantrisant (*Parva Lantrissan*), Trelleck (*Trillek*), Mitchel Troy (*Troye*), Llangwm (*Lancom*), and Undy (*Woundy*) and the advowsons of the churches of Tredunnock (*Tredenauch*), Llansoy (*Landisseye*), Mitchel Troy, Llangybi, Panteg (*Pentek*), Kemeys (*Kemmeys*), and Llandegveth (*Landegewych*), of the chapel of Cwmcarvan (*Concarvan*), of the abbey of Caerleon, of the priory of Usk, and of the hospital of Usk. Right of Elizabeth. Remise and quitclaim, specifying Eleanor's heirs, to her. (Warranty.) Cons. £1,000.

77/58/55

[The fine is labelled *Gloucestr'* although the places mentioned are not in Gloucestershire, but in Monmouthshire, adjoining Gloucestershire. Cf. above, no. 411.]

528. Morrow [3 Feb.] of the Purification. Richard de Bagendon (*Baginden*) and Agnes his wife quer. by John de Bledisloe (*Bledelawe*) in Agnes's place by the king's writ; Roger de Pedwardine (*Pedewardyn*) def. The manor of Bagendon and the advowson of the church of the same manor, GLOS., and a messuage, a mill, 3 ploughlands, 40 a. of meadow, and 26*s*. 8*d*. rent in Wellington (*Welynton*), HEREFS. Grant and render to Richard and Agnes. To hold to them and their heirs in tail. Contingent remainder to Richard's heirs. *Labelled* Glouc', Hereford'.

286/35/50

529. Two weeks [22 April] from Easter. John le Butler (*Botiller*) of Shustoke (*Shustoke*) quer.; John son of Milisent de Morton def. A messuage, 4 yardlands, 18 a. of meadow, and 24*s*. rent in Lechlade (*Lecchelade*). Right of John son of Milisent by John le Butler's gift. For this, grant back and render to John le Butler. To hold during his life, of John son of Milisent, paying a rose a year at St. John the Baptist and doing service to the chief lords. Remainder to John de Quelesbergh and Beatrice his wife and their heirs in tail. Contingent reversion to John son of Milisent.

77/57/50

1330

530. Two weeks [22 April] from Easter. John de Weston quer.; Thomas de Dowdeswell (*Doudeswell*) and Isabel his wife def. A messuage, 2½ yardlands, and 8 a. of meadow in Olveston (*Olveston*). Right of John. Render to him. (Warranty, specifying Isabel's heirs.) Cons. 10 marks.

77/58/51

531. Two weeks [22 April] from Easter. (Made one week from Hilary 18 Edward II [20 Jan. 1325].) John de Haudlo and Matilda his wife quer.; Robert de Haudlo clerk def. The manors of Suckley (*Suckeleye*), Upton Snodsbury (*Snodesbury*), and Wick (*Wyke*) and 8 a. of meadow and half of two mills in Kidderminster (*Kyderministre*), WORCS., the manors of Bidford (*Bideford*) and Broom (*Brome*), WARWS., the manor of Little Rissington (*Rysyndon Basset*), GLOS., the manor of Compton Dando (*Cumpton Dauno*), SOM., the manor of East Wickham (*Estwykham*), KENT, and the manors of Ryston (*Ryston*) and Thurning (*Thernyng*), NORF. Right of Robert. For this, grant of the reversion of the manors of Suckley, Bidford, and Broom held in dower by Aline who was wife of Edward Burnel, the manors of Little Rissington, Compton Dando, Ryston, and Thurning held by the same Aline for term of life, the manors of Upton Snodsbury, Wick, and East Wickham held by Alice who was wife of Walter de Beauchamp (*de Bello Campo*) for term of life, and the meadow and the half held by Clement de Dunclent (*Dounclent*) and Avice his wife for term of life, all of Robert's inheritance, to John and Matilda and their heirs in tail male. To hold the manors of Suckley, Bidford, Broom, and Little Rissington and the meadow and the half of the king and the residue of the chief lords. Contingent remainder to Matilda's heirs. Made by the king's order as to the manors etc. held in chief, and with the consent of Aline, Alice, Clement, and Avice, and they did fealty to John and Matilda. *Labelled* Wygorn', Warr', Gloucestr', Somers', Kanc', Norff'.

286/36/53

[Cf. *Som. Fines, 1307–46*, p. 239; *Warws. Fines, 1284–1345*, pp. 140–1, no. 1691.]

532. Two weeks [22 April] from Easter. The king quer. by Peter de Liddington (*Ludyngton*) his clerk who answers for him; William la Zouche (*Zousche*) de Mortimer and Eleanor his wife def. The manor of Hanley Castle (*Hanle*), WORCS., the land of Glamorgan (*Glamorgan*) and Margam (*Margannon*) in the march of Wales (*Wall'*), and the manor of Tewkesbury (*Teukesbury*), GLOS. Right of the king. Remise and quitclaim, specifying Eleanor's heirs, to him. *Labelled* Wygorn', Glouc'.

286/36/54

[For the identity of Hanley Castle, *V.C.H. Worcs.* iv. 96.]

533. Two weeks [22 April] from Easter. William de Carswall (*Kareswell*) and Mary his wife quer.; Mr. Thomas de Langley (*Langeleye*) def. The manors of Lower Siddington (*Nethersodynton*), Tarlton (*Torleton*), and Weston Maudit (*Weston Mauduyt*), GLOS., and the manors of Milcote (*Mulcote*), Little Dorsington (*Parva Dersynton*), Pinley (*Pynnele*), Stivichall (*Styvychale*), and Wyken (*Wykene*), a messuage and £10 rent in Harborough Magna (*Herdebarewe*), and the advowsons of the churches of Wolfhamcote (*Welhamcote*) and Harborough, WARWS. Grant and render to William and Mary. To hold during their lives. Remainder to Geoffrey son of Geoffrey de Langley and his heirs in tail. Contingent remainder to William's heirs. (Warranty.) Cons. £100. *Labelled* Glouc', Warr'.

286/36/55

[Cf. *Staffs. Fines, 1327–1547*, p. 183; *Warws. Fines, 1284–1345*, p. 141, no. 1692.]

1330

534. Two weeks [22 April] from Easter. Amaury de St. Amand (*de sancto Amando*) and Joan his wife quer. by William de Coleshill (*Coleshull*) Joan's guardian in her place by the king's writ; William de Harwell (*Harewell*) chaplain def. The manor of South Cerney (*Cerneye*), GLOS., and the manors of West Woodhay (*Westwydehay*) and East Ilsley (*Hildesle*), BERKS. Grant and render to Amaury and Joan, except for a messuage and 1½ ploughlands in West Woodhay. To hold to Amaury and Joan and their heirs in tail. And grant to them of the reversion of the messuage and 1½ ploughlands held by William de Holt and Emmeline his wife for term of life, of William's inheritance. To hold as above. Contingent remainder to Amaury's heirs. Cons. 100 marks. *Labelled* Glouc', Berk'.

286/36/56

[For the identity of South Cerney, Rudder, *Glos.* p. 327; of East Ilsley, *V.C.H. Berks.* iv. 26.]

535. Morrow [18 May] of Ascension. Walter Prentice (*Prentyz*) of Bristol (*Bristoll'*) quer. by John de Milton; Hugh de Ludwell (*Ludewell*) and Margaret his wife def. A messuage in the suburb of Bristol. Right of Walter. Render to him. (Warranty, specifying Margaret's heirs.) Cons. 100*s*.

77/58/60

[Cf. *Bristol Gt. Red Book*, p. 216, no. 123.]

536. Morrow [18 May] of Ascension. John son of Maurice de Saltmarsh (*de Salso Marisco*) quer.; Roger de Radnor (*Radenore*) and Agnes his wife def. A messuage in Bristol (*Bristoll'*). Right of John. Remise and quitclaim, specifying Roger's heirs, to him. (Warranty, by Roger alone.) Cons. 100*s*.

77/58/61

[Cf. *Bristol Gt. Red Book*, p. 216, no. 124.]

537. One week [10 June] from Trinity. John le Butler (*Botiller*) of Llantwit (*Lanultyt*) and Beatrice his wife quer. by Henry le Butler in Beatrice's place by the king's writ; Alice de Park of Hardwicke (*Herdwyk*) def. The manors of Park (*Park*) and Brawn (*Brewern*) and a messuage and 1 ploughland in Murcott (*Morcote*). Right of John. Remise and quitclaim to John and Beatrice and John's heirs. (Warranty.) Cons. 100 marks.

77/58/53

[For the identity of Brawn, *Glos. Fines, 1199–1299*, no. 562; geographical proximity indicates Murcott, in Minsterworth.]

538. One week [10 June] from Trinity. John le Butler (*Botiller*) of Llantwit (*Lanultyt*) and Beatrice his wife quer. by Henry le Butler in Beatrice's place by the king's writ; Simon son of Eleanor de Park def. The manors of Park (*Park*) and Brawn (*Brewern*) and a messuage and 1 ploughland in Murcott (*Morcote*). Right of John. Remise and quitclaim to John and Beatrice and John's heirs. (Warranty.) Cons. 100 marks.

77/58/56

[Cf. above, no. 537.]

539. One week [10 June] from Trinity. Thomas atte Green (*Grene*) of Gloucester (*Gloucestr'*) and Joan his wife quer. by John de Winstone (*Wynston*) in Joan's place; Robert Michel and Margery his wife def. A messuage and 3 shops in Gloucester. Right of Thomas. Render to Thomas and Joan. To hold to them and Thomas's heirs. (Warranty, specifying Margery's heirs.) Cons. 20 marks.

77/58/58

1330

540. One week [10 June] from Trinity. John Lucas quer.; Robert son of Laurence le White (*Whyte*) of Edgeworth (*Eggeworth*) and Cristina his wife def. Twenty-seven acres of land in Baunton (*Baudynton*). Right of Cristina. For this, Robert and Cristina granted and rendered the land to John. To hold during his life. Remainder to John's son John and his heirs in tail. Successive contingent remainders to that John's brother Richard and his heirs in tail, to Richard's sister Margaret and her heirs in tail, to Margaret's sister Alice and her heirs in tail, and to John Lucas's heirs.

77/58/59

541. Two weeks [17 June] from Trinity. Walter Abey and Felicia his wife quer. by John de Winstone (*Wynston*) in Felicia's place by the king's writ; Walter de Yoxall (*Yoxhale*) and Cristina his wife def. A messuage in Cirencester (*Cyrencestre*). Grant and render to Walter Abey and Felicia. To hold to them and their heirs in tail. Contingent remainder to Felicia's heirs. Cons. 100*s*.

77/58/52

542. Morrow [25 June] of St. John the Baptist. Robert son of Edward de Frayn (*de Fraxino*) of Lechlade (*Lechelade*) quer.; William son of Robert son of Edward de Frayn of Lechlade and Hugh brother of the same William def. Two messuages, 14½ a. of land, and 2 a. of meadow in Lechlade. Right of William, as those which William and Hugh had by Robert's gift. For this, grant and render to Robert. To hold during his life, of William and Hugh and William's heirs, paying a rose a year at St. John the Baptist and doing service to the chief lords. Reversion to William and Hugh and William's heirs.

77/58/54

543. One week [6 Oct.] from Michaelmas. (Made one month from Easter 3 Edward III [21 May 1329].) Giles de Beauchamp (*de Bello Campo*) and Katherine his wife quer.; John de Bures and Hawise his wife def. Half of the manors of Kemerton (*Kenemarton*) and Down Hatherley (*Dounhatherleye*) held by John de Annesley (*Aunesleye*) and Lucy his wife for term of life. Giles acknowledged the right of Hawise. For this, John and Hawise granted the reversion, of Hawise's inheritance, to Giles and Katherine and their heirs in tail. To hold of John de Bures and Hawise and Hawise's heirs, paying a rose a year at St. John the Baptist and doing service to the chief lords. Contingent reversion to John de Bures and Hawise and Hawise's heirs. Made in the presence of John de Annesley and Lucy and with their consent, and they did fealty to Giles and Katherine. [*Worn.*]

77/57/43

544. One week [6 Oct.] from Michaelmas. John Mautravers the younger quer.; John de Cailly (*Caillewe*) def. The castle of Carreg Cennen (*Careckenyn*) and the manor of Carreg Cennen in South Wales (*Suthwall*), the castle of Brimpsfield (*Brymesfeld*), the manors of Brimpsfield, King's Stanley (*Kyngestanleye*), Rockhampton (*Rokhampton*), Stonehouse (*Stonhouse*), Stoke Gifford (*Stoke Giffard*), Syde (*Side*), and Walls (*Walles*), 12 a. of meadow in Badgeworth (*Begeworth*), and the advowsons of the churches of Winterbourne (*Wynterbourn*) and of the said manors of King's Stanley, Rockhampton, Stonehouse, Stoke Gifford, and Syde, GLOS., and the manors of Boyton (*Boyton*), Elston (*Eliston*), Broughton Gifford (*Broghton*), Corton (*Corton*), Sherrington (*Sharnton*), Stapleford (*Stapelford*), and Codford St. Peter (*Codeford*) and the advowsons of the

1330

churches of the said manors of Boyton, Elston, Broughton, Sherrington, Stapleford, and Codford, WILTS. Right of John de Mautravers. Remise and quitclaim to him of the castles, the manors of Carreg Cennen, Brimpsfield, King's Stanley, Rockhampton, Sherrington, Stapleford, and Codford, the meadow, and the advowsons of the churches of Winterbourne and of the manors of King's Stanley, Rockhampton, Sherrington, Stapleford, and Codford. And grant to him of the reversion of the manors of Stonehouse, Stoke Gifford, Elston, and Broughton and the advowsons of the churches of the same manors held by Margaret who was wife of John Giffard of Brimpsfield in dower, of the manors of Syde, Walls, and Boyton and the advowsons of the churches of the manors of Syde and Boyton held by the same Margaret for term of life, and of the manor of Corton, held by Robert le Bor for term of life, of John de Cailly's inheritance. To hold the castles and the manors of Carreg Cennen, Brimpsfield, King's Stanley, Rockhampton, Stoke Gifford, Walls, Elston, Sherrington, and Stapleford and the advowsons of the churches of Winterbourne and of the said manors of King's Stanley, Rockhampton, Elston, Sherrington, and Stapleford, of the king, and all the other manors, the meadow, and the advowsons of the chief lords. Cons. £1,000. Made by the king's order as to the castles, manors, and advowsons held in chief, and with the consent of Robert and Margaret, and they did fealty to John Mautravers. *Labelled* Glouc', Wiltes'. *Endorsed* Henry Sturmy put in his claim. Henry son of Henry Sturmy and Margaret his wife put in their claim. James son of Nicholas de Audley (*Audelegh*) and John son of Fulk le Strange (*lestraunge*) put in their claim. Roger Bavent, Richard Dauntsey (*Dansey*), Thomas de Benton and Margaret his wife put in their claim. Robert de Condicote put in his claim.

286/36/67

[Cf. *Wilts. Fines, 1327–77*, pp. 26–7, no. 65.]

545. Two weeks [13 Oct.] from Michaelmas. John de Bures and Hawise his wife and Giles de Beauchamp (*de Bello Campo*) and Katherine his wife quer.; John de Sollers (*Solers*) def. The manor of English Bicknor (*Bykenore*) and 20 messuages, 4 ploughlands, 60 a. of meadow, and £13 rent in Longford (*Langeford*) by Gloucester (*Gloucestr'*). John de Bures and Hawise acknowledged the right of John de Sollers by gift of John de Bures and Hawise. For this, grant back and render to John de Bures and Hawise of the holdings and manor except for £10 rent in the same manor. To hold the manor to John and Hawise and Hawise's heirs, of the king, and the holdings in Longford to them during their lives, of the chief lords. Remainder of the holdings to Giles and Katherine and their heirs in tail, with contingent remainder to Hawise's heirs. And John de Sollers granted and rendered the £10 rent excepted above to Giles and Katherine, to hold during the lives of John de Bures and Hawise, of the king, with remainder to Hawise's heirs. Made by the king's order. [*Worn.*]

77/57/45

546. Three weeks [20 Oct.] from Michaelmas. William de Cheltenham (*Chiltenham*) and Elena his wife quer. by John de Cheltenham in Elena's place by the king's writ; Thomas ap Adam def. The manor of Purton (*Puryton*) by Newnham (*Newenham*). William acknowledged the right of Thomas by William's gift. For this, grant and render to William and Elena. To hold to them and William's heirs. (Warranty.)

77/57/39

[Cf. *Berkeley Castle Mun.* i, pp. 480–1, A2/36/4 (counterpart).]

1330

547. Three weeks [20 Oct.] from Michaelmas. Maurice de Berkeley (*Berkeleye*) quer.; Thomas ap Adam def. The manors of King's Weston (*Kyngesweston*) and Elberton (*Ailberton*). Right of Thomas by Maurice's gift. For this, grant back and render to Maurice. (Warranty.)

77/57/40

548. Three weeks [20 Oct.] from Michaelmas. Thomas de Berkeley (*Berkeleye*) quer.; John le Freeman (*Freman*) and Margaret his wife def. One fifth of a messuage and of 2 ploughlands in Iron Acton (*Irenacton*). Right of Margaret. For this, John and Margaret granted and rendered the holding to Thomas. (Warranty, specifying Margaret's heirs.) *Endorsed* John de Acton 'chivaler' put in his claim.

77/57/41

[Cf. *Berkeley Castle Mun.* i, p. 430, A2/9/1 (counterpart).]

549. Three weeks [20 Oct.] from Michaelmas. Thomas de Berkeley (*Berkeleye*) and Margaret his wife quer. by John de Cheltenham (*Chiltenham*) in Margaret's place by the king's writ; Thomas ap Adam (*Apadam*) def. The castle of Beverston (*Beverston*) and the manors of Beverston and Over (*Oure*), GLOS., and the manor of Barrow Gurney (*Barewe*), SOM. Thomas de Berkeley acknowledged the right of Thomas ap Adam by gift of Thomas de Berkeley. For this, grant and render to Thomas de Berkeley and Margaret. To hold to them and Thomas de Berkeley's heirs. (Warranty.) *Labelled* Glouc', Somers'. *Endorsed* John Inge put in his claim.

286/35/45

[Cf. *Som. Fines, 1307–46*, p. 238; *Berkeley Castle Mun.* i, p. 148, A1/13/5 (counterpart). For the identity of Barrow Gurney, Collinson, *Som.* ii. 309.]

550. One month [27 Oct.] from Michaelmas. William Corbet quer.; Walter Power and Margery his wife def. A messuage, 60 a. of land, and 7 a. of meadow in Thornbury (*Thornbury*). Right of Margery. For this, Walter and Margery granted and rendered the holdings to William. To hold during his life. Successive remainders to Juliana de Yately (*Yatele*) during her life and to Roger Corbet of Tytherington (*Tyderington*) and his heirs in tail male. Contingent remainder to William's daughter Petronilla. (Warranty, specifying Margery's heirs.)

77/57/49

551. Morrow [3 Nov.] of All Souls. William Owen (*Uwayne*) quer. by William Read (*Rede*); William 'the handelsetter' and Alice his wife def. A messuage in the suburb of Bristol (*Bristoll'*). Right of William Owen by gift of William 'the handelsetter' and Alice. To hold to William Owen. (Warranty, specifying Alice's heirs.) Cons. 10 marks.

77/57/42

[Cf. *Bristol Gt. Red Book*, p. 216, no. 122.]

552. Morrow [12 Nov.] of St. Martin. Reynold de Botreaux and Isabel his wife quer.; Mr. Walter de Botreaux def. The manor of Alcester (*Alyncestr'*), WARWS., and 1 ploughland, 22 a. of meadow, and 6 a. of pasture in Redwick (*Raddewyk*), GLOS. Reynold acknowledged the right of Mr. Walter, of which he had the manor by Reynold's gift. For this, grant and render of the manor to Reynold and Isabel. To hold to them and their heirs

1330

in tail male, of the king. And grant to Reynold and Isabel and their said heirs of the reversion of the land, meadow, and pasture held by Joan who was wife of Hugh de Gurney (*Gourney*) and Hugh her son for term of life, of Mr. Walter's inheritance. To hold as above, of the chief lords. Contingent remainder to Reynold's heirs. Made, as to the manor, by the king's order. *Labelled* Warr', Gloucestr'.

286/36/71

[Cf. *Warws. Fines, 1284–1345*, p. 141, no. 1693.]

553. Two weeks [25 Nov.] from St. Martin. William le Semes vicar of the church of Down Hatherley (*Donhatherleye*) quer.; Walter le Southern (*Southerne*) of Gloucester (*Gloucestr'*) and Alice his wife def. Two messuages, 18 a. of land, and 2 a. of meadow in Down Hatherley. Right of William by gift of Walter and Alice. To hold to William. (Warranty, by Walter alone.) Cons. 20 marks.

77/57/44

1331

554. One week [20 Jan.] from Hilary. Hugh Poyntz of Curry Mallet (*Corymalet*) and Margaret his wife quer.; Nicholas Poyntz parson of the church of St. Mary's Hoo (*Sancta Maria de Hoo*) and Hugh de Melplash (*Meliplash'*) parson of the church of Curry Mallet def. The manor of Tockington (*Tokynton*), GLOS., and a messuage, 1 ploughland, 27 a. of meadow, 40 a. of wood, and 40*s.* rent in Isle Abbots (*Ile Abbatis*), SOM. Hugh de Poyntz acknowledged the right of Nicholas, as those which Nicholas and Hugh de Melplash had by gift of Hugh Poyntz. For this, grant and render to Hugh Poyntz and Margaret. To hold during their lives. Remainder to that Hugh's son Nicholas and his heirs in tail. Successive contingent remainders to that Nicholas's brother Hugh and his heirs in tail, to that Hugh's brother Walter and his heirs in tail, to Walter's brother Henry and his heirs in tail, to Henry's brother Thomas and his heirs in tail, and to the heirs of Hugh Poyntz. *Labelled* Glouc', Somers'.

286/36/74

[Cf. *Som. Fines, 1307–46*, pp. 239–40.]

5 Edward III

1331

555. One week [9 Feb.] from the Purification. John de la Mare of Rendcomb (*Rendecoumbe*) quer.; Walter son of Roger de Chandos (*Chaundos*) def. Three messuages, 60 a. of land, and 20*s.* rent in North Cerney (*North Sarneye*) and two thirds of the manor of Rendcomb. Right of Walter by John's gift. For this, grant back and render to John. To hold during his life. Remainder to John's son Thomas and his heirs in tail. Successive contingent remainders to Thomas's brother William and his heirs in tail and to John's heirs.

77/59/76

556. Two weeks [14 April] from Easter. John son of Roger la Warre and John son of the same John and Margaret his wife quer.; John de Claydon (*Cleydon*) parson of the church of Mancetter (*Maincestre*) def. The manor of Allington (*Alyngton*), WILTS., the manor of Wickwar (*Wykewarre*), GLOS., and the manor of Brislington (*Brustlyngton*), SOM. John son of Roger acknowledged the right of John de Claydon by gift of John son of Roger.

1331

For this, grant back and render to John son of Roger. To hold during his life, the manor of Allington of the king, and the other manors of the chief lords. Remainder to John son of John and Margaret his wife and their heirs in tail. Contingent remainder to the heirs of John son of Roger. Made by the king's order as to the manor of Allington. *Labelled* Wiltes', Glouc', Somers'.

286/36/82

[Cf. *Som. Fines, 1307–46*, p. 240; *Wilts. Fines, 1327–77*, p. 30, no. 79.]

557. Two weeks [14 April] from Easter. Henry de Harnhill (*Harnhull*) 'chevaler' quer.; John de Anne parson of the church of Pennington (*Penyton*) def. The manor of Harnhill and the advowson of the church of the same manor. Right of John by Henry's gift. For this, grant back and render to Henry. To hold during his life. Remainder to John de Winchester (*Wynton*') and Joan his wife and Joan's heirs in tail. Successive contingent remainders to John de Stonor (*Stonore*) 'chivaler' and his heirs in tail male and to Henry's heirs.

77/59/77

558. One month [28 April] from Easter. Nicholas de Newland (*Newelond*) the elder and Edith his wife quer. by John Winstone (*Wynstan*) in their place by the king's writ; John de Putford (*Podeford*) def. A messuage, a toft, 1 yardland, and ½ a. of meadow in Frampton on Severn (*Frompton super Sabrinam*) held by Richard Veal (*Vyel*) and Agnes daughter of Henry de Rodley (*Rodleye*) for term of life. Grant of the reversion to Nicholas and Edith and their heirs in tail. Contingent remainder to Nicholas's heirs. (Warranty.) Cons. 20 marks. *Endorsed* Walter Wrytye and Joan his wife put in their claim.

77/59/80

559. One month [28 April] from Easter. Peter le Marshal (*Mareschal*) of Withy Bridge (*Wythybrugg*) quer.; Thomas atte Stowe of Uckington (*Okynton*) and Agnes his wife def. Six acres of land, 1 a. of meadow, 1 a. of pasture, and half of a messuage and a mill in Uckington. Right of Peter. Render to him. (Warranty, specifying Agnes's heirs.) Cons. 20 marks.

77/59/81

560. One week [2 June] from Trinity. Mr. Richard de Chaceley (*Chaddesleye*) clerk quer. by John de Winstone (*Wynston*); Richard de Blewbury (*Blebury*) and Isabel his wife def. A messuage, 36 a. of land, 13 a. of meadow, 7 a. of pasture, and 4*s.* 6*d.* rent in Tirley (*Trynleye*) and Chaceley. Right of Mr. Richard by gift of Richard and Isabel. To hold to Mr. Richard. (Warranty, by Richard de Blewbury alone.) Cons. 20 marks.

77/58/73

[Chaceley adjoins Tirley but was in Worcs. until 1931.]

561. One week [2 June] from Trinity. Matilda who was wife of Gilbert de Blouham quer.; John le Good (*Gode*) of Cheltenham (*Chiltenham*) and Alice his wife def. A messuage in Cirencester (*Cyrencestre*). Right of Matilda. Render to her. (Warranty, specifying Alice's heirs.) Cons. 100*s.*

77/58/74

1331

562. One week [2 June] from Trinity. John de Berkeley (*Berkeleye*) of Dursley (*Derseleye*) and Hawise his wife quer.; William de Berkeley and John de Gloucester (*Gloucestr'*) def. The manors of Dursley, Newington Bagpath (*Coldenewynton*), and Dodington (*Dodynton*) and a messuage, 1 yardland, 10 a. of meadow, 5 a. of wood, and 40*s.* rent in Leonard Stanley (*Stanleye Sancti Leonardi*). John de Berkeley acknowledged the right of William and John de Gloucester by John de Berkeley's gift. For this, grant and render to John de Berkeley and Hawise. To hold to them and their heirs in tail, of the king. Contingent remainder to John de Berkeley's heirs. Made by the king's order.

77/58/75

[A copy of this fine is filed as CP 25/1/288/51, 2nd nos., no. 3.]

563. One week [2 June] from Trinity. John de St. Philbert (*de Sancto Philiberto*) quer.; Roger de Aspley (*Asperle*) and Juliana his wife def. The manor of Westwell (*Westwell*), OXON., 18 marks rent in Farmington (*Thermerton*), GLOS., and 5 a. of meadow in Eaton Hastings (*Etonhastynges*), BERKS. Grant, remise, and quitclaim to John of whatever Roger and Juliana had in the manor and holdings in the name of Juliana's dower. For this, John granted that he would pay to Roger and Juliana during Juliana's life 20 marks a year, at St. John the Baptist, Michaelmas, St. Martin, and Easter, with right of distraint for non-payment. *Labelled* Oxon', Glouc', Berk'.

286/36/92

564. Two weeks [9 June] from Trinity. Robert Camp (*Caumpe*) and Alice his wife quer.; Ralph de Filton def. Two messuages and 2 yardlands in Winterbourne (*Wynterbourne*). Robert acknowledged the right of Ralph by Robert's gift. For this, grant and render to Robert and Alice. To hold to them and their heirs in tail. Contingent remainder to Robert's heirs.

77/58/69

565. Two weeks [9 June] from Trinity. William de Pedmore (*Pedemor*) 'orfevre' [*i.e. goldsmith*] and Margaret his wife quer.; Walter Pope of Gloucester (*Gloucestr'*) 'chapeleyn' def. A messuage in Gloucester. William acknowledged the right of Walter by William's gift. For this, grant and render to William and Margaret. To hold to them and their heirs in tail. Contingent remainder to William's heirs.

77/58/71

566. Two weeks [9 June] from Trinity. Robert de Sapy (*Sapi*) and Aline his wife quer. by John de Bledisloe (*Bledelowe*) in Aline's place by the king's writ; John son of Adam de Anne def. The advowson of the church of Westbury on Severn (*Westbury*). Right of Aline. Render to Robert and Aline. To hold to them and Aline's heirs. (Warranty.) Cons. 100*s.*

77/58/72

567. Two weeks [9 June] from Trinity. Owen (*Audoenus*) de Oakley (*Ocle*) and Joan his wife quer.; Henry Joye chaplain def. A messuage, a mill, 1 ploughland, 12 a. of meadow, 3 a. of wood, and 20*s.* rent in Oakley. Owen acknowledged the right of Henry by Owen's gift. For this, grant and render to Owen and Joan. To hold to them and their heirs in tail. Contingent remainder to Owen's heirs

77/59/78

1331

568. Two weeks [9 June] from Trinity. (Made one week from Hilary 4 Edward III [20 Jan. 1331].) John de Haudlo quer.; Eustace de Eton chaplain and Geoffrey de Scarborough (*Skardeburgh'*) chaplain def. The manors of Coln St. Aldwyn (*Colne Sancti Ailwini*), Hatherop (*Hathrop*), and Wick (*Wyke*), GLOS., the manors of Chadlington (*Chadelynton*), Shippenhull (*Shupenhull*), and Lew (*Leawe*), 20 messuages and 2 ploughlands in Headington (*Hedyndon*), and the bailiwick of the forests of Shotover (*Shettore*) and Stowood (*Stowode*), OXON., and the manors of Trimworth (*Tremworth Haudlo*), Crundale (*Crundale*), Fenn (*Vanne*), Oare (*Ore*), and Ashenden (*Assheden*), £10 rent in Canterbury (*Cantuar'*), and the advowson of the church of the manor of Crundale, KENT. Right of Eustace, of which Eustace and Geoffrey had the manors of Coln, Hatherop, Wick, Chadlington, Shippenhull, Trimworth, Crundale, and Fenn, and the messuages, land, rent, bailiwick, and advowson (except for 2 messuages and 110 a. of land in the manors of Coln and Wick) by John's gift. For this, grant back and render to John. To hold during his life, the messuage, ploughlands, and bailiwick of the king, the other manors and the rent of the chief lords. And grant to John of the reversion of 2 messuages and 84 a. of land in Coln St. Aldwyn held by Henry Dun for term of life, of 8 a. of land in the manor of Wick held by Robert le Mouner for term of life, of 18 a. of land in the same manor of Wick held by William atte Ford (*Forde*) for term of life, of the manor of Lew held by Richard de Chastillon (*Chastilloun*) for term of life, and of the manors of Oare and Ashenden held by Isabel who was wife of John le FitzNeil (*fitz Nel'*) for term of life, of Eustace's inheritance. To hold during his life of the chief lords. Remainder to John de Haudlo's son Richard and Isabel his wife and to Richard's heirs in tail. Successive contingent remainders to Richard's brother Nicholas and his heirs in tail, to Nicholas's brother Thomas and his heir in tail, and to Thomas's heirs. Made by the king's order as to the messuages, land and bailiwick held in chief, and with the consent of Richard de Chastillon, and he did fealty to John. *Labelled* Glouc', Oxon', Kanc'. [*Worn.*]

286/36/96

569. Morrow [25 June] of St. John the Baptist. Ralph Hammond (*Hamond*) of Dowdeswell (*Doudeswell*) and Matilda his wife quer. by Peter de Edgeworth (*Eggeworth*); John de Banbury (*Bannebury*) and Alice his wife def. Five messuages, 3½ yardlands, 3 a. of meadow, 1 a. of pasture, and 4*s*. rent in Stowell (*Stowell*). Right of Ralph, as those which Ralph and Matilda had by gift of John and Alice. To hold to Ralph and Matilda and Ralph's heirs. (Warranty, by John alone.) Cons. 20 marks. *Endorsed* Emma daughter of William de Swardeston (*Swerdeston*) and Cecily, Emma's sister, put in their claim

77/59/79

570. One week [1 July] from St. John the Baptist. John de Bradley (*Bradelegh*) and Isabel his wife, quer.; John de Westbury def. A messuage, 1 ploughland and 30 a. of land, 12 a. of meadow, 6 a. of pasture, and 12 a. of wood in Bradford-on-Avon (*Bradeford*), WILTS., 2 messuages, 3 gardens, 1 ploughland and 40 a. of land, 14 a. of meadow, 4 a. of wood, 7 marks rent, and half of a mill in Lawrence Weston (*Weston Sancti Laurencii*), Charlton (*Cherletone*), and Redland (*Thridelonde*), GLOS. Right of John de Westbury by gift of John de Bradley and Isabel. For this, grant back and render to John and Isabel.

1331

To hold during their lives. Remainder to John de Bradley's brother Walter and his heirs in tail. Successive contingent remainders to Walter's brother Roger and his heirs in tail, to Roger's brother Thomas and his heirs in tail, and to John de Bradley's heirs. *Labelled* Wiltes', Glouc'.

286/36/99

[Cf. *Wilts. Fines, 1327–77*, p. 31, no. 86.]

571. Morrow [3 Nov.] of All Souls. John Francis (*Frounceys*) of Bristol (*Bristoll'*) the younger and Agnes his wife quer. by the said John; John Francis of Bristol the elder def. A messuage, a toft, and 2 shops in the suburb of Bristol. John the younger acknowledged the right of John the elder by gift of John the younger. For this, grant and render of the messuage and shops to John the younger and Agnes. To hold to them and Agnes's heirs. And grant and render of the toft to John the younger. (Warranty.) *Endorsed* Margery who was wife of Gilbert Francis (*Frounceis*) the younger of Bristol put in her claim.

77/58/62

[Cf. *Bristol Gt. Red Book*, pp. 216–17, no. 125.]

572. Morrow [3 Nov.] of All Souls. Gilbert Francis (*Frounceys*) of Bristol (*Bristoll'*) quer. by John Manship; John Francis of Bristol the elder def. Two messuages in Bristol. Right of Gilbert. Render to him. Cons. 20 marks.

77/58/67

[Cf. *Bristol Gt. Red Book*, pp. 217–18, no. 128.]

573. Morrow [3 Nov.] of All Souls. Ranulph de Beckford (*Beckeford*) quer.; Robert Michel and Margery his wife def. A messuage in Gloucester (*Gloucestr'*) Right of Ranulph. Render to him. (Warranty, specifying Margery's heirs.) Cons. 100*s*.

77/58/70

574. Morrow [12 Nov.] of St. Martin. Thomas de Cannings (*Kanynges*) parson of the church of Tarrant Monkton (*Tarente Monachorum*) quer.; Joan Bigod (*Bygot*) def. A messuage, 1 ploughland, and 3½ a. of meadow in Gotherington (*Goderyngton*) and Bishop's Cleeve (*Clyve Episcopi*). Right of Thomas. Render to him. (Warranty.) Cons. 100 marks. *Endorsed* Joan, Margery, Alice, Elizabeth, and Robergia, coheirs of Odo de Dumbleton (*Dummelton*), put in their claim.

77/58/64

575. Morrow [12 Nov.] of St. Martin. Roger Turtle of Bristol (*Bristoll'*) quer. by John Manship; John Horshale and Matilda his wife def. Rent of 20*s*. in the suburb of Bristol. Right of Roger by gift of John and Matilda. Remise and quitclaim, specifying Matilda's heirs, to Roger. (Warranty.) Cons. 30 marks.

77/58/66

[Cf. *Bristol Gt. Red Book*, p. 217, no. 127.]

576. One week [18 Nov.] from St. Martin. Richard de Hurtesleye and Clemency his wife quer.; Thomas de Whitwick (*Whytewyk*) def. A messuage, 1 ploughland, and 13*s*. rent in Newent (*Newent*). Right of Thomas by gift of Richard and Clemency. For this, grant back

1331

and render to Richard and Clemency. To hold during their lives. Remainder to their son John and his heirs in tail. Successive contingent remainders to John's brother Walter and his heirs in tail and to Richard's heirs.

77/58/63

577. One week [18 Nov.] from St. Martin. William Beauflour of Bristol (*Bristoll'*) quer.; Roger Savekyn and Agnes his wife def. A messuage and a shop in Bristol. Right of William. Render to him. (Warranty, specifying Agnes's heirs.) Cons. 20 marks.

77/58/65

[Cf. *Bristol Gt. Red Book*, p. 217, no. 126.]

578. Two weeks [25 Nov.] from St. Martin. John le Mercer of Worcester (*Wygorn'*) and Agnes his wife quer. by Nicholas Rook in Agnes's place by the king's writ; Richard de Clent clerk def. A messuage, 1 ploughland, 20 a. of meadow, 30 a. of wood, and 65*s.* rent in Powick (*Poywyk*) and Farley (*Farnleye*) by Mathon (*Matheme*), WORCS., and rents of 26*s.* and 1 lb. of pepper in Colesborne (*Colesbourn*), GLOS. John acknowledged the right of Richard by John's gift. For this, grant and render to John and Agnes. To hold to them and their heirs in tail. Successive contingent remainders to Thomas de la Barre and Isabel his wife and their heirs in tail, and to Isabel's heirs. *Labelled* Wygorn', Glouc'.

286/37/109

6 Edward III

1332

579. Two weeks [27 Jan.] from Hilary. (Made two weeks from Michaelmas 5 Edward III [13 Oct. 1331].) Robert de Goldhill (*Goldhull*) and Isabel his wife quer. by Peter de Edgeworth (*Eggerworth*) in Isabel's place by the king's writ; Walter le Mariner (*Marener*) chaplain and John de Putloe (*Puttleye*) chaplain def. Three messuages, a mill, 100 a. of land, 3 a. of meadow, and 1½*d.* rent in Down Hatherley (*Dunhatherleye*) and Churchdown (*Chirchesdon*). Robert acknowledged the right of Walter, as those which Walter and John had by Robert's gift. For this, grant and render to Robert and Isabel. To hold during their lives. Remainder to Edmund son of Roger Turtle of Bristol (*Bristoll'*) and his heirs in tail male. Contingent remainder to Roger Turtle.

77/58/68

580. Two weeks [3 May] from Easter. (Made one month from Easter 4 Edward III [6 May 1330].) John Moryn of Winchcombe (*Wynchecombe*) and Margery his wife quer.; John de Alre and Hawise his wife def. Half of a messuage, 1 ploughland, and 18*d.* rent in Moreton in Marsh (*Moreton Hennemersh*). John Moryn acknowledged the right of Hawise. For this John de Alre and Hawise granted and rendered two thirds of the half to John Moryn and Margery. To hold to them and their heirs in tail, of John de Alre and Hawise and Hawise's heirs, paying a rose a year at St. John the Baptist and doing service to the chief lords. And John and Hawise granted to John and Margery the reversion of the one third of the half, held by Robert Pygace (*Pygaz*) and Joan his wife in Joan's dower, of Hawise's inheritance. To hold as above. (Warranty.) Contingent reversion to John and Hawise and Hawise's heirs.

77/59/83

1332

581. Two weeks [3 May] from Easter. Margery who was wife of John de Chippenham (*Cyppenham*) quer.; Thomas de Evesham clerk def. A messuage and 1 ploughland in Naunton (*Newenton*) by Slaughter (*Sloughtre*). Right of Thomas by Margery's gift. (Warranty.) Cons. £20.

77/59/89

582. Morrow [29 May] of Ascension. Thomas son of Thomas Beaumond of Dorsington (*Dorsyntone*) and Margery his wife quer. by John de Willersey (*Willereseye*) in Margery's place; Thomas Beaumond of Dorsington the elder def. A messuage, 94 a. of land, and 2 a. of meadow in Dorsington. Thomas son of Thomas acknowledged the right of Thomas Beaumond. For this, grant and render to Thomas son of Thomas and Margery. To hold to them and their heirs in tail, of Thomas Beaumond, paying a rose a year at St. John the Baptist and doing service to the chief lords. Contingent reversion to Thomas Beaumond.

77/59/90

583. Morrow [29 May] of Ascension. John Nicol of Pebworth (*Pebbeworth*) quer.; Thomas Beaumond of Dorsington (*Dorsyntone*) the elder def. A messuage, 1 ploughland, 10 a. of meadow, and 6s. 8d. rent in Dorsington. Right of John by Thomas's gift. For this, grant back and render to Thomas. To hold during his life. Remainder to Thomas's son Thomas and his heirs in tail. Contingent remainder to Thomas Beaumond's heirs.

77/59/91

584. One week [21 June] from Trinity. The prior of Bath (*Bathon'*) quer.; Mr. Ellis de St. Albans (*de Sancto Albano*) parson of the church of Wethersfield (*Wetheresfeld*) def. Half of the manor of Tadwick (*Tatewyk*). Right of the prior and his church of the apostles Peter and Paul, Bath. Render to him. To hold of the chief lords by the services due and accustomed and finding two chaplains, one a monk chaplain in the cathedral church of the priory aforesaid and the other a secular chaplain in the parish church of Cold Ashton (*Coldasshton*), to celebrate divine service daily for the souls of the same Ellis and of John de Sodbury (*Sobbury*) clerk and their ancestors and all the faithful departed, also paying 20s. every year on the day of Ellis's anniversary, for celebrating masses for his soul, and 5s. on the same day in a distribution to the poor. (Warranty.) Cons. (paid by the prior to Ellis) 100 marks. Made by the king's order.

77/59/92

[Tadwick was in Somerset. The fine, which is labelled *Gloucestr'*, was filed as a Glos. fine presumably because Cold Ashton is concerned, though less directly.]

585. One week [21 June] from Trinity. (Made two weeks [3 May] from Easter in the said year.) Thomas de Hatherley (*Hatherleye*) and Katherine his wife quer. by William de Tutshill (*Tyddeshull*) in Katherine's place by the king's writ; John le Widow (*Wedewe*) chaplain def. Two messuages, 1 ploughland, 4 a. of meadow, 4 a. of pasture, 1 a. of wood, and 11s. rent in Up Hatherley (*Uphatherleye*) and Great Bentham (*Magna Benetham*). Grant and render to Thomas and Katherine. To hold to them and their heirs in tail. Contingent remainder to Thomas's heirs.

77/59/98

1332

586. Morrow [25 June] of St. John the Baptist. Nicholas de Morton of Tewkesbury (*Teukesbury*) quer. by William Guge in his place by the king's writ; Thomas de Birmingham (*Burmyngham*) of Shropshire (*Salop'*) and Matilda his wife def. Half of a messuage in Tewkesbury. Right of Nicholas by gift of Thomas and Matilda. (Warranty, specifying Matilda's heirs.) Cons. 100*s*.

77/59/93

587. Two weeks [28 June] from Trinity. (Made three weeks [10 May] from Easter in the said year.) John le Butler (*Botiller*) of Llantwit (*Lanultyt*) and Beatrice his wife quer. by Walter Murymouth in Beatrice's place; John de Didbrook (*Dudebrok*) and Joan his wife def. The manors of Park (*Park*) and Brawn (*Bruerne*) and a messuage and 1 ploughland in Murcott (*Morcote*). Right of John le Butler. Remise and quitclaim, specifying Joan's heirs, to John le Butler and Beatrice and John le Butler's heirs. (Warranty.) Cons. 100 marks.

77/59/94

[For Brawn and Murcott cf. above, no. 537.]

588. Two weeks [28 June] from Trinity. (Made three weeks [10 May] from Easter in the said year.) Emery Pauncefoot (*Pauncefot*) quer.; Geoffrey de Stoke and Adam Eseger parson of the church of Hasfield (*Hasfeld*) def. The manor of Hasfield. Right of Geoffrey. For this, Geoffrey and Adam granted to Emery the reversion of the manor held by Clemency who was wife of Grymbald Pauncefoot in dower, of Geoffrey's inheritance. To hold to Emery during his life. Remainder to Emery's son Grymbald and Elena daughter of Alan de Charlton (*Cherleton*) 'chivaler' and the heirs of Grymbald and Elena in tail. Successive contingent remainders to Grymbald's heirs in tail, to Grymbald's brother Hugh and his heirs in tail, and to Emery's heirs. Made in Clemency's presence and with her consent, and she did fealty to Emery.

77/59/95

589. One week [6 Oct.] from Michaelmas. (Made two weeks from Easter, 8 Edward II [6 April 1315].) John de Chester (*Chestr'*) of Broad Campden (*Brodecampeden*) and Agnes his wife quer. by William de Charingworth (*Chaveryngworth*) in Agnes's place by the king's writ (John was dead by the time that the fine was granted and recorded and was replaced by his son and heir Henry); John Alexander (*Alysaundres*) def. A messuage and 2 yardlands in Broad Campden. Right of John Alexander by gift of John de Chester. For this, grant and render to John de Chester and Agnes. To hold to them and their heirs in tail. Contingent remainder to the heirs of John de Chester. (Warranty.) [*Badly worn.*]

77/59/82

590. One week [6 Oct.] from Michaelmas. (Made two weeks [3 May] from Easter in the said year.) Roger Turtle of Bristol (*Bristoll'*) quer.; John de Cardiff (*Kerdyf*) the elder def. A messuage and £8 rent in Bristol and the suburb of the same town. Right of Roger. Render to him of the rent and one eighth of the messuage. And grant to him of the reversion of seven eighths of the messuage held by Thomas Belcher (*Belecher*) and Cristina his wife for term of life, of John's inheritance. (Warranty.) Cons. 100 marks.

77/59/97

[Cf. *Bristol Gt. Red Book*, p. 218, no. 129.]

1332

591. One week [6 Oct.] from Michaelmas. (Made one week from St. John the Baptist 4 Edward III [1 July 1330].) William de Whittington (*Whityngton*) 'chivaler' quer.; Reynold de Abenhall (*Abehale*) def. The manors of Sollers Hope (*Hopsolers*) and Hopton Sollers (*Hopton*), HEREFS., and the manor of Pauntley (*Paunteleye*), GLOS. Right of Reynold, of which he had two thirds of the manors of Sollers Hope and Pauntley by gift of William. For this, grant back and render to William. To hold during his life. And grant to William of the reversion of the manor of Hopton Sollers held by Juliana who was wife of Thomas de Sollers (*Solers*) for term of life and of one third of the manors of Sollers Hope and Pauntley held by the said Juliana in dower, of Reynold's inheritance. To hold as above. Remainder to William's son William and Joan daughter of William son of William Maunsell (*Maunsel*) and the heirs of William son of William [de Whittington]. *Labelled* Hereford', Glouc'.

286/37/122

[Joan was presumably the intended wife of William de Whittington's son William, whose heirs, rather than those of William son of William Maunsell, were presumably to have the remainder.]

592. Two weeks [13 Oct.] from Michaelmas. William son of John de Heyford and of his wife Joan quer.; John de Heyford and Joan his wife def. A messuage and 5 yardlands in Radbrook (*Rodbrok*). Right of William. Render to him. (Warranty, specifying Joan's heirs.) Cons. 20 marks.

77/59/85

[That the first mention of Joan is as William's mother is clear, her name being in the genitive not the accusative case; it is unusual but was made evidently because the holding was of her inheritance.]

593. Two weeks [13 Oct.] from Michaelmas. (Made two weeks from St. John the Baptist 3 Edward III [8 July 1329].) James le Butler (*Botiller*) earl of Ormond (*Dormound*) and Eleanor his wife quer.; James Lawless (*Laules*) def. The manor of Withington (*Wytheton*), LANCS., the manors of Shere (*Shire*) and the Vachery (*La Vacherie*) and the advowson of the church of the manor of Shere, SURREY, the manors of Great Linford (*Lynford*), Twyford (*Twyford*), and Aylesbury (*Ayllesbury*) and the advowson of the church of the manor of Linford, BUCKS., the manor of Smeetham (*Smytheton*) and the advowson of the chapel of East Tilbury (*Est Tillebury*), ESSEX, the manor of Finborough (*Fynebergh*), SUFF., the manor of Cold Ashton (*Coldaston*), GLOS., the manor of Long Compton (*Cumpton in Hennemersh*), WARWS., the manors of Rotherfield Peppard (*Retherfeld Pippard*) and Fritwell (*Fretewell*) and the advowson of the church of the manor of Rotherfield Peppard, OXON., the manor of Sopley (*Sopele*), HANTS., and the manors of Belluton (*Belveton*) and Brean (*Brene*), SOM. The earl acknowledged the right of James Lawless, of which he had the manors of Withington, Shere, the Vachery, Linford, and Twyford and the advowsons of the churches of Shere and Linford and of the chapel of East Tilbury by the earl's gift. For this, grant and render to the earl and Eleanor. To hold to them and their heirs in tail. And grant to them of the reversion of the manor of Aylesbury held by Robert de Montalt (*Monte Alto*) and Emma his wife in Emma's dower, of the manors of Smeetham and Finborough held by Edmund le Butler for term of life, of the manors of Cold Ashton, Long Compton, and Rotherfield Peppard and of the advowson of the church of Rotherfield Peppard held by John

1332

Peppard (*Pippard*) for term of life, of the manor of Fritwell held by John de Alneton for term of life, of the manor of Sopley held by Thomas West for term of life, and of the manors of Belluton and Brean held by Cecily de la Hay (*Haye*) for term of life, of James's inheritance. To hold as above. Contingent remainder to the earl's heirs. Made in the presence of Edmund, John Peppard, John de Alneton, Thomas, and Cecily and with their consent, and they did fealty to the earl and Eleanor. *Labelled* Lanc', Buk', Suff', Warr', Sutht', Surr', Essex', Glouc', Oxon', Somers'. [*Worn*.]

286/37/124

[Cf. *Essex Fines, 1327–1422*, pp. 27–8; *Som. Fines, 1307–46*, p. 241; *Warws. Fines, 1284–1345*, pp. 151–2, no. 1740.]

594. Three weeks [20 Oct.] from Michaelmas. John le Usher (*Ussher*) and Alice his wife quer.; John de Dean (*Dene*) def. Two messuages in Mitcheldean (*Magna Dene*). Right of John de Dean by gift of John le Usher and Alice. For this, grant back and render to John le Usher and Alice. To hold to them and John le Usher's heirs.

77/59/86

595. One month [27 Oct.] from Michaelmas. (Made one week [1 July] from St. John the Baptist in the said year.) William de Kingscote (*Kyngescote*) and Mathea his wife quer. by Robert de Saul (*Salle*) in Mathea's place by the king's writ; Robert le Cornwalsh parson of the church of Uley (*Iweley*) def. The manor of Kingscote (*Kynggescote*). William acknowledged the right of Robert by William's gift. For this, grant and render to William and Mathea. To hold to them and their heirs in tail. Contingent remainder to William's heirs.

77/59/87

596. One month [27 Oct.] from Michaelmas. (Made two weeks [8 July] from St. John the Baptist in the said year.) Walter Bellamy (*Belamy*) and Gunnilda his wife quer. by John Winstone (*Wynstan*) in Gunnilda's place; Richard son of Nicholas atte Grove of North Nibley (*Nubbeleye*) def. A messuage, 59 a. of land, and 1 a. of meadow in Wotton under Edge (*Wotton*) by Kingswood (*Kyngeswode*) and Nibley. Right of Walter, as those which Walter and Gunnilda had by Richard's gift. To hold to Walter and Gunnilda and Walter's heirs. (Warranty.) Cons. 100 marks.

77/59/88

597. Morrow [12 Nov.] of St. Martin. (Made two weeks [13 Oct.] from Michaelmas in the said year.) Theobald Russel and Thomas his son quer. by William de Bery, Thomas's guardian; Walter Waleys def. A toft and 4 yardlands in Dyrham (*Durham*). Theobald acknowledged the right of Walter. For this, grant and render to Thomas of the toft and 2 yardlands. To hold to Thomas during his life. And grant to Thomas of the reversion of the following portions of land in the remaining 2 yardlands: 11 a. held by John le Bedel, 20 a. held by Roger de Dyrham (*Derham*), 10 a. held by William Cope, 4½ a. held by Nicholas le Tailor (*Taillour*), and 34 a. held by John Borard, all for term of life, of Walter's inheritance. To hold as above. Remainder to Theobald and his heirs. [*Worn*.]

77/59/84

[The fine was granted and recorded in the same term as that in which it was made.]

1333

598. One week [20 Jan.] from Hilary. (Made one week from Michaelmas in the said year [6 Oct. 1332].) William de Syde quer. by John de Winstone (*Wynston*); William Sewyn and Alice his wife def. Two messuages, 70 a. of land, 3 a. of meadow, and 10*s.* rent in Badgeworth (*Beggeworthe*), Great Bentham (*Magna Benetham*), and Shurdington (*Shurdynton*). Right of William de Syde. Remise and quitclaim, specifying Alice's heirs, to him. (Warranty.) Cons. £40.

77/59/96

[Cf. *Berkeley Castle Mun.* i, p. 436, A2/13/2 (counterpart).]

599. One week [20 Jan.] from Hilary. (Made one week from Michaelmas in the said year [6 Oct. 1332].) William le Archer quer.; Nicholas le Archer def. A messuage and ¾ yardland in *Lavynsaid*. Grant and render to William. To hold to him and his heirs in tail, of Nicholas, paying a rose a year at St. John the Baptist and doing service to the chief lords. Contingent remainder to William's brother Thomas and his heirs in tail. Contingent reversion to Nicholas. Cons. 10 marks.

77/59/99

[The lower part of the last four (or five) letters of *Lavynsaid* have been removed by the filing hole. The *s* is clearly not *f*, the *a* is fairly certain, and the top of the *d* is clear; there may be another letter after it. The document is labelled *Glouc'*.]

7 Edward III

1333

600. Two weeks [27 Jan.] from Hilary. (Made two weeks from Michaelmas 6 Edward III [13 Oct. 1332].) Robert le Franklin (*Fraunkelayn*) of Meysey Hampton (*Hampton Meysy*) and Matilda his wife quer.; William le Knight (*Knyght*) of Meysey Hampton def. A messuage, 2 a. of meadow, and a quarter of 1 yardland in Meysey Hampton. Right of William by Robert's gift. For this, grant and render to Robert and Matilda. To hold to Robert and Matilda and their heirs in tail. Contingent remainder to Robert's heirs. *At the foot* Egreworth.

77/60/101

[The name at the foot, which is small and faint, is presumably a personal surname.]

601. Two weeks [27 Jan.] from Hilary. (Made the morrow of St. Martin 6 Edward III [12 Nov. 1332].) Edmund du Cellar (*Celer*) of Bristol (*Bristoll'*) and Lucy his wife quer.; Thomas de Lydiard (*Lydyard*) and Alice his wife def. Three messuages in Gloucester (*Gloucestr'*). Right of Edmund, of which Edmund and Lucy had one messuage by gift of Thomas and Alice. To hold to Edmund and Lucy and Edmund's heirs. And grant to them of the reversion of a messuage held by John le Glasswright (*Glasewrighte*) of Gloucester for term of life and of a messuage held by Richard Pope 'fisshere' and William his son for term of life, of Alice's inheritance. To hold as above. (Warranty.) Cons. 20 marks. [*Worn.*]

77/60/103

602. Morrow [3 Feb.] of the Purification. (Made one week from St. Martin, 6 Edward III [18 Nov. 1332].) Robert de Gloucester (*Gloucestr'*) and Amice his wife quer.; William Toyt def. Half of the manor of Alkerton (*Alcrynton*). Robert acknowledged the right of William by Robert's gift. For this, grant and render to Robert and Amice. To hold to them and their heirs in tail. Successive contingent remainders to Robert's brother John

1333

and his heirs in tail, to John's brother Roger and his heirs in tail, to John de Breadstone (*Bradeston*) and Cristina his wife and their heirs in tail, and to John de Breadstone's heirs.

77/59/100

603. One week [6 June] from Trinity. (Made the morrow [14 May] of Ascension in the said year.) Roger Norman (*Normaund*) of Southampton (*Suthampton*) quer.; Hugh Sampson and William Loveraz def. Two messuages, 3 ploughlands, 30 a. of meadow, 20 a. of wood, and 6s. 6d. rent in Kemble (*Kemele*), Morley (*Morlegh*), and Malmesbury (*Malmesbury*), WILTS., and 7 messuages, 3½ yardlands, and 2s. rent in Arlington (*Alurynton*) by Bibury (*Bibury*) and half and one fifth of half of the manor of Arlington, GLOS. Right of Hugh, of which Hugh and William had the holdings in Arlington by Roger's gift. For this, grant back and render to Roger. To hold during his life. And grant to Roger of the reversion of the half and one fifth of half held by Alice who was wife of John de Pembridge (*Penbrigg*) in dower and of the holdings in Wilts. held by Geoffrey de Morley (*Mourle*) for term of life, of Hugh's inheritance. To hold as above. Remainder to Roger's son Roger and his heirs in tail. Contingent remainder to Roger Norman's heirs. *Labelled* Wiltes', Glouc'.

286/37/137

[Cf. *Wilts. Fines, 1327–77*, pp. 39–40, no. 127.]

604. Morrow [25 June] of St. John the Baptist. (Made one month [2 May] from Easter in the said year.) Nicholas de Stoke Edith (*Edithestoke*) quer.; Stephen de Grandene of Gloucester (*Gloucestr'*) and Elena his wife def. A messuage in Gloucester. Right of Nicholas by gift of Stephen and Elena. (Warranty, specifying Elena's heirs.) Cons. 100s.

77/60/105

605. Two weeks [8 July] from St. John the Baptist. John Daubeney (*de Albiniaco*) and Cecily his wife quer.; Ellis de Godley (*Godeleye*) def. The manor of Kingsholm (*Kyngeshome*) by Gloucester (*Gloucestr'*). John acknowledged the right of Ellis by John's gift. For this, grant and render to John and Cecily. To hold to them and their heirs in tail, of the king. Contingent remainder to John's heirs. Made by the king's order.

77/60/112

606. York. One week [6 Oct.] from Michaelmas. (Made Westminster, one week [6 June] from Trinity in the said year.) Richard de Aston quer. by John de Winstone (*Wynston*); John de Shobdon (*Shobedon*) 'pestour' [*i.e. baker*] and Cristina his wife def. A messuage in Gloucester (*Gloucestre*). Right of Richard. Remise and quitclaim, specifying Cristina's heirs, to him. (Warranty.) Cons. 100s.

77/60/104

607. York. Two weeks [13 Oct.] from Michaelmas. (Made Westminster, two weeks [13 June] from Trinity in the said year.) Gilbert de Alne and Elizabeth his wife quer. by William de Christchurch (*Cristechirche*) in Elizabeth's place; Richard de Lypiatt (*Lupyate*) def. Twelve messuages, 2½ ploughlands, 50 a. of meadow, and 20 a. of wood in Elmington (*Almynton*) and Rodmarton (*Rodemerton*). Right of Richard by Gilbert's

1333

gift. For this, grant and render to Gilbert and Elizabeth. To hold during their lives. Remainder as to 3 messuages, 1½ ploughlands, and the meadow and wood in Elmington to Gilbert's son Drew (*Drogo*) and his heirs in tail. Contingent remainder to Gilbert's heirs. Remainder as to the residue, sc. 9 messuages and 1 ploughland in Rodmarton, to Gilbert's sons Edmund and John during their lives and to Gilbert's heirs. [*Worn.*]

77/60/107

[The upper part of the first two letters of *Lupyate* have been lost to the filing hole. What remains of the first letter is not very convincing as *L* and might be *E, G,* or *W.*]

608. York. Two weeks [13 Oct.] from Michaelmas. (Made Westminster, two weeks [8 July] from St. John the Baptist in the said year.) Reynold de Abenhall (*Abbehale*) 'chivaler' and Joan his wife and Hugh son of the same Reynold quer. by John Durrant (*Durant*) in Joan's place and by the same John as Hugh's guardian; John le Marshal (*Mareschal*) parson of the church of Blaisdon (*Blechedon*) def. A messuage, 60 a. of land, and 6*s.* rent in Blaisdon. Reynold acknowledged the right of John by Reynold's gift. For this, grant and render to Reynold and Joan. To hold during their lives. Remainder to Hugh during his life and to Reynold's heirs.

77/60/110

609. York. Two weeks [13 Oct.] from Michaelmas. (Made Westminster, two weeks [13 June] from Trinity in the said year.) Richard de Stonehouse (*Stonhouse*) and Agnes his wife quer. by John de Winstone (*Wynston*) in Agnes's place; John le Widow (*Wedewe*) def. A messuage in Cirencester (*Cyrencestre*). Richard acknowledged the right of John by Richard's gift. For this, grant and render to Richard and Agnes. To hold to them and their heirs in tail. Contingent remainder to Richard's heirs.

77/60/111

610. York. One month [27 Oct.] from Michaelmas. William Atworth (*atte Vorde*) quer.; John son of Ellis Brown (*Broun*) of Bristol (*Bristoll'*) imp. A messuage in Bristol. (Warranty of charter.) Right of William. Remise and quitclaim to him. (Warranty.) Cons. 100*s.*

77/60/102

[Cf. *Bristol Gt. Red Book*, p. 218, no. 130.]

611. York. One month [27 Oct.] from Michaelmas. (Made Westminster, two weeks [8 July] from St. John the Baptist in the said year.) Reynold de Abenhall (*Abbehale*) 'civaler' [*sic*] and Joan his wife and Reynold son of the same Reynold quer. by John Durrant (*Durant*) in Joan's place and by the same John as guardian of Reynold son of Reynold; John le Marshal (*Mareschal*) parson of the church of Blaisdon (*Blechedon*) def. A messuage, a mill, 1 ploughland, 4 a. of meadow, 30 a. of wood, and 6 marks rent in Blaisdon and the advowson of half of the church of Blaisdon. Reynold de Abenhall acknowledged the right of John by Reynold de Abenhall's gift. For this, grant and render to Reynold de Abenhall and Joan. To hold during their lives. Remainder to Reynold son of Reynold and John his brother during their lives and to Reynold de Abenhall's heirs.

77/60/108

1333

612. York. One month [27 Oct.] from Michaelmas. (Made Westminster, two weeks [8 July] from St. John the Baptist in the said year.) Reynold de Abenhall (*Abbehale*) 'chivaler' and Joan his wife and Reynold son of the same Reynold quer. by John Durrant (*Durant*) in Joan's place and by the same John as guardian of Reynold son of Reynold; John le Marshal (*Mareschal*) parson of the church of Blaisdon (*Blechedon*) def. A messuage, a mill, 1 ploughland, 4 a. of meadow, 30 a. of wood, and 6 marks rent in Blaisdon and the advowson of half of the church of Blaisdon. Reynold de Abenhall acknowledged the right of John by Reynold de Abenhall's gift. For this, grant and render to Reynold de Abenhall and Joan. To hold during their lives. Remainder to Reynold son of Reynold and John his brother during their lives and to Reynold de Abenhall's heirs. [*Worn.*]

77/60/109

[Nos. 611 and 612 are virtual duplicates. Both are clearly feet of fines, not indentures. It is not clear whether they represent a single transaction or separate transactions relating to two exactly equal halves of an estate. The most substantial difference is that one has 'civaler' instead of 'chivaler; otherwise the only difference in wording is that no. 611 uses slightly more abbreviation than no. 612, e.g. a slapdash for the final *m* of *idem* and *cum*.]

613. York. Morrow [3 Nov.] of All Souls. (Made Westminster, two weeks [8 July] from St. John the Baptist in the said year.) The bailiffs and community of Gloucester (*Gloucestr'*) quer. by John de Winstone (*Wynston*); William Trenchant (*Trenchaunt*) of Alton (*Aulton*) and Alice his wife and Richard Channon (*Chaunyn*) and Margery his wife def. Rent of 100*s*. in Gloucester. Right of the community. Remise and quitclaim, specifying Alice's and Margery's heirs, to the bailiffs and community. Cons. 100 marks.

77/60/106

8 Edward III

1334

614. York. Two weeks [10 April] from Easter. (Made there the morrow of All Souls 7 Edward III [3 Nov. 1333].) Hugh Mustel and Isabel his wife quer. by Richard de Clent in Isabel's place by the king's writ; John son of Thomas le Butler (*Botiller*) 'chivaler' def. A messuage, a shop, 1 ploughland and 10 a. of land, 16 a. of meadow, 9 a. of pasture, 20 a. of wood, and 51*s*. 1*d*. rent in Habberley (*Haberleye*), Kidderminster (*Kyderminister*), and Puxton (*Pokelston*), WORCS., and 4 messuages, a mill, 5 ploughlands, 20 a. of meadow, 4 a. of pasture, 20 a. of wood, and 110s. rent in Boddington (*Botynton*), Guiting Power (*Gutynge Parva*), and Hardwicke (*Herdewyk*), GLOS. Hugh acknowledged the right of John, of which he had a messuage, 1 ploughland, 4 a. of meadow, and 2*s*. rent in Hardwicke and two thirds of all the other holdings by gift of Hugh and Isabel. For this, grant back and render to Hugh and Isabel. To hold to them and their heirs in tail. And grant to them of the reversion of the one third of the 4 messuages, the shop, the mill, 5 ploughlands and 10 a. of land, 32 a. of meadow, 13 a. of pasture, 40 a. of wood, 161*s*. 1*d*. rent [*sic, recte* 159*s*. 1*d*. rent?] held by John de la Mare of Rendcomb (*Ryndecombe*) and Anne his wife in Anne's dower in Habberley, Kidderminster, Puxton, Boddington, and Guiting Power. To hold as above. Contingent remainder to Hugh's heirs. *Labelled* Wygorn', Glouc'. [*Worn.*] *Endorsed* William de Homme of Stoke Orchard (*Stoke Archer*) put in his claim.

286/38/152

1334

615. York. Two weeks [10 April] from Easter. Elizabeth de Burgh (*de Burgo*) quer.; Thomas de Chedworth (*Chedeworth*) clerk and Henry de Collingham (*Colyngham*) def. The manor of Bardfield (*Berdefeld*), ESSEX, the advowson of the priory of Anglesey (*Angleseye*), CAMBS., and the castles of Usk (*Usk*) and Caerleon (*Kaerlyon*), the manors of Usk, Caerleon, Liswerry (*Lyswyry*), Tintern Parva (*Tynterne Parva*), New Grange (*Nova Grangia*), Little Llantrisant (*Parva Lantrissan*), Trelleck (*Trillek*), Mitchel Troy (*Troye*), Llangwm (*Lancom*), and Undy (*Woundy*), and the advowsons of the abbey of Caerleon, the priories of Usk and Anglesey, the hospital of Usk, the churches of Tredunnock (*Tredenagh'*), Llansoy (*Landisseye*), Mitchel Troy, Llangybi (*Tregruk'*), Panteg (*Pentek'*), Kemeys (*Kemmeys*), and Llandegveth (*Landegewyth'*), and the chapel of Cwmcarvan (*Concarvan'*). Right of Thomas and Henry by Elizabeth's gift. For this, grant back and render to Elizabeth. To hold during her life, of the king. Remainder to Henry de Ferrers (*de Ferariis*) and Isabel his wife and their heirs in tail. Contingent remainder to Elizabeth's heirs. Made by the king's order. *Labelled* Essex', Cantebr', Glouc'.

286/38/153

[Cf. *Essex Fines, 1327–1422*, p. 34. The fine is labelled for Gloucestershire because of the places named that are in Monmouthshire. Cf. above, nos. 411, 527. Anglesey priory is named twice, evidently in error.]

616. York. One week [29 May] from Trinity (Made Westminster, one week from St. Martin 4 Edward III [18 Nov. 1330].) Mr. Simon de Bittiscombe (*Bitlescombe*) quer.; Richard le Blunt (*Blount*) 'chivaler' and Aline his wife def. A messuage, 1 ploughland, 10 a. of meadow, 10 a. of pasture, 60 a. of wood, and 30*s*. rent in Cromhall (*Cromhale*). Right of Richard, of which Richard and Aline had the messuage, land, meadow, pasture, wood and 19*s*. 4*d*. rent by Mr. Simon's gift. And grant to Richard and Aline of 10*s*. 8*d*. rent with the homage and all services of the abbot of St. Augustine's of Bristol (*Bristoll'*) and of William de Walton (*Wauton*), William atte Hay, Richard Colwich (*Colewych*), and John de Berkeley (*Berkele*) 'chivaler' from all the holdings which they held of Mr. Simon in the said township. To hold to Richard and Aline and Richard's heirs. For this, grant to Mr. Simon of the said messuage, land, meadow, pasture, wood, and 19*s*. 4*d*. rent, to hold during his life, of Richard and Aline and Richard's heirs, paying a rose a year at St. John the Baptist and doing service to the chief lords. Reversion to Richard and Aline and Richard's heirs. [*Worn.*]

77/58/57

617. York. One week [29 May] from Trinity. Richard de Aston quer.; William Laurence and Olive his wife def. A messuage in the suburb of Gloucester (*Gloucestr'*). Right of Richard. Render to him. (Warranty, specifying Olive's heirs.) Cons. 10 marks.

77/60/115

618. York. Three weeks [20 Oct.] from Michaelmas. (Made there one week [1 July] from St. John the Baptist in the said year.) Thomas atte Cross (*Croys*) and Rose his wife quer.; Adam de Campden (*Caumpeden*) chaplain def. Five messuages, 2 shops, 1 yardland, 5 a. of meadow, and 8*s*. rent in [. . .] Campden. Right of Adam [. . .] by gift of Thomas and Rose. For this, grant back and render to Thomas and Rose. To hold during their lives. And grant to them of the reversion of [. . .] held by Robert de Han[. . .] for term of life, of

1334

a messuage held by Nicholas le Ma[. . .], of [. . .] held by William de Farndon for term of life, of a shop held by Thomas Colin (*Colyn*) for term of life, and of [. . .] held by Richard le Tailor (*Taillour*) for term of life, of Adam's inheritance. To hold as above. Remainder to Robert son of the same Thomas atte Cross and Joan his wife and Robert's heirs in tail. Contingent remainder to Rose's heirs. [*Badly worn and stained.*]

77/60/113

619. One month from the day [*date of grant and record largely illegible*]. (Made York, one week [1 July] from St. John the Baptist in the said year.) William Pygace and Alice his wife quer.; Philip de Betrich of Gotherington (*Goderynton*) def. Two messuages, 24 a. of land, and 1 a. of meadow in Gotherington. Right of Philip, as to a messuage and the land and meadow by gift of William and Alice. For this, grant back and render of that messuage and the land and meadow to William and Alice. To hold during Alice's life. And grant to William and Alice of the reversion of a messuage held by Matilda Whetherherde for term of life, of Philip's inheritance. To hold as above. Remainder of a third, except for 4 a. of land, to William son of Adam Barron (*Baroun*), during his life, of another third to Alice's daughter Juliana during her life, and of the last third to Thomas son of William Foxcote during his life, and to Alice's heirs. [*Badly worn.*]

77/60/114

[Parts of this fine are illegible even under ultra-violet light, and the abstract offered above is uncertain with respect to the remainders.]

9 Edward III

1335

620. York. Two weeks [27 Jan.] from Hilary. Cecily who was wife of William le Roper (*Ropare*) of Bristol (*Bristoll'*) quer.; Henry de Berkeley (*Berkele*) and Joan his wife def. Two shops in Bristol. Right of Cecily. Remise and quitclaim, specifying Joan's heirs, to her. (Warranty.) Cons. 10 marks.

77/60/119

[Cf. *Bristol Gt. Red Book*, p. 219, no. 132.]

621. York. Two weeks [27 Jan.] from Hilary. Robert Grundy and Agnes his wife quer.; John Tynte and Isabel his wife def. A messuage and 2½ a. of land in Ham (*Hamme*) by Berkeley (*Berkeley*). Right of Robert, as those which Robert and Agnes had by gift of John and Isabel. Remise and quitclaim, specifying Isabel's heirs, to Robert and Agnes and Robert's heirs. (Warranty.) Cons. 20 marks.

77/60/123

622. York. Morrow [3 Feb.] of the Purification. (Made there one week from St. Martin 8 Edward III [18 Nov. 1334].) John de Stonor (*Stonore*) quer.; Henry de Harnhill (*Harnhull*) 'chivaler' def. The manor of Condicote (*Cundicote*) and 24 messuages, 3 ploughlands and 260 a. of land, 60 a. of meadow, 20 a. of pasture, 100 a. of wood, and 40s. rent in Doughton (*Doughton*), Tetbury (*Tettebury*), and Henbury (*Hembury in Salso Marisco*) and the advowson of the church of the same manor of Condicote. Right of Henry by John's gift. For this, grant back and render to John. To hold during his life. Remainder to John's sons John, Thomas, William, and Adam and to the heirs in tail male

1335

of John son of John. Successive contingent remainders to the heirs in tail male of John de Stonor, to his heirs in tail, and to his right heirs. [*Worn and stained.*]

77/60/124

[John de Stonor's four sons were presumably to hold jointly during their lives, but the wording of the fine is not explicit.]

623. York. Two weeks [30 April] from Easter. Alexander le Hatter (*Hattare*) clerk quer.; Margaret who was wife of William de Pedmore (*Pedemore*) 'orfevre' [*i.e.* goldsmith] def. A messuage in Gloucester (*Gloucestre*). Right of Alexander by Margaret's gift. For this, grant back and render to Margaret. To hold during her life, of Alexander, paying a rose a year at St. John the Baptist and doing service to the chief lords. Reversion to Alexander.

77/60/117

624. York. One week [18 June] from Trinity. (Made there two weeks [30 April] from Easter in the said year.) John de Marcle of Gloucester (*Gloucestr'*) quer.; Andrew de Pendock (*Pendok*) of Gloucester. def. Two messuages in Gloucester. Right of John, of which John had one messuage by Andrew's gift. And grant to John of the reversion of the other messuage, held by William Crisp 'webbe' [*i.e. weaver*] and Agnes his wife for term of life, of Andrew's inheritance. (Warranty.) Cons. 20 marks.

77/60/116

625. York. Two weeks [25 June] from Trinity. (Made there three weeks [7 May] from Easter in the said year.) Robert de Wrington (*Wryngton*) quer.; Gilbert Pokerel and Isabel his wife def. A toft in the suburb of Bristol (*Bristoll'*). Right of Robert by gift of Gilbert and Isabel. (Warranty, specifying Isabel's heirs.) Cons. 100*s.*

77/60/118

[Cf. *Bristol Gt. Red Book*, p. 219, no. 131.]

626. York. Morrow [25 June] of St. John the Baptist. (Made there one month [14 May] from Easter in the said year.) Andrew le Walsh (*Walshe*) and Isabel his wife quer.; Thomas de Berkeley (*Berkeleye*) of Coberley (*Cubberleye*) def. Six messuages, a toft, 4 ploughlands, 32 a. of meadow, and 14*s.* 1*d.* rent in Woolstrop (*Wolvesthrop*) and Hempsted (*Heghamstud*). Andrew acknowledged the right of Thomas by Andrew's gift. For this, grant and render to Andrew and Isabel. To hold to them and their heirs in tail. Contingent remainder to Andrew's heirs.

77/60/125

627. York. One week [6 Oct.] from Michaelmas. John Capel the elder quer.; Thomas de Wick (*Wyke*) and Thomas Allen (*Aleyn*) def. A messuage, 80 a. of land, 5 a. of meadow, and 2 a. of pasture in Ham (*Hamme*) and Alkington (*Alkynton*). Right of Thomas de Wick, as those which Thomas de Wick and Thomas Allen had by John's gift. For this, grant back and render to John. To hold during his life. Remainder to John's son John and Joan his wife and their heirs in tail. Contingent remainder to the heirs of John Capel.

77/60/121

1335

628. York. Two weeks [13 Oct.] from Michaelmas. (Made there the morrow [26 May] of Ascension in the said year.) Richard Gatwick (*Gatewyk*) of Broad Marston (*Brodemerston*) quer.; Walter Beaumont of Broad Marston def. One yardland in Broad Marston held by Henry Beaumont for term of life. Right of Richard. Grant to him of the reversion, of Walter's inheritance. (Warranty.) Cons. 100*s*. Made in Henry's presence and with his consent, and he did fealty to Richard.

77/60/120

629. York. One month [27 Oct.] from Michaelmas. (Made there two weeks [8 July] from St. John the Baptist in the said year.) Richard de Hangleton (*Hangelton*) and Alice his wife quer.; John de Winstone (*Wynston*) def. A messuage, a garden, 300 a. of land, 100 a. of meadow, 20 a. of wood, and 13 marks rent in Wightfield (*Wyghtfeld*) and Apperley (*Apperle*). Right of John by Alice's gift. For this, grant and render to Richard and Alice. To hold during their lives. Remainder to James son of John de Helion (*Helyoun*) and his heirs in tail. Contingent remainder to Alice's heirs. *Endorsed* Walter de Helion put in his claim. [*Badly worn.*]

77/60/122

1336

630. York. One week [20 Jan.] from Hilary. (Made there two weeks from St. Martin in the said year [25 Nov. 1335].) William Curtis (*Curteys*) of Wotton (*Wotton*) and Agnes his wife quer.; Thomas de Elberton (*Aylberton*) chaplain and William le Bowyer (*Bowyare*) of Wotton chaplain def. Two messuages and 2 yardlands in Elberton and Alveston (*Aleweston*) by Thornbury (*Thornbury*). Right of Thomas as those which Thomas and William le Bowyer had by gift of William Curtis and Agnes. For this, grant back and render to William Curtis and Agnes. To hold to them and their heirs in tail. Contingent remainder to William Curtis's heirs.

77/61/126

10 Edward III

1336

631. York. Two weeks [9 June] from Trinity. (Made there two weeks [14 April] from Easter in the said year. William le Salter (*Saltare*) and Agnes his wife quer.; Walter le Mariner (*Maryner*) parson of the church of St. John within the north gate of Gloucester (*Gloucestr'*) and John de Putloe (*Putteleye*) chaplain def. Eight acres of land, 1½ a. of meadow, and one third of a messuage in Wotton (*Wotton*) by Gloucester. Right of Walter, as those which Walter and John had by gift of William and Agnes. For this, grant back and render to William and Agnes. To hold to them and William's heirs.

77/61/133

632. York. Morrow [25 June] of St. John the Baptist. (Made there one month [28 April] from Easter in the said year.) William de Bentham (*Benetham*) and Agnes his wife quer.; Agnes de la Chamber (*Chaumbre*) def. A messuage, a mill, 4½ yardlands, 4 a. of meadow, 63 a. of wood, and 13*s*. 4*d*. rent in Badgeworth (*Beggeworth*) and Brockworth (*Brokworth*). Right of Agnes de la Chamber. For this, grant and render to William and

1336

Agnes his wife. To hold during their lives. Remainder to their son Thomas and his heirs in tail male. Successive contingent remainders to Thomas's brother William and his heirs in tail male, to William's brother Richard and his heirs in tail male, to Richard's brother Robert and his heirs in tail male, and to William de Bentham's heirs. [*Worn.*]

77/61/132

633. York. Two weeks [9 June] from Trinity. (Made there three weeks [21 April] from Easter in the said year.) John son of Maurice de Weston of Cirencester (*Cyrencestre*) and Margery his wife quer.; Richard Laurence and Avice his wife def. A messuage in Cirencester. Right of John. Remise and quitclaim, specifying Avice's heirs, to John and Margery and John's heirs. (Warranty.) Cons. 100*s*.

77/61/131

634. York. Two weeks [9 June] from Trinity. (Made there three weeks [21 April] from Easter in the said year.) John Athelam of Tewkesbury (*Teukesbury*) and Joan his wife quer.; Robert atte Wood (*Wode*) of Tewkesbury and Alice his wife def. A messuage in Tewkesbury. Right of John, as that which John and Joan had by gift of Robert and Alice. To hold to John and Joan and John's heirs. (Warranty, specifying Alice's heirs.) Cons. 20 marks.

77/61/134

635. York. Two weeks [9 June] from Trinity. John de Horncastle (*Horncastel*) of Bristol (*Bristoll'*) 'vyneter' [*i.e.* vintner] quer.; Richard Estmere of Bristol and Agnes his wife def. Half of a messuage in Bristol. Right of John. Render to him. (Warranty, specifying Agnes's heirs.) Cons. 100*s*.

77/61/135

[Cf. *Bristol Gt. Red Book*, p. 219, no. 133.]

636. York. Two weeks [13 Oct.] from Michaelmas. (Made there two weeks [9 June] from Trinity in the said year.) Henry de Aston quer.; Henry Wyville and Katherine his wife def. Two messuages and 6 yardlands in *Coldaston* [Cold Ashton or Aston Blank]. Grant, remise, and quitclaim to Henry de Aston of whatever Henry Wyville and Katherine had in the holdings for term of Katherine's life. Cons. 20 marks.

77/61/130

637. York. Three weeks [20 Oct.] from Michaelmas. (Made there the morrow [3 Feb.] of the Purification in the said year.) William de Eynsford (*Eynesford*) 'chivaler' quer.; Roger de Burghill (*Burghhull*) def. Thirteen messuages, 132 a. of land, and 50*s*. rent in Westbury on Severn (*Westbury*), held by William de Stinchcombe (*Styntescombe*) for term of life. Right of William de Eynsford. Grant to him of the reversion, of Roger's inheritance. (Warranty.) Cons. 100 marks. Made in William de Stinchcombe's presence and with his consent, and he did fealty to William de Eynsford.

77/61/129

[William de Eynsford's surname occurs elsewhere as Eylsford: cf. e.g. *V.C.H. Glos*. x. 87.]

1336

638. York. Morrow [12 Nov.] of St. Martin. (Made there two weeks [13 Oct.] from Michaelmas in the said year.) Thomas de Seymour (*de Sancto Mauro*) 'chivaler' quer.; Henry Wyville (*Wyvill*) and Katherine his wife def. Two messuages, 75 a. of land, and 4*s*. rent in Up Ampney (*Upameneye*). Grant, remise, and quitclaim to Thomas. Cons. 100 marks.

77/61/127

[The fine was granted and recorded in the same term as that in which it was made. Up Ampney is either Ampney Crucis or Ampney St. Mary.]

639. York. Morrow [12 Nov.] of St. Martin. (Made there two weeks [13 Oct.] from Michaelmas in the said year. Thomas de Seymour (*de Sancto Mauro*) 'chivaler' quer.; Henry Wyville (*Wyvill*) and Katherine his wife def. Four messuages, 215½ a. of land, 10½ a. of meadow, and 2*s*. 6*d*. rent in Up Ampney (*Upameneye*). Right of Thomas by gift of Henry and Katherine. (Warranty, specifying Henry's heirs.) Cons. 100 marks.

77/61/128

[The fine was granted and recorded in the same term as that in which it was made.]

1337

640. York. One week [20 Jan.] from Hilary. (Made there one week from Michaelmas in the said year [6 Oct. 1336].) John son of Geoffrey de Weston and Agnes his wife quer.; Geoffrey de Weston Subedge (*Weston Underegge*) the elder def. A messuage, 5 yardlands, 10 [. . .] a. of meadow, and 30*s*. rent in Weston Subedge, held by Thomas de Evesham for term of the life of Geoffrey de Weston of Kennett (*Kenette*). Grant of the reversion to John and Agnes and their heirs in tail. To hold of Geoffrey de Weston Subedge, paying a rose a year at St. John the Baptist and doing service to the chief lords. Contingent reversion to Geoffrey de Weston Subedge. Cons. 100 marks.

77/61/136

[The number of acres of meadow was more than 10: the word *decem* is followed by the sign for *et* and a space, now lost in the filing hole, before *acris*.]

11 Edward III

1337

641. York. Two weeks [27 Jan.] from Hilary. (Made there two weeks from Michaelmas 10 Edward III [13 Oct. 1336].) Henry Elyvaunt and Petronilla his wife quer.; William le Long (*Longe*) 'chapeleyn' def. Five messuages, 1 yardland and 12 a. of land, 5 a. of meadow, and 1½ a. of wood in Minchinhampton (*Hampton Monialium*). Henry acknowledged the right of William, of which William had a messuage, 1 yardland, 4 a. of meadow, and the wood by Henry's gift. For this, grant and render of those holdings to Henry and Petronilla. To hold during their lives. And grant to them of the reversion of 8 a. of land held by Richard de Brimscombe (*Bremescombe*) for term of life, of a messuage and 1 a. of land held by Adam Clavill for term of life, of a messuage held by Robert le Hooper (*Hopere*) for term of life, of a messuage and 1 a. of land held by Margery la Soper (*Sapiare*) for term of life, and of a messuage, 2 a. of land, and 1 a. of meadow held by Agnes daughter of Henry Elyvaunt and Justina her sister for term of life, of William's inheritance. To hold as above. Remainder to Henry's son John and his heirs in tail. Successive contingent remainders to John's brother Nicholas and his heirs in tail, to Nicholas's brother Richard and his heirs in tail, to Richard's sister Agnes and her heirs in tail, to Agnes's sister Justina and her heirs in tail, and to Henry's heirs. [*Worn.*]

77/61/142

1337

642. York. Two weeks [27 Jan.] from Hilary. (Made there two weeks from Michaelmas 10 Edward III [13 Oct. 1336].) Roger Head (*Heved*) of Gloucester (*Gloucestr'*) quer.; John Cannon (*Canoun*) and Alice his wife and John de Lydbrook (*Lodebrok*) and Juliana his wife def. A messuage in the suburb of Gloucester. Right of Roger. Render to him. (Warranty, specifying Alice's and Juliana's heirs.) Cons. £40.

77/61/143

643. York. Two weeks [27 Jan.] from Hilary. (Made there two weeks from Michaelmas 10 Edward III [13 Oct. 1336].) Richard de Coombs (*Coumbes*) and Matilda his wife quer.; William le Long (*Longe*) 'chapeleyn' def. Three messuages, 2 yardlands, 4 a. of meadow, and rents of 7*d*. and 1 lb. of pepper in Minchinhampton (*Hampton Monialium*). Right of William by gift of Richard and Matilda. For this, grant back and render to Richard and Matilda. To hold to them and their heirs in tail. Contingent remainder to Matilda's heirs.

77/61/145

644. York. Two weeks [27 Jan.] from Hilary. Hugh abbot of Flaxley (*Flaxleye*) quer.; John le Butler (*Botiller*) of Llantwit (*Lanultyt*) and Beatrice his wife def. Rent of 5 marks in Brawn (*Brewerne*). Right of John. Remise and quitclaim to John and Beatrice and John's heirs. Cons. 20 marks.

77/61/146

645. York. Two weeks [4 May] from Easter. (Made there two weeks [27 Jan.] from Hilary in the said year.) John Payn of Baunton (*Baudynton*) and Alice his wife quer.; Thomas de Chalford (*Chalkford*) chaplain def. A messuage and half of 1 yardland in Hankerton (*Hanekynton*), WILTS., and a messuage and 60 a. of land in Baunton, GLOS. John acknowledged the right of Thomas by John's gift. For this, grant and render to John and Alice. To hold to them and their heirs in tail. Contingent remainder to John's heirs. *Labelled* Wiltes', Glouc'.

287/39/226

[Cf. *Wilts. Fines, 1327–77*, p. 49, no. 173.]

646. York. Two weeks [4 May] from Easter. (Made there two weeks [27 Jan.] from Hilary in the said year.) Robert Hereward quer.; Gilbert de Candover (*Candeure*) and Agnes his wife def. A messuage, 24 a. of land, and 3 a. of meadow in Chelworth (*Cheleworth*), Hailstone (*Haleweston*), and Ashton Keynes (*Ayshton*), WILTS., and 4 a. of meadow in South Cerney (*Southcerneye*), GLOS. Right of Robert. Remise and quitclaim, specifying Agnes's heirs, to him. Cons. 40 marks. *Labelled* Wiltes', Glouc'.

287/39/227

[Cf. *Wilts. Fines, 1327–77*, p. 49, no. 174.]

647. York. Two weeks [4 May] from Easter. (Made there two weeks [27 Jan.] from Hilary in the said year.) Robert Hereward quer.; Henry Wyville (*Wyvill*) and Katherine his wife def. A messuage, 24 a. of land, and 3 a. of meadow in Chelworth (*Cheleworth*), Hailstone (*Haleweston*), and Ashton Keynes (*Ayshton*), WILTS., and 4 a. of meadow in

1337

South Cerney (*Southcerneye*), GLOS. Right of Robert. Remise and quitclaim (specifying Henry's heirs) to him. (Warranty.) Cons. 40 marks. *Labelled* Wiltes', Gloucestr'.

287/39/229

[Cf. *Wilts. Fines, 1327–77*, p. 49, no. 175.]

648. York. Three weeks [11 May] from Easter. (Made there two weeks from Easter 10 Edward III [14 April 1336].) Roger Corbet of Hadley (*Hadleye*) quer.; John son of Richard de Clopton and Alice his wife def. The manor of Clopton (*Clopton*). John acknowledged the right of Roger by John's gift, except for 4 messuages and 2½ yardlands in the same manor. For this, grant and render of the manor as aforesaid to Richard and Alice. To hold to them and their heirs in tail, of Roger, paying a rose a year at St. John the Baptist, doing suit to Roger's court of Ebrington (*Ebriston*) every three weeks, and doing service to the chief lords. And grant to John and Alice of the reversion of a messuage and 1 yardland held by John le Young (*Younge*) for term of life, of a messuage and ½ yardland held by the same John and Joan his wife for term of Joan's life, of a messuage and ½ yardland held by Nicholas Wilkins (*Wylkyns*) and Alice his wife for term of life, and of a messuage and ½ yardland held by Walter Hopkins (*Hobekyns*) and Cecily his wife for term of Cecily's life, of Roger's inheritance. To hold as above. Contingent remainder to Thomas son of John son of Richard de Clopton and his heirs in tail. Contingent reversion to Roger. [*Worn.*]

77/61/144

649. York. Two weeks [29 June] from Trinity. (Made there three weeks [11 May] from Easter in the said year.) Henry de Haddon quer.; Thomas de Marlborough (*Marlebergh'*) and John de Haddon def. Thirteen messuages, 260½ a. of land, 6 a. of meadow, and 5*s*. 1*d*. rent in Ravensthorpe (*Ravenesthorp*), NORTHANTS., and 9 messuages, 172 a. and 1 rood of land, 4 a. of meadow, 4 a. of pasture, 6 a. of wood, 8*s*. 10½*d*. rent, and one eighth of the hundred of Winterbourne (*Wynterbourn*) in Winterbourne and the advowson of one eighth of the church of the same township, GLOS. Right of Thomas, as those which Thomas and John had by Henry's gift. For this, grant back and render to Henry. To hold during his life. Remainder to William FitzWarren (*Fitz Waryn*) and Amice his wife and their heirs in tail. Contingent remainder to Henry's heirs. *Labelled* Norht', Glouc'. [*Faded.*]

287/39/208

650. York. Two weeks [29 June] from Trinity. (Made there one month [18 May] from Easter in the said year.) John de Navestock (*Navestok'*) parson of the church of Willingale Doe (*Willinghale*) quer.; William de Walton (*Wauton*) of Cromhall (*Crumhale*) def. The manor of Cromhall and the advowson of the church of the same manor, GLOS., and 3 messuages, 2 mills, 5 ploughlands, 24 a. of meadow, 40 a. of pasture, 6 a. of wood, and £10 rent in Sutton Veny (*Fennysutton*), Little Sutton (*Litelsutton*), and Newnham (*Newenham*), WILTS. Right of John by William's gift. For this, grant back and render to William. To hold during his life. Remainder to Thomas son of William de Walton of Horham (*Horham*) and Elizabeth his wife and their heirs in tail. Contingent remainder to John son of William Gerald (*Geraud*) of Matson (*Mattesdon*). *Labelled* Glouc', Wiltes'.

287/39/209

[Cf. *Wilts. Fines, 1327–77*, p. 50, no. 178.]

1337

651. York. One week [1 July] from St. John the Baptist. Simon de Dean (*Deene*) of Kemerton (*Kenemarton*) quer.; Adam de Ashcroft (*Asshecroft*) of Twyning (*Twenynge*) def. Two messuages, 2 yardlands and 2 a. of land, 1 a. of meadow, and 10*s*. rent in Kemerton and Westmancote (*Westmuncote*). Right of Adam, of which he had a messuage and the said yardlands, meadow, and rent by Simon's gift. For this, grant back and render to Simon. To hold during his life. And grant to Simon of the reversion of the messuage and 1 a. of land in Westmancote held by Richard Guiting (*Gutynge*) and Matilda his wife for term of life, and of 1 a. of land in the same township held by Richard Chaukyn and Agnes his wife for term of life, of Adam's inheritance. To hold as above. Remainder to Geoffrey le Spenser of Upton on Severn (*Upton super Sabrinam*) and Elena his wife and their heirs in tail. Contingent remainder to Geoffrey's son Robert. (Warranty.) [*Worn.*]

77/61/147

[Westmancote was largely if not entirely in Bredon parish, in Worcs.]

652. York. One week [1 July] from St. John the Baptist. John le Butler (*Botiller*) of Llantwit (*Lanultyt*) and Beatrice his wife quer.; Hugh abbot of Flaxley (*Flasleye*) def. The manor of Brawn (*Brewerne*). Right of John. Remise and quitclaim to John and Beatrice and John's heirs. Cons. 100 marks.

77/61/148

653. York. One week [6 Oct.] from Michaelmas. Thomas de Braose (*Brewes*) and Beatrice his wife quer. by John de Stopham in Beatrice's place; Robert de Harpford (*Harperdesford*) def. The manors of Chesworth (*Cherresworth*), Sedgewick (*Seggewyk*), and Bidlington (*Bydlyngton*), SUSSEX, the manors of Bookham (*Bokham*) and Bramley (*Bromlegh*), SURREY, the manor of Manningford Bruce (*Manygford*), WILTS., the manor of Weaverthorpe (*Wyrthorp*), YORKS., and the manor of Tetbury (*Tettebury*), GLOS. Thomas acknowledged the right of Robert by Thomas's gift. For this, grant and render to Thomas and Beatrice. To hold to them and their heirs in tail. Contingent remainder to Thomas's heirs. Made by the king's order. *Labelled* Sussex', Surr', Wiltes', Ebor', Gloucestr'.

287/39/211

[Cf. *Sussex Fines, 1307–1509*, p. 90, no. 1860; *Wilts. Fines, 1327–77*, p. 50, no. 179.]

654. York. One week [6 Oct.] from Michaelmas. (Made there the morrow [25 June] of St. John the Baptist in the said year.) Roger Turtle of Bristol (*Bristoll'*) quer.; Roger Spert and Margery his wife def. A messuage in the suburb of Bristol. Right of Margery. For this, Roger Spert and Margery granted and rendered the messuage to Roger Turtle. (Warranty, specifying Margery's heirs.)

77/61/149

[Cf. *Bristol Gt. Red Book*, pp. 219–20, no. 134.]

655. York. Two weeks [13 Oct.] from Michaelmas. (Made there one week [22 June] from Trinity in the said year.) Richard Avening (*Avenyng*) and Agnes his wife quer.; William de Prestbury (*Prestebury*) parson of the church of Minchinhampton (*Munechenehampton*) def. A messuage, 3 tofts, 6 cottages, and 1 ploughland in Avening.

1337

Richard acknowledged the right of William by Richard's gift. For this, grant and render to Richard and Agnes. To hold to them and their heirs in tail. Contingent remainder to Richard's heirs.

77/61/137

656. York. Two weeks [13 Oct.] from Michaelmas. (Made there the morrow [25 June] of St. John the Baptist in the said year.) Maurice de Berkeley and Margery his wife quer.; William de Syde def. The manors of Elberton (*Aylberton*) and King's Weston (*Kyngesweston*). Maurice acknowledged the right of William by Maurice's gift. For this, grant and render to Maurice and Margery. To hold to them and Maurice's heirs.

77/61/138

657. York. Two weeks [13 Oct.] from Michaelmas. (Made there two weeks [29 June] from Trinity in the said year.) Thomas son of Robert de Grafton of Broad Marston (*Brodemerston*) quer.; Robert de Grafton of Broad Marston def. A messuage, 1 yardland, and 3 a. of meadow in Broad Marston. Right of Thomas. Remise and quitclaim to him. (Warranty.) Cons. £20.

77/61/139

658. York. Two weeks [13 Oct.] from Michaelmas. William de Cheltenham (*Chiltenham*) quer.; Gilbert Chasteleyn and Elizabeth his wife def. Rent of 20*s*. in Winterbourne (*Wynterbourne*). Grant to William, with the homages and all the services of John de la River (*Ryvere*) and John de Brokenborough (*Brokenbergh*) from all the holdings which they held of Gilbert and Elizabeth in the said township. (Warranty, specifying Elizabeth's heirs.) Cons. 20 marks.

77/61/140

659. York. Two weeks [13 Oct.] from Michaelmas. John de Sodbury (*Sobbury*) clerk quer.; Alexander de Hunsingore (*Hunsyngoure*) and Isabel his wife def. The manor of West Marshfield (*Westmarsfeld*). Grant, remise, and quitclaim to John of whatever Alexander and Isabel had in the said manor for term of their lives. (Warranty.) For this, John granted that he would pay to Alexander and Isabel during their lives £10 a year, at Michaelmas, Christmas, Easter, and St. John the Baptist, with the right of distraint in the said manor for any arrears. [*Worn.*]

77/61/141

660. York. Two weeks [13 Oct.] from Michaelmas. (Made there two weeks [27 Jan.] from Hilary in the said year.) Roger de Pedwardine (*Pedwardyn*) and William parson of the church of Bagendon (*Baggynden*) quer.; Richard son of Richard de Bagendon def. One third of the manor of Bagendon, GLOS., and one third of a messuage, 4 ploughlands, 10 a. of meadow, and 20*s*. rent in Wellington (*Welynton*), HEREFS., held by Lucy who was wife of Richard de Bagendon in dower, of Richard's inheritance. Right of Roger. Grant of the reversion to him and William and Roger's heirs. (Warranty.) Cons. 40 marks. *Labelled* Glouc', Hereford'.

287/39/240

12 Edward III

1338

661. York. Two weeks [27 Jan.] from Hilary. (Made there three weeks from Michaelmas 11 Edward III [20 Oct. 1337].) Richard Talbot and Elizabeth his wife quer; Thomas Talbot clerk def. The castle and manor of Goodrich Castle (*Chastelgodrich'*) except for a messuage, a mill, 1 ploughland and 100 a. of land, 40 a. of meadow, 160 a. of wood, and a fishery in the waters of the Wye (*Weye*) from the new ditch as far as the wood of Welsh Bicknor (*Bykenore*), and the advowson of the vicarage of the same township of Goodrich Castle, HEREFS., and the manor of Painswick (*Payneswyk'*) except for 10 messuages, 4 mills, 14 yardlands, 10 a. of meadow, and 1 a. of wood in the same manor, GLOS. Right of Thomas by gift of Richard and Elizabeth. For this, grant back and render to Richard and Elizabeth. To hold to them and their heirs in tail, of the king. Contingent remainder to Richard's heirs. Made by the king's order. *Labelled* Hereford', Gloucestr'. [*Stained.*]

287/39/247

662. York. Two weeks [27 Jan.] from Hilary. Thomas de Chedworth and John de Hatfield (*Haytfeld*) clerk quer.; Elizabeth de Burgh (*de Burgo*) def. The castle of Llangybi (*Tregruk*) [MON.]. Right of Thomas, as that which Thomas and John had by Elizabeth's gift. For this, grant back and render to Elizabeth. To hold during her life, of the king. Remainder to Henry de Ferrers (*de Ferariis*) and Isabel his wife and their heirs in tail, to hold of the king. Contingent remainder to Elizabeth's heirs. Made by the king's order.

77/62/157

[Like other fines relating to Monmouthshire, this was filed as a Glos. fine.]

663. York. Three weeks [3 May] from Easter. Alexander Reynald of Bristol (*Bristoll'*) quer.; John de Biddestone (*Budeston*) of Bristol and Isabel his wife def. A messuage in the suburb of Bristol. Right of Alexander by gift of John and Isabel. (Warranty, specifying Isabel's heirs.) Cons. 20s.

77/62/152

[Cf. *Bristol Gt. Red Book*, pp. 220–1, no. 137.]

664. York. Three weeks [3 May] from Easter. William le Newmaster (*Niwemaister*) of Bristol (*Bristoll'*) quer.; Walter de Tockington (*Tokynton*) and Joan his wife def. A messuage in the suburb of Bristol. Right of William. Remise and quitclaim, specifying Joan's heirs, to him. (Warranty.) Cons. 20s.

77/62/153

[Cf. *Bristol Gt. Red Book*, p. 221, no. 138.]

665. York. Three weeks [3 May] from Easter. Nicholas de Frampton (*Frompton*) quer.; Gilbert Pokerel and Isabel his wife def. A messuage in the suburb of Bristol (*Bristoll'*). Right of Nicholas by gift of Gilbert and Isabel. (Warranty, specifying Isabel's heirs.) Cons. 100s. *Endorsed* Florence who was wife of William Bagge of Bristol (*Bristollia*) put in her claim.

77/62/154

[Cf. *Bristol Gt. Red Book*, p. 221, no. 139.]

1338

666. York. Three weeks [3 May] from Easter. Fulk FitzWarren (*Fitz Waryn*) quer.; William de Cheltenham (*Chiltenham*) and Elena his wife def. Sixteen messuages, 2 ploughlands, 10 a. of meadow, 7 a. of pasture, 40 a. of wood, and 60*s.* rent in Great Bentham (*Magna Bentham*), Little Bentham (*Parva Bentham*), Great Shurdington (*Magna Shurdyngton*), Little Shurdington (*Parva Shurdyngton*) and Badgeworth (*Beggeworth*). Right of Fulk. Remise and quitclaim, specifying Elena's heirs, to him. Cons. 100 marks.

77/62/160

667. York. One week [14 June] from Trinity. Robert Selyman quer.; Thomas de Thornhill (*Thornhulle*) and John de Dagnall (*Dagenhale*) def. A messuage, 2 ploughlands, 10 a. of meadow, and 44*s.* rent in Shipton Moyne (*Shiptone Moygne*). Right of Thomas, as those which Thomas and John had by Robert's gift. For this, grant back and render to Robert. To hold during his life. Remainder to John le Moyne (*Moygne*).

77/62/165

668. York. Two weeks [21 June] from Trinity. (Made there three weeks [3 May] from Easter in the said year.) Richard Francis (*Fraunceys*) quer.; Thomas Launce of Hawkesbury (*Hauekesbury*) and Alice his wife def. A messuage, 2 yardlands, 6 a. of meadow, and 12*d.* rent in Moreton Valence (*Morton Valence*). Right of Richard. Remise and quitclaim, specifying Alice's heirs, to him. (Warranty.) Cons. 20 marks.

77/62/158

669. York. Two weeks [21 June] from Trinity. (Made there one month [10 May] from Easter in the said year.) Henry de Clifford and Matilda his wife quer.; William le Long (*Longe*) chaplain def. Three messuages, 3 ploughlands, 10 a. of meadow, 10 a. of wood, and 30*s.* rent in Tunley (*Tonleye*), Over Lypiatt (*Overlepeyate*), and Frampton Mansell (*Frompton*). Right of William by gift of Henry and Matilda. For this grant back and render to Henry and Matilda. To hold to them and their heirs in tail. Contingent remainder to Henry's heirs.

77/62/159

670. York. Two weeks [21 June] from Trinity. (Made there three weeks [3 May] from Easter in the said year.) Robert d'Abitot (*Dabetot*) and Matilda his wife quer.; Edmund de Kinnersley (*Kynardesleye*) def. The manor of Leigh (*la Leye*) by Boddington (*Botyntone*). Robert acknowledged the right of Edmund. For this, grant and render to Robert and Matilda. To hold to them and Robert's heirs. (Warranty.) *Endorsed* Richard son of John de Kinnersley put in his claim.

77/62/161

671. York. One week [6 Oct.] from Michaelmas. John Giffard of Leckhampton (*Lechampton*) and Joan his wife quer.; William de Cheltenham (*Chiltenham*) and Elena his wife def. The manor of Leckhampton and the advowson of the church of the same manor. Right of John. Remise and quitclaim, specifying Elena's heirs, to John and Joan and John's heirs. Cons. 100 marks.

77/62/156

1338

672. York. Two weeks [13 Oct.] from Michaelmas. Robert de Wrington (*Wrynketon*) of Bristol (*Bristoll'*) quer.; Walter Cote and Margaret his wife, William Corry and Joan his wife, and John Page and Margery his wife def. Three quarters of a messuage and of a toft in the suburb of Bristol. Right of Robert by gift of Walter and Margaret, William and Joan, and John and Margery. Remise and quitclaim, specifying Margaret's, Joan's, and Margery's heirs, to him. (Warranty.) Cons. 100*s*.

77/61/150

[Cf. *Bristol Gt. Red Book*, p. 220, no. 135.]

673. York. Three weeks [20 Oct.] from Michaelmas. Isabella queen of England quer.; Geoffrey le Spenser (*Spencer*) and Elena his wife def. One third of 3 messuages, 1 ploughland, 40 a. of meadow, 20 a. of pasture, 10 a. of wood, and 20*s*. rent in Over, Highnam (*Ovrehynehomme*), Lassington (*Lassyndon*), and Maisemore (*Mayesmore*). Right of the queen. Remise and quitclaim, specifying Elena's heirs, to her. Cons. 20 marks.

77/62/155

[The fusion in the document of the names Over and Highnam is presumably a mistake, since no other record of Over or Upper Highnam is known: cf. *P.-N.G.* iii. 159.]

674. York. Morrow [12 Nov.] of St. Martin. William de Whitfield (*Whitefeld*) 'chivaler' and Constance his wife quer.; Robert [Wyville] bishop of Salisbury (*Sar'*) and John de Chamber (*Camera*) def. The manor of Woodsford (*Werdesford Belet*), 3 a. of meadow in Moreton (*Morton*), and the bailiwick of guarding the banks of the waters of Frome (*Frome*) and Stour (*Stoure*), DORSET, the manor of Shockerwick (*Shokerwyk*) and 7 messuages, 160 a. of land, 12 a. of meadow, 20 a. of wood, and 28*s*. 8*d*. rent in Batheaston (*Batheneston*), SOM., and the manor of Bromsberrow (*Brommesbergh'*) and 62*s*. rent in Bromsberrow and the advowson of the church of the same township, GLOS. Right of the bishop, of which he and John had the manors, the bailiwick, and 3 a. of meadow in Moreton and the advowson by gift of William and Constance. For this, grant back and render to William and Constance. To hold to them and their heirs in tail. And grant to them of the reversion of the messuages, land, meadow, wood, 12 a. of meadow, and rent in Batheaston held by John Cole for term of life, of 40*s*. rent in Bromsberrow held by Thomas de Whitfield for term of life, and of 22*s*. rent in the same township held by William Dickon (*Dycoun*) for term of life, all of the bishop's inheritance, to hold as above. Successive contingent remainders to John son of William de Whitfield and Eve his wife and their heirs in tail and to William's heirs. *Labelled* Dors', Somers', Glouc'. [*Worn and stained.*]

287/39/245

[Cf. *Som. Fines, 1307–46*, p. 247; *Dorset Fines, 1327–1485*, p. 142.]

1339

675. One week [20 Jan.] from Hilary. William le Hawker (*Haukare*) of Bristol (*Bristoll'*) quer.; John Selk 'peautrer' [*i.e. pewterer*] and Joan his wife def. A messuage in the suburb of Bristol. Right of William. Remise and quitclaim, specifying Joan's heirs, to him. (Warranty.) Cons. 100*s*.

77/62/151

[Cf. *Bristol Gt. Red Book*, p. 220, no. 136.]

1339

676. One week [20 Jan.] from Hilary. (Made two weeks from Michaelmas 6 Edward III [13 Oct. 1332].) Thomas son of Maurice de Berkeley (*Berkele*) quer.; William de Syde def. The manor of Syde (*Syde*) and the advowson of the church of the same manor, held by Margaret who was wife of John Giffard of Brimpsfield (*Brymmesfeld*) for term of life. Right of Thomas. Grant to him of the reversion, of William's inheritance. Cons. 100 marks.

77/62/162

677. One week [20 Jan.] from Hilary. (Made York, two weeks from Trinity 11 Edward III [29 June 1337].) Philip Calf of Chipping Campden (*Chepyngcaumpeden*) quer.; Richard Lettice (*Letice*) of Chipping Campden chaplain def. A messuage in Chipping Campden held by John le Reeve (*Reve*) of Aston Subedge (*Aston under Egge*) and Isabel his wife for term of life. Right of Philip. Grant to him of the reversion, of Richard's inheritance. (Warranty.) Cons. 100*s.*

77/62/163

678. One week [20 Jan.] from Hilary. Henry Scot of Tewkesbury (*Teukesbury*) quer.; John de Tirley (*Trynleye*) and Joan his wife def. A messuage in Tewkesbury. Right of Henry by gift of John and Joan. (Warranty, specifying Joan's heirs.) Cons. 10 marks.

77/62/164

13 Edward III

1339

679. One week [9 Feb.] from the Purification. Robert Bruse (*Bruyse*) and Joan his wife and Robert's daughter Joan quer.; Walter son of Walter Goldwin (*Goldwyne*) and Nichola his wife def. A messuage, 18 a. of land, and 1½ a. of meadow in Hardwicke (*Herdewyke*) by Boddington (*Botynton*). Right of Robert. Remise and quitclaim, specifying Nichola's heirs, to Robert, Joan, and Joan and to Robert's heirs. (Warranty.) Cons. 20 marks.

77/62/172

680. Two weeks [11 April] from Easter. John Sampson of Bristol (*Bristoll'*) quer.; Walter le Whittier (*Whittawiare*) and Stephana his wife and Richard Capy 'cordewaner' and Margery his wife def. A messuage in the suburb of Bristol. Right of John by gift of Walter and Stephana and Richard and Margery. Remise and quitclaim, specifying Stephana's and Margery's heirs, to him. (Warranty.) Cons. 10 marks.

77/62/168

[Cf. *Bristol Gt. Red Book*, pp. 221–2, no. 141.]

681. Two weeks [11 April] from Easter. Philip de Torrington (*Toryton*) and Isabel his wife quer.; Everard le Francis (*Fraunceys*) of Bristol (*Bristoll'*) def. Seven messuages and half of 1 a. of land in Bristol and the suburb of the same town. Philip acknowledged the right of Everard by Philip's gift. For this, grant and render to Philip and Isabel. To hold to them and their heirs in tail. Contingent remainder to Philip's heirs.

77/62/170

[Cf. *Bristol Gt. Red Book*, p. 222, no. 143.]

1339

682. Two weeks [11 April] from Easter. Odo de Acton and Anne his wife quer.; Robert de la Field (*Felde*) def. A messuage, 1 ploughland, 30 a. of meadow, 30 a. of pasture, and 100*s*. rent in Gossington (*Gosynton*), Hurst (*Hurste*), and Kingston (*Kyngeston*) by Slimbridge (*Slymbrugge*). Odo acknowledged the right of Robert by Odo's gift. For this, grant and render to Odo and Amy. To hold during their lives. Remainder to Odo's daughter Isabel during her life and to Odo's heirs.

77/62/174 [bis]

[Cf. *Berkeley Castle Mun.* i, p. 280, A1/43/54 (counterpart).]

683. Two weeks [11 April] from Easter. Edmund le Blunt (*Blount*) and Agnes his wife quer.; John de Abson (*Abbedeston*) and John Scot of Upton (*Upton*) def. Two thirds of the manor of Mangotsfield (*Manegodesfeld*). Edmund acknowledged the right of John de Abson, as those which John and John had by Edmund's gift. For this, grant and render to Edmund and Agnes. To hold to them and their heirs in tail. Contingent remainder to Edmund's heirs.

77/62/175

684. Two weeks [11 April] from Easter. Walter de Cirencester (*Cyrencestr'*) quer.; Henry Wyville (*Wyvill*) and Katherine his wife def. A messuage, 2 mills, 2 ploughlands, 6 a. of meadow, 20 a. of wood, and 24*s*. rent in Great Taynton (*Magna Teynton*) and Byfords (*Byfare*). Right of Walter. Remise and quitclaim, specifying Katherine's heirs, to him. Cons. 100 marks.

77/63/176

685. Three weeks [18 April] from Easter. Robert le White of Bristol (*Bristoll'*) and Cristina his wife quer.; William de Woodhill (*Wodehull*) and Alice his wife def. One third of a messuage in Bristol. Right of Cristina. Remise and quitclaim, specifying Alice's heirs, to Robert and Cristina and Cristina's heirs. (Warranty.) Cons. 10 marks.

77/62/169

[Cf. *Bristol Gt. Red Book*, p. 222, no. 142.]

686. Three weeks [18 April] from Easter. William Saunders (*Saundres*) and Margaret his wife quer.; Robert son of Robert de Draycott (*Dreycote*) def. A messuage and 1 a. of land in Alkington (*Alkynton*). Right of Robert by gift of William and Margaret. For this, grant back and render to William and Margaret. To hold to them and William's heirs.

77/62/174

687. One month [25 April] from Easter. Robert Hereward quer.; William de Frome of Cirencester (*Cirencestr'*) and Matilda his wife def. Two shops in Cirencester. Right of Robert by gift of William and Matilda. (Warranty, specifying William's heirs.) Cons. £10.

77/62/173

688. One week [30 May] from Trinity. (Made two weeks [11 April] from Easter in the said year.) John Spilman (*Spylemon*) the elder and Katherine his wife quer.; John Lescy of Ebley (*Ebbaleye*) def. Rent of 8 marks and 2s. 4*d*. in Oxlinch (*Hoxlynge*) and

1339

Minchinhampton (*Munechene Hampton*). John Spilman acknowledged the right of John Lescy by John Spilman's gift. For this, grant to John Spilman and Katherine. To hold during their lives. Remainder to John Spilman's son Henry and Henry's brother Edward during their lives and to John Spilman's heirs.

77/63/178

689. One week [30 May] from Trinity. (Made two weeks [11 April] from Easter in the said year.) Richard le Clarkson (*Clerkessone*) of Paganhill (*Pagenhull*) and Eve his wife quer.; Henry Seryd of Paganhill chaplain def. A messuage, a garden, 1 yardland and 9 a. of land, 1 a. of meadow, 1 a. of pasture, 4 a. of wood, and 6s. 2d. rent in Paganhill. Richard acknowledged the right of Henry by Richard's gift. For this, grant and render to Richard and Eve. To hold to them and their heirs in tail. Contingent remainder to Richard's heirs.

77/63/179

690. Two weeks [6 June] from Trinity. Ralph [de Shrewsbury] bishop of Bath and Wells (*Bathon' et Wellen'*) quer.; Thomas de Breadstone (*Bradeston*) and Isabel his wife def. One hundred acres of pasture, 80 a. of heath (*bruere*), and 20 a. of furze (*janicie*) in Pucklechurch (*Pokelecherche*). Right of the bishop. Remise and quitclaim, specifying Thomas's heirs, to the bishop and his heirs. (Warranty.) Cons. 100 marks.

77/63/177

691. One week [6 Oct.] from Michaelmas. John Mautravers the elder quer.; Henry de Forneaux and Thomas de Homere def. The manors of Hill Deverill (*Hulle Deverel*), Great Somerford (*Somerford Mautravers*), and Coate (*Cotes*) and the advowson of the church of the same manor of Somerford, WILTS., the manors of Witchampton (*Wychampton*), Langton Matravers (*Langeton*), Woolcombe (*Wollecombe*), and Hampreston (*Hammeprestone*) and the advowsons of the churches of the same manors of Witchampton and Langton and of the church of Melbury Bubb (*Melebury Bobbe*), DORSET, and the manor of Woodchester (*Wodechestre*) and the advowson of the church of the same manor, GLOS. Right of Henry, as those which Henry and Thomas had by John's gift. For this, grant back and render to John. To hold during his life. Remainder to his son John Mautravers the younger and his heirs in tail male. Contingent remainder to John the younger's heirs. *Labelled* Wiltes', Dors', Glouc'. *Endorsed* The prioress of Kington St. Michael (*Kyngton*) put in her claim.

287/40/261

[Cf. *Dorset Fines, 1327–1485*, pp. 142–3; *Wilts. Fines, 1327–77*, p. 59, no. 220.]

692. Two weeks [13 Oct.] from Michaelmas. John de Sollers (*Solers*) and Margery his wife quer.; John de Bures and Hawise his wife def. Rent of 60s. in Longford (*Longeford*) by Gloucester (*Gloucestr'*). Right of Hawise. For this, John de Bures and Hawise granted and rendered the rent to John de Sollers and Margery. To hold to them and their heirs in tail, of John de Bures and Hawise and Hawise's heirs, paying a rose a year at St. John the Baptist and doing service to the chief lords. Contingent remainder to Giles de Beauchamp (*de Bello Campo*) and Katherine his wife and their heirs in tail. (Warranty.) Contingent reversion to John de Bures and Hawise and Hawise's heirs. [*Worn.*]

77/62/166

1339

693. Two weeks [13 Oct.] from Michaelmas. William de Cheltenham (*Chiltenham*) quer.; Walter de Horton and Eleanor his wife def. A messuage, 2 ploughlands, 3 a. of meadow, and 24s. rent in Hawkesbury (*Haukesbury*). Grant to William and remise and quitclaim to him of whatever Walter and Eleanor had in the holdings in the name of Eleanor's dower. Cons. £20.

77/62/171

[Cf. *Berkeley Castle Mun.* i, p. 469, A2/26/1 (counterpart).]

694. Morrow [12 Nov.] of St. Martin. Everard le Francis (*Fraunceys*) of Bristol (*Bristoll'*) quer.; William Jeu of Monmouth (*Monemuth*) and Alice his wife def. A messuage in Bristol. Grant and render to Everard. (Warranty, specifying Alice's heirs.) Cons. 100s.

77/62/167

[Cf. *Bristol Gt. Red Book*, p. 221, no. 140.]

1340

695. One week [20 Jan.] from Hilary. (Made one week [6 Oct.] from Michaelmas in the said year.) Hugh son of Robert atte Mill (*Milne*) of Lechlade (*Lecchelade*) and Margery his wife quer.; John Lydiard (*Lydyard*) of Wotton under Edge (*Wotton Underegge*) def. Two messuages, 2 tofts, 14½ a. of land, and 2 a. of meadow in Lechlade. Grant and render to Hugh and Margery. To hold to them and their heirs in tail. Contingent remainder to Hugh's heirs. Cons. 20 marks.

77/63/180

14 Edward III

1340

696. Two weeks [27 Jan.] from Hilary. (Made the morrow of St. Martin 13 Edward III [12 Nov. 1339].) Edward de St. John (*de sancto Johanne*) 'le neveu' quer.; Matthew son of Herbert def. The manor of Wolverton (*Wolferton*) and the advowson of the church of the same manor, HANTS., a messuage and 1 ploughland in *Morhalle*, NORF., and a messuage and 1 ploughland in Haresfield (*Harsefeld*), GLOS. Right of Edward by Matthew's gift. For this, grant back and render to Matthew. To hold to Matthew and his heirs in tail, of Edward, paying a rose a year at St. John the Baptist and doing service to the chief lords. Contingent remainder to Matthew's brother Reynold, to hold during his life, with reversion to Edward. *Labelled* Sutht', Norff', Gloucestr'.

287/40/288

697. Two weeks [27 Jan.] from Hilary. (Made two weeks from Michaelmas 13 Edward III [13 Oct. 1339].) John de Brokenborough (*Brokenbergh*) and Alice his wife quer.; Robert de Brokenborough parson of the church of North Wraxall (*Wroxhale*) def. A messuage, a mill, 2 ploughlands and 1 yardland, 16 a. of meadow, 3 a. of wood, and £10 3s. rent in Hempton (*Hempton*), Tockington (*Tokynton*), Winterbourne (*Wynterbourne*), and Lee (*La Lee*). John acknowledged the right of Robert by John's gift. For this, grant and render to John and Alice. To hold to them and John's heirs.

77/63/184

[For the identity of North Wraxall, *Reg. Martival*, i. 364.]

1340

698. Two weeks [27 Jan.] from Hilary. (Made two weeks from Michaelmas 13 Edward III [13 Oct. 1339].) Thomas Prick (*Pricke*) of Staverton (*Staverton*) and Alice his wife quer.; William Milnes (*Mylns*) of Dolton (*Doulton*) and Isolda his wife def. Eight acres of land, 2 a. of meadow, 1 a. of pasture, 2*s*. rent, and one quarter of a messuage in Evington (*Yevynton*). Right of Thomas, of which Thomas and Alice had 4 a. of land, 1 a. of meadow, the pasture, 7*d*. rent, and the said quarter by gift of William and Isolda. To hold to Thomas and Alice and Thomas's heirs. And grant to Thomas and Alice of the reversion of 2 a. of land held by Adam atte Grove and Ralph his brother for term of life, of 1 a. of land held by William de Durnford (*Derneford*) for term of life, of 1 a. of land held by John atte Stoke and Agnes his wife and Richard their son for term of life, of 1 a. of meadow held by William Devereux (*Devereus*) for term of life, of 9*d*. rent held by William le Broudare for term of life, and of 8*d*. rent held by Richard Gabbe for term of life, of Isolda's inheritance. To hold as above. (Warranty.) Cons. 20 marks. [*Worn*.]

77/63/186

699. Two weeks [27 Jan.] from Hilary. (Made two weeks from St. Martin 13 Edward III [25 Nov. 1339].) William Crisp of Gloucester (*Gloucestr'*) merchant quer.; Geoffrey le Spenser and Elena his wife def. A messuage in Gloucester. Right of William. Remise and quitclaim, specifying Elena's heirs, to him. Cons. 20 marks.

77/63/187

700. One week [18 June] from Trinity. (Made two weeks [30 April] from Easter in the said year.] Geoffrey de Scarborough (*Scardeburgh*) parson of the church of Onibury (*Onebury*) and Thomas Asselote parson of the church of Wolstanton (*Wolstanston*) quer.; John de Haudlo def. The manors of Billingford (*Billyngford*), Ryston (*Ryston*), and Thurning (*Thernynge*), 20 a. of land in Foxley (*Foxle*), and the advowson of the church of the same manor of Billingford, NORF., the manor of Little Rissington (*Rysyndon Basset*) and 8 messuages, 12 shops, 15 cellars (*celaria*), 2 gardens, and 62*s*. rent in Bristol (*Bristoll'*), GLOS., the manors of Bidford (*Bydeford*) and Broom (*Brome*), WARWS., and the manor of Compton Dando (*Compton Dauno*), SOM. Right of Geoffrey, of which Geoffrey and Thomas had the manor of Billingford and the holdings and the advowson by John's gift. For this, grant back and render to John. To hold during his life. And grant to John of the reversion of the manors of Ryston, Thurning, Little Rissington, Bidford, Broom, and Compton Dando, held by Aline who was wife of Edward Burnel for term of life, of Geoffrey's inheritance. To hold as above. Remainder to John's son Nicholas. *Labelled* Norff', Glouc', Warr', Somers'.

287/40/275

[Cf. *Som. Fines, 1307–46*, p. 248; *Warws. Fines, 1284–1345*, pp. 181–2, no. 1875.]

701. Two weeks [25 June] from Trinity. John de la River (*Ryvere*) 'chivaler' and Margaret his wife quer.; Henry vicar of the church of Old Sodbury (*Sobbery*) and William Edward def. The manors of Acton Turville (*Acton Turbervill*), Tormarton (*Tormerton*), and West Littleton (*Lutleton*). John acknowledged the right of Henry, as those which Henry and William had by John's gift. For this, grant and render to John and Margaret. To hold to them and John's heirs.

77/63/185

1340

702. One week [6 Oct.] from Michaelmas. (Made two weeks [8 July] from St. John the Baptist in the said year.) Matilda who was wife of John Marmion (*Marmyoun*) quer.; Robert Norris (*Noreys*) parson of the church of West Retford (*Westretford*) and Simon de Winteringham (*Wyntryngham*) master of the hospital of St. Giles by Catterick (*Catryk'*) def. The manor of Berwick (*Berewyk*), SUSSEX, the manor of Winteringham, LINCS., and the manor of Quinton (*Quenton*), GLOS. Right of Robert, as those which Robert and Simon had by Matilda's gift. For this, grant back and render to Matilda. To hold during her life. Remainder to Robert son of John Marmion during his life. Remainder to John de Grey (*Gray*) of Rotherfield Greys (*Retherefeld*) and Avice his wife and their heirs in tail. Successive contingent remainders to Avice's heirs in tail, to John de Barnack (*Bernak*) and Joan his wife and Joan's heirs in tail, and to the heirs of Robert son of John Marmion. *Labelled* Sussex', Lincoln', Glouc'.

287/40/285

[Cf. *Sussex Fines, 1307–1509*, p. 99, no. 1914.]

703. Two weeks [13 Oct.] from Michaelmas. (Made one week [18 June] from Trinity in the said year.) Robert Selyman quer.; Thomas de Thornhill (*Thornhull*) and John de Dagnall (*Dagenhale*) def. Twelve messuages, 1 yardland and 29½ a. of land, 1 a. of meadow, and 3s. 3d. rent in Shipton Moyne (*Shipton Moigne*). Right of Thomas. For this, Thomas and John granted to Robert the rent with all the homage and service of William Mile from all the holdings which he formerly held of Thomas and John in the said township. To hold during Robert's life. And they granted to Robert the reversion of 2 messuages, 6 a. of land, and ½ yardland held by Margery Bernard and William her son for term of life, of 1½ a. of land held by the same Margery for term of life, of a messuage and ½ yardland held by Ralph Bernard and Agnes his wife for term of life, of a messuage and 2 a. of land held by Alice atte Hill (*Hulle*) for term of life, of a messuage held by Alice Hidbury and Isolda Hidbury for term of life, of a messuage held by John le Tailor (*Taillour*) and Alice his wife and Alice's son John for term of Alice's and John's life, of a messuage held by Robert Douce for term of life, of a messuage held by William Beale (*Bele*) for term of life, of a messuage held by Robert Couste and Joan his wife for term of life, of a messuage held by Alice Smithers (*Smythes*) for term of life, of a messuage and 2½ a. of land held by John de Thornhill and Matilda his wife and Matilda's daughter Isabel for term of Matilda's and Isabel's life, of 4½ a. of land held by Roger le Doume for term of life, of 4 a. of land and 1 a. of meadow held by William Knap for term of life, of a messuage and 3 a. of land held by William Joce and Felicia his wife for term of Felicia's life, of 4 a. of land held by John Heath (*Hethe*) for term of life, of 1 a. of land held by William le Monk for term of life, and of 1 a. of land held by William le Hooper (*Hopere*) for term of life, all of Thomas's inheritance. To hold as above. Remainder to John le Moyne (*Moygne*).

77/63/182

704. Two weeks [13 Oct.] from Michaelmas. Roger Beaver (*Beauver*) of Bristol (*Bristoll'*) quer.; William Lydiard of Bristol and Juliana his wife def. A toft in Bristol. Right of Roger. Remise and quitclaim, specifying Juliana's heirs, to him. (Warranty.) Cons. 10 marks.

77/63/189

[Cf. *Bristol Gt. Red Book*, p. 223, no. 145.]

1340

705. Three weeks [20 Oct.] from Michaelmas. John Hughes (*Hugges*) of Bristol (*Bristoll'*) 'burgeys' quer.; Robert le Rich (*Ryche*) of Bristol 'burgeys' and Alice his wife def. A messuage and 2 shops in the suburb of Bristol. Right of John. Remise and quitclaim, specifying Alice's heirs, to him. (Warranty.) Cons. 10 marks.

77/63/188

[Cf. *Bristol Gt. Red Book*, pp. 222–3, no. 144.]

706. Morrow [3 Nov.] of All Souls. (Made two weeks [13 Oct.] from Michaelmas in the said year.) William de Clinton (*Clynton*) earl of Huntingdon (*Huntyngdon*) and Juliana his wife quer.; Pancius de Controne physician (*medicus*) def. (Pancius was dead by the time that the agreement was granted and recorded and was replaced as def. by James de Controne his cousin and heir). The manor of Temple Guiting (*Gutyng*). Pancius acknowledged the right of the earl, as that which the earl and Juliana had by Pancius's gift. To hold to the earl and Juliana and the earl's heirs. (Warranty, by Pancius.) Cons. (given to Pancius) 100 marks. *Endorsed* Hugh le Despenser put in his claim.

77/63/183

[The fine was granted and recorded in the same term as that in which it was made. It refers to a writ of covenant, instead of the usual plea of covenant.]

707. Two weeks [25 Nov.] from St. Martin. Roger [Northburgh] bishop of Coventry and Lichfield (*Coventr' et Lych'*) quer.; John son of Thomas le Irish (*Irreys*) of Anstey (*Ansty*) and Alice his wife def. Six messuages, 6 yardlands, and 40*s*. rent in Dorsington (*Dersyngton*) and one third of the manor of Dorsington. Grant to the bishop. Remise and quitclaim to him and his heirs of whatever John and Alice had in the holdings for term of Alice's life. Cons. 100 marks.

77/63/181

15 Edward III

1341

708. Two weeks [27 Jan.] from Hilary. Robert de Wrington (*Wryngton*) quer.; Gilbert Pokerel the younger def. A messuage and a toft in the suburb of Bristol (*Bristoll'*), held by Gilbert Pokerel the elder and Isabel his wife for term of life. Right of Robert. Grant to him of the reversion, of the inheritance of Gilbert the younger. (Warranty.) Cons. 20 marks.

77/63/190

[Cf. *Bristol Gt. Red Book*, p. 223, no. 146.]

709. Two weeks [27 Jan.] from Hilary. John de Besemountsel and Isabel his wife quer.; Thomas de Besford (*Besseford*) parson of the church of Beverston (*Beverston*) and Robert de Brinsley (*Brinnesleye*) def. A messuage, 1 ploughland, 8 a. of meadow, 8 a. of pasture, and 40*s*. rent in Alderton (*Aldrynton*) and Gretton (*Gretton*) by Winchcombe (*Wynchecombe*). Grant and render to John and Isabel. To hold to them and John's heirs. Cons. 40 marks.

77/63/197

710. One week [10 June] from Trinity. Roger Crook (*Crouk*) clerk quer.; Reynold de Deerhurst (*Derhurst*) and Agnes his wife def. Two messuages in Gloucester (*Gloucestr'*). Right of Roger. Remise and quitclaim, specifying Agnes's heirs, to him. (Warranty.) Cons. 20 marks.

77/63/194

1341

711. Two weeks [17 June] from Trinity. (Made three weeks [29 April] from Easter in the said year. John de Berkeley (*Berkeleye*) of Dursley (*Durseleye*) and Hawise his wife quer. by William de Stanley in Hawise's place by the king's writ; Richard le Walsh (*Walshe*) chaplain def. A messuage, 100 a. of land and 10 a. of moor in Dursley, Cam (*Camme*), and Slimbridge (*Slymbrugge*). John acknowledged the right of Richard by John's gift. For this, grant and render to John and Hawise. To hold to them and their heirs in tail. Successive contingent remainders to John's son Nicholas and his heirs in tail, to Nicholas's brother John and his heirs in tail, and to John de Berkeley's heirs. [*Worn.*]

77/63/198

712. Morrow [25 June] of St. John the Baptist. Robert de Barrow (*Barewe*) quer.; Robert le Norris (*Norreys*) of Bristol (*Bristoll'*) def. A messuage in the suburb of Bristol. Right of Robert de Barrow. Remise and quitclaim to him. (Warranty.) Cons. 100*s.*

77/63/193

[Cf. *Bristol Gt. Red Book*, p. 224, no. 149.]

713. One week [6 Oct.] from Michaelmas. John Horncastle (*Horncastel*) of Bristol (*Bristoll'*) quer.; Geoffrey Methelan of Bristol and Agnes his wife def. A messuage in the suburb of Bristol. Right of John by gift of Geoffrey and Agnes. (Warranty, specifying Agnes's heirs.) Cons. 10 marks.

77/63/192

[Cf. *Bristol Gt. Red Book*, p. 224, no. 148.]

714. Two weeks [13 Oct.] from Michaelmas. Richard atte Wall (*Walle*) burgess of Bristol (*Bristoll'*) quer.; Geoffrey Methelan burgess of Bristol and Agnes his wife def. A garden in the suburb of Bristol. Right of Richard by gift of Geoffrey and Agnes. (Warranty, specifying Agnes's heirs.) Cons. 10 marks.

77/63/191

[Cf. *Bristol Gt. Red Book*, pp. 223–4, no. 147.]

715. Two weeks [13 Oct.] from Michaelmas. John Bars and Alice his wife quer.; William Bruyn def. A messuage in Gloucester (*Gloucestr'*). Right of William by gift of John and Alice. For this, grant back and render to John and Alice. To hold to them and John's heirs.

77/63/196

716. Two weeks [13 Oct.] from Michaelmas. (Made two weeks from Michaelmas 14 Edward III [13 Oct. 1340].) William de Cheltenham (*Chiltenham*) quer.; John de la Mare of Langley Burrell (*Langele Burel*) def. The manor of Abson (*Abboteston*), held by Cecily de Uphay for term of life. Right of William. Grant to him of the reversion, of John's inheritance. (Warranty.) Cons. 100 marks. Made in Cecily's presence and with her consent, and she did fealty to William.

77/63/200A

1341

717. Two weeks [13 Oct.] from Michaelmas. John de Brickhampton (*Bruggehampton*) and Joan his wife quer.; William Warin (*Waryn*) def. A messuage and 1 yardland in Rockhampton (*Rokhampton*). Right of William by gift of John and Joan. For this, grant back and render to John and Joan. To hold to them and their heirs in tail [*sc.* male], of William, paying a rose a year at St. John the Baptist and doing service to the chief lords. Successive contingent remainders of the half of the holding towards the east to Joan daughter of the same John and Joan and her heirs in tail, to that Joan's sister Isabel and her heirs in tail, and to John's brother Richard and his heirs in tail, with contingent reversion to William. Successive contingent remainders of the other half of the holding to the said Isabel and her heirs in tail, to the said Joan daughter of John and Joan and her heirs in tail, and to the said Richard and his heirs in tail, with contingent reversion to William. [*Worn.*]

77/63/200B

[In neither place where it might have done so does the fine specify that the holding should be held in tail *male*, but the intention is clear from the contingent remainders of the two halves to the female issue of John and Joan.]

718. Morrow [3 Nov.] of All Souls. (Made one week [10 June] from Trinity in the said year.) John Coggeshall (*Coggeshale*) and Elizabeth his wife quer.; John Loholt (*Lohout*) def. The manor of Colesborne (*Colesbourne*). John Coggeshall acknowledged the right of John Loholt by John Coggeshall's gift. For this, grant and render to John Coggeshall and Elizabeth. To hold to them and their heirs in tail, of John Loholt, paying a rose a year at St. John the Baptist and doing service to the chief lords. Contingent remainder to Matilda daughter of John Loholt and her heirs in tail. To hold as above. (Warranty.) Contingent reversion to John Loholt. [*Worn.*]

77/63/199

1342

719. One week [20 Jan.] from Hilary. (Made two weeks from Michaelmas in the said year [13 Oct. 1341].) Henry le Draper of Gloucester (*Gloucestre*) and Denise his wife quer.; Walter son of Walter le Smith (*Smyth*) 'webbe' [*i.e. weaver*] and Agnes his wife def. A messuage in the suburb of Gloucester. Right of Henry, as that which Henry and Denise had by gift of Walter and Agnes. To hold to Henry and Denise and Henry's heirs. (Warranty, specifying Agnes's heirs.) Cons. 100*s*.

77/63/195

16 Edward III

1342

720. Morrow [3 Feb.] of the Purification. John atte Hall (*Halle*) of Shenington (*Shenyndon*) and Edith his wife quer.; John Heritage (*Eritage*) of Alkerton (*Alcrynton*) and Alice his wife def. A messuage and 2 yardlands in Shenington. Right of John Heritage, as those which John and Alice had by gift of John atte Hall and Edith. For this, grant back and render to John atte Hall and Edith. To hold to them during their lives, of John Heritage and Edith and John's heirs, paying a rose a year at St. John the Baptist and doing service to the chief lords. Reversion to John Heritage and Edith and John's heirs.

77/64/202

1342

721. Morrow [3 Feb.] of the Purification. John de Wickham (*Wykham*) and Petronilla his wife quer.; Richard le Young (*Yonge*) of Shenington (*Shenyndon*) def. A messuage, 2 yardlands, and 3 a. of meadow in Shenington. John acknowledged the right of Richard. For this, grant and render to John and Petronilla of two thirds of the messuage and [the whole of] 1½ yardlands. To hold to them and their heirs in tail. And grant to them of the reversion of one third of the messuage and [the whole of] ½ yardland and the meadow held by William le Young, Robert his brother, and Alice and Agnes his sisters for term of life, of Richard's inheritance. To hold as above. Contingent remainder to John's heirs. (Warranty.) *Endorsed* William son of Richard le Young of Shenington put in his claim. [*Worn.*]

77/64/204

722. Two weeks [14 April] from Easter. Thomas le Clerk of Bristol (*Bristoll'*) quer.; Simon Tumbrel and John son of Robert Tumbrel of Bristol def. A messuage in the suburb of Bristol. Right of Thomas by gift of Simon and John. (Warranty, specifying Simon's heirs.) Cons. 100*s*.

77/64/209

[Cf. *Bristol Gt. Red Book*, p. 224, no. 150.]

723. One month [28 April] from Easter. John Upoure quer.; Nicholas Seymour (*Seymore*) of Bristol (*Bristoll'*) 'bowyer' and Cristina his wife def. A toft in the suburb of Bristol. Right of John by gift of Nicholas and Cristina. (Warranty, specifying Cristina's heirs.) Cons. 100*s*.

77/64/210

[Cf. *Bristol Gt. Red Book*, pp. 224–5, no. 151.]

724. Morrow [25 June] of St. John the Baptist. (Made two weeks from Michaelmas 15 Edward III [13 Oct. 1341].) Roger de Acton and John his brother quer. by Thomas de Tochewyk in John's place; Ralph Russel def. The manor of Aust (*Auste*), held by Roger de Quantock (*Cantok*) for term of life and for two years beyond that. Grant of the reversion by Ralph to Roger de Acton and John. To hold during their lives, of Ralph, paying 1*d.* a year at Michaelmas and doing service to the chief lords. (Warranty.) Reversion to Ralph. Cons. 10 marks. Made in Roger Quantock's presence and with his consent, and he did fealty to Roger de Acton and John. [*Worn.*]

77/64/201

725. Two weeks [13 Oct.] from Michaelmas. (Made one week from St. Martin 14 Edward III [18 Nov. 1340].) William de Shareshill (*Shareshull*) 'chivaler' quer.; Ellis Lyvet def. The manor of Hillesley (*Hildesleye*) and the advowson of the chapel of the same manor held by Eleanor who was wife of John Lyvet of Haselor (*Haselore*) for term of life. Right of William. Grant to him of the reversion, of Ellis's inheritance. (Warranty.) Cons. 100 marks. [*Worn.*]

77/64/203

726. Two weeks [13 Oct.] from Michaelmas. Walter son of Walter de Gloucester (*Gloucestre*) and Petronilla his wife quer.; John de Ingleby (*Ingelby*) chaplain and Robert

1342

de Bridgford (*Bruggeford*) def. The hundred of Langley (*Langele*) and the manors of Alveston (*Alveston*) and Earthcott (*Erdecote*). Walter acknowledged the right of John and Robert, of which they had two thirds of the hundreds and of the manors by Walter's gift. For this, grant and render to Walter and Petronilla. To hold to them and their heirs in tail, of the king. And grant to them of the reversion of the one third of the hundred and manors held by Eleanor who was wife of Fulk FitzWarren (*le Fitz Waryn*) in dower, of the inheritance of John and Robert. To hold as above. Contingent remainder to Peter Corbet of Siston (*Syston*). Made by the king's order. [*Worn and stained.*]

77/64/208

727. One month [27 Oct.] from Michaelmas. John de Sodbury (*Sobbury*) clerk quer.; John son of William Manser of Docking (*Dokkyngge*) and Isabel his wife def. The manor of West Marshfield (*Westmarsfeld*). Right of John de Sodbury. Remise and quitclaim, specifying Isabel's heirs, to him. (Warranty.) Cons. 100 marks. *Endorsed* Richard son and heir of John de Hedon put in his claim.

77/64/205

1343

728. One week [20 Jan.] from Hilary. (Made two weeks from Michaelmas in the said year [13 Oct. 1342].) John Burne and Alice his wife quer.; William Marshal (*Mareschal*) parson of the church of Dorsington (*Dersynton*) def. Two messuages and 2¾ yardlands in Dorsington and Pebworth (*Pebbeworth*). Right of William by gift of John and Alice. For this, grant back and render to John and Alice. To hold during their lives. Remainder to Thomas Burne, Thomas's brothers Richard and Robert, and Robert's sisters Alice, Juliana, Hawise, Margery, Joan, and Eleanor [jointly] during their lives. Remainder to the heirs of Alice wife of John de Burne.

77/64/207

17 Edward III

1343

729. Two weeks [27 Jan.] from Hilary. (Made two weeks from Michaelmas 16 Edward III [13 Oct. 1342].) Thomas Snyte and Matilda his wife quer. by John Durrant (*Durant*) in Matilda's place; Philip Pontoise and Joan his wife def. Ten acres of land in Ham (*Hamme*). Thomas acknowledged the right of Joan, as that which Philip and Joan had by Thomas's gift. For this, grant and render to Thomas and Matilda. To hold to them and Thomas's heirs. (Warranty, specifying Joan's heirs.)

77/64/211a (formerly 77/64/206)

730. Two weeks [27 April] from Easter. Robert de Wrington (*Wryngton*) and Juliana his wife quer.; John de Barton and Elizabeth his wife def. A messuage in the suburb of Bristol (*Bristoll*). Right of Robert. Remise and quitclaim, specifying Elizabeth's heirs, to Robert and Juliana and Robert's heirs. (Warranty.) Cons. 100*s*.

77/64/211b

[Cf. *Bristol Gt. Red Book*, p. 225, no. 152.]

1343

731. Two weeks [27 April] from Easter. William Reynald and Simon Sandwich (*Sandwych*) quer.; Ranulph Newmaster (*Newemaystre*) and Alice his wife def. A messuage and 28s. rent in Bristol (*Bristoll'*). Right of William, as those which William and Simon had by gift of Ranulph and Alice. To hold to William and Simon and William's heirs. (Warranty, specifying Alice's heirs.) Cons. 20 marks.

77/64/212

[Cf. *Bristol Gt. Red Book*, p. 224, no. 153.]

732. One month [11 May] from Easter. Robert de Apperley (*Apperleye*) 'chivaler' and Margaret his wife quer.; William Bruyn of Gloucester (*Gloucestr'*) and Juliana his wife def. A messuage, 80 a. of land, and 2 a. of meadow in Tirley (*Trynleye*) and Hasfield (*Hasfeld*). Grant, remise, and quitclaim of whatever William and Juliana had in the holdings for term of their lives to Robert and Margaret and Robert's heirs. Cons. 40 marks.

77/64/218

733. Morrow [23 May] of Ascension. Laurence Martin (*Martyn*) of Fairford (*Fairford*) quer.; John son of Philip Devereux (*Devereusse*) of Eastleach Turville (*Lechturvill*) and Agnes his wife def. A messuage and 40 a. of land in Eastleach Turville. Right of Laurence by gift of John and Agnes. (Warranty, specifying John's heirs.) Cons. £20. *Endorsed* John Devereux (*Deverous*) put in his claim.

77/64/221

734. One week [15 June] from Trinity. (Made one month [11 May] from Easter in the said year.) William de Cheltenham (*Chiltenham*) and Robert his son quer.; William de Shareshill (*Shareshull*) 'chivaler' def. The manor of Hillesley (*Hildesleye*). Grant and render to William de Cheltenham and Robert. To hold to them and Robert's heirs in tail. Contingent remainder to William de Cheltenham's heirs. Cons. 100 marks.

77/64/219

735. One week [15 June] from Trinity. (Made three weeks [4 May] from Easter in the said year.) Thomas de Breadstone (*Bradeston*) 'chivaler' quer.; Robert Selyman (*Selymon*) and Alice his wife and John Selyman and Isabel his wife def. Sixteen acres of land, 2½ a. of meadow, and 3 a. of wood in Cam (*Camme*) and Stinchcombe (*Styntescombe*). Right of Thomas. Remise and quitclaim, specifying Alice's and Isabel's heirs, to him. (Warranty.) Cons. 20 marks.

77/64/220

736. One week [6 Oct.] from Michaelmas. William de Bohun earl of Northampton (*Norhampton*) and Elizabeth his wife quer.; Edmund de Bohun 'chivaler' def. The manor of Haresfield (*Harisfeld*). Right of the earl, as that which the earl and Elizabeth had by Edmund's gift. To hold to the earl and Elizabeth and the earl's heirs. (Warranty.) Cons. £100.

77/64/215

1343

737. Two weeks [13 Oct.] from Michaelmas. William de Bohun earl of Northampton (*Norhampton*) and Elizabeth his wife quer.; Edmund de Bohun 'chivaler' def. The manor of Haresfield (*Harisfeld*). Right of the earl, as that which the earl and Elizabeth had by Edmund's gift. For this, grant back and render to Edmund. To hold during his life, of the earl and Elizabeth and the earl's heirs, paying a rose a year at St. John the Baptist and doing service to the chief lords. (Warranty, specifying the earl's heirs.) Reversion to the earl and Elizabeth and the earl's heirs. *Endorsed* Glouc'.

77/64/214

738. Two weeks [13 Oct.] from Michaelmas. Thomas Sewell (*Sewale*) of Wickham (*Wykham*) and John de la Brooke (*Broke*) parson of the church of Ditteridge (*Dycherigg*) quer.; John de Knovill and Margery his wife def. by Gilbert de Bardfield (*Berdefeld*) in Margery's place by the king's writ. The manors of Kilcot (*Killecote*) and Little Taynton (*Parva Teynton*). John de Knovill acknowledged the right of Thomas, as those which Thomas and John de la Brooke had by John de Knovill's gift. For this, grant and render to John de Knovill and Margery. To hold to them and their heirs in tail. Contingent remainder to John de Knovill's heirs.

77/64/216

739. Morrow [3 Nov.] of All Souls. Thomas Belcher (*Belechere*) of Bristol (*Bristoll'*) quer. by Geoffrey Martin (*Martyn*); John Horshale and Matilda his wife def. A messuage in the suburb of Bristol. Right of Thomas by gift of John and Matilda. (Warranty, specifying Matilda's heirs.) Cons. 100*s*.

77/64/213

[Cf. *Bristol Gt. Red Book*, p. 225, no. 154.]

1344

740. One week [20 Jan.] from Hilary. Adam Martel and Cecily his wife quer. by William de Westhall (*Westhale*) in Cecily's place; Michael de Ash (*Asshe*) def. The manor of Stowell (*Stowell*) and the advowson of the church of the same manor. Adam acknowledged the right of Michael by Adam's gift. For this, grant and render to Michael and Cecily. To hold to them and their heirs in tail. Contingent remainder to Robert de Staverton.

77/64/217

18 Edward III

1344

741. Two weeks [*27* Jan.] from Hilary. (Made three weeks from Michaelmas 17 Edward III [20 Oct. 1343].) Robert de Prestbury (*Prestebury*) 'chivaler' quer.; William Maunsell (*Maunsel*) of Lypiatt (*Lupyate*) def. Two messuages and 2 ploughlands in Prestbury. Right of William by Robert's gift. For this, grant back and render to Robert. To hold during his life. Remainder to Robert's son John and Eleanor his wife and their heirs in tail. Successive contingent remainders to John's brother Robert and his heirs in tail, to Robert's brother William and his heirs in tail, and to William's brother Thomas.

77/64/223

1344

742. Two weeks [27 Jan.] from Hilary. (Made two weeks from Michaelmas 17 Edward III [13 Oct. 1343].) Robert d'Abitot (*Dabetot*) quer.; William Chichele (*Chichely*) of Gloucester (*Gloucestre*) and Matilda his wife def. A messuage and ½ yardland in Withington (*Wythyndon*) and Hilcot (*Huldecote*). Right of Robert by gift of William and Matilda. (Warranty, specifying Matilda's heirs.) Cons. 10 marks.

77/64/224

743. Two weeks [27 Jan.] from Hilary. (Made two weeks from Michaelmas 17 Edward III [13 Oct. 1343].) William de Cheltenham (*Chiltenham*) and Elena his wife quer.; Ellis de Elberton (*Aylbrighton*) and Joan his wife def. The manor of Purton (*Piriton*). Right of William. Remise and quitclaim, specifying Joan's heirs, to William and Elena and William's heirs. (Warranty.) Cons. 100 marks.

77/64/225

744. Two weeks [27 Jan.] from Hilary. (Made two weeks from Michaelmas 17 Edward III [13 Oct. 1343].) Thomas son of Maurice de Berkeley (*Berkele*) 'chivaler' quer.; Ellis de Elberton (*Aylbrighton*) and Joan his wife def. The manors of Beverston (*Beverston*) and Over (*Oure*). Right of Thomas. Remise and quitclaim, specifying Joan's heirs, to him. (Warranty.) Cons. £100.

77/65/226

[Cf. *Berkeley Castle Mun.* i, p. 148, A1/13/6 (counterpart).]

745. Two weeks [18 April] from Easter. Thomas de Dumbleton (*Dumbelton*) chaplain quer.; Edmund le Freeman (*Fremon*) and Emma his wife def. A messuage, 36 a. of land, 6 a. of meadow, and 6*d.* rent in Quedgeley (*Quedesle*). Right of Thomas by gift of Edmund and Emma. For this, grant back and render to Edmund and Emma. To hold during their lives. Remainder to Nicholas son of Thomas de Amersham (*Agmondesham*) the elder and his heirs in tail. Successive contingent remainders to Nicholas's brother Edward and his heirs in tail, to Edward's brother John and his heirs in tail, and to John's heirs.

77/65/233

746. Three weeks [25 April] from Easter. (Made one week [9 Feb.] from the Purification in the said year.) John son of Walter de Basing (*Beysyn*) and Margaret his wife quer.; Walter de Basing 'chivaler' and Alice his wife def. The manor of Eyford (*Eyford*) and the advowson of the church of the same manor, held by Geoffrey de Wickham (*Wikkewane*) for term of life, of Alice's inheritance. Grant of the reversion to John and Margaret and their heirs in tail. To hold of Walter and Alice and Alice's heirs, paying a rose a year at St. John the Baptist and doing service to the chief lords. Contingent reversion to Walter and Alice and Alice's heirs.

77/65/231

747. Three weeks [25 April] from Easter. Isabel de Broadwell (*Bradewall*) quer.; James de Audley (*Audeleye*) def. Half of the manor Badgeworth (*Beggesworth*). Grant and render to Isabel. To hold during her life, of James, paying a rose a year at St. John the Baptist and doing service to the chief lords. Remainder to Isabel's son James and his heirs in tail. To hold as above. (Warranty.) Contingent reversion to James de Audley. Cons. 100 marks.

77/65/232

1344

748. One week [6 June] from Trinity. (Made one month [2 May] from Easter in the said year.) Philip le Marshal (*Mareschal*) and Joan his wife quer.; Ellis de Blakeney (*Blakeneye*) clerk def. Three acres of land and 44*s.* rent in Blaisdon (*Blechedon*). Right of Joan, as those which Philip and Joan had by Ellis's gift. For this, grant back and render to Ellis. To hold during his life, of Philip and Joan and Joan's heirs, paying a rose a year at St. John the Baptist and doing service to the chief lords. (Warranty.) Reversion to Philip and Joan and Joan's heirs.

77/65/236

749. One week [6 June] from Trinity. (Made one month [2 May] from Easter in the said year.) Philip le Marshal (*Mareschal*) and Joan his wife quer.; Geoffrey le Marshal vicar of the church of Longhope (*Longehope*) def. A messuage, 1 ploughland, and 8*s.* rent in Longhope. Philip acknowledged the right of Geoffrey by Philip's gift. For this, grant and render to Philip and Joan. To hold to them and their heirs in tail. Contingent remainder to Philip's heirs.

77/65/240

750. One week [6 June] from Trinity. (Made one month [2 May] from Easter in the said year.) Philip le Marshal (*Mareschal*) and Joan his wife quer.; Geoffrey le Marshal vicar of the church of Longhope (*Longehope*) def. A messuage, 1 ploughland, 12 a. of wood and 40*s.* rent in Blaisdon (*Blechedon*) and the advowson of the church of the same township. Right of Geoffrey by gift of Philip and Joan. For this, grant back and render to Philip and Joan. To hold to them and their heirs in tail. Contingent remainder to Joan's heirs.

77/65/238

751. Two weeks [13 June] from Trinity. (Made three weeks [25 April] from Easter in the said year.) William de Tytherington (*Tyderynton*) the younger and Isabel his wife quer. by John de Winstone (*Wynstan*) in Isabel's place; William de Tytherington (*Tiderynton*) and Lucy his wife def. A messuage, 60 a. of land, 4 a. of meadow, and 6*d.* rent in Tytherington. Grant and render to William the younger and Isabel. To hold to them and their heirs in tail. Contingent remainder to the heirs of William the younger. (Warranty, specifying the heirs of William the elder.) Cons. 100 marks.

77/65/234

752. Two weeks [13 June] from Trinity. (Made three weeks [25 April] from Easter in the said year.) Robert son of Thomas Stevens (*Stevenes*) of Edgeworth (*Eggesworthe*) and Alice and Joan his sisters quer.; Thomas Stevens of Edgeworth and Joan his wife def. A messuage, 1 ploughland, 4 a. of meadow, 6 a. of pasture, 20 a. of wood, 8*s.* rent, and one third of 12 a. of pasture in Edgeworth. Right of Thomas, as those which Thomas and Joan had by gift of Robert, Alice, and Joan. For this, grant back and render to Robert, Alice, and Joan. To hold to them and Robert's heirs in tail, of Thomas and Joan and Thomas's heirs, paying a rose a year at St. John the Baptist and doing service to the chief lords. Contingent remainder to Thomas's younger daughter Joan and her heirs in tail. Contingent reversion to Thomas and Joan and Thomas's heirs.

77/65/235

1344

753. Two weeks [13 June] from Trinity. (Made two weeks [18 April] from Easter in the said year.) Richard Talbot knight quer.; Thomas son of Thomas de Huntley (*Huntele*) knight def. The manor of Huntley and the advowson of the church of the same manor. Right of Richard. Remise and quitclaim to him. (Warranty.) Cons. 100 marks.

77/65/237

754. Two weeks [13 June] from Trinity. (Made three weeks [25 April] from Easter in the said year.) Richard Home and John Butter (*Boter*) parson of the church of *Staundon* [Staunton?] quer.; William Hook (*Hoke*) of Littledean (*Parva Dene*) and Matilda his wife def. Sixteen acres of land and 2 a. of meadow in Lydney (*Lydeneye*). Right of John. Remise and quitclaim, specifying Matilda's heirs, to Richard and John and John's heirs. (Warranty.) Cons. 10 marks.

77/65/239

755. Two weeks [8 July] from St. John the Baptist. Hugh le Despenser and Elizabeth his wife quer.; Edmund de Grimsby (*Grymesby*) and William de Osberston clerks def. The manors of Martley (*Martelegh*) and Bushley (*Bisshelegh*), WORCS., the manors of Shipton under Wychwood (*Shypton*) and Burford (*Burford*), OXON., the manor of Stanford in the Vale (*Stanford*), BERKS., the manor of Ashley (*Asshelegh*), HANTS., the manor of Rotherfield (*Rotheresfeld*), SUSSEX, and the manor of Old Sodbury (*Sobbury*), GLOS. Hugh acknowledged the right of Edmund and William by Hugh's gift. For this, grant and render to Hugh and Elizabeth. To hold to them and Hugh's heirs, of the king. Made by the king's order. *Labelled* Wygorn', Oxon', Berk', Sutht', Sussex', Glouc'. *Endorsed* William de Clinton (*Clynton*) earl of Huntingdon (*Huntyndon*) and Juliana his wife and Laurence de Hastings (*Hastynges*) earl of Pembroke (*Pembr'*) put in their claims.

287/41/338

[Cf. *Sussex Fines, 1307–1509*, p. 112, no. 1997. For the identity of Shipton, *Cal. Inq. p.m.* x, p. 415; of Stanford, above, no. 391.]

756. Two weeks [13 Oct.] from Michaelmas. Everard le French (*Frensh*) of Bristol (*Bristoll'*) quer. by Geoffrey Martin (*Martyn*); Thomas de Bury chaplain def. A messuage in Bristol. Right of Everard by Thomas's gift. (Warranty.) Cons. 100*s.*

77/64/222

[Cf. *Bristol Gt. Red Book*, p. 226, no. 155.]

757. Two weeks [13 Oct.] from Michaelmas. (Made two weeks [13 June] from Trinity in the said year.) Thomas Flory and Joan his wife quer. by John de Winstone (*Wynstan*) in Joan's place; John de Pixley (*Pykesleye*) clerk def. A messuage, 40 a. of land, 6 a. of meadow, and 10*s.* 9¼*d.* rent in Wotton (*Wotton*) by Gloucester (*Gloucestr'*). Thomas acknowledged the right of John by Thomas's gift. For this, grant and render to Thomas and Joan. To hold to them and their heirs in tail. Contingent remainder to Thomas's heirs.

77/65/227

758. Two weeks [13 Oct.] from Michaelmas. Maurice son of Maurice de Berkeley (*Berkele*) 'chivaler' quer.; Walter son of Walter de Gloucester (*Gloucestr'*) 'chivaler' def. The manor of Uley (*Iweleye*). Right of Maurice. Remise and quitclaim to him. Cons. 100 marks.

77/65/230

1344

759. Two weeks [13 Oct.] from Michaelmas. (Made two weeks [13 June] from Trinity in the said year.) John de la River (*Ryvere*) 'chivaler' and Margaret his wife quer.; William de Cheltenham (*Chiltenham*) and William Edward' def. The manor of East Horrington (*Esthornyngdon*), SOM., and the manors of Tormarton (*Tormerton*), West Littleton (*Littelton*), and Acton Turville (*Acton Turvill'*) and the advowsons of the churches of the manors of Tormarton and Acton Turville, GLOS. Right of William de Cheltenham, of which the same William and William Edward' had the manor of West Littleton, half and two thirds of half of the manor of Acton Turville, and two thirds of the manors of Tormarton and East Horrington and the advowsons by gift of John and Margaret. For this, grant back and render to John and Margaret of the manor of West Littleton, the half and two thirds of the manor of Acton Turville, and two thirds of the manor of Tormarton except a messuage and 2 ploughlands in the manor of Tormarton. To hold to John and Margaret and John's heirs. And grant and render to John of the messuage and 2 ploughlands above excepted, the advowsons, and the two thirds of the manor of East Horrington. To hold to John and his heirs. And grant to John and Margaret and John's heirs of the reversion of one third of the manor of Tormarton and of one third of half of the manor of Acton Turville, held by Denise who was wife of John son of Richard de la River in dower, and grant to John and his heirs of the reversion of one third of the manor of East Horrington held by the same Denise in dower, of the inheritance of William de Cheltenham. *Labelled* Somers', Glouc'. [*Worn.*]

287/41/342

[Cf. *Som. Fines, 1307–46*, p. 251.]

760. One month [27 Oct.] from Michaelmas. Henry Hereward and Joan his wife quer.; Robert de Louth (*Louthe*) and Elena his wife def. Half of a messuage in Cirencester (*Cirencestre*). Right of Henry. Remise and quitclaim, specifying Elena's heirs, to Henry and Joan and Henry's heirs. (Warranty.) Cons. 100*s*.

77/65/229

761. Two weeks [25 Nov.] from St. Martin. Fulk de Birmingham (*Bermyngham*) 'chivaler' quer.; Richard de Hangleton (*Hangelton*) and Alice his wife def. Two messuages, 400 a. of land, 110 a. of meadow, 20 a. of wood, and 9 marks rent in Wightfield (*Whitfelde*) and Apperley (*Apperle*). Right of Fulk. Render to him. (Warranty, specifying Alice's heirs.) For this, Fulk granted that he would pay to Richard and Alice during their lives £30 a year, at the Annunciation and Michaelmas, with right of distraint for non-payment.

77/65/228

1345

762. One week [20 Jan.] from Hilary. (Made one week from Michaelmas in the said year [6 Oct. 1344].) Richard son of Gilbert Talbot knight quer.; Thomas Fabian and Eve his wife def. One third of the manor of Ley (*Leye*) and 6 messuages, 160 a. of land, 30 a. of meadow, 12 a. of wood, and £10 rent in Upper Ley (*Overleye*), Lower Ley (*Netherleye*), Westbury on Severn (*Westbury*), Elton (*Elftone*), and Denny (*Dunye*). Right of Richard. Remise and quitclaim, specifying Eve's heirs, to him. (Warranty.) Cons. 100 marks.

77/65/241(a)

1345

763. One week [20 Jan.] from Hilary. (Made two weeks from Michaelmas in the said year [13 Oct. 1344].) Henry de Cosham and Cristiana his wife quer.; William Haynes of Standlake (*Stanlake*) and Agnes his wife def. A messuage and 13 a. of land in Eastleach Turville (*Lech Turville*). Right of Henry, as those which Henry and Cristiana had by gift of William and Agnes. To hold to Henry and Cristiana and Henry's heirs. (Warranty, specifying Cristiana's heirs.) Cons. 20 marks.

77/65/241

19 Edward III

1345

764. Two weeks [27 Jan.] from Hilary. (Made two weeks from Michaelmas 18 Edward III [13 Oct. 1344].) Robert Hereward quer.; Abraham de Hailey (*Haylye*) and Alice his wife def. A messuage in Cirencester (*Cirencestr'*). Right of Robert. Remise and quitclaim, specifying Alice's heirs, to him. (Warranty.) Cons. 100*s*.

77/65/243

765. Two weeks [27 Jan.] from Hilary. Henry de Willington (*Wylyngton*) and Isabel his wife quer. by William de Medewell in Isabel's place; Robert Ewyas parson of the church of *Lomene* [Uplowman?] and Nicholas Warre def. The manor of Coverdine (*Culverdene*). Henry acknowledged the right of Robert, as that which Robert and Nicholas had by Henry's gift. For this, grant and render to Henry and Isabel. To hold to them and Henry's heirs.

77/65/244

766. Two weeks [27 Jan.] from Hilary. (Made the morrow of All Souls 18 Edward III [3 Nov. 1344].) Peter de Montfort (*Monte Forti*) quer.; Thomas de Compton and John de Middleham (*Middelham*) def. The manor of Meon (*Mune*), GLOS., and the manor of Leigh Castle (*Castellegh*), WORCS. Right of Thomas, as that which Thomas and John had by Peter's gift. For this, grant back and render to Peter. To hold during his life. Remainder to Alice wife of Richard de Nowers (*Novers*) during her life and to Robert de Pembridge (*Pembrugg'*). *Labelled* Glouc', Wygorn'.

287/42/367

767. Morrow [3 Feb.] of the Purification. (Made two weeks from Easter 17 Edward III [27 April 1343].) Roger Turtle quer. by Geoffrey Martin (*Martyn*); Ellis son of John Daubeney (*Daubeneye*) def. Sixty-five acres of land and 7 a. of meadow in Hatherley (*Hatherlegh*), Wallsworth (*Wallesworth*), and Twigworth (*Tygworth* [sic]). Right of Roger. Grant to him of the reversion of 55 a. of land and 4 a. and 3 roods of meadow held by John le Walsh (*Walshe*) for term of life, and of 10 a. of land and 2 a. and 1 rood of meadow held by William atte Marsh (*Mershe*) and Cecily his wife for term of life, of Ellis's inheritance in the said townships. (Warranty.) Cons. 20 marks.

77/65/242

768. Two weeks [10 April] from Easter. (Made two weeks [27 Jan.] from Hilary in the said year.) Hugh Mustel and Isabel his wife quer. by Peter de Edgeworth (*Eggeworth)* in Isabel's place; Ralph de Boulsdon (*Bullesdon*) of Clifton (*Clifton*) chaplain def. Four

1345

messuages, a mill, 5 ploughlands, 20 a. of meadow, 4 a. of pasture, 20 a. of wood, and 100*s*. rent in Boddington (*Botynton*), Guiting Power (*Parva Gutynge*), and Hardwicke (*Herdewyk*), GLOS., and a messuage, 2 ploughlands and 10 a. of land, 16 a. of meadow, 9 a. of pasture, 20 a. of wood, and 51*s*. 1*d*. rent in Habberley (*Haberleye*), Kidderminster (*Kyderministre*), Trimpley (*Trimpeleye*), and Puxton (*Pokeston*), WORCS. Hugh acknowledged the right of Ralph, of which he had a messuage, 1 ploughland, 4 a. of meadow and 2*s*. rent in Ha[bberley] and two thirds of all the other holdings by Hugh's gift. For this, grant and render to Hugh and Isabel. To hold to them and their heirs in tail. And grant to Hugh and Isabel of the reversion of one third of 4 messuages, the mill, 6 ploughlands and 10 a. of land, 32 a. of meadow, the pasture in the said wood, and £7 9*s*. 1*d*. rent in Boddington, Guiting Power, Habberley, Kidderminster, Trimpley, and Puxton held by John son of John de la Mare of Rendcomb (*Ryndecombe*) and Anne his wife in Anne's dower, of Ralph's inheritance. To hold as above. Successive contingent remainders to Thomas son of Thomas le Butler (*Botiller*) 'chivaler' and his heirs in tail, to that Thomas's brother Alan and his heirs in tail, and to Thomas le Butler 'chivaler'. *Labelled* Glouc', Wygorn'. [*Worn and stained.*]

287/42/373

769. Two weeks [10 April] from Easter. (Made one week from St. John the Baptist 18 Edward III [1 July 1344].) John atte Wood (*Wode*) of Winchcombe (*Wynchecumbe*) and Amice his wife quer.; William de Fontenay (*Founteneye*) parson of the church of Swindon (*Swyndon*) def. A messuage, 40 a. of land, and 2 a. of meadow in Winchcombe and Gretton (*Gretton*). Right of William. For this, grant and render to John and Amice. To hold to them and Amice's heirs.

77/65/247

770. Two weeks [10 April] from Easter. John de Dowdeswell (*Doudeswelle*) quer.; Thomas de Weston the younger and Joan his wife def. The manor of Dowdeswell, 9 messuages, a mill, 2 ploughlands and 7 yardlands, 20 a. of meadow, 20 a. of pasture, 100 a. of wood, and 7*s*. 8*d*. rent in Castlett (*Catslade*) and Cutsdean (*Cotesdene*), and the advowson of the church of the same manor. Right of John. Remise and quitclaim, specifying Joan's heirs, to him. Cons. 200 marks.

77/65/249

771. Three weeks [17 April] from Easter. John de Eastleach (*Estlecche*) and Cristiana his wife quer.; John Plusabele of Littleton Drew (*Lutlynton Dreu*) and Edith his wife def. A messuage, 1 ploughland, and 6*s*. rent in Eastleach. Right of John de Eastleach, as those which John and Cristiana had by gift of John Plusabele and Edith. To hold to John de Eastleach and Cristiana and that John's heirs. (Warranty, specifying Edith's heirs.) Cons. 40 marks.

77/65/248

772. One month [23 April] from Easter. Thomas de Berkeley (*Berkelee*) 'chivaler' quer.; Anselm de Farndon and Matilda his wife def. A messuage and ¾ yardland in Over (*Overe*). Grant to Thomas. Remise and quitclaim to him of whatever Anselm and Matilda had in the said holdings for term of Matilda's life. Cons. 20 marks.

77/66/251

1345

773. Morrow [6 May] of Ascension. Simon de Apperley (*Apperleye*) 'smyth' quer.; John atte Hole and Alice his wife def. Two shops in Gloucester (*Gloucestr'*). Right of Simon. Remise and quitclaim, specifying Alice's heirs, to him. (Warranty.) Cons. 20 marks.

77/65/250

774. Two weeks [5 June] from Trinity. (Made three weeks [17 April] from Easter in the said year.) John de Milcombe (*Mildecombe*) and Alice his wife quer. by Ralph Friday in Alice's place; Robert son of Robert de Wickham (*Wykham*) def. One fifth of the manor of Shenington (*Shenindon*) [*reading uncertain*]. John acknowledged the right of Robert by John's gift, except for 3 messuages, 4*s.* rent, and 1½ yardlands. For this, grant and render of the one fifth as aforesaid to John and Alice. To hold to them and their heirs in tail. And grant to them of the reversion of the excepted messuages, land, and rent, held by Alice who was wife of Philip le Soor in dower, of Robert's inheritance. To hold as above. Contingent remainder to John's heirs. (Warranty.) [*Worn.*]

77/65/245

775. One week [1 July] from St. John the Baptist. John de Peyto the younger and Beatrice his wife quer.; Mr. Roger de Grafton def. The manor of Lark Stoke (*Larkestok*). Right of Mr. Roger by gift of John and Beatrice. For this, grant back and render to John and Beatrice. To hold during their lives. Remainder to Walter son of Richard de Clodeshale and Alice his wife and their heirs in tail. Successive contingent remainders to Roger de Bishopstone (*Bisshoppesdon*) and his heirs in tail, to John de Bishopstone and his heirs in tail, and to Roger de Bishopstone's heirs. [*Worn and stained.*]

77/65/246

776. Two weeks [13 Oct.] from Michaelmas. Robert de Staverton and Margaret his wife quer.; James de Wilton and Elizabeth his wife def. Two messuages, 40 a. of land, 5 a. of meadow, 8 a. of wood, and 79*s.* 6*d.* rent, and one third of a messuage and 1 ploughland in Arlingham (*Erlyngham*), Coaley (*Coveley*), Cam (*Camme*), Slimbridge (*Slymbrige*), and Up Hatherley (*Uphatherleye*). Grant and render to Robert and Margaret of [a messuage], 23 a. of land, 3 a. of meadow, the wood, the one third of the messuage and ploughland, and the rent, with the homages and all the services of Richard Dun, Walter [de Middleton (*Middelton*)] the younger, Walter le Ferrar (*Ferour*), Richard Reynald, Walter Jakeman (*Jakemon*), Walter le Fisher (*Fisshare*), Alice Bertram, John Huyetes, Richard le Tailor (*Taylour*), Walter Bill (*Byl*), Matilda atte Wood (*Wode*), [John Blackford (*Blakeford*)], Thomas de Berkeley (*Berkeleye*), Mariot Fallewolle, Walter Beoleystrete, William Ramsbury (*Remmesbury*) and Joan his wife, and Matilda Sealey (*Sely*). To hold to Robert and Margaret and their heirs in tail. And grant to Robert and Margaret of the reversion of a messuage and 10 a. of land held by [Mariot Fallewolle] for term of life, of 7 a. of land held by Matilda atte Wood for term of life, and of 2 a. of meadow held by John de Blackford (*Blakeforde*) for term of life, of Elizabeth's inheritance. To hold as above. Contingent remainder to Robert's heirs. (Warranty.) Cons. £40. [*Worn and stained.*]

77/66/252

[Some of the details, as indicated above by square brackets, have been supplied from the note of fine, CP 26/1/9, Mich. 19 Edw. III.]

1345

777. Two weeks [13 Oct.] from Michaelmas. Robert de Staverton and Margaret his wife quer.; John Sergeant and Michael de Ash (*Assh*) def. Two messuages, 28 a. of land, 12 a. of wood, 57*s*. 9*d*. rent, and one third of a messuage and 1 ploughland in Arlingham (*Erlyngham*), Slimbridge (*Slymbrugge*), Coaley (*Coveleye*), Cam (*Camme*), and Up Hatherley (*Uphatherleye*). Right of John, of which John and Michael had a messuage, the land, wood, rent, and the one third by gift of Robert and Margaret. For this, grant back and render to Robert and Margaret. To hold to them and their heirs in tail. And grant to them of the reversion of a messuage in Arlingham held by John le Shepherd (*Shepehurd*) for term of life, of John's inheritance. To hold as above. Contingent remainder to Robert's heirs. [*Worn.*]

77/66/253

778. Two weeks [13 Oct.] from Michaelmas. Joan daughter of Nicholas de Morton of Tewkesbury (*Teukesbury*) quer.; William de Cleeve (*Clyve*) and Margery his wife and Margery's sister Agnes def. Half of two messuages in Tewkesbury. Right of Joan. Remise and quitclaim, specifying Margery's and Agnes's heirs, to Joan. (Warranty.) Cons. 20 marks.

77/66/254

779. Three weeks [20 Oct.] from Michaelmas. William Cailly (*Kaylewey*) and Alice his wife quer.; Robert Murdoch (*Murdak*) def. The manor of Luckington (*Lokynton*) and the advowson of the church of the same manor, WILTS., and a messuage, 2 ploughlands, 24 a. of meadow, 10 a. of wood, and 5*s*. rent in Horton (*Horton*) [*reading uncertain*], GLOS. Right of Robert, of which he had two thirds of two thirds of the manor and holdings, one third of the manor and holdings, and the advowson by gift of William and Alice. For this, grant back and render to William and Alice. To hold to them and Alice's heirs in tail. And grant to William and Alice of the reversion of the one third of two thirds held by Ellis atte Hall (*Halle*) and Felicia his wife in Felicia's dower, of Robert's inheritance. To hold as above. Contingent remainder to Thomas de Breadstone (*Bradeston*). *Labelled* Wiltes', Glouc'. [*Torn and worn.*]

287/42/363

[Cf. *Wilts. Fines, 1327–77*, p. 77, no. 306.]

20 Edward III

1346

780. Two weeks [27 Jan.] from Hilary. (Made one week from the Purification 18 Edward III [9 Feb. 1344].) Henry le Draper of Gloucester (*Gloucestr'*) and Denise his wife quer.; John son of Richard de Huntley (*Hunteleye*) def. Three messuages in Gloucester and the suburb of the same town, held by Denise who was wife of Richard de Huntley for term of life. Right of Henry. Grant of the reversion, of John's inheritance, to Henry and Denise. To hold to them and Henry's heirs. (Warranty.) Cons. £20.

77/66/255

781. Two weeks [27 Jan.] from Hilary. (Made the morrow of St. Martin 19 Edward III [12 Nov. 1345].) Walter atte Hall (*Halle*) and Margery his wife quer.; Thomas parson of the church of Beverston (*Beovereston*) and Henry le Fisher (*Fisshere*) of Malmesbury (*Malmesbury*) def. Ten messuages, 4 tofts, 290 a. of land, 7 a. of meadow, and 12*s*. rent

1346

in Hawkesbury (*Haukesbury*). Right of Thomas and Henry, of which they had a messuage, 2 tofts, 100 a. of land, 1 a. of meadow, and the rent by gift of Walter and Margery. For this, grant back and render to Walter and Margery. To hold during their lives. And grant to them of the reversion of 8 messuages, 157 a. of land, and 5 a. of meadow held by Alesia who was wife of John atte Hall for term of life, of a messuage and 7 a. of land held by John Derby and Edith his wife and Isabel their daughter for term of life, of a messuage and 7 a. of land held by Agnes atte Hall and Isabel her daughter for term of life, of a messuage and 8 a. of land held by Ellis atte Hall and Felicia his wife for term of life, of 4 a. of land held by Richard Harre and Matilda his wife for term of life, of 7 a. of land held by Alice Turk for term of life, and of 1 a. of meadow held by John de Tytherington (*Tyderyngton*) for term of life, of the inheritance of Thomas and Henry. To hold as above. Remainder to the abbot of Pershore (*Pershore*) and his successors. Made by the king's order. [*Worn.*]

77/66/256

[The total extent of the holdings given at the beginning of the fine includes two messuages fewer and two tofts more than the sum of the constituent parts. Presumably two of the tofts are described as messuages in the later part of the fine.]

782. Two weeks [27 Jan.] from Hilary. (Made two weeks from Michaelmas 19 Edward III [13 Oct. 1345].) Robert Coly chaplain and Elizabeth who was wife of John Coly quer.; Thomas Beaumond parson of the church of Weeting (*Wetynge*) def. Two messuages, 2 tofts, 90 a. of land, 3 a. of meadow, 8*d.* rent, and half of 1 a. of wood and 1 a. of moor in Taynton (*Teynton*). Right of Thomas by gift of Robert and Elizabeth. For this, grant back and render to Robert and Elizabeth. To hold during their lives. Remainder to John son of John Coly, the younger, and his heirs in tail. Successive contingent remainders to the same John's sister Juliana and her heirs in tail and to the said John's heirs.

77/66/258

783. Two weeks [27 Jan.] from Hilary. (Made two weeks from Michaelmas 19 Edward III [13 Oct. 1345].) James le Millward (*Muleward*) of Fairford (*Fayreford*) and Cristina his wife quer.; Henry James of Fairford and Alice his wife def. A messuage in Fairford. Right of James, as that which James and Cristina had by gift of Henry and Alice. To hold to James and Cristina and James's heirs. (Warranty, specifying Alice's heirs.) Cons. 10 marks.

77/66/259

784. Two weeks [27 Jan.] from Hilary. William de Syde quer.; Richard de Henley (*Henle*) of Newport (*Neweport*) 'carpenter' and Isabel his wife def. A messuage, a toft, 12 a. of land, 2 a. of meadow, and 1 a. of wood in Alkington (*Alkynton*). Right of William. Remise and quitclaim, specifying Isabel's heirs, to him. (Warranty.) Cons. 20 marks.

77/66/260

785. Two weeks [27 Jan.] from Hilary. (Made two weeks from Michaelmas 19 Edward III [13 Oct. 1345].) William Bruyn of Gloucester (*Gloucestr'*) 'burgeys' quer.; Thomas Merryman (*Maryman*) of Gloucester 'burgeys' and Joan his wife and Hugh Dymock (*Dymmok*) of Gloucester and Alice his wife def. A messuage in Gloucester held by

1346

Reynold de Tutshill (*Tydeshull*) and Alice his wife for term of Alice's life. Right of William. Grant of the reversion, of Joan's and Alice's inheritance, to him. (Warranty.) Cons. 100*s*.

77/66/270

786. Two weeks [30 April] from Easter. John Horncastle (*Horncastell*) of Bristol (*Bristoll'*) quer.; Geoffrey Methelan of Bristol and Agnes his wife def. A messuage in the suburb of Bristol. Right of John by gift of Geoffrey and Agnes. (Warranty, specifying Agnes's heirs.) Cons. 10 marks.

77/66/261

[Cf. *Bristol Gt. Red Book*, p. 226, no. 156.]

787. Two weeks [30 April] from Easter. John de Acton 'chivaler' and Joan his wife quer. by Richard Beynon (*Beynyn*) in Joan's place; Reynold de Stoke parson of the church of *Bere* def. The manor of Iron Acton (*Irenacton*) and the advowson of the church of the same manor. John acknowledged the right of Reynold by John's gift. For this, grant and render to John and Joan. To hold to them and their heirs in tail. Contingent remainder to John's heirs.

77/66/266

788. Three weeks [7 May] from Easter. William Hook (*Hoke*) of Bristol (*Bristoll'*) quer.; Thomas Lampner and Cristina his wife def. A messuage in Bristol. Right of William by gift of Thomas and Cristina. (Warranty, specifying Cristina's heirs.) Cons. 100*s*.

77/66/262

[Cf. *Bristol Gt. Red Book*, p. 226, no. 157.]

789. One month [14 May] from Easter. William le Felter (*Feltere*) of Bristol (*Bristoll'*) quer.; Richard de Sutton of Bristol and Cecily his wife def. A messuage in the suburb of Bristol. Right of William by gift of Richard and Cecily. (Warranty, specifying Richard's heirs.) Cons. 100*s*.

77/66/263

[Cf. *Bristol Gt. Red Book*, pp. 226–7, no. 158.]

790. One month [14 May] from Easter. William le Felter (*Feltere*) and Edith his wife quer.; Isabel who was wife of John le Whittier (*Whittaillour*) of Bristol (*Bristoll'*) 'toukere' [*i.e. fuller*] def. Three shops in the suburb of Bristol. Right of William, as those which William and Edith had by Isabel's gift. To hold to William and Edith and William's heirs. (Warranty.) Cons. 20 marks.

77/66/264

[Cf. *Bristol Gt. Red Book*, p. 227, no. 159.]

791. Morrow [26 May] of Ascension. (Made one week [9 Feb.] from the Purification in the said year.) John de Garston and Joan his wife quer.; John de Callaughton (*Calweton*) and Alice his wife def. One and a half ploughlands, 6½ a. of meadow, 11 a. of wood, and 18*s*. 0½*d*. rent in Stone (*Stone*) by Berkeley (*Berkele*). Right of John de Garston. Render to the same John and Joan. To hold to them and John's heirs. (Warranty, specifying Alice's heirs.) Cons. £20. [*Faded.*]

77/66/257

1346

792. Two weeks [25 June] from Trinity. (Made three weeks from Easter 18 Edward III [25 April 1344].) Henry de Brockworth (*Brokworth*) and Walter son of John de Brockworth quer.; John le Spenser of Defford (*Defford*) and Margery his wife def. A messuage, 40 a. of land, 3 a. of meadow, and 3*s.* rent in Brockworth, held by Richard Ernes (*Erneys*) for term of life. Grant of the reversion, of Margery's inheritance, to Henry and Walter and Walter's heirs in tail. Successive contingent remainders to Thomas son of Robert de la Mare and his heirs in tail and to Walter de Frome. (Warranty.) Cons. 20 marks. [*Worn.*]

77/66/269

793. One week [6 Oct.] from Michaelmas. (Made two weeks [30 April] from Easter in the said year.) William de Syde and William parson of the church of Olveston (*Olveston*) quer.; John de la River (*Ryvere*) 'chivaler' and Margaret his wife def. The manors of Tormarton (*Tormarton*), West Littleton (*Lutileton*), Acton Turville (*Torevylesacton*), Coomb's End (*Cotelescombe*), and Shirehill (*Shirewelle*). Right of William de Syde, as those which William de Syde and William the parson had by gift of John and Margaret. For this, grant back and render to John and Margaret. To hold during their lives. Remainder to Thomas their son and Emma daughter of Maurice de Berkeley (*Berkeleye*) and their heirs in tail male. Successive contingent remainders to John's heirs in tail male and to his heirs. [*Worn.*]

77/66/267

794. One week [6 Oct.] from Michaelmas. (Made two weeks [30 April] from Easter in the said year.) William de Syde quer.; Walter Goldmere (*Goldemere*) def. The manor of Over (*Oure*) and a messuage, 1 ploughland, 30 a. of meadow, and £8 rent in King's Weston (*Kyngesweston*) and Lawrence Weston (*Weston Sancti Laurencii*). Right of Walter by William's gift. For this, grant back and render to William. To hold during his life. Remainder to Thomas son of Maurice de Berkeley (*Berkeleye*) 'chivaler', to hold during his life, and then to Thomas's son Thomas and his heirs in tail male. Contingent remainder to the heirs of Thomas son of Maurice. [*Worn.*]

77/66/268

795. One week [6 Oct.] from Michaelmas. John [Stratford] archbishop of Canterbury (*Cantuar'*), John Engayne 'chivaler', Oliver de Bohun 'chivaler', Robert de Teye, Peter Favelore, William de Pembridge (*Penbrigge*), and William de Dersham quer.; William de Bohun earl of Northampton (*Norhampton*) and Elizabeth his wife def. The manors of Hinton Waldrist (*Henton*) and Speen (*Spene*), BERKS., the manors of Pyrton (*Pyriton*), Haseley (*Hasle*), Kirtlington (*Kertlyngton*), Ascott-under-Wychwood (*Ascote*), and Deddington (*Dadyngton*), OXON., the town and manor of High Wycombe (*Wycombe*), BUCKS., the manor of Long Bennington (*Longebenyngton*), LINCS., the manor of Kneesall (*Kneshale*), NOTTS., the manor of Newnham (*Newenham*), GLOS., the manor of Wix (*Wykes*), ESSEX, and £42 rent in Bosham (*Bosham*), SUSSEX. The earl acknowledged the right of the archbishop and the other quer. by the earl's gift. For this, grant and render to the earl and Elizabeth. To hold to them and the earl's heirs in tail, of the king. Contingent remainder to the king. Made

1346

by the king's order. *Labelled* Berk', Notyngh', Oxon', Glouc', Buk', Essex', Lincoln', Sussex'. [*Worn*.]

287/42/382

[Cf. *Essex Fines, 1327–1422*, p. 84; *Sussex Fines, 1307–1509*, p. 120, no. 2044. For the identity of Ascot and Wix, *Cal. Inq. p.m.* x, pp. 525, 568, 781.]

796. Two weeks [13 Oct.] from Michaelmas. Stephen de Stowe of Bristol (*Bristoll'*) quer.; Robert de Cameley (*Cameleye*) and Sarah his wife def. Rent of 20*s*. in the suburb of Bristol. Right of Stephen. Render to him. Cons. 10 marks. [*Worn*.]

77/66/265

[Cf. *Bristol Gt. Red Book*, p. 227, no. 160.]

797. Two weeks [13 Oct.] from Michaelmas. Everard le Francis (*Fraunceys*) burgess of Bristol (*Bristoll'*) quer.; William Kynewyne burgess of Bristol and Joan his wife def. Three messuages and 20*d*. rent in Bristol. Right of Everard by gift of William and Joan. (Warranty, specifying Joan's heirs.) Cons. £10.

77/66/271

[Cf. *Bristol Gt. Red Book*, p. 227, no. 161.]

798. Two weeks [25 Nov.] from St. Martin. John de Wysham 'chivaler' and Joan his wife quer. by Gilbert de Bardfield (*Berdefeld*); Richard de Morton chaplain def. The manor of Tedstone Delamere (*Tedesterne de la Mare*) and the advowson of the church of the same manor, HEREFS., and 2 messuages, 200 a. of land, 30 a. of pasture, and 60 a. of wood in the township of St. Briavels (*de Sancto Briavello*) and Newland (*la Newelonde*) by the township of St. Briavels in the forest of Dean (*Dene*), GLOS. Grant and render to John and Joan. To hold to them and John's heirs in tail. Contingent remainder to John de Bures, son of Andrew de Bures. *Labelled* Hereford', Glouc'. *Endorsed* Richard son of Richard de Bagendon (*Baggynden*) put in his claim. [*Worn*.]

287/42/389

21 Edward III

1347

799. Two weeks [27 Jan.] from Hilary. (Made the morrow of All Souls 20 Edward III [3 Nov. 1346].) John de Acton quer.; Reynold de Stoke (*Stok*) parson of the church *Bere* def. The manors of Elkstone (*Elkeston*) and Winstone (*Wynston*). Right of Reynold by John's gift. For this, grant back and render to John. To hold during his life, of the king. Remainder to John Poyntz and Elizabeth his wife and John Poyntz's heirs in tail male. Successive contingent remainders to John Poyntz's heirs in tail and to John de Acton's heirs. Made by the king's order. [*Worn*.]

77/66/272

800. Morrow [3 Feb.] of the Purification. Robert de Staverton quer.; Ralph de Abenhall (*Habenhale*) def. Three messuages, a mill, 4 ploughlands, 55 a. of meadow, 43 a. of wood, and £7 2*s*. 2*d*. rent in Blaisdon (*Blechesdon*), Rodley (*Rodleye*), Stantway (*Stayntweye*), and Westbury on Severn (*Westbury*) and the advowson of half of the church of Blaisdon. Right of Robert. Render to him of a messuage, 40½ a. of meadow, 3 a. of wood, and 2 ploughlands in Rodley and Westbury except for 66 a. of land in the same ploughlands, and grant to him of 16*s*. 2*d*. rent together with the homages and all the

1347

services of Thomas Chaxhill (*Chaxhull*), Thomas Abenhall, Henry de Rodley, Henry Helyotes, Juliana Hook (*Hok'*), Richard Hook, Richard Martin, John Cope (*Coppe*), Richard le Holder (*Holdare*), Walter Cope, John de Wick (*Wyk*), John Bird (*Bryd*), Henry le Young (*Yong*), John le Sawyer (*Sawyare*), Aline Sapy, and Alexander Basse for all the tenements formerly held by them of Ralph in the township of Rodley. And Ralph granted to Robert the reversion of a messuage, 1 ploughland, a mill, 5 a. of meadow, 40 a. of wood, and £6 6s. rent in the township of Blaisdon and the said advowson, all held by John de Abenhall and Reynold his brother for term of life, of a messuage and 1 ploughland in the same township held by Hugh de Abenhall for term of life, of the following holdings in Rodley, 3 a. of land held by Helena Eynolf', 1 a. of land held by Sarah daughter of John Tuyles, 3 a. of land held by William de Haydon, 2 a. of land held by John Robins (*Robynes*), 3 a. of land held by Helena Eynolf' of Cleeve (*Clyve*) and Richard her son, 2 a. of land held by Adam atte Oak (*Oke*), 5 a. of land held by Richard Veal (*Fyel*) and Thomas his son, 2 a. of land held by Richard Tryg of Cleeve, 2 a. of land held by John son of John Baderon, 2 a. of land held by John Baderon, 3 a. of land held by Thomas Hockley (*Hockleye*), 2 a. of land held by John Hemming (*Hemmyng*), 7 a. of land held by Thomas Chaxhill, 5 a. of land held by Thomas Ladbrook (*Lodebrok*), 15 a. of land held by Robert Brown (*Broun*), 10 a. of land and 1½ a. of meadow held by Richard le Bays, ½ a. of meadow held by Walter Richard, and 1½ a. of meadow held by John Fylote, all for term of life, and of 6 a. of meadow in Rodley and Westbury held by Richard Veal for term of life, all of Ralph's inheritance. (Warranty.) Cons. 100 marks. [*Stained.*]

77/67/278

[The sum of the acres of land of which the remainder was granted is 67, not 66 as stated to be excepted from the 2 ploughlands. The surname le Yong and the name John le Sawyare have been supplied from the note of fine, CP 26/1/10, Hil. 21 Edw. III.]

801. Two weeks [15 April] from Easter. Everard le Francis (*Fraunceys*) of Bristol (*Bristoll'*) quer.; John Silk' of Bristol 'balauncer' and Joan his wife and William de Eddeston and Margery his wife def. A messuage in the suburb of Bristol. Right of Everard. Remise and quitclaim, specifying Joan's and Margery's heirs, to him. (Warranty.) Cons. 10 marks.

77/67/285

[Cf. *Bristol Gt. Red Book*, p. 229, no. 167.]

802. One month [29 April] from Easter. John Pirie (*Pirye*) chaplain and Richard Veal (*Viel*) of Rodley (*Rodleye*) quer.; Joan who was wife of William Scaward of Gloucester (*Gloucestr'*) and Walter her son def. A messuage, a toft, and 2s. rent in Gloucester and the suburb of the same town. Right of John. Render to John and Richard. To hold to them and John's heirs. (Warranty, specifying Joan's heirs.) Cons. £10.

77/67/281

803. Two weeks [10 June] from Trinity. Philip de Torrington (*Torynton*) quer.; John de Ottery (*Otery*) the elder def. A messuage in Bristol (*Bristoll'*). Right of Philip by John's gift. (Warranty.) Cons. 100s.

77/67/283

[Cf. *Bristol Gt. Red Book*, pp. 228–9, no. 165.]

1347

804. Two weeks [10 June] from Trinity. John Horncastle (*Horncastel'*) quer.; John Richman (*Rycheman*) of Chepstow (*Chypstowe*) and Margaret his wife def. A messuage in Bristol (*Bristoll'*). Right of John Horncastle by gift of John Richman and Margaret. (Warranty, specifying Margaret's heirs.) Cons. 100*s*.

77/67/284

[Cf. *Bristol Gt. Red Book*, p. 229, no. 166.]

805. One week [6 Oct.] from Michaelmas. John de Horncastle (*Horncastel*) of Bristol (*Bristoll'*) and James his son. quer.; John de Priddy (*Pridie*) and Elisia his wife def. Two messuages in the suburb of Bristol. Right of John de Horncastle, as those which John and James had by gift of John de Priddy and Elisia. To hold to John de Horncastle and James and that John's heirs. (Warranty, specifying Elisia's heirs.) Cons. 20 marks.

77/66/273

[Cf. *Bristol Gt. Red Book*, p. 228, no. 162.]

806. Two weeks [13 Oct.] from Michaelmas. Everard le Francis (*Fraunceys*) burgess of Bristol (*Bristoll'*) quer.; Walter de Wellington (*Welyngton*) son of Nicholas de Wellington and Matilda wife of Walter def. A messuage in the suburb of Bristol. Right of Everard by gift of Walter and Matilda. (Warranty, specifying Matilda's heirs.) Cons. 100*s*.

77/66/274

[Cf. *Bristol Gt. Red Book*, p. 228, no. 163.]

807. Two weeks [13 Oct.] from Michaelmas. Roger son of Roger de Barley (*Berleye*) and Sibyl daughter of James Hussey (*Husee*) of Hampton quer.; Roger de Barley def. A messuage, 1 ploughland, 200 a. of pasture, and 18*s*. rent in Calmsden (*Calmondesdene*). Roger de Barley granted the reversion of the holding, held by James Hussey for term of ten years at a rent of 1*d*. a year, to Roger son of Roger and Sibyl and their heirs in tail. To hold of Roger de Barley, paying to him during his life 13*s*. 4*d*. a year, at Christmas and St. John the Baptist, and to his heirs a rose a year at St. John the Baptist, and doing service to the chief lords. Contingent reversion to Roger de Barley. Cons. 100 marks. [*Worn and stained.*]

77/66/275

808. Two weeks [13 Oct.] from Michaelmas. Richard atte Wall (*Walle*) of Bristol (*Bristoll'*) quer.; Geoffrey Methelan and Agnes his wife def. Four shops and 2 gardens in the suburb of Bristol. Right of Richard by gift of Geoffrey and Agnes. (Warranty, specifying Agnes's heirs.) Cons. 100*s*.

77/67/282

[Cf. *Bristol Gt. Red Book*, p. 228, no. 164.]

809. Two weeks [13 Oct.] from Michaelmas. David Bennett (*Benet*) quer.; Stephen atte Cellar (*Celer*) and Isabel his wife def. Rent of 40*s*. in Bristol (*Bristoll'*) held by Isabel Passer (*Passour*) for term of life. Right of David. Grant to him of the reversion, of the inheritance of Stephen's wife Isabel. (Warranty.) Cons. 20 marks.

77/67/286

[Cf. *Bristol Gt. Red Book*, pp. 229–30, no. 168.]

1347

810. Two weeks [13 Oct.] from Michaelmas. Thomas Kennett (*Kenet*) and Margaret his wife quer. by John de Crewkerne (*Crukern'*), Margaret's guardian; John Oliver (*Olyver*) 'clerc' and Ralph son of Nicholas de Hill (*Hulle*) def. Two messuages and 2 ploughlands in Hill and Tresham (*Tresham*), GLOS., and a messuage and 1 ploughland in Henstridge (*Hengstrygge*), SOM. Thomas acknowledged the right of John, as those which John and Ralph had by Thomas's gift. For this, grant and render to Thomas and Margaret. To hold to them and their heirs in tail male. Contingent remainder to Thomas's heirs. *Labelled* Glouc', Somers'.

287/43/403

[Cf. *Som. Fines, 1347–99*, p. 177.]

811. Morrow [3 Nov.] of All Souls. William de Cheltenham (*Chiltenham*) quer.; John de Lichfield (*Lichesfeld*) and Margery his wife def. Five acres of land and 1 a. of meadow in Hawkesbury (*Haukesbury*). Right of William by gift of John and Margery. (Warranty, specifying Margery's heirs.) Cons. 20 marks.

77/67/276

812. Morrow [3 Nov.] of St. Martin. (Made one week [1 July] from St. John the Baptist in the said year.) Thomas de Amersham (*Agmondesham*) quer.; Richard Davy of Clapley (*Cloppeley*) and Alice his wife def. A messuage, 13 a. of land, and 1½ a. of meadow in Bishop's Cleeve (*Clyve*) and Brockhampton (*Brokhampton*). Right of Thomas by gift of Richard and Alice. (Warranty, specifying Alice's heirs.) Cons. 20 marks.

77/67/277

813. One week [18 Nov.] from St. Martin. Henry Hussey (*Husee*) 'chivaler' quer.; Thomas de Sherborne (*Shirbourn*) parson of the church of Sapperton (*Saperton*) and Robert de Taynton (*Teynton*) parson of the church of Great Rissington (*Broderysyndon*) def. The manor of South Moreton (*Morton*) and 65s. rent in Long Wittenham (*Westwyttenham*), BERKS., and half of the manors of Great Rissington and Sapperton except for 1 a. of meadow in Great Rissington, GLOS. Right of Thomas and Robert by Henry's gift. For this, grant back and render to Henry. To hold during his life, the manor and the half of the king, the rent of the chief lords. Remainder to Henry's son Henry and Elizabeth daughter of John de Bohun and their heirs in tail. Successive contingent remainders to Henry the son's heirs in tail, to Henry the father's son Richard and his heirs in tail, to the heirs in tail of Henry the father by Katherine his wife, to Henry the father's daughter Elizabeth and her heirs in tail, and to John de Huntingfield (*Huntyngfeld*). Made by the king's order as to the manor and the half. *Labelled* Berk', Glouc'. [*Worn.*]

287/43/407A

[For the identity of Moreton, *V.C.H. Berks*. iii. 500.]

814. One week [18 Nov.] from St. Martin. Walter de Isle (*Idle*) and Joan his wife quer.; Thomas de Sherborne (*Shirbourn*) parson of the church of Sapperton (*Saperton*) and Robert de Taynton (*Teynton*) parson of the church of Great Rissington (*Broderysyndon*) def. Half of the manors of Great Rissington and Sapperton and the advowsons of the churches of the same manors, GLOS., and half of the manor of Pulborough (*Pulbergh'*), SUSSEX. Walter acknowledged the half of the manors and the advowsons to be the right of Thomas and Robert by Walter's gift. For this, grant and render to Walter and

1347

Joan of the same half, of the half of the manor of Pulborough, and of the advowsons. To hold to Walter and Joan and Walter's heirs in tail, the half of the manors of Great Rissington and Sapperton and the advowsons of the king, the half of the manor of Pulborough of the chief lords. Successive contingent remainders to Henry Hussey (*Husee*) 'chivaler' during his life and then to Henry's son Henry and his heirs in tail, to the heirs in tail of Henry the father by Katherine his wife, to Henry the father's daughter Elizabeth and her heirs in tail, and to Walter's heirs. Made by the king's order as to the half of the manors of Great Rissington and Sapperton and the advowsons. *Labelled* Glouc', Sussex'. [*Worn.*]

287/43/407B

[Cf. *Sussex Fines, 1307–1509*, p. 124, no. 2064.]

1348

815. One week [*20* Jan.] from Hilary. John Delerobe and Alice his wife quer.; Hawise de Bitton (*Button*) def. Six messuages, 108 a. of land, 8 a. of meadow, rent of 18*d.* and 3 cloves, and half of a dovecot and rent of 1 lb. of cumin in Bitton, Oldland (*Oldlonde*), East Hanham (*Esthanam*), Churchley (*Cherchesleye*) and Abson (*Abbodestone*) by Pucklechurch (*Pokelchirche*). Right of Hawise, of which she had 3½ messuages, 79 a. of land, 5 a. of meadow, and the half of the dovecot by gift of John and Alice. For this, grant back and render to John and Alice, together with the homages and all the services of Thomas Haynes (*Heynes*) and Joan his wife for the holdings which they held of Hawise in Oldland. To hold during their lives of Hawise, paying a rose a year at St. John the Baptist and doing service to the chief lords. And grant to John and Alice of the reversion of 8 a. of land, 1½ a. of meadow, and half of a messuage held by William de Morton and Isabel his wife for term of life, of 13 a. of land, 1½ a. of meadow, and half of a messuage held by John atte Fenne for term of life, of 2 a. of land held by William Horston for term of life, of 4 a. of land and half of a messuage held by Richard Mynge for term of life, and of a messuage and 2 a. of land held by Thomas Shortfrend for term of life, all of Hawise's inheritance. To hold as above. Reversion to Hawise.

77/67/279

22 Edward III

1348

816. Two weeks [27 Jan.] from Hilary. (Made two weeks from Michaelmas 21 Edward III [13 Oct. 1347].) Roger de Kingslane (*Kyngeslone*) quer.; Nicholas de Linton (*Lynton*) of Gloucester (*Gloucestre*) 'shetare' and Agnes his wife def. A messuage, a toft, and 2 shops in the suburb of Gloucester (*Gloucestr'*). Right of Roger, of which he had the toft and shops by gift of Nicholas and Agnes. And grant to Roger of the reversion of the messuage, held by Alice Fisher (*Fissh'*) for term of life, of Agnes's inheritance. (Warranty.) Cons. 100 marks.

77/67/280

817. Morrow [3 Feb.] of the Purification. Ralph de Grey 'chivaler' quer.; John Wlysp' of Southrop (*Southrop*) def. One and half acres of meadow in Kelmscott (*Kelmescote*), OXON., and a messuage and 1 yardland in Southrop, GLOS. Right of Ralph. Remise and quitclaim to him. (Warranty.) Cons. 20 marks. *Labelled* Oxon', Glouc'.

287/43/412

1348

818. Two weeks [4 May] from Easter. Giles de Beauchamp (*de Bello Campo*) 'chivaler' and Katherine his wife quer.; John de Bures 'chivaler' and Hawise his wife def. The advowson of the church of Kemerton (*Kynemarton*). Grant and render to Giles and Katherine. To hold to Giles and Katherine and their heirs in tail, of John and Hawise and Hawise's heirs, paying a rose a year at St. John the Baptist and doing service to the chief lords. Contingent reversion to John and Hawise and Hawise's heirs. Cons. £20.

77/67/291

819. One week [22 June] from Trinity. (Made two weeks [27 Jan.] from Hilary in the said year.) Richard son of Richard de Baskerville (*Baskervill*) and Joan daughter of Adam de Everingham (*Everyngham*) quer. by John de Stretton her guardian; Richard de Baskerville knight def. The manor of Combe Baskerville (*Combe Baskervill*). Grant and render to Richard son of Richard and Joan. To hold to them and their heirs in tail, of Richard de Baskerville, paying a rose a year at St. John the Baptist and doing service to the chief lords. (Warranty.) Contingent reversion to Richard de Baskerville. Cons. 100 marks.

77/67/289

820. Morrow [25 June] of St. John the Baptist. Richard de Stafford 'chivaler' quer.; Ralph de Stafford 'chivaler' and Margaret his wife def. One quarter of the manor of Chipping Campden (*Chepyng Caumpedene*). Right of Richard by gift of Ralph and Margaret. (Warranty, specifying Margaret's heirs.) Cons. 20 marks.

77/67/290

821. One week [6 Oct.] from Michaelmas. (Made two weeks [27 Jan.] from Hilary in the said year.) John atte Wood (*Wode*) of Winchcombe (*Wynchecombe*) quer.; John Spilman (*Spilleman*) of Randwick (*Ryndewyk*) def. A messuage, 9½ a. of land, and 9s. 6d. rent in Swindon (*Swyndon*), held by Margery Mayel for term of life. Right of John atte Wood. Grant to him of the reversion, of the inheritance of John Spilman. (Warranty.) Cons. 20 marks.

77/67/288

822. Two weeks [13 Oct.] from Michaelmas. (Made three weeks [11 May] from Easter in the said year.) Everard le French (*Frensh*) of Bristol (*Bristoll*) quer.; Walter de Tockington (*Tokynton*) 'tanner' and Joan his wife and Adam le Clerk 'corviser' and Margaret his wife def. A messuage in the suburb of Bristol. Right of Everard by gift of Walter and Joan and Adam and Margaret. (Warranty, specifying only Joan's heirs.) Cons. 100s.

77/67/287

[Cf. *Bristol Gt. Red Book*, p. 230, no. 169.]

1349

823. One week [20 Jan.] from Hilary. (Made two weeks from Easter in the said year [4 May 1348].) Richard Talbot knight quer.; Robert de Staverton def. Two messuages, a mill, 2 ploughlands, 5 a. of meadow, 60 a. of wood, and £6 6s. rent in Blaisdon (*Blechedon*) and the advowson of half of the church of the same township. Right of

1349

Richard. Grant to him of the reversion of a messuage, the mill, 1 ploughland, the meadow, the wood, and the rent, held by John de Abenhall (*Abehale*) and Reynold de Abenhall for term of life, and of a messuage and 1 ploughland, held by Hugh de Abenhall for term of life, of Robert's inheritance. Cons. 100 marks.

77/67/292

23 Edward III

1349

824. Two weeks [26 April] from Easter. (Made two weeks from Michaelmas 22 Edward III [13 Oct. 1348].) William Bruyn of Gloucester (*Gloucestre*) quer.; Peter le Wild (*Wylde*) and Elena his wife, William Smart and Matilda his wife, and Robert Lethenard and Joan his wife def. A messuage, 16 a. of land, and 2 a. of meadow in Longney (*Longeneye*). Right of William Bruyn by gift of Peter and Elena, William Smart and Matilda, and Robert and Joan. (Warranty, specifying Elena's, Matilda's, and Joan's heirs.) Cons. 40 marks.

77/67/296

825. Two weeks [26 April] from Easter. (Made two weeks from Michaelmas 22 Edward III [13 Oct. 1348].) Robert de Aston quer.; Philip Crook (*Crok'*) and Alice his wife def. A messuage in the suburb of Gloucester (*Glouc'*). Right of Robert. Render to him. (Warranty, specifying Philip's heirs.) Cons. 10 marks.

77/67/297

826. Two weeks [26 April] from Easter. (Made two weeks from Michaelmas 21 Edward III [13 Oct. 1347].) William de Stowell chaplain quer.; John de Banbury (*Bannebury*) and Alice his wife def. A messuage and 1 yardland in Coln St. Denis (*Culne Sancti Dionisii*). Right of William by gift of John and Alice. (Warranty, specifying Alice's heirs.) Cons. 20 marks.

77/67/298

827. One month [10 May] from Easter. Thomas de Berkeley (*Berkele*) quer.; William de Syde, Walter Goldmere, and David de Melksham (*Milkesham*) def. The castle of Berkeley and the manors of Berkeley, Ham (*Hamme*), Appleridge (*Appelrugge*), Alkington (*Alkynton*), Hinton (*Hyneton*), Wotton under Edge (*Wotton*), Symond's Hall (*Simondeshale*), Cam (*Cam*), Coaley (*Couelye*), Slimbridge (*Slymburgge*), and Upton St. Leonards (*Upton Sancti Leonardi*), the hundred of Berkeley, the views of frankpledge belonging to the said manors, and the advowsons of the churches of the manors of Wotton and Slimbridge (*Slymbrugge*). Right of William, David, and Walter by Thomas's gift. For this, grant back and render to Thomas. To hold to Thomas during his life, of the king. Remainder to Maurice de Berkeley, Thomas's son, and his heirs in tail. Successive contingent remainders to the heirs in tail male of Thomas and Katherine his wife and to Thomas's heirs. Made by the king's order. [*Worn and torn.*]

77/67/294

[Cf. *Berkeley Castle Mun.* i, p. 5, A1/1/20 (counterpart), where the date is given differently.]

828. One month [10 May] from Easter. Thomas son of Maurice de Berkeley (*Berkele*) 'chivaler' and Thomas son of the same Thomas son of Maurice quer.; Thomas de Besford

1349

(*Besseford*) parson of the church of Beverston (*Beverston*), Roger de Eastham (*Estham*), and John le Vey clerk def. The manors of Syde (*Side*) and Weston Birt (*Westonebrut'*) and the advowson of the church of the manor of Syde. Right of Thomas de Besford, Roger, and John by gift of Thomas son of Maurice. For this, grant and render to Thomas son of Maurice and Thomas his son. To hold to them and the heirs in tail male of Thomas son of Thomas. Successive contingent remainders to the heirs in tail male of Thomas son of Maurice and Katherine his wife and to the heirs of Thomas son of Maurice.

77/67/295

829. One week [6 Oct.] from Michaelmas. John le Felter (*Feltere*) of Bristol (*Bristoll'*) and Alice his wife quer.; Philip Gille (*Gylle*) of Bristol and Benedicta his wife def. Two messuages and 10*s.* rent in the suburb of Bristol. Right of Benedicta. For this, Philip and Benedicta granted back and rendered the holdings and rent to John and Alice. To hold to John and Alice and their heirs in tail. Contingent remainder to John's heirs. (Warranty, specifying Benedicta's heirs.)

77/67/299

[Cf. *Bristol Gt. Red Book*, p. 230, no. 170.]

830. Two weeks [13 Oct.] from Michaelmas. John de Fretherne (*Frethorn*) of Childrey (*Chelereye*) and Elizabeth his wife quer.; Walter de Worth parson of the church of Childrey and William de Cotes chaplain def. The manor of Fretherne and the advowson of the church of Fretherne. John acknowledged the right of Walter, as those which Walter and William had by John's gift. For this, grant and render to John and Elizabeth. To hold to them and their heirs in tail. Contingent remainder to John's heirs.

77/67/293

24 Edward III

1350

831. Two weeks [11 April] from Easter. John Shipman quer.; Agnes de Methelan (*Medelane*) def. A messuage, 5 shops, and 20*s.* rent in the town of Bristol (*Bristoll'*) and the suburb of the same town. Right of John by Agnes's gift. (Warranty.) Cons. 10 marks.

77/68/303

[Cf. *Bristol Gt. Red Book*, p. 231, no. 173.]

832. One month [25 April] from Easter. Robert Seward and Thomas Babcary (*Babecary*) quer.; Geoffrey Beauflour and Agnes his wife def. Two messuages in the suburb of Bristol (*Bristoll'*). Right of Robert. Render to Robert and Thomas. To hold to them and Robert's heirs. (Warranty, specifying Agnes's heirs.) Cons £10.

77/68/302

[Cf. *Bristol Gt. Red Book*, p. 231, no. 172.]

833. Morrow [7 May] of Ascension. John Head (*Hevod'*) of Gloucester (*Gloucestr'*) quer.; John le Marshal (*Marchal'*) of Bristol (*Bristoll'*) and Alice his wife def. A messuage in the suburb of Gloucester. Right of John Head by gift of John le Marshal and Alice. (Warranty, specifying Alice's heirs.) Cons. 100*s.*

77/67/300

1350

834. One week [30 May] from Trinity. William son of Henry de Frampton (*Frompton*) quer. by William Hale (*Hayl*) his guardian; Walter Bacton (*Bakton*) and Edith his wife def. Two messuages in the suburb of Bristol (*Bristoll'*). Right of William. Render to him. (Warranty, specifying Edith's heirs.) Cons. 20 marks.

77/68/301

[Cf. *Bristol Gt. Red Book*, pp. 230–1, no. 171.]

835. One week [6 Oct.] from Michaelmas. (Made one week from Hilary 23 Edward III [20 Jan. 1350].) Walter Catewy of Harwell (*Harewell*), John Chelsey, and Robert Dagnall (*Dagenhale*) chaplain quer.; Thomas Catewy and Joan his wife def. Six messuages, a mill, 2½ ploughlands, 18 a. of meadow, and 35*s*. rent in Elkstone (*Elkston*), Colesborne (*Colesbourn*), Longford (*Langeford*), Brockworth (*Brokworth*), and Wotton (*Wotton*). Right of Walter, of which Walter, John, and Robert had the said holdings by gift of Thomas and Joan. And grant to Walter, John and Robert of the rent, with the homages and all the services of the prior of Llanthony (*Launtony*), William de Sollers (*Solers*), John Alsy, Matilda Alsy, and John Droys from the holdings which they held of Thomas and Joan. To hold to Walter, John, and Robert and Walter's heirs. (Warranty, specifying Joan's heirs.) Cons. 100 marks.

77/68/304

25 Edward III

1351

836. Two weeks [1 May] from Easter. Edmund Blanket and Alice his wife quer.; Philip Gille and Benedicta his wife def. Two shops and a garden in the suburb of Bristol (*Bristoll'*). Right of Edmund, as those which Edmund and Alice had by gift of Philip and Benedicta. To hold to Edmund and Alice and Edmund's heirs. (Warranty, specifying Benedicta's heirs.) Cons. 20 marks.

77/68/310

[Cf. *Bristol Gt. Red Book*, p. 231, no. 174.]

837. Three weeks [8 May] from Easter. Richard de Stafford 'chivaler' quer.; John Turville (*Turvyll*) and Joan his wife def. The manor of Aston Subedge (*Aston subtus Egge*) and the advowson of the church of the same manor. Right of Richard by gift of John and Joan. (Warranty, specifying Joan's heirs.) Cons. 200 marks.

77/68/308

838. Morrow [27 May] of Ascension. William de Edington (*Edyndon*) bishop of Winchester (*Wynton'*) quer.; John de St. Philbert (*de Sancto Philberto*) knight def. The manor Westwell (*Westwell*), OXON., and the manor of Farmington (*Thormarton*) and the advowson of the church of the same manor, GLOS. Right of the bishop, and render to him. To hold to him and his heirs. (Warranty.) Cons. 200 marks. *Labelled* Oxon', Glouc'.

287/44/457

839. One week [19 June] from Trinity. Ralph [de Stafford] earl of Stafford (*Stafford*) quer.; Mr. Edmund Mortain (*Morteyn*) and William de Rothwell (*Rothewell*) clerk def.

1351

The manor of Thornbury (*Thornebury*). Right of Mr. Edmund and William by the earl's gift. For this, grant back and render to the earl. To hold during his life, of the king. Remainder to the earl's son Hugh and Philippa daughter of Thomas de Beauchamp (*de Bello Campo*) earl of Warwick (*Warr'*) and Hugh's heirs in tail. Contingent remainder to Hugh's heirs. Made by the king's order.

77/68/306

840. Two weeks [26 June] from Trinity. Henry atte More and Emma his wife quer.; Anselm de Gurney (*Gorney*), and Joan his wife def. A messuage, 1 ploughland, and 8 a. of meadow in King's Weston (*Kyngesweston*). Right of Henry, as those which Henry and Emma had by gift of Anselm and Joan. To hold to Henry and Emma and Henry's heirs. (Warranty, specifying Anselm's heirs.) Cons. 100 marks.

77/68/307

841. Two weeks [26 June] from Trinity. John Castleacre (*Castelacre*) and Cecily his wife quer.; William Moorslade (*Morslade*) and Katherine his wife def. Half of a messuage and shop in the suburb of Bristol (*Bristoll'*). Right of John, as that which John and Cecily had by gift of William and Katherine. To hold to John and Cecily and John's heirs. (Warranty, specifying Katherine's heirs.) Cons. 20 marks.

77/68/312

[Cf. *Bristol Gt. Red Book*, p. 232, no. 176.]

842. Two weeks [13 Oct.] from Michaelmas. James de Audley (*Audeleye*) knight and Adam de St. John (*de Sancto Johanne*) chaplain quer.; Ellis Daubeney (*Daubeneye*) and Agnes his wife def. A messuage, 60 a. of land, and 10 a. of meadow in Alkerton (*Alcrynton*). Right of James. Remise and quitclaim, specifying Agnes's heirs, to James and Adam and James's heirs. (Warranty.) Cons. 100 marks.

77/68/305

843. Two weeks [13 Oct.] from Michaelmas. John Peers (*Peres*) and Amice his wife quer.; Richard de Mickley (*Mickelegh*) and Cecily his wife def. A messuage and 3 shops in Bristol (*Bristoll'*). Grant and render to John and Amice. To hold to them and their heirs in tail. Contingent remainder to John's brother William Peers. (Warranty, specifying Cecily's heirs.) Cons. 20 marks

77/68/311

[Cf. *Bristol Gt. Red Book*, p. 232, no. 175.]

1352

844. One week [20 Jan.] from Hilary. John son of Giles de Beauchamp (*de Bello Campo*) and Joan his wife quer.; Giles de Beauchamp 'chivaler' and Katherine his wife def. The manor of Down Hatherley (*Dounhatherleye*). Grant and render to John and Joan. To hold to them and their heirs in tail, of Giles and Katherine and Katherine's heirs, paying a rose a year at St. John the Baptist and doing service to the chief lords. (Warranty, specifying Katherine's heirs.) Contingent reversion to Giles and Katherine and Katherine's heirs. Cons. 200 marks.

77/68/309

26 Edward III

1352

845. Two weeks [27 Jan.] from Hilary. Walter de Poulton (*Pulton*) quer.; Philip de Oo of Hereford (*Hereford*) and Florence his wife def. A messuage, 12 a. of land, and 8 a. of meadow in Wightfield (*Wythfeld*) and Tirley (*Trynle*). Grant and render to Walter. (Warranty, specifying Florence's heirs.) Cons. 20 marks.

77/68/313

846. Two weeks [27 Jan.] from Hilary. (Made two weeks from Michaelmas 25 Edward III [13 Oct. 1351].) Edmund Blanket and Alice his wife quer.; Lucy daughter of Nicholas de Farleigh (*Farleye*) def. A messuage in the suburb of Bristol (*Bristoll'*). Right of Edmund, as that which Edmund and Alice had by Lucy's gift. Remise and quitclaim to Edmund and Alice and Edmund's heirs. (Warranty.) Cons. 10 marks.

77/68/321

[Cf. *Bristol Gt. Red Book*, p. 233, no. 178.]

847. Two weeks [22 April] from Easter. Lionel de Antwerp (*Andewerp*) the king's son quer.; John Mautravers 'chivaler' def. The castle and manor of Brimpsfield (*Brymmesfeld*) and the advowson of the priory of Brimpsfield. Right of Lionel. Render to him. Cons. £200. *Endorsed* John Hammond (*Hamond*) of Shangton (*Shanketon*) and Mabel his wife and John Swan of Shangton and Isabel his wife put in their claim.

77/68/314

[The endorsement is repeated, in the same hand, on the next fine in the file, no. 849 below, presumably in error on one of the two. The indentures of this fine are filed in CP 25/1/288/51, the right-hand one as no. 5 and the left-hand one as no. 6. No. 5 is endorsed 'Between Lionel of Antwerp and . . .', incomplete.]

848. Two weeks [22 April] from Easter. Roger le Chamberlain (*Chaumberleyn*) and Margaret his wife quer.; Robert Murdoch (*Murdak*) parson of the church of Winterbourne (*Wynterbourne*) def. Three messuages in Gloucester (*Gloucestr'*). Right of Robert by gift of Roger and Margaret. For this, grant back and render to Roger and Margaret. To hold to them and Roger's heirs. *Endorsed* John Hammond (*Hamond*) of Shangton (*Shanketon*) and Mabel his wife and John Swan of Shangton and Isabel his wife put in their claim.

77/68/315

[On the endorsement, see note to no. 847 above.]

849. Two weeks [22 April] from Easter. Thomas de Breadstone (*Bradeston*) 'chivaler' quer.; William FitzWarren (*fitz Waryn*) 'chivaler' and Amice his wife def. One eighth of the manor of Winterbourne (*Wynturbourne*). Right of Thomas. Render to him. (Warranty, specifying William's heirs.) Cons. 20 marks.

77/68/317

850. One week [10 June] from Trinity. Matthew Seward and Isabel his wife quer.; Robert de Cheddar (*Cheddre*) and Walter Kebbe def. A messuage and 2 shops in the suburb of Bristol (*Bristoll'*). Right of Robert, as those which Robert and Walter had by gift of Matthew and Isabel. For this, grant back and render to Matthew and Isabel. To hold to them and Matthew's heirs.

77/68/322

[Cf. *Bristol Gt. Red Book*, p. 233, no. 179.]

1352

851. Two weeks [17 June] from Trinity. Nicholas Freeman (*Freoman*) and Juliana his wife quer.; Thomas Dollyng def. Two messuages and 72 a. of land in Hambrook (*Hambrok*), Frenchay (*Fromshawe*), and Hinton (*Henton*). Right of Thomas by gift of Nicholas and Juliana. For this, grant back and render to Nicholas and Juliana. To hold to them and their heirs in tail. Contingent remainder to Nicholas's heirs.

77/68/316

852. One week [6 Oct.] from Michaelmas. (Made two weeks [22 April] from Easter in the said year.) John de Coggeshall (*Coggeshale*) quer.; Ellis Daubeney (*Daubeny*) and Agnes his wife def. The manor of Matson (*Mattesdon*). Grant and render to John. To hold during his life, of Ellis and Agnes and Agnes's heirs, paying a rose a year at St. John the Baptist and doing service to the chief lords. Remainder to John's son John. To hold during his life, of Ellis and Agnes, as above. Remainder to Ellis's son Richard and his heirs in tail. To hold of Ellis and Agnes and Agnes's heirs, as above. (Warranty, specifying Ellis's heirs.) Contingent reversion to Ellis and Agnes and Agnes's heirs. Cons. 200 marks. [*Worn.*]

77/68/319

[That the clause of warranty specifies Ellis's heirs conflicts with the tenure from Agnes's heirs and the contingent reversion to them.]

853. Two weeks [13 Oct.] from Michaelmas. (Made two weeks [17 June] from Trinity in the said year.) Thomas de Breadstone (*Bradeston*) and Agnes his wife quer.; Robert Coyny and Robert Murdoch (*Murdak*) parson of the church of Winterbourne (*Wynterbourn*) def. The manor of Winterbourne and the advowson of the church of the same manor. Thomas acknowledged the right of Robert Coyny, as those which that Robert and Robert Murdoch had by Thomas's gift. For this, grant and render to Thomas and Agnes. To hold to them and their heirs in tail male. Successive contingent remainders to Robert de Breadstone and his heirs in tail male, to John de Breadstone and his heirs in tail male, and to Thomas's heirs. [*Worn.*]

77/68/318

854. One week [18 Nov.] from St. Martin. John Stoke quer.; Robert Prentice (*Prentys*) and Joan his wife def. A messuage in the suburb of Bristol (*Bristoll'*). Right of John by gift of Robert and Joan. (Warranty, specifying Robert's heirs.) Cons. 10 marks.

77/68/320

[Cf. *Bristol Gt. Red Book*, p. 232, no. 177.]

27 Edward III

1353

855. Two weeks [7 April] from Easter. Richard Hurrell (*Hurel*) 'spicer' quer.; William Mason (*Maschoun*) and Joan his wife def. A messuage in the suburb of Bristol (*Bristoll'*). Right of Richard. Remise and quitclaim, specifying Joan's heirs, to him. (Warranty.) Cons. 10 marks.

77/68/323

[Cf. *Bristol Gt. Red Book*, p. 233, no. 180.]

1353

856. Two weeks [7 April] from Easter. Walter Derby quer.; Thomas Ottery (*Otery*) and Elena his wife def. A messuage in Bristol (*Bristoll'*). Right of Walter by gift of Thomas and Elena. (Warranty, specifying Elena's heirs.) Cons. 10 marks.

77/68/324

[Cf. *Bristol Gt. Red Book*, p. 234, no. 181.]

857. Two weeks [7 April] from Easter. Walter Frampton (*Frompton*) quer.; William Somerton of Bristol (*Bristoll'*) and Margery his wife def. Rent of 13*s.* 4*d.* in the suburb of Bristol. Right of Walter by gift of William and Margery. Cons. 20 marks.

77/68/325

[Cf. *Bristol Gt. Red Book*, p. 234, no. 182.]

858. Two weeks [7 April] from Easter. (Made two weeks from St. John the Baptist 26 Edward III [8 July 1352].) Gilbert le Despenser 'chivaler' and John de Leigh (*Legh*) the elder quer. by Thomas de Peddyng in John's place; Fulk de Birmingham (*Bermyngeham*) 'chivaler' def. Two messuages, 400 a. of land, 110 a. of meadow, 20 a. of wood, and £6 rent in Wightfield (*Wightfeld*) and Apperley (*Apperlee*). Right of Gilbert. Render to him and John, together with the homage and all the service of Nicholas de Apperley from the holdings which he held of Gilbert in the said townships. To hold to Gilbert and John and Gilbert's heirs. (Warranty.) Cons. 100 marks.

77/69/328

859. Two weeks [7 April] from Easter. (Made one month from Easter 23 Edward III [10 May 1349].) Thomas son of Maurice de Berkeley (*Berkele*) and Katherine his wife and Thomas son of the same Thomas and Katherine quer.; Thomas de Besford (*Besseford*) parson of the church of Beverston (*Beverston*), Roger de Eastham (*Estham*), and John le Vey clerk def. The manors of Over (*Oure*) and King's Weston (*Kyngesweston*), held by William de Syde (*Side*) for term of life. Grant of the reversion, of the inheritance of Thomas de Besford, to Thomas son of Maurice and Katherine and Thomas their son and to the son Thomas's heirs in tail male. Successive contingent remainders to the heirs in tail male of Thomas son of Maurice and Katherine, and then of Over to the heirs of Thomas son of Maurice, and of King's Weston to Alphonse de Berkeley and his heirs in tail male and to the heirs of Thomas son of Maurice. Made in William's presence and with his consent, and he did fealty to Thomas son of Maurice and Katherine and Thomas their son. [*Worn.*]

77/69/330

[Cf. *Berkeley Castle Mun.* i, pp. 477–8, A2/35/5 (counterpart).]

860. Two weeks [7 April] from Easter. (Made two weeks [27 Jan.] from Hilary in the said year.) Henry le Moyne and Joan his wife quer.; John de Oldland (*Oldelond*) parson of the church of King's Stanley (*Stanlegh*) and Peter le Hayward chaplain def. The manor of Shipton Moyne (*Shypton Moyne*) and the advowson of the church of the same manor. Right of John and Peter by Henry's gift. For this, grant and render to Henry and Joan. To hold to them and their heirs in tail, of the king. Contingent remainder to Henry's heirs. Made by the king's order.

77/69/331

1353

861. Two weeks [7 April] from Easter. William Marny of Gloucester (*Gloucestre*) and Agnes his wife quer.; Andrew le Walsh (*Walshe*) of Woolstrop (*Wolvesthrop*) and Walter le Mariner (*Maryner*) chaplain def. A messuage, 3½ shops, and a toft in Gloucester. Right of Walter, as those which Walter and Andrew had by gift of William and Agnes. For this, grant back and render to William and Agnes. To hold to them and William's heirs.

77/69/336

862. Three weeks [14 April] from Easter. (Made two weeks [27 Jan.] from Hilary in the said year.) Thomas de Haukesok and Alice his wife quer.; Hugh Housom and Amice his wife def. A messuage, 1 yardland, 10 a. of meadow, and 2 a. of wood in Deerhurst Walton (*Derhurstis Walton*). Grant, remise, and quitclaim of whatever Hugh and Amice had in the holdings for term of Amice's life to Thomas and Alice and Thomas's heirs. (Warranty during Amice's life.) Cons. 100 marks.

77/69/329

863. One week [26 May] from Trinity. Richard de Stafford 'chivaler' quer.; John Turville (*Turvill*) and Joan his wife def. Seventeen messuages, 13 yardlands, and 18*s*. rent in Aston Subedge (*Aston under Egge*). Right of Richard. Remise and quitclaim, specifying Joan's heirs, to him. (Warranty.) Cons. 100 marks.

77/69/332

864. One week [26 May] from Trinity. Richard de Stafford 'chivaler' quer.; Thomas de Thorney (*Thorneye*) citizen and pepperer of London and Joan his wife def. Four messuages and 4 yardlands in Aston Subdege (*Aston under Egge*). Right of Richard. Remise and quitclaim, specifying Joan's heirs, to him. Cons. 20 marks.

77/69/333

865. Two weeks [2 June] from Trinity. Thomas Moyne (*Moigne*) 'chivaler' quer.; John Wick (*Wyke*) 'toukere' [*i.e. fuller*] and Isabel his wife def. Two messuages in Bristol (*Bristoll'*). Right of Thomas by gift of John and Isabel. (Warranty, specifying Isabel's heirs.) Cons. 10 marks.

77/69/326

[Cf. *Bristol Gt. Red Book*, p. 234, no. 183.]

866. One week [1 July] from St. John the Baptist. The king quer. by John Gaunt who sues for him; John de St. Philbert (*de Sancto Philberto*) def. The manor of Southrop (*Southorp*), GLOS., and the manors of Eaton Hastings (*Eton Hastyngs*) and Carswell (*Karswell*) and the advowson of the church of the same manor of Eaton Hastings, BERKS. Right of the king, and render to him. (Warranty.) Cons. 100 marks. *Labelled* Glouc', Berk'.

287/44/488

[The right-hand and left-hand parts of the indenture of which the above is the foot are filed with the feet of fines and are respectively 287/44/485 and 287/44/487.]

1353

867. One week [6 Oct.] from Michaelmas. William de Peyto and Isabel his wife quer.; Roger atte Hall (*Halle*) chaplain and Simon de Walton def. Forty messuages in Bristol (*Bristoll'*) and the suburb of the same town. Right of Roger, as those which Roger and Simon had by gift of William and Isabel. To hold to Roger and Simon and Roger's heirs. (Warranty, specifying Isabel's heirs.) Cons. 40 marks.

77/69/327

[Cf. *Bristol Gt. Red Book*, p. 234, no. 184.]

868. Two weeks [13 Oct.] from Michaelmas. (Made two weeks from Trinity [2 June] in the said year.) Gilbert Chasteleyn knight and Margaret his wife quer.; John de Nowers knight def. The manor of Charingworth (*Charyngworth*). Gilbert acknowledged the right of John, of which he had two thirds of one third of the manor by Gilbert's gift. For this, grant and render of the two thirds to Gilbert and Margaret. To hold during their lives, of John, paying a rose a year at St. John the Baptist and doing service to the chief lords. And grant to Gilbert and Margaret of the reversion of two thirds of the manor held by John de Moorhall (*Morhall*) and Petronilla his wife for term of Petronilla's life and of the third part of one third held by the same John and Petronilla in Petronilla's dower, of the inheritance of John de Nowers. To hold as above. (Warranty.) Reversion on the death of Gilbert and Margaret to John de Nowers. [*Worn.*]

77/69/334

869. Two weeks [13 Oct.] from Michaelmas. (Made one week from St. John the Baptist 24 Edward III [1 July 1350].) Ellis de Blakeney (*Blakeneye*) parson of the church of Colwall (*Colewalle*) quer.; John son of Richard de Blakeney def. Four messuages, 2 ploughlands, 6 a. of meadow, 30 a. of wood, and 36*s.* rent in Blaisdon (*Blechesdon*) and half of the advowson of the church of the same township, held by Philip le Marshal (*Mareschal*) for term of life. Right of Ellis. Grant to him of the reversion. (Warranty.) Cons. 100 marks.

77/69/335

870. Two weeks [13 Oct.] from Michaelmas. Robert Palet quer.; John de Clifford and Erneburga his wife def. A messuage, 40 a. of land, 6 a. of meadow, and 10*s.* 9¼*d.* rent in Wotton (*Wotton*) by Gloucester (*Gloucestr'*). Right of Robert by gift of John and Erneburga. (Warranty, specifying John's heirs.) Cons. 20 marks.

77/69/337(a)

871. Two weeks [13 Oct.] from Michaelmas. (Made two weeks from Trinity 26 Edward III [17 June 1352].) Thomas de Berkeley (*Berkele*) quer.; William de Syde (*Side*) and Walter Goldmere (*Goldemere*) def. The manor of Barrow Gurney (*Barewe*) and 2 messuages and 3 ploughlands in Cheddar (*Cheddre*) and Tickenham (*Tikenham*), SOM., and a messuage and 1 ploughland in Falfield (*Falevelde*), GLOS. Right of William, of which William and Walter had the manor and the messuage and ploughland in Falfield by Thomas's gift. For this, grant back and render to Thomas. To hold to him during his life. And grant to Thomas of the reversion of a messuage and 2 ploughlands in Cheddar held by John de Acton 'chivaler' for term of life and of a messuage and 1 ploughland in Tickenham held by Roger de Eastham (*Estham*) for term of life, of William's inheritance.

1353

To hold as above. Remainder to Thomas's son Edmund and his heirs in tail male. Successive contingent remainders to the heirs in tail male of Thomas and Katherine his wife and to Thomas's heirs. *Labelled* Somers', Glouc'. [*Worn and stained.*]

287/44/492A

[Cf. *Som. Fines, 1347–99*, p. 181.]

1354

872. One week [20 Jan.] from Hilary. Edmund Blanket and Alice his wife quer.; John Castleacre (*Castelacre*) and Cecily his wife def. A messuage in the suburb of Bristol (*Bristoll'*). Right of Edmund, as that which Edmund and Alice had by gift of John and Cecily. To hold to Edmund and Alice and Edmund's heirs. (Warranty, specifying John's heirs.) Cons. 10 marks.

77/69/337(b) (formerly 77/69/342)

[Cf. *Bristol Gt. Red Book*, p. 235, no. 185.]

28 Edward III

1354

873. Two weeks [27 Jan.] from Hilary. (Made three weeks from Easter 27 Edward III [14 April 1353].) John Mautravers 'chivaler' quer.; Edmund de Barford (*Bereford*), Henry de Tingewick (*Tyngwych*), and Nicholas Pinnock (*Pynnok*) clerk def. The manors of Stoke Gifford (*Stoke Giffard*) and Walls (*Walle*). Right of Edmund, as those which Edmund, Henry, and Nicholas had by John's gift. For this, grant back and render to John. To hold to him and his heirs in tail male. Successive contingent remainders to Thomas son of Maurice de Berkeley (*Berkele*), the younger, and his heirs in tail male, to Thomas's brother Maurice and his heirs in tail male, to Maurice's brother Edward and his heirs in tail male, and to Thomas son of Maurice de Berkeley, the elder. [*Worn.*]

77/69/344

[The syntax makes it clear that 'the younger' and 'the elder' apply to Thomas in each instance, not to Maurice.]

874. Two weeks [27 Jan.] from Hilary. (Made two weeks from Michaelmas 27 Edward III [13 Oct. 1353].) John atte Lode chaplain quer.; John Hawote and Margery his wife def. A messuage, 12 a. of land, 4 a. of meadow, and 6*d.* rent in Deerhurst (*Derhurst*), Chaceley (*Chadesley*), and Wightfield (*Wyghtfeld*). Right of John atte Lode by gift of John Hawote and Margery. (Warranty, specifying Margery's heirs.) Cons. 20 marks.

77/69/345

[*Chadesley* is evidently Chaceley, which adjoins Deerhurst but is on the other side of the Severn and was in Worcestershire.]

875. Morrow [3 Feb.] of the Purification. Roger la Warre and Elizabeth his wife quer.; Thomas de Wick (*Wyke*) and John his son def. The manor of Isfield (*Isefeld*), SUSSEX, and the manor Wickwar (*Wykewarre*) and the advowson of the church of the same manor, GLOS. Roger acknowledged the right of Thomas, as those which Thomas and John had by Roger's gift. For this, grant and render to Roger and Elizabeth. To hold to them and their heirs in tail. Successive contingent remainders to Roger's son John and his heirs in tail and to Roger's heirs. *Labelled* Sussex', Gloucestr'.

287/44/497

[Cf. *Sussex Fines, 1307–1509*, p. 137, no. 2146.]

1354

876. Two weeks [27 April] from Easter. Reynold Pearl (*Peerle*) of Shropshire (*Salop'*) and Joan his wife quer.; Richard de Lawley (*Laueley*) chaplain and Thomas de Tyford chaplain def. Two messuages in Bristol (*Bristoll'*). Right of Richard, as those which Richard and Thomas had by gift of Reynold and Joan. For this, grant back and render to Reynold and Joan. To hold to them and their heirs in tail. Contingent remainder to Reynold's heirs.

77/69/340

[Cf. *Bristol Gt. Red Book*, pp. 235–6, no. 188.]

877. Two weeks [27 April] from Easter. (Made two weeks [27 Jan.] from Hilary in the said year.) Thomas de Berkeley (*Berkele*) the elder and Katherine his wife quer.; Walter Goldmere and John de Cleeve (*Clyve*) def. The castle and manor of Beverston (*Beverston*). Thomas acknowledged the right of Walter and John by Thomas's gift. For this, grant and render to Thomas and Katherine. To hold to them and their heirs in tail male, of the king. Contingent remainder to Thomas's heirs. Made by the king's order.

77/69/347

[Cf. *Berkeley Castle Mun.* i, p. 148, A1/13/7 (counterpart).]

878. Three weeks [4 May] from Easter. Walter de Frampton (*Frompton*) burgess of Bristol (*Bristoll'*) quer.; Thomas Moyne (*Moigne*) knight def. Two messuages in Bristol. Right of Walter by Thomas's gift. Remise and quitclaim to Walter. (Warranty.) Cons. 20 marks.

77/69/338

[Cf. *Bristol Gt. Red Book*, p. 235, no. 186.]

879. Three weeks [4 May] from Easter. Edmund Blanket and Alice his wife quer.; Philip Gille and Benedicta his wife def. A messuage in the suburb of Bristol (*Bristoll'*). Right of Edmund, as that which Edmund and Alice had by gift of Philip and Benedicta. To hold to Edmund and Alice and Edmund's heirs. (Warranty, specifying Benedicta's heirs.) Cons. 10 marks.

77/69/341

[Cf. *Bristol Gt. Red Book*, p. 236, no. 189.]

880. Three weeks [4 May] from Easter. Maurice son of Maurice de Berkeley (*Berkelee*) 'chivaler' and Joan his wife quer.; William Corbridge (*Corbrugge*) and Richard Warbleton (*Warbulton*) def. The manors of Deep Moor (*More*), Dodscot St. Giles (*Dodescote*), and Blinsham (*Blemesham*), DEVON, the manor of Pencarrow (*Pencarrou*), CORNW., and the manor of Compton Greenfield (*Compton Grenevill*), GLOS. Right of William, as those which William and Richard by gift of Maurice and Joan. For this, grant back and render to Maurice and Joan. To hold to them and their heirs in tail. Contingent remainder to Joan's heirs. *Labelled* Devon', Cornub', Glouc'. [*Worn.*]

287/44/499

[Cf. *Cornwall Fines, 1195–1377*, p. 435, no. 689; *Berkeley Castle Mun.* i, p. 456, A2/20/3 (iv) copy).]

881. Two weeks [22 June] from Trinity. (Made two weeks [27 Jan.] from Hilary in the said year.) Henry atte More and Emma his wife quer.; Stephen de Stroud (*Strode*) 'harpour' and Margaret his wife def. A messuage, 8 a. of land, 1 a. of wood, 50*s.* rent, and one sixth of a mill in Lawrence Weston (*Weston Sancti Laurencii*). Henry

1354

acknowledged the right of Margaret. For this, Stephen and Margaret granted and rendered the holdings to Henry and Emma. To hold to Henry and Emma and Henry's heirs. (Warranty, specifying Margaret's heirs.)

77/69/346

[The fine was granted and recorded in the same term as that in which it was made.]

882. Two weeks [13 Oct.] from Michaelmas. Humphrey de Bohun earl of Hereford (*Hereford*) and Essex (*Essex*) quer.; William de Bohun earl of Northampton (*Norhampton*) and Elizabeth his wife def. The manor of Haresfield (*Harsefeld*) and a messuage and 1 ploughland in Haresfield. Grant and render to the earl of Hereford and Essex. To hold to him and his heirs in tail, of the earl of Northampton and Elizabeth and that earl's heirs, paying a clove a year at St. John the Baptist and doing service to the chief lords. (Warranty.) Contingent reversion to the earl of Northampton and Elizabeth and that earl's heirs. Cons. 200 marks.

77/69/343

883. Two weeks [25 Nov.] from St. Martin. Walter le King (*Kyng*) and Agnes his wife quer.; John Peers (*Peres*) of Bristol (*Bristoll'*) and Amice his wife def. A messuage in Bristol. Right of Walter. Render to Walter and Agnes. To hold to them and Walter's heirs. (Warranty, specifying John's heirs.) Cons. 10 marks. [*Worn.*]

77/69/339

[Cf. *Bristol Gt. Red Book*, p. 235, no. 187.]

1355

884. One week [20 Jan.] from Hilary. (Made [one week] from Michaelmas in the said year [6 Oct. 1354].) John de Bromwich quer.; Thomas Warin (*Waryn*) and Juliana his wife def. Rent of 14*s.* 4*d.* in Taynton (*Teynton*) and Bulley (*Bulleye*). Grant to John with the homages and all the services of [. . .] and John Heddnet from the holdings which they held of Thomas and Juliana [. . .]. (Warranty, specifying Juliana's heirs.) Cons. 20 marks. [*Torn and stained.*]

77/69/348

[This fine, the two following in the file, and all those in files 78/70, 78/71, and 78/72 have been damaged apparently by damp and are missing the lower left-hand portion and in many instances the lower right-hand portion, the surviving edges being stained by damp.]

29 Edward III

1355

885. Two weeks [27 Jan.] from Hilary. (Made two weeks from Michaelmas 28 Edward III [13 Oct. 1354].) William de Cheltenham (*Chiltenham*) and John de Coggeshall (*Cokeshale*) quer.; John Mautravers knight def. The manor of Rockhampton (*Rokhampton*) and the advowson of the church of the same manor. Right of William and John de Coggeshall by gift of John Mautravers. For this, grant back and render to John Mautravers. To hold to him and his heirs in tail male, of the king. Contingent remainder to Thomas son of Maurice de Berkeley (*Berkele*) of Uley (*Ule*) knight. Made by the king's order. [*Torn and stained.*]

77/69/350

[The name of Thomas's father has been supplied from the note of fine, CP 26/1/14, Hil. 29 Edw. III.]

1355

886. Two weeks [14 June] from Trinity. (Made one month from Michaelmas 28 Edward III [27 Oct. 1354].) William de Sherston and Margery his wife quer. by the same William; Thomas le Freeman (*Freman*) of Brockhampton (*Brocamton*) and Matilda his wife def. A messuage, 22 a. of land, and 2 a. of meadow in Bishop's Cleeve (*Bisshopesclyve*) held by Joan [. . .] for term of life, of Matilda's inheritance. Right of William. Grant to William and Margery and William's heirs of the reversion. (Warranty.) Cons. 20 marks. [*Torn and stained.*]

78/70/351

887. Two weeks [14 June] from Trinity. John son of Robert de Yate and Margaret his wife quer.; William [. . .] vicar of the church of Westbury on Severn (*Westbury*) and Matthew de Yate chaplain def. Twenty acres of land, 10 a. of meadow [. . .]*s.* rent and one third of one quarter of a weir (*gurgitis*) in Arlingham (*Erlyngham*) and one third of [. . .]. Right of Matthew, as those which William and Matthew had by gift of John and Margaret. For this, grant back and render to John and Margaret. To hold to them and their heirs in tail. Successive contingent remainders to the heirs in tail of Robert [. . .] and to Margaret's heirs. [*Torn and stained.*]

78/70/352

888. Two weeks [14 June] from Trinity. Robert Barron (*Baroun*) of Great Taynton (*Magna Teynton*) and Isabel his wife quer.; Thomas Warin (*Waryn*) and Juliana his wife def. A messuage, 1 yardland, 1 a. of [. . .], 6 a. of marsh, and 2*d.* rent in Great Taynton. Right of Robert, as those which Robert and Isabel had by gift of Thomas and Juliana. To hold to Robert and Isabel and [. . .]'s heirs. (Warranty, specifying Juliana's heirs.) Cons. 10 marks. [*Torn and stained.*]

78/70/355

889. Two weeks [14 June] from Trinity. John Ergleis of Bristol (*Bristoll'*) quer.; John Free (*Freo*) and Margaret his wife. A messuage in the suburb of Bristol. Right of John Ergleis. Remise and quitclaim, specifying [. . .]'s heirs, to him. Cons. 10 marks. [*Torn and stained.*]

78/70/356

[Cf. *Bristol Gt. Red Book*, p. 236, no. 191.]

890. Morrow [25 June] of St. John the Baptist. John Fowkes (*Foukes*) of Long Marston (*Drymershton*) quer.; Adam Aylemund of Stratford on Avon (*Stretford super Avene*) and Alice his wife def. A messuage and 1 yardland in Long Marston. Right of John. Remise and quitclaim, specifying Alice's heirs, to him. (Warranty.) Cons. [. . .]. [*Torn and stained.*]

78/70/354

891. Two weeks [8 July] from St. John the Baptist. Stephen Granger (*Graunger*) of [. . .] quer. by Stephen de Edgeworth (*Egesworth*); Richard [. . .] def. A messuage, 26 a. of land, and 2 a. of meadow in [. . .]. Right of Stephen. Remise and quitclaim to him. (Warranty.) Cons. [. . .] marks. [*Torn and stained.*]

78/70/353

1355

892. One week [6 Oct.] from Michaelmas. Walter de Thornhill (*Thornhull*) and Elizabeth his wife quer.; William de Thornhill clerk and Richard de Thornhill def. Two thirds of one quarter of the manors of Stathe (*Stathe*) and Wanstrow (*Wondestr'*), SOM., and one third of the manor of Arlingham (*Erlyngham*) and one third of a fishery in the water of Severn (*Severn'*) in Arlingham, GLOS. Right of William, as those which William and Richard had by gift of Walter and Elizabeth. For this, grant back and render to Walter and Elizabeth. To hold to them and their heirs in tail. Successive contingent remainders to Elizabeth's son James [de Wilton] and his heirs in tail, to James's sister Joan and her heirs in tail, and to Elizabeth's heirs. *Labelled* Somers', Glouc'.

287/45/514

[Cf. *Som. Fines, 1347–99*, p. 183. Elizabeth was the widow of James de Wilton: *Berkeley Castle Mun.* i, p. xxxi.]

893. One week [6 Oct.] from Michaelmas. (Made [. . .] in the same year.) Walter Haldane (*Haldayn*) chaplain quer.; Thomas Fabian and Eve his wife def. One third of the manors of Lassington (*Lassyngdon*), [. . .], and Norcott (*Northcote*) by Cirencester (*Cyrencestr'*). Right of Walter by gift of Thomas and Eve. For this, grant back and render to Thomas and Eve. To hold to them and their heirs in tail. Contingent remainder to Thomas's heirs. [*Torn and stained.*]

78/70/358

894. Two weeks [13 Oct.] from Michaelmas. John Peers (*Peres*) of Bristol (*Bristoll'*) quer.; Walter Waldyng and Alice his wife def. Half of a messuage in Bristol. Right of John. Remise and quitclaim, specifying Alice's heirs, to him. (Warranty.) Cons. 10 [marks]. [*Torn and stained.*]

78/70/360

[Cf. *Bristol Gt. Red Book*, p. 237, no. 192.]

895. Three weeks [20 Oct.] from Michaelmas. John Read (*Rede*) burgess of [. . .] quer.; Reynold Cornwall (*Cornwaille*) of London (*London'*) 'sherman' and Joan his wife def. A messuage in Baldwin Street (*Baldewynestrete*) in the suburb of Bristol (*Bristollie*). Right of John by gift of Reynold and Joan. Remise and quitclaim, specifying Joan's heirs, to John. (Warranty.) Cons. [. . .] marks. [*Torn and stained.*]

78/70/359

[Omitted from *Bristol Gt. Red Book*.]

896. [. . .]. (Made [. . .] 28 Edward III [1354–5].) Walter Derby of Bristol (*Bristoll'*) quer.; Geoffrey Bardney (*Bardeneye*) def. A messuage in Bristol. Right of Walter by Geoffrey's gift. Remise and quitclaim to Walter. (Warranty.) Cons. 20 marks. [*Torn and stained.*]

77/69/349

[Cf. *Bristol Gt. Red Book*, p. 236, no. 190. Only the regnal years are legible of the dates on which the fine was granted and recorded (29 Edward III) and was made.]

897. [. . .]. John de Oldland (*Oldelonde*) quer.; Thomas de Berkeley (*Berkele*) and Katherine his wife def. The manor of Woodmancote (*Wodemancote*). Grant to John.

1355

Remise and quitclaim to him of whatever Thomas and Katherine had in the manor for term of Katherine's life. Cons. 100 marks. [*Torn and stained.*]

78/70/357

[Only the regnal year of the date is legible.]

1356

898. One week [20 Jan.] from Hilary. John de [. . .]pe of Gloucester (*Gloucestr'*) clerk quer.; Thomas Warin (*Waryn*) of Purton (*Pyriton*) by Lydney (*Lydeneye*) and Juliana his wife def. Rent of 26*s*. 8*d*. in Minsterworth (*Ministeworth*). Right of John by gift of Thomas and Juliana. (Warranty, specifying Juliana's heirs.) Cons. [. . . marks]. [*Torn and stained.*]

78/70/361 (formerly 78/70/362)

[In the file the fines numbered 361 and 362 have been renumbered, to accord with their dates, but they have not been re-ordered.]

30 Edward III

1356

899. Two weeks [27 Jan.] from Hilary. John Tracy 'chivaler' quer.; William Tracy parson of the church of Toddington (*Todynton*) and John Butler (*Botiller*) chaplain def. The manor of Toddington except 2 messuages and [. . .] yardlands in the same manor and the advowson of the church of the same manor. John Tracy acknowledged the manor to be the right of William, as that which William and John Butler had by John Tracy's gift. For this, grant back and render to John Tracy. To hold during his life. Remainder to William [? son of John] Tracy and Hawise his wife and William's heirs in tail male. Contingent remainder to John Tracy's heirs. [*Torn and stained.*]

78/70/362 (formerly 78/70/361)

[The acknowledgement makes clear that the advowson was excepted from the agreement.]

900. Two weeks [27 Jan.] from Hilary. John de Wysham and Joan his wife quer.; Thomas de Morton parson of the church of Shelsley Beauchamp (*Sheldeslegh Beauchamp*) def. A messuage, 1½ ploughlands and 8 a. of land, 20 a. of wood, and 3*s*. rent in Noxon (*Noxton*) and Newland (*Neulond*), GLOS., and a messuage, 1½ ploughlands, 6 a. of meadow, 8 a. of wood, and 6*s*. 8*d*. rent in Tedstone Delamare (*Teddesternelamare*) and the advowson of the church of the same township, HEREFS. Grant and render to John and Joan. To hold to them and their heirs in tail. Successive contingent remainders to John's heirs in tail and to Robert de Bures 'chivaler'. Cons. 200 marks. *Labelled* Glouc', Hereford'.

287/45/529

901. Morrow [3 Feb.] of the Purification. Maurice son of Maurice de Berkeley (*Berkele*) 'chivaler' and Joan his wife quer.; John Vey clerk and William de Corbridge (*Corbrigge*) def. The manors of Deep Moor (*More*), Dodscot St. Giles (*Dodescote*), and Blinsham (*Blythemesham*), DEVON, and the manor of Compton Greenfield (*Cumpton Grenevill*) and the advowson of the chapel of the same manor, GLOS. Right of John, as those which John and William had by gift of Maurice and Joan. For this, grant back and render to Maurice and Joan. To hold to them and Joan's heirs in tail. Successive contingent remainders to Thomas son of Maurice de Berkeley the elder 'chivaler' and Katherine his wife and their heirs in tail male and to Joan's heirs. *Labelled* Devon', Glouc'.

287/45/521

[Cf. *Berkeley Castle Mun*. i, p. 456, A2/20/3 (copy).]

1356

902. Two weeks [8 May] from Easter. Richard Ketford (*Ketforde*) of Staunton (*Staunton*) quer.; Thomas Stowell and Cristiana his wife def. Two messuages, 70 a. of land, 2 a. of meadow, 4 a. of wood, and 12*d.* rent in Staunton (*Staunton*) by English Bicknor (*Bykenore Engleys*). Right of Richard by gift of Thomas and Cristiana. (Warranty, specifying Cristiana's heirs.) Cons. 100 marks. [*Torn and stained.*]

78/70/363

[The amount of rent and of the consideration have been supplied from the note of fine, CP 26/1/14, Easter 30 Edw. III.]

903. Two weeks [8 May] from Easter. John Sergeant (*Sergeaunt*) the younger quer.; Walter Hurst (*Hurste*) and Joan his wife def. A messuage, 26 a. of land, 2 a. of meadow, and 2*s.* rent in Ham (*Hamme*), Alkington (*Alkynton*), and Cam (*Camme*). Right of John. Remise and quitclaim, specifying Joan's heirs, to him. (Warranty.) Cons. 100 marks. [*Torn and stained.*]

78/70/364

[The acreage of meadow has been supplied from the note of fine, CP 26/1/14, Easter 30 Edw. III.]

904. Three weeks [15 May] from Easter. Walter de Hurst (*Hurste*) quer.; Walter de Nass (*Nasse*) def. Twenty acres of meadow, 12*d.* rent, 3 a. of pasture, and the free fishery of Nass. Right of Walter de Hurst. Remise and quitclaim to him. (Warranty.) Cons. 20 marks. [*Torn and stained.*]

78/70/365

[The amounts of rent and of the consideration have been supplied from the note of fine, CP 26/1/14, Easter 30 Edw. III.]

905. One week [26 June] from Trinity. Geoffrey Beauflour quer.; Richard de Poulesham and Margaret his wife def. Ten messuages, 10*s.* rent, and half of 1 a. of land in the suburb of Bristol (*Bristoll'*). Right of Geoffrey. Remise and quitclaim, specifying Margaret's heirs, to him. (Warranty.) Cons. 20 marks. [*Torn and stained.*]

78/70/370

[Cf. *Bristol Gt. Red Book*, p. 237, no. 193. Geoffrey's surname, some details of the holding and the amount of the consideration have been supplied from the note of fine, CP 26/1/14, Trin. 30 Edw. III.]

906. Two weeks [3 July] from Trinity. (Made three weeks [15 May] from Easter in the said year.) Walter de Hurst (*Hurste*) quer.; Richard Home of Lydney (*Lydeneye*) def. Two messuages, 3 a. of land, and 3 a. of wood in Lydney, held by Joan Home of Lydney for term of life. Right of Walter. Grant to him of the reversion, of Richard's inheritance. (Warranty.) Cons. 20 marks. [*Torn and stained.*]

78/70/366

[The holding of land has been supplied from the note of fine, CP 26/1/14, Trin. 30 Edw. III.]

907. One week [6 Oct.] from Michaelmas. John Mautravers 'chivaler' and Agnes his wife quer.; Henry de Tingewick (*Tyngwyk*) parson of the church of Langton Matravers (*Langeton*) and John Sturmy def. The manors of Philipston (*Phelpeston*), Wimborne St. Giles (*Upwymbourn*), Lytchett Matravers (*Lychet Mautravers*), Matravers (*Lodres*

1356

Mautravers), Frome Whitfield (*Frome Whitefield*), Langton Matravers (*Langeton in Purbyk*), and Wootton Fitzpaine (*Wodetone in Mershwodeval*), the advowsons of the churches of the same manors of Lytchett Matravers, Frome Whitfield, Langton, and Wootton, 2 ploughlands, 22 a. of meadow, 20 a. of pasture, and 6 a. of wood in Eggardon (*Ekerdon*), Woolcombe (*Owelcombe*), and West Moors (*la More*), and the advowson of half of the church of the manor of Wimborne, DORSET, the manors of Coate (*Cotes*), Winterbourne Stoke (*Wynterbournestoke*), Hill Deverill (*Hulle Deverel*), and Great Somerford (*Somerford Mautravers*) and the advowson of the church of the same manor of Somerford, WILTS., the manors of Woodchester (*Wodechestre*), Stonehouse (*Stonhouse*), and Shurdington (*Shurdyngton*), the advowson of the church of the said manor of Woodchester, and a messuage, 1 ploughland, 10 a. of meadow, and 20s. rent in Minchinhampton (*Munechenehampton*), GLOS., and the manor of Childrey (*Chelreye*), BERKS. John Mautravers acknowledged the right of Henry, as that which Henry and John Sturmy had by John Mautravers's gift. For this, grant and render to John Mautravers and Agnes. To hold to them and their heirs in tail. Contingent remainder to John Mautravers's heirs. *Labelled* Dors', Wiltes', Glouc', Berk'. *Endorsed* Roger Siston and Joan his wife put in their claim. John Bartlett (*Bartelot*) put in his claim.

287/45/524

[Cf. *Dorset Fines, 1327–1485*, pp. 150–1; *Wilts. Fines, 1327–77*, p. 109, no. 443.]

908. Morrow [12 Nov.] of St. Martin. Robert Palet quer.; Thomas Spicer and Amice his wife def. Seven messuages, 2 shops, and 7s. rent in Gloucester (*Gloucestre*). Right of Robert by gift of Thomas and Amice. For this, grant back and render to Thomas and Amice. To hold to them and their heirs in tail. Contingent remainder to Thomas's heirs. *Endorsed* The prior of St. Oswald's, Gloucester (*Gloucestr'*), and the convent of the same place put in their claim. [*Torn and stained.*]

78/70/367

[Thomas's surname has been supplied from the note of fine, CP 26/1/14, Trin. 30 Edw. III.]

909. Morrow [12 Nov.] of St. Martin. William atte Wynyard of Gloucester (*Gloucestr'*) and Katherine his wife quer. by the same William; Thomas le Porter of Gloucester 'spicer' and Amice his wife def. A messuage in the suburb of Gloucester. Right of William, as that which William and Katherine had by gift of Thomas and Amice. To hold to William and Katherine and William's heirs. (Warranty, specifying Thomas's heirs.) Cons. 10 marks. [*Torn and stained.*]

78/70/368

[Thomas's surname and address and the amount of the consideration have been supplied from the note of fine, CP 26/1/14, Mich. 30 Edw. III.]

910. One week [18 Nov.] from St. Martin. Alexander Meys (*Moys*) of Bristol (*Bristoll'*) quer.; John Richard of Bristol and Amy his wife def. A messuage in Bristol. Right of Alexander by gift of John and Amy. (Warranty, specifying Amy's heirs.) Cons. 20 marks. [*Torn and stained.*]

78/70/371

[Cf. *Bristol Gt. Red Book*, p. 237, no. 194. John's surname and address have been supplied from the note of fine, CP 26/1/14, Trin. Edw. III.]

1357

911. One week [20 Jan.] from Hilary. (Made two weeks from Michaelmas in the said year [13 Oct. 1356].) Robert Harvey (*Hervy*) quer.; Matthew de Saniger (*Swonhungre*) and Joan his wife def. A messuage, 1 yardland, 2½ a. of meadow, and 4 a. of wood in Ham (*Homme*). Right of Robert. Remise and quitclaim, specifying Joan's heirs, to him. Cons. 20 marks. [*Torn and stained.*]

78/70/369

[The acreage of meadow and the fact that the remise and quitclaim specified Joan's heirs have been supplied from the note of fine, CP 26/1/14, Hil. 30–1 Edw. III.]

31 Edward III

1357

912. One week [1 July] from St. John the Baptist. John Pirie parson of the church of Staunton (*Staunton*) by Corse (*Cors*) quer. by William de Westhall (*Westhale*); James King (*Kyng*) and Agnes his wife def. A messuage in Gloucester (*Gloucestr'*). Right of John. Remise and quitclaim, specifying Agnes's heirs, to him. (Warranty.) Cons. 10 marks. [*Torn and stained.*]

78/70/374

[The attorney's surname has been supplied from the note of fine, CP 26/1/14, 31 Edw. III (mixed).]

913. Two weeks [13 Oct.] from Michaelmas. William Somerville (*Somerwelle*) quer.; Thomas son of Thomas Richman (*Richeman*) def. Rent of 42*s.* in Bristol (*Bristoll'*) and the suburb of the same town. Right of William. Render to him. (Warranty.) Cons. 100 marks. [*Torn and stained.*]

78/70/372

[Cf. *Bristol Gt. Red Book*, p. 237, no. 195. The surname Richman and the amount of the consideration have been supplied from the note of fine, CP 26/1/14, Mich. 31 Edw. III.]

914. Two weeks [13 Oct. *or* 25 Nov.] from [Michaelmas *or* St. Martin]. (Made two weeks [18 June] from Trinity in the said year.) John son of William de Clifford quer.; John son of Henry de Clifford def. A messuage and 40 a. of land in Frampton on Severn (*Frompton super Sabrinam*). Right of John son of William. Remise and quitclaim to him. (Warranty.) Cons. 20 marks. [*Torn and stained.*]

78/70/375

[The amount of land has been supplied from the note of fine, CP 26/1/14, Mich. 31 Edw. III.]

915. One month [27 Oct.] from Michaelmas. John More chaplain and John de Batsford (*Batesford*) quer.; Philip Gille and Benedicta his wife def. A messuage in the suburb of Bristol (*Bristoll'*). Right of John de Batsford, as that which John Batsford and John More had by gift of Philip and Benedicta. To hold to John and John and John de Batsford's heirs. (Warranty, specifying Benedicta's heirs.) Cons. 20 marks. [*Torn and stained.*]

78/70/373

[Cf. *Bristol Gt. Red Book*, p. 238, no. 196.]

32 Edward III

1358

916. Two weeks [27 Jan.] from Hilary. (Made two weeks from Michaelmas 31 Edw. III [13 Oct. 1357].) Thomas de Ledbury (*Ledebury*) and Amice his wife quer.; Thomas de Corse (*Cors*) and Isabel his wife and Richard de Salisbury (*Salesbury*) and Margaret his wife def. A messuage in Gloucester (*Gloucestr'*). Right of Thomas de Ledbury, as that which Thomas and Amice had by gift of Thomas de Corse and Isabel and Richard and Margaret. To hold to Thomas de Ledbury and Amice and that Thomas's heirs (Warranty, specifying [Isabel's and Margaret's] heirs.) Cons. 10 marks. [*Torn and stained.*]

78/71/378

917. Two weeks [27 Jan.] from Hilary. (Made two weeks from Michaelmas 31 Edw. III [13 Oct. 1357].) Thomas Ledbury (*Ledebury*) of Gloucester (*Gloucestr'*) and Amice his wife quer. by John de Stretton in Amice's place; Richard d'Abitot (*Dabetot*) def. Ten messuages, 45 a. of land, and 10 a. of meadow in Elmore (*Elemor*) and Minsterworth (*Munestreworth*) held by Matilda who was wife of Robert d'Abitot for term of life. Right of Thomas. Grant of the reversion to Thomas and Amice and Thomas's heirs. (Warranty.) Cons. 100 marks. [*Torn and stained.*]

78/71/379

[The messuages and the forename of Matilda's husband have been supplied from the note of fine, CP 26/1/15, Hil. 31–2 Edw. III.]

918. Two weeks [27 Jan.] from Hilary. John de Wycombe of Bristol (*Bristoll'*) the elder quer.; John le Felter (*Feltere*) of Bristol and Alice his wife def. A messuage and 13*s*. 4*d*. rent in the suburb of Bristol. Right of John de Wycombe. Remise and quitclaim, specifying Alice's heirs, to him. (Warranty.) Cons. 100 marks. [*Torn and stained.*]

78/71/388

[Cf. *Bristol Gt. Red Book*, p. 238, no. 197.]

919. One week [8 Feb.] from the Purification. Robert le Walour and Margery his wife quer.; William le Hayberare chaplain and Roger Weynleye clerk def. Six and a half messuages in Gloucester (*Gloucestr'*). Right of William, as those which William and Roger had by gift of Robert and Margery. For this, grant back and render to Robert and Margery. To hold during their lives. Remainder to John and Robert sons of Robert and Margery and Robert the son's heirs in tail. Contingent remainder to Margery's heirs. [*Torn and stained.*]

78/71/377

[Roger's surname and status and John's name and parentage have been supplied from the note of fine, CP 26/1/15, Hil. 31–2 Edw. III.]

920. Two weeks [15 April] from Easter. Walter le Mariner (*Maryner*) parson of the church of St. John, Gloucester (*Gloucestr'*), quer.; William Churchdown (*Chirchesdon*) and Alice his wife def. Two messuages in Gloucester. Right of Walter by gift of William and Alice. (Warranty, specifying Alice's heirs). Cons. 20 marks. [*Torn and stained.*]

78/71/376

1358

921. Two weeks [15 April] from Easter. Thomas de Berkeley (*Berkeleye*) of Coberley (*Coberleye*) and Joan his wife quer.; John le Butler (*Botiller*) [. . .] and William de Westhall (*Westhale*) def. Half of the manor of Stoke Orchard (*Archerstoke*). Right of John and William by gift of Thomas and Joan. For this, grant back and render to Thomas and Joan. To hold to them and their heirs in tail, of the king. Contingent remainder to [. . .]'s heirs. Made by the king's order. [*Torn and stained.*]

78/71/380

922. Morrow [11 May] of Ascension. The king quer. by John Gaunt who sues for him; John de St. Philbert (*de Sancto Philberto*) 'chivaler' and Margaret his wife def. The manors of Eaton Hastings (*Eton Hastynges*) and Carswell (*Carsewell*), BERKS., and the manor of Southrop (*Souththrop*), GLOS. Right of the king. Remise and quitclaim, specifying John's heirs, to him. (Warranty.) Cons. 300 marks. *Labelled* Berk', Glouc'.

287/45/547

[The left-hand and right-hand parts of the indenture of which the above is the foot are filed with the feet of fines and are respectively 287/45/548 and 287/45/549.]

923. Two weeks [10 June] from Trinity. (Made three weeks [22 April] from Easter the said year). Henry Pratt of Newland (*la Newelonde*) quer.; Thomas Haynes (*Heynes*) and Joan his wife def. A messuage, 4 a. of land, 2 a. of pasture, and 1 a of wood in Newland (*Newelonde*). Right of Henry. Remise and quitclaim, specifying Joan's heirs, to him. (Warranty.) Cons. 20 marks. [*Torn and stained.*]

78/71/382

[The messuage has been supplied from the note of fine, CP 26/1/15, Trin. 32 Edw. III.]

924. Two weeks [10 June] from [Trinity]. (Made three weeks [22 April] from Easter in the said year.) Henry atte More and Emma his wife quer.; Robert de Bradley (*Bradeleye*) brother and heir of John de Bradley def. A messuage, 40 a. of land, 8 a. of meadow, 2 a. of wood, 6 marks rent, and half of a mill in Lawrence Weston (*Weston Sancti Laurencii*), Charlton (*Cherleton*), Redland (*Tridelond*), and Redwick (*Redewyke*). Right of Robert. Remise and quitclaim to him, specifying Henry's heirs. (Warranty.) Cons. 100 marks. [*Torn and stained.*]

78/71/381

[The acreage of land and meadow, the mill, and the first letters of the location have been supplied from the note of fine, CP 26/1/15, Trin. 32 Edw. III.]

925. Two weeks [13 Oct.] from Michaelmas. John Sergeant the younger quer.; Thomas atte Cellar (*Celere*) of Evesham (*Evesham*) and Alice his wife def. A messuage and 7 a. of land in Ham (*Hamme*). Right of John. Remise and quitclaim, specifying Alice's heirs, of the messuage and 5 a. to John. Grant to him of the reversion of 1½ a. held by John Badcock (*Badecok*) for term of life and of ½ a. held by William Baker (*Bakere*) for term of life, of Alice's inheritance. (Warranty). Cons. 10 marks. [*Torn and stained.*]

78/71/383

[The amount of the consideration has been supplied from the note of fine, CP 26/1/15, Mich. 32 Edw. III.]

1358

926. Two weeks [13 Oct.] from Michaelmas. (Made two weeks [10 June] from Trinity in the said year.) Robert Harvey (*Hervy*) quer.; William atte Wood (*Wode*) and Alice his wife and Robert Wayfer def. A messuage, 1 yardland, 2½ a. of meadow, and 4 a. of wood in Ham (*Homme*). Right of Robert Harvey. Remise and quitclaim, specifying Robert Wayfer's heirs, to him. (Warranty.) Cons. 100 marks. [*Torn and stained.*]

78/71/384

[The location of the holdings has been supplied from the note of fine, CP 26/1/15, Mich. 32 Edw. III.]

927. Two weeks [13 Oct.] from Michaelmas. James Thickness (*Thiknesse*) and Margaret his wife quer.; Ellis Daubeney (*Daubeneye*) and Agnes his wife def. A messuage, 40 a. of land and 3 a. of meadow in Alkerton (*Alkrynton*). Right of James. Remise and quitclaim, specifying Agnes's heirs, to James and Margaret and James's heirs. (Warranty.) Cons. 100 marks. [*Torn and stained.*]

78/71/385

[James's surname has been supplied from the note of fine, CP 26/1/15, Mich. 32 Edw. III.]

928. Two weeks [13 Oct.] from Michaelmas. Richard Scot quer.; John son of Roger Daniel atte Hill (*Hulle*) of Rodley (*Rodeleye*) and Agnes his wife def. A messuage in Westbury on Severn (*Westbury*) by Newnham (*Newenham*). Right of Richard by gift of John and Agnes. (Warranty, specifying Agnes's heirs.) Cons. 10 marks. [*Torn and stained.*]

78/71/386

[Richard's surname and the location of the messuage have been supplied from the note of fine, CP 26/1/15, Mich. 32 Edw. III.]

929. Two weeks [13 Oct.] from Michaelmas. William de Matson (*Mattesdon*) and Matilda his wife quer.; John le Spenser of Defford (*Defford*) and Margery his wife and John Wych and Joan his wife def. A messuage, 1½ ploughlands, 7 a. of meadow, 1 a. of wood, and 6*s*. 8*d*. rent in Brockworth (*Brokworth*). Right of William. Remise and quitclaim, specifying Margery's and Joan's heirs, to William and Matilda and William's heirs. (Warranty.) Cons. [. . .]. [*Torn and stained.*]

78/71/387

[William's surname and the full amount of the rent have been supplied from the note of fine, CP 26/1/15, Mich. 32 Edw. III, which is itself damaged: the reading of William's surname is uncertain, and the amount of the consideration is illegible.]

33 Edward III

1359

930. Two weeks [27 Jan.] from Hilary. Edward de Bohun quer.; John de Bohun of Midhurst (*Midhurst*) def. The manor of Magor (*Magor*) [MON.] held by Richard Laxman for term of life by John's demise. Grant of the reversion to Edward. To hold to him and his heirs in tail, of John, paying a rose a year. Contingent remainder to John's heirs. Cons. [. . .]. [*Torn and stained.*]

78/71/391

[Labelled and filed as a Glos. fine.]

1359

931. Two weeks [5 May] from Easter. John FitzNichol (*Fitz Nichol*) and Eve his wife quer.; John parson of the church of St. Pierre (*Seintpere*) and Walter parson [. . .] def. The manors of Hill (*Hulle*) and Nympsfield (*Nymdesfeld*) and the advowson of the chantry of Kinley (*Kynleye*). John FitzNichol acknowledged the right of John the parson and Walter by gift of John FitzNichol. For this, grant and render of the manors and the advowson to John FitzNichol and Eve. To hold to them and their heirs in tail male, of the king. Contingent remainder to John FitzNichol's heirs. Made by the king's order. [*Torn and stained.*]

78/71/393

932. Two weeks [5 May] from Easter. Richard de Bristol (*Bristowe*) of Gloucester (*Gloucestre*) and Amice his wife quer.; Richard Keys of Gloucester and Agnes his wife def. A messuage in the suburb of Gloucester (*Gloucestr'*). Right of Richard de Bristol, as that which Richard and Amice had by gift of Richard Keys and Agnes. To hold to Richard de Bristol and Amice and Richard's heirs. (Warranty, specifying Agnes's heirs.) Cons. 10 marks. [*Torn and stained.*]

78/71/395

933. Three weeks [12 May] from Easter. Henry Drake of Gloucester (*Gloucestr'*) quer.; John Cluet of Gloucester and Cristina his wife def. A messuage, 4 a. of land, and 3s. rent in Gloucester and Upton St. Leonard (*Upton Sancti Leonardi*). Right of Henry by gift of John and Cristina. For this, grant back and render to John and Cristina. To hold to them during their lives, of Henry, paying a rose a year at St. John the Baptist and doing service to the chief lords. Reversion to Henry. [*Torn and stained.*]

78/71/394

[The 3s. rent has been supplied from the note of fine, CP 26/1/15, Easter 33 Edw. III.]

934. Three weeks [12 May] from Easter. John Yawan of Frogpool (*Froggepol*) quer.; Geoffrey le French (*Frenssh*) and Joan his wife def. A messuage, 5 a. of land, and ½ a. of meadow in Lydney (*Lydeneye*). Right of John. Remise and quitclaim, specifying Joan's heirs, to him. (Warranty.) Cons. 10 marks. [*Torn and stained.*]

78/71/397

[Geoffrey's surname and the amount of the consideration have been supplied from the note of fine, CP 26/1/15, Easter 33 Edw. III.]

935. Three weeks [12 May] from Easter. Thomas de Berkeley (*Berkele*) quer.; John Puttock (*Pottok*) and Alice his wife def. A messuage and 3 a. of land in Wotton under Edge (*Wotton Underegge*). Right of Thomas. Remise and quitclaim, specifying Alice's heirs, to him. (Warranty.) Cons. 10 marks. [*Torn and stained.*]

78/71/398

[Cf. *Berkeley Castle Mun.* i, p. 355, A1/56/13 (counterpart).]

936. Three weeks [12 May] from Easter 33 Edw. III (Made two weeks from Easter 32 Edw. III [15 April 1358].) Robert de Passelewe and John de Bruton quer.; Thomas Fabian and Eve his wife def. One third of the manors of Lassington (*Lassyndon*), Edgeworth (*Eggesworth*), and Norcott (*Northcote*) and the advowson of one third of the churches of the same manors of Lassington and Edgeworth, GLOS., and one third of the manor of Westhide (*Westhide*), HEREFS. Right of Robert. Render to Robert and John of

1359

one third of the one third of the manor of Lassington and two thirds of two thirds of the same one third and the advowson. To hold to them and Robert's heirs. Grant, specifying Eve's heirs, to Robert and John and Robert's heirs of the reversion of one third of the one third of the manors of Edgeworth and Norcott and two thirds of two thirds of the same one third held by Thomas de Ralegh of Charles (*Charles*) for term of life, of the one third of the manor of Westhide held by John de Hyde for term of life, and of the one third of two thirds of the said one third of the manors of Lassington, Edgeworth, and Norcott held by Margaret who was wife of Walter de Helion (*Helyoun*) in dower, of Eve's inheritance. (Warranty.) Cons 200 marks. Made, as to the one third of the manor of Westhide and one third of two thirds of one third of the manors of Lassington, Edgeworth, and Norcott, in the presence and with the consent of John de Hyde and Margaret, who did fealty to Robert and John de Bruton. *Labelled* Glouc', Hereford'

288/46/564

937. One week from [. . .]. (Made one month [19 May] from Easter in the said year. Walter son of Robert Millward (*Muleward*) quer.; John Cocker (*Cokir*) and Isabel his wife def. A messuage in the suburb of Bristol (*Bristoll'*). Right of Walter by gift of John and Isabel. (Warranty, specifying Isabel's heirs.) Cons. 10 marks. [*Torn and stained.*]

78/71/389

[Cf. *Bristol Gt. Red Book*, p. 238, no. 198.]

938. One month [19 May] from Easter. John Willing (*Willyng*) of Boseley (*Boseleye*) quer.; Hugh Arthur and Joan his wife def. Two messuages, 46 a. of land, 6 a. of meadow, 18 a. of wood, and 10*d*. rent in Westbury on Severn (*Westbury*). Right of John by gift of Hugh and Joan. (Warranty, specifying Joan's heirs.) Cons. 100 marks. [*Torn and stained.*]

78/71/392

[John's surname, the amount of land, and the location of the holdings have been supplied from the note of fine, CP 26/1/15, Easter 33 Edw. III.]

939. One week [6 Oct.] from Michaelmas. John atte Mill (*Mulle*) of Oxlinch (*Hoxlynge*) quer.; Roger Norris (*Norreys*) of Haresfield (*Harsefeld*) and Clarice his wife def. A messuage, 20 a. of land, 1 a. of meadow, and 5 a. of moor in Oxlinch. Right of John by gift of Roger and Clarice. Cons. 20 marks. [*Torn and stained.*]

78/71/400

940. One week [6 Oct.] from Michaelmas. Robert de la Marche and Agnes his wife and Thomas son of the same Robert quer.; John de Stanbourn and Mabel his wife def. Four messuages, 10 a. of land, 9*s*. 6*d*. rent, and one quarter of a messuage in Tewkesbury (*Teukisbury*) and Southwick (*Southwyk*). Grant to Robert and Agnes and Thomas. Render to them. To hold to Robert and Agnes and Thomas and Thomas's heirs in tail. Successive contingent remainders to Thomas's brother Edmund and his heirs in tail and to Robert's heirs. (Warranty, specifying John's heirs.) Cons. £100. [*Torn, worn, and holed.*]

78/72/402

[The messuages and the acreage of land have been supplied from the note of fine, CP 26/1/15, Mich. 33 Edw. III.]

1359

941. Two weeks [13 Oct.] from Michaelmas. William Child of Gloucester (*Gloucestre*) 'mercer' quer.; John Rolves of Madeley (*Maddeleye*) and Clemency his wife and Nicholas de Minsterworth (*Menstreworth*) 'peyntour' and Alice his wife def. A messuage in Gloucester. Right of William by gift of John and Clemency and Nicholas and Alice. (Warranty, specifying Clemency's and Alice's heirs.) Cons. 10 marks. [*Torn and stained.*]

78/71/396

[The location of the messuage has been supplied from the note of fine, CP 26/1/15, Mich. 33 Edw. III.]

942. Morrow [3 Nov.] of All Souls. John Blanket quer.; Thomas Ottery (*Otery*) and Elena his wife def. A messuage and a shop in the town of Bristol (*Bristoll'*) and the suburb of the same. Right of John by gift of Thomas and Elena. (Warranty, specifying Thomas's heirs.) Cons. 20 marks. [*Torn and stained.*]

78/71/390

[Cf. *Bristol Gt. Red Book*, p. 239, no. 199.]

943. Morrow [3 Nov.] of All Souls. John de Nowers 'chivaler' quer.; Robert de Vernon (*Vernoun*) and Galiana his wife def. One third of two thirds of the manor of Charingworth (*Charyngworth*). Grant to John. Remise and quitclaim to him of whatever Robert and Galiana had in the one third in Galiana's dower. Cons. 20 marks. [*Torn.*]

78/72/401

[Robert's surname, the grant, the subject of the quitclaim, and the amount of the consideration have been supplied from the note of fine, CP 26/1/15, Mich. 33 Edw. III.]

944. Two weeks [13 Nov.] from Michaelmas. William Andrews (*Andreus*) and Isabel his wife quer.; John Noblepas and William Atkyns (*Adekyns*) def. A messuage, 13 a. of land, 1½ a. of meadow, and 2 a. of wood in Ham (*Hamme*). William Andrews acknowledged the right of John, as those which John and William Atkyns had by William Andrews's gift. For this, grant to William Andrews and Isabel. Render to them. To hold to them and their heirs in tail. Contingent remainder to the heirs of William Andrews. (Warranty.) [*Torn.*]

78/72/403

945. One week [18 Nov.] from St. Martin. Peter Corbet 'chivaler' and Eleanor his wife by Nicholas Chamberlain (*Chamberleyn*) in Eleanor's place; John de Ingleby (*Ingelby*) [*reading uncertain*] of Lawrenny (*Laurenny*) and Robert Forestel def. The manor of Siston (*Ciston*). Peter acknowledged the right of John, as that which John and Robert had by Peter's gift. For this, grant and render to Peter and Eleanor. To hold to Peter and Eleanor and Peter's heirs. [*Torn and stained.*]

78/71/399

[Nicholas's forename has been supplied from the note of fine, CP 26/1/15, Mich. 33 Edw. III.]

INDEX OF PERSONS AND PLACES

References are to entry-numbers. Successive references to names that are not differentiated have been separated only where identity is unlikely or impossible.

Harwell (Berks.), 835
Harwell, William de, 534
Haselbech (Northants.), advowson, 292; manor, 292
Haseley (Oxon.), manor, 795
Haselor (Warws.), 725
Hasfield, 394, 470, 732; manor, 588; parson, 588
Hasfield, William de, vicar of Henbury, 451
Hastang, Thomas, and Matilda his wife, 241
Hastings, Laurence de, earl of Pembroke, 755
Hatfield [*unspecified*], 266
Hatfield, John de, 662
Hathaway, Agnes wife of William de, 501
— Ralph, 30
— William de, 501
Hatherley, Down, 224, 274, 320, 366, 425, 498, 501, 553, 579; manor, 543, 844; Hatherley Wood, 498; vicar, 553
Hatherley, Up, 154, 498, 585, 776–7; manor, 309, 332
Hatherley [*unspecified*], 15, 767
Hatherley, Henry de, 309
— Katherine wife of Thomas de, 585
— Richard de, 131
— Thomas de, 585
Hatherley, Up, John de, 332
— Thomas son of John de, 332
Hatherop, 452; manor, 568
Hatley St. George (Cambs.), advowson, 504; manor, 504
Hatter, Alexander le, 623
— Amice wife of Richard le, 458
— Richard le, 458
Haudlo, Isabel wife of Richard, 568
— John de, 292, 421, 531, 568, 700
— Matilda wife of John de, 292, 421, 531
— Nicholas son of John de, 568, 700
— Richard son of John de, 568
— Robert de, 421, 531
— Thomas son of John de, 568
— William de, 292
Hauekescumbe, 8
Haukesok, Thomas, and Alice his wife, 862
Haurugge, Walter de, and Alice his wife, 98
Hauville, Henry de, 473
Haw, the, in Tirley, 252, 394–5, 503
Hawker, William le, 675
Hawkesbury, 66, 227, 668, 693, 781, 811; *and see* Badminton, Little; Hillesley; Kilcott; Tresham
Hawkesbury, John de, 288
Hawley, Robert, and Matilda his wife, 353
Hawote, John, and Margery his wife, 874
Hay, Agnes wife of Richard atte, 342
— Cecily de la, 593

— Joan wife of Laurence de, 406
— John de la, 93, 351
— John son of William de la, 451
— Laurence de la, 406
— Richard atte, 342
— Thomas de la, 247
— William (atte) (de la), 451, 616
— William son of William de la, 451
Hayberare, William le, 919
Haydon, in Boddington, 503
Haydon, William de, 800
Hayl, William, and Matilda his wife, 51; *and see* Hale
Haynes, Agnes wife of William, 763
— Joan wife of Thomas, 815, 923
— Thomas, 815, 923
— William, 763
Hayward, Peter le, 860
— Richard le, 274
Hazel, John atte, and Joan his wife, 321, 339, 346
Hazleton, 214
Head, John, 833
— Roger, 642
Headington (Oxon.), 568
Heath, Geoffrey atte, 308
— John, 703
Heddnet, John, 884
Hedon, John de, 727
— Richard son of John de, 727
Helion, Isabel wife of Robert de, 65
— James son of John de, 629
— John de, 629
— Margaret wife of Walter de, 936
— Reynold brother of Robert de, 65
— Robert de, 65
— Walter de, 629, 936
Helpston, John de, 513
Helyotes, Henry, 800
Hemming, John, 800
Hempsted, 626; *and see Wykeham*
Hempton, in Almondsbury, 697
Henbury, 83, 247, 622; vicar, 266, 451; *and see* Charlton; Elmington; Lee; Redwick; Saltmarsh; Shirehampton; Weston, King's; Weston, Lawrence
Hengham, Jordan de, 295
Henley, Richard, and Isabel his wife, 784
Henry vicar of Old Sodbury, 701
Henstridge (Som.), 452, 810
Herbert son of John, and Eleanor his wife, 278
Herbert, Matthew son of, *see* Matthew
Herdman, Geoffrey, and Edith his wife, 408, 410
Hereford, 845
Hereford, Little (Herefs.), 501
Hereford, earl of, *see* Bohun, Humphrey de

Malmesbury, William de, 111
Malpas (Mon.), priory, 371
Malswick, in Newent, 179
Malvern, Robert de, 206, 403
Mancetter (Warws.), parson, 556
Mandeville, Isabel wife of Robert, 422–3
— John son of Robert, 422
— Robert, 422–3
— Thomas son of Robert, 422
— William son of Robert, 422
Mangotsfield, manor, 683
Manningford Bruce (Wilts.), manor, 653
Mansell Gamage, Richard de, 462; *and see* Maunsell
Manser, Isabel wife of John, 727
— John son of William, 727
— William, 727
Manship, John, 486, 572, 575
Maperton [Maperton (Som.) or Mapperton (Dorset)?], 452
Marche, Agnes wife of Robert de la, 940
— Edmund son of Robert de la, 940
— Richard de la, 196
— Robert de la, 940
— Thomas son of Robert de la, 940
Marcle, John de, 624
Mare, Anne wife of John de la, of Rendcomb, 614
— Anne wife of John son of John de la, 768
— John de la, of Langley Burrell, 716
— John de la, of Rendcomb, 555, 614, 768
— John son of John de la, of Rendcomb, 768
— Lucy wife of Robert de la, 224
— Peter son of Robert de la, 445
— Reynold de la, 501
— Robert de la, 224, 445, 792
— Thomas son of John de la, of Rendcomb, 555
— Thomas son of Robert de la, 445, 792
— William son of John de la, of Rendcomb, 555
Margam (Glam.), 532
Marine, John de la, 116
Mariner, Walter le, (parson of St. John's within the north gate, Gloucester), 579, 631, 861, 920
Marky, John, 417
— Juliana wife of William, 417
— William son of John, 417
Marlborough, Thomas de, 649
Marmion, Elicia wife of Thomas, 246
— John, 447, 702
— Matilda wife of John, 702
— Robert son of John, 702
— Thomas, 246
Marny, William, and Agnes his wife, 861
Marsh, Cecily wife of William atte, 767
— John de, 507

— William atte, 767
Marshal, Adam le, 96
— Agnes wife of Adam le, 96
— Agnes wife of William le, 483
— Alice wife of John le, 833
— Geoffrey, vicar of Longhope, 749–50
— Gunnilda wife of John le, 485
— Joan wife of Philip le, 748–50
— John le, 485, 833
— John le, parson of Blaisdon, 608, 611–12
— Peter le, 559
— Philip le, 748–50, 869
— William le, 483
— William, parson of Dorsington, 728
Marshfield, 416, 433; West Marshfield, manor, 659, 727; *and see* Shirehill
Marshfield, John de, 236
Marston, Broad, in Pebworth, 341, 628, 657
Marston, Long, 890
Marston, Ralph de, and Eleanor his wife, 428
Martel, Adam, and Cecily his wife, 740
Marten, in Grafton (Wilts.), 452
Martin, Geoffrey, 739, 756, 767
— Laurence, 733
— Richard, 800
Martley (Worcs.), manor, 755
Masindon, Robert de, and Margery his wife, 366
Masinton, Gilbert de, and Cristina his wife, 442
Mason, Adam le, 173
— Agnes wife of Adam le, 173
— Joan wife of William, 855
— Matilda wife of Mr. Richard le, 498
— Mr. Richard le, 498
— Robert le, 471
— William, 855
Mathon (Worcs.), 578; *and see* Farley
Matravers, in Loders (Dorset), manor, 907
Matson, 242, 650; manor, 242, 852
Matson, Agnes de, 21, 242
— Eve sister of Agnes de, 21
— Matilda wife of William de, 929
— William de, 929
Matthew son of Herbert, 696
   his brother, *see* Reynold
Maunsell, Joan daughter of William son of William, 591
— William, 82, 374, 591
— William, of Lypiatt, 741
— William son of William, 82, 374, 591
— *and see* Mansell Gamage, Richard de
Mautravers, Agnes wife of John de, 907
— Eleanor wife of John de, 150
— John (de), 150, 847, 873, 885, 907
— John, the elder, 212, 691
— John, the younger, 212, 544, 691

Moreton (Dorset), 452, 674
Moreton, South (Berks.), manor, 813
Moreton in Marsh, 181, 580; *and see* Coldicote
Moreton Valence, 442, 668; manor, 484
Morhalle (Norf.), 696
Morley, in Crudwell (Wilts.), 603
Morley, Geoffrey de, 603
Morris, Richard, 516
Mortain, Mr. Edmund, 839
— Isabel wife of Roger de, 195
— Roger de, 195
Mortimer, *see* Zouche
Morton, in Churcham, 516
Morton, Cristiana wife of John de, 312
— Eleanor wife of John son of John de, 312
— Elizabeth wife of John de, 74
— Isabel wife of William de, 815
— Joan daughter of Nicholas de, 778
— John de, 74, 312
— John son of John de, 312
— John son of Milisent de, 529
— Milisent de, 529
— Nicholas de, 329, 586, 778
— Richard de, 798
— Thomas de, parson of Shelsley Beauchamp, 900
— William de, 815
Morwent, in Hartpury, 40
Morwent, William de, 40
Moryn, Eleanor wife of Walter, 428
— John, 580
— Margaret wife of Robert, 218
— Margery wife of John, 580
— Robert, 218
— Walter, 428
Mouner, Robert le, 568
Mount Gilbert, John de, 518
Mountain, Thorald de la, and Joan his wife, 46–7, 50
Moyne, Henry le, 141, 860
— Joan wife of Henry le, 141, 860
— John le, 667, 703
— Thomas, 865, 878
— *and see* Monk
Mucegros, Agnes de, 88
Munning, Robert, 417
Murcott, in Minsterworth, 330, 537–8, 587
Murdoch, Geoffrey, 60
— Margery wife of Geoffrey, 60
— Robert, 779
— Robert, parson of Winterbourne, 848, 853
Murymouth, Walter, 587
Musard, Malcolm, 186
— Reynold, 512

Musket, Walter, 340
Mustel, Hugh, and Isabel his wife, 614, 768
Mynge, Richard, 815

Nabal's, in Sutton Benger (Wilts.), 452
Nash, *see* Ash
Nass, in Lydney, 904
Nass, Robert son of Walter de, 280
— Walter de, 280, 904
Naunton, 581
Navestock, John de, parson of Willingale Doe, 650
Neel, Geoffrey son of Thomas, 203
— Nicholas, 377
— Thomas, 36, 203
— Thomas [*another*], 203
Netheravon (Wilts.), 144, 452
Netton, in Durnford (Wilts.), 452
Neville, Philip de, 195
— Robert son of Philip de, 195
New Grange (Mon.), manor, 411, 527, 615
Newent, 182, 304, 576; *and see* Cugley; Kilcot; Malswick; Okle; Stallion
Newington Bagpath, manor, 562
Newington, Mr. Henry de, 192
— Joan wife of John de, 192
— Joan wife of Thomas, 251
— John de, 192, 251
— Thomas son of John de, 251
Newland, 229, 364, 378, 798, 900, 923; *and see* Noxon
Newland, Nicholas de, and Edith his wife, 558
Newmaster, Alice wife of Ranulph, 731
— Ranulph, 731
— William le, 664
Newnham (Glos.), manor, 795
Newnham, in Sutton Veny (Wilts.), 650
Newport (Mon.), castle, 371; manor, 371; *and see* Stow
Newport, in Berkeley, 784
Newton, John de, 522
Nibley, North, 596
Nicholas, abbot of Stanley, 23
Nicol, John, 583
Noblepas, John, 944
Noke, in Hucclecote, 354
Norcott, in Preston (near Cirencester), manor, 893, 936
Norcott, Reynold de, and Lucy his wife, 100
Norfolk, *see* Barton Bendish; Billingford; Caldecote; Docking; Foxley; *Morhalle*; Ryston; Thurning; Weeting
Norman, Roger le, of Cirencester, 350, 358–9
— Roger, of Southampton, 603

SELECTIVE INDEX OF SUBJECTS

References are to entry-numbers.

223

CORRIGENDA

to *Abstracts of Feet relating to Gloucestershire, 1199–1299*
(Gloucestershire Record Series volume 16)

page 8, no. 46, *line* 1 *omit* [de Bohun]

page 8, no. 47, *line* 2 *for* D(ownton?) *read* (Willington?)

page 28, no. 150, *line* 5 *for* d'E[. . .] *read* d'E[vercy]

page 30, no. 158, *lines* 3–4 *for* Quenton [Quenington or Quinton] *read* Quinton (*Quenton*)

page 32, no. 165, *line* 6 *for* life, of Robert *read* life, of Richard

page 45, no. 220, *line* 1 *for* Meyey *read* Meysey

page 50, no. 242, *line* 5 *for* Grownegrave *read* Grimmesgrave *and line* 6 *for* Gates *read* Yate (*Gate*)

page 68, line 6, *for* For his, grant *read* For this, grant

page 77, no. 389, *lines* 1–2 *for* Baudrun, pet.; Ralph de Wilton *read* Baderon (*Baudrun*), pet.; Ralph de Willington

page 79, no. 400. *The date is in fact three weeks* [*15 July*] *from St. John the Baptist, as shown by no.* 1017.

page 84, no. 425 *for* William de Welton (*five times*) *read* William de Weston *and in line* 4 *for* Welton *read* Weston on Avon (*Weston*)

page 101, no. 513, *line* 3 *after* Esse *add* [in Prestbury?]

page 105, no. 528, *line* 1 *for* Kaylly *read* Cailly (*Kaylly*)

page 123, no. 619, *lines* 3--4 *for* in Tohinton [Tockington, Glos.?] *read* in Taynton (*Tohinton*)

page 123, no. 619, *line* 19 *for* Kikpeck *read* Kilpeck

page 142, no. 708, *line* 3 *for* Sturidon [Sturden (GLOS.)?] *read* Sturden (*Sturidon*) [GLOS.]

page 156, line 7 *for* Hampton? *read* Acton? *and line* 10 *for* Margey *read* Margery

page 156, no. 776, *note, omit* if not entirely

page 166, line 9, *for* presence hat *read* presence that

page 172, no. 847, *line* 15 *for* Haresfield *read* Hasfield

page 205, no. 1017, *note, for the last sentence read* The foot of fine is above, no. 400, and no. 1017 was included in error.

page 207, column 1, *s.v.* Acton Turville *add at end* ; manor, 776

page 209, column 2, *before last line add new entry* Baderon, Philip, 389

page 210, column 2, *s.v.* Baudrun *omit whole entry*

page 212, column 1, *line* 23 *move* Bussage, in Chalford, 917 *to page* 215, *column* 1, *line* 16

page 212, column 2, *s.v.* Bohun *omit* Cecily de, countess of Hereford, 46 / —

page 215, column 1, *s.v.* Cailly *add* — Mabel de, 528

page 216, column 1, *between* Cave *and* Cecily *add* Cecily countess of Hereford, 46

page 221, column 1, *s.v.* Downton *omit whole entry*

page 221, column 2, *s.v.* Dyrham *add at end* ; *and see* Hinton

page 221, column 2, *s.v.* E[. . .], Robert d' *omit whole entry*

page 222, column 2, *s.v.* Esse, *to read* Esse [in Prestbury?], 513

page 222, column 2, *s.v.* Evercy *after* Robert de, 64 *add* , 150

page 224, column 2, *s.v.* Gates *omit whole entry*

page 227, column 2, *s.v.* Haresfield *omit* ; manor, 847

page 227, column 2, *s.v.* Hasfield [*first entry*] *add at end* ; manor, 847

page 228, column 2, *s.v.* Hereford [*second entry*] *for* Bohun, Cecily de *read* Cecily

page 229, *column* 1, *s.v.* Hinton, *second entry to read* Hinton, in Dyrham and Hinton, 708

page 229, *column* 1, *s.v.* Horton *omit* Gates, 242;

page 231, *column* 1, *s.v.* Kaylly *omit whole entry*

page 238, *column* 2, *s.v.* Olveston *omit* ; *Tohinton*

page 241, *column* 1, *s.v.* Prestbury [*first entry*] *add at end* ; *and see Esse*

page 241, *column* 2, *s.v.* Quenington *omit* 158,

page 247, *column* 1, *penultimate line to read* Sturden, in Winterbourne, 708

page 248, *column* 1, *s.v.* Taynton *after* 523, *add* 619,

page 249, *column* 1, *s.v.* Tockington *omit* ; *and see Tohinton*

page 249, *column* 1, *s.v. Tohinton omit whole entry*

page 251, *column* 2, *s.vv. Welton and* Welton *omit the whole of both entries*

page 252, *column* 1, *s.v.* Weston on Avon *add reference* 425,

page 252, *column* 1, *s.v.* Weston, William *add reference* 425,

page 253, *column* 1, *s.v.* Willington *after* wife of Ralph de *add* 47, *and after* — Ralph de *add references* 47, *and* 389,

page 253, *column* 1, *s.v.* Wilton *omit* — Ralph de, 389

page 253, *column* 2, *s.v.* Winterbourne *for Sturidon read* Sturden

page 254, *column* 2, *s.v.* Yate *after* 71, *add* 242,